Software Synthesizers

The Definitive Guide to Virtual Musical Instruments

Edited by Jim Aikin

Backbeat Books

San Francisco

Published by Backbeat Books
600 Harrison Street, San Francisco, CA 94107
www.backbeatbooks.com
email: books@musicplayer.com

An imprint of the Music Player Group
Publishers of *Guitar Player, Bass Player, Keyboard,* and other magazines
United Entertainment Media, Inc.
A CMP Information company

CMP
United Business Media

Distributed to the book trade in the US and Canada by
Publishers Group West, 1700 Fourth Street, Berkeley, CA 94710

Distributed to the music trade in the US and Canada by
Hal Leonard Publishing, P.O. Box 13819, Milwaukee, WI 53213

Cover and Text Design: Doug Gordon

Library of Congress Cataloging-in-Publication Data

Aikin, Jim.
   Software synthesizers: the definitive guide to virtual musical instruments / by Jim Aikin.
      p. cm.
   Includes indexes.
   ISBN 0-87930-752-8 (alk. paper)
   1. Synthesizer (Musical instrument). 2. Electronic musical instruments. 3. Computer sound processing. 4. Computer music—instruction and study. I. Title.
ML74.A54 2003
786.7'419–dc21

                                                     2003040441

Printed in the United States of America

03 04 05 06 07   5 4 3 2 1

Contents

Foreword

I've been an electronic/musical instrument designer for half a century. There were two types of computers when I began—analog and digital. Analog computers had "computational modules" that performed mathematical operations on voltages, such as adding and multiplying. For instance, if you applied two volts to one input of an adder module and three volts to another input, the adder's output would be five volts. By using the appropriate modules and connecting them together with patch cords in the right way, you could solve mathematical equations in real time. At a summer job that I had in the mid '50s, one of my co-workers was developing an analog computer to figure out how sound waves would travel through the ocean, and then display the results as a graph on a cathode-ray tube. It was a high-tech, high-price, high-secrecy military project.

A decade or so after seeing analog computers in operation at that summer job, I designed and built my first modular analog synthesizer. Basically, it was a direct descendent of "general-purpose" analog computers. You could start with a simple waveform and perform various operations on it to shape it into an interesting musical sound. Technically speaking, each of the modules performed a specific mathematical operation on the voltages that it produced or processed. Musically speaking, however, it was a new musical instrument, capable of producing an amazing variety of fat, expressive sounds. That technology is still used in many "hardware synthesizers."

Digital computers perform mathematical operations directly on numbers, rather than on voltages. Yes, it was possible to use one of the early digital computers to calculate "musical functions" (sounds). But the computer couldn't go fast enough to generate the numbers for a typical musical waveform in real time, so you had to record the numbers on tape and then play them back at high speed through a digital-to-analog converter to create a musical sound. Back when musicians first began experimenting with "digital music," a computer filled a whole room, digital tape recorders were the size of refrigerators, and digital-to-analog converters were exotic, state-of-the-art devices. What's more, the software for these early "software synthesizers" was encoded on hundreds of punched cards, each of which contained just one instruction.

We've come a long way, baby. And fast! Digital computers went personal just 25 years ago. My old beloved Apple II provided me not only with a software emulation of a typewriter (a.k.a. a word processor) that enabled me to edit my typing without using an eraser, but also with the Mountain Computer Music System, one of the earliest affordable software synthesizers. To be sure, the MCMS required extra hardware, you set it up by typing instructions, and its eight-bit waveform resolution put a fog of grunge over the sounds it produced. But it was a synthesizer! You could program your own sounds and then play them in real time.

Fast-forward to the present. My current laptop bristles with software emulations. I can call up a complete calculator, operate any electronic circuit that I can think of, and touch up photographs to my heart's content. I can walk around in an imaginary room and transplant bushes in an imaginary garden. And yes, I can connect patch cords and turn knobs on a virtual modular analog synthesizer, and then play it with my MIDI keyboard. With all of these, the graphics are realistic and the sound is amazingly clean. These are more than experiments or novelties. These are real tools that I can use to get my work done and have some fun.

At times, all of this capability has a bittersweet flavor for me. My present laptop replaced a computer that was five years old and hopelessly obsolete. All my software is new too. What will happen in another five years? No matter how wonderful my current software is, I don't think I should become too attached to it, because I will soon abandon it in favor of the Next Big Thing. But then I realize that today's technology is not about permanence. It's about constantly learning and exploring. For learning and exploring software synthesizers, you can have no better guide than Jim Aikin. Jim is an accomplished master at explaining technical subjects to musicians, and he has real in-depth experience with synthesizers of all kinds. Whatever your level of familiarity with software synthesizers is, this book will help you use and enjoy them.

Keep synthesizin'!

—Bob Moog
November 27, 2002

Introduction

Thanks to MTV and the World Wide Web, linear narrative is a thing of the past. So why should a book have only one introduction? This one has four. Feel free to jump back and forth.

The three-and-a-half-second sneak preview

Why a book on software synthesizers? Because they're the coolest thing that's happened to music since, like, the invention of the electric guitar. Don't believe me? Keep reading.

The long zoom in

For as long as there have been musical instruments, musicians and instrument designers have worked closely with one another to improve the sound of the instruments. The violin was a pivotal expression of 17th-century Italian woodworking technology, the piano with its hundreds of moving parts a triumph of 19th Century mechanical engineering.

The piano and the violin, like all other pre-20th-century instruments, had one thing in common: The mechanism that produced the sound was inextricably linked to the physical activity of the musical performer. True, it was possible to capture a performance and reproduce it mechanically, as on a player piano, or even punch the piano roll by hand, with no performer in the picture at all. But the mechanism of the player piano still had to be attached to a physical piano in order to produce music. Moreover, the mechanism was specific to the piano: Attached (somehow) to a violin or trumpet, it would have produced no sound at all.

Today, the linkage between physical activity and the production of musical tone is no longer a necessity; it's optional (though many would argue it's a desirable option). In the last 25 years, the evolution of electronic instruments has abstracted the process of tone production — with amazing results, as the instruments discussed in these pages will attest. At the same time, devices called sequencers, which can play electronic instruments untouched by human hands, have abstracted the process of musical performance to the point where it would be all but unrecognizable to musicians of an earlier era.

Music-making will never be the same again. And none of these groundbreaking changes could have taken place prior to the birth of the computer.

Even in the 1960s and 1970s, when synthesizers first reached the public ear, a synthesizer needed a separate knob for each type of change that the performer wanted to make in the sound. The knob was physically attached to a circuit that effected the change. Rerouting signals within a synth meant flipping switches or even plugging in patch cords (hence the term "patch," which is still used to refer to the group of settings that produce a given sound in a synthesizer). The performer was no more abstracted from the production of tone than when playing a piano.

But then the computer got into the act. For the first time it became not only possible but easy to store, edit, and reproduce both musical gesture (the act of drawing the bow across the violin's strings) and the tone-producing mechanism that responds to the gesture.

Computers, it has to be said, are very good at some things and not nearly as good at others. There are satisfactions in making music with a computer, but they're irretrievably different from the satisfactions of making music with a conventional instrument. Computers — let's be frank — are balky, unresponsive things. If your goal is to lay your hands on a keyboard, or, even moreso, on some other type of performance interface, thereby to express your innermost soul unburdened of any form of intellectual effort, computer-based music-making is not for you. The process is often tweaky. What matters are the results. And the results can be awe-inspiring.

If you're new to the possibilities of computer-based music-making, this book, and the demo software and music files on the accompanying CD, will blow your doors off. If you're an old hand, there may still be a few items that will surprise and delight you. Be warned, though: It would be impossible to cover everything about computer-based music in one book: The topic is far too vast. The focus in these pages is on a relatively recent development: Within the past five years, it has become practical for the first time to use the computer itself not simply for recording and editing music but as a musical instrument in its own right. The age of computer-based sound synthesis has arrived.

The close-up

In the late 1980s, I had a fairly well-equipped electronic music studio in my living room. It occupied most of the living room, in fact. On a black metal A-frame stand resided no less than four synthesizers (all with keyboards, naturally). To the left of the keyboards was a computer — an Atari ST, with a floppy disk drive and a whole megabyte of RAM — in which I recorded and edited MIDI sequences. On the other side stood an 8-track reel-to-reel tape deck, the kind with 12-inch spools and ½-inch tape.

Today I get by with one keyboard, and the tape deck has long since disappeared. But my studio (now compact enough to fit in a small bedroom) has at least ten times as much music power as it did then — depending on how you calculate "music power," I suppose. I'm not a big fan of pseudo-scientific jargon. No matter how you figure it, I can produce more types of sound than I could 15 years ago, produce many of the same types of sound with higher quality and less background noise, edit my recordings with infinitely more precision, and format the finished music for distribution with a kind of ease and flexibility that were unthinkable then.

I can't claim any of the credit. The magic comes from a computer — the same computer on which I'm writing these words, on which I cruise the Internet, play games, and do my taxes. Eight or ten amazing synthesizers sit quietly on my hard drive, waiting for me to call them up to do my bidding. I also have an assortment of recording software at my disposal.

You can be jealous if you like. Since I make my living writing about this stuff, companies send me software for evaluation. Most musicians neither have, nor need, both Cubase and Sonar on their PCs at the same time, or both Reason and Storm. These programs duplicate many of one another's functions. On the other hand, there are cogent musical reasons for wanting to have a variety of softsynths. As with their hardware cousins, every model has, to a greater or lesser extent, its own unique sound and capabilities.

It has to be said that my music probably isn't much better than it was 15 years ago. In spite of some of the more optimistic advertising claims you'll encounter from time to time, technology does not provide an adequate substitute for talent. If anything, we've reached a point where having more technology can make it more difficult to produce a finished piece of music, rather than easier. First, there are an awful lot of options to sift through. Second, listeners' expectations have been ratcheted upward by the fact that everyone has access to the same high-tech tools. And then there are the hours you spend tracking down system conflicts inside the computer . . . no, let's not get into that.

Even with the occasional crash, glitch, or compatibility collision, though, I'm ridiculously happy with my computer-based music setup. As you read through the software profiles in these pages, I think you'll see why.

The establishing shot

The music industry goes through cycles. I suppose any industry does. In the pioneering phase, a groundbreaking product is introduced: It does something cool that has never been possible before. Excitement is generated. A year or two later, the boom phase has started: Six manufacturers, or twenty, are pushing products that do pretty much what the pioneering product did. Each offers a few new features, or a bundle of older features in a new package, that manufacturers hope will entice consumers to buy. As the public becomes more familiar with the new product type, the market grows, but eventually it becomes glutted. In the consolidation phase, many of the competing manufacturers fall by the wayside, leaving a few stodgy giants and a few smaller "boutique" companies who offer items that wouldn't be economical for the giants.

Right now, software synthesis is deep in the boom phase. Eight or ten years ago, there just about wasn't any such thing. The few software synths that existed either responded to MIDI input with an annoying time lag, or didn't respond to realtime input at all. Today there are at least a hundred developers, large and small, pursuing their own visions of musical magic and/or madness. No matter whether you want a faithful replication of a hardware synth from days of yore or a toolbox with which you can do things no one else has ever imagined, someone will be happy to sell you the software.

Almost from the beginning, *Keyboard* magazine has been chronicling the development of software synthesizers. In several dozen Keyboard Reports over the past five years, *Keyboard's* editors and freelance product reviewers have poked and prodded assorted softsynths, revealing their quirks, singing their praises, and encouraging the industry to strive for even greater heights.

If I had tried to write a whole book about software synthesizers from scratch, the research would have taken me so long that the first part of the book would have been years out of date by the time I finished the last chapter. The field is changing much too rapidly for such a leisurely approach. Fortunately, I was able to turn to the *Keyboard* archives for much of my source material. The profiles of individual instruments in Chapters 2 through 7 of this book are based almost entirely on product reviews that first appeared in *Keyboard*.

Where necessary, I've updated the reviews with information provided by the manufacturers — lists of new features, explanations of bugfixes, and so on. In the interest of journalistic integrity as well as historical accuracy, however, I have not deleted from the reviews any discussion of problems that the manufacturer told me have been fixed since the review was first published. In reading the reviews, then, you'll need to bear in mind both the date on which it was initially published and any information on updates that may have addressed the problems.

Since considerable segments of this book were written at various times and by various authors, it's necessary to make explicit another important *caveat:* Not every feature of every instrument is mentioned in the product profiles. Not only that, but the fact that a given feature is not mentioned in a given profile should *not* be taken as a conclusive indication that the product under discussion doesn't have that feature.

Product reviewer A, let's say, may be very concerned with feature X and make a point of discussing it in his review of instrument N. Reviewer B, however, may ignore feature X in his review of instrument M, *even though feature X is implemented in instrument M*. This can happen for any of several reasons. Feature X may be of little personal concern to reviewer B. Given the need to write to a limited word count (and many of the profiles in these pages are pretty darn short, for reasons having more to do with the exigencies of magazine production than with the merits of the software itself), other features may have seemed more in need of discussion. Or by the time instrument M was released, feature X may have become so nearly an industry standard that reviewer B felt it no longer warranted discussion.

While the profiles gathered here provide a broad-based and hands-on introduction to the field, then, they can't be considered definitive. A few significant instruments, in fact, are not profiled at all. For more information, I'd urge you to visit the websites of the respective developers (you'll find the URLs in Appendix B), as well as visiting public bulletin boards or relevant newsgroups and asking other musicians about their experiences.

I'd like to thank Greg Rule, *Keyboard's* editor, and Debbie Greenberg, executive editor, for their support throughout the process of putting together this book. I'd also like to thank the writers who contributed one or more reviews — Craig Anderton, Julian Colbeck, Marty Cutler, Joe Gore, Angela Hill, Ken Hughes, John Krogh, Francis Preve, Ernie Rideout, and Greg Rule. Needless to say, any mistakes that may have been introduced during the editing of the book are my responsibility, not theirs.

Thanks are also due to the many manufacturers who graciously allowed us to include demo versions of their software on the CD-ROM that accompanies this book. Whether you use a Macintosh or a Windows PC, you're about to make some wonderful discoveries.

And now — let the oscillators oscillate! Let the filters resonate! Let the modulation routings route and the envelope generators generate. On with the show!

—Jim Aikin

The Softsynth Revolution

Maybe Gil Scott-Heron was half-right: Maybe the revolution won't be televised — but it may be downloadable. Only a few short years ago, the best sounds you could get from your computer were the tacky, lo-fi synthesizer tones dribbling from a consumer-grade soundcard. Today, thanks to screaming-fast CPUs and a lot of clever software engineering, the world of music-making has been turned on its head.

If you'd like to make music with your computer and want to know about the coolest and most intriguing options for high-quality synthesized sound, you've come to the right place. While this book doesn't cover by any means all of the tools you can use to get music from a computer (at the end of this chapter you'll find a brief explanation of what's not covered, and why), most of the best and the brightest are lined up in these pages. Also on tap: clear, concise explanations of what you need to get started and a step-by-step tutorial of synthesizer terminology. Oh, and let's not forget the CD-ROM filled with demo software you can install and try out.

But first — the title of the book is *Software Synthesizers*. Most of you probably know what software is and what a synthesizer is. Even so, I'm going to do my best to avoid making glib assumptions that will create confusion. In the world of music software, I've found, far too many people — even experienced people — get frustrated and bewildered and eventually give up because no one took the time to explain to them exactly what's what. If I want you to share my enthusiasm for softsynths (and I do), it's up to me to make sure you're on the bus. So let's start by defining what we're going to be talking about.

What's a synthesizer?

In the broadest sense, any musical instrument that makes its sounds electronically can be called a synthesizer. We'll want to narrow that definition a bit — but first you need to understand the difference between "electrical" and "electronic."

An electric guitar is not an electronic instrument. Why? Because the sound originates in physically vibrating strings, which are excited (by the fingers or a pick) in a mechanical way. Put your ear close to the strings, and you'll hear the music even if the guitar is unplugged. The same is true of a genuine electric piano: Physical tines or reeds inside the body of the instrument are struck by physical hammers, thus producing tones. The tones of the strings, tines, or reeds are captured electrically with electromagnetic pickups so that they can be amplified. (Note, however, that most electrically operated pianos built today are electronic, not electric: They have no physical reeds or tines. Their "electric piano" sounds are electronically simulated.)

In an electronic instrument, the tones originate in an electronic circuit of some sort, be it analog or digital. If you were to listen to the circuit, you'd hear, at most, a faint background hum and the whir of the cooling fan. The tones become sound only when the output of the instrument is sent to an amplifier and emerges from a loudspeaker.

All synthesizers are electronic instruments, but not all electronic instruments are synthesizers. To qualify as a synthesizer, an instrument has to have one of two characteristics: (1) Its sound-producing circuitry offers a significant number of options to the user, enabling the user to shape the tone color as needed, and/or (2) it makes a class of sounds traditionally associated with synthesizers.

Not all of the instruments discussed in this book are synthesizers. In Chapter 2 we'll meet some software that doesn't conform to either of the definitions above, and in Chapters 5 and 7 we'll encounter instruments that do conform to definition 1, but that aren't usually called synthesizers.

Don'tcha just love hair-splitting arguments over terminology? Let's dig a little deeper, and see if we can clarify matters.

The first synthesizers that became widely known to the public, in the late 1960s, used analog electronic circuits — circuits built of discrete resistors, capacitors, diodes, and so on. The Minimoog (see **Figure 1-1**) is perhaps the best-known example, but more than a dozen similar instruments were in production by 1975. They had a limited, but very distinctive, palette of sounds. Today, any instrument that makes this type of sound arguably qualifies as a synthesizer, whether or not it has the types of sound-shaping controls associated with those early instruments and whether or not it uses true analog circuits.

In the early 1980s, some other types of synths appeared. Yamaha produced a series of synths that used FM technology, the leader of the pack being the DX7. (I'll have more to say about FM and other types of synthesis in Chapter 8.) The FM sound was quite different from that of analog instruments, but FM synths still provide plenty of user control over the sound, so they meet the definition: They're synthesizers.

At about this same time, the falling price of computer memory and the availability of faster digital circuits made it possible to store sampled sounds digitally. (A sample is a recording of an actual sound — see Chapter 5.) Synthesizers such as the Roland D-50 and Korg M1 began to appear; they made sounds by playing samples stored on ROM (read-only memory) chips. For instance, a synth might have recordings of real trumpet, guitar, and electric piano notes, which could be

Figure 1-1.
The Minimoog, produced between 1970 and 1981, was the first commercially successful synthesizer. It generated sounds using discrete analog circuits (nothing computerized), and its keyboard could play only one note at a time. *Photo courtesy Mark Vail.*

played from the keyboard. These instruments were also known as synthesizers, *but only if they offered the kinds of tone controls usually associated with their analog predecessors.* An instrument that played samples from ROM but didn't have synth-type tone controls was not generally considered a synthesizer, except perhaps by the marketing department of the company that built it.

A year or two later, we began to see instruments such as the E-mu Emulator and Ensoniq Mirage, which could store sampled sounds in RAM (random-access memory). New samples could be loaded by the user from a floppy diskette, or recorded directly into the instrument using a microphone. Although these instruments typically had the kinds of tone controls associated with synthesizers, they weren't *called* synthesizers. They were called samplers. Samplers are still an important type of instrument; several software samplers are covered in Chapter 5.

We'll meet other variations on the formula as we go along. You won't go too far wrong, though, if you look at it this way: It's a synthesizer if it sounds like a synthesizer, or if it has the types of controls usually associated with a synthesizer. But if it lets you load the pre-recorded sounds of your choice from a disk or other external medium, it's a sampler, not a synthesizer.

A note for insiders: Yes, you're right. This handy rule of thumb pretty much ignores physical modeling synthesizers. The Yamaha VL-1, which was the first commercially available synth based on physical modeling, did not have most of the traditional types of controls, nor did it sound like a traditional synth, but it was a synth all the same.

Why the confusion? Basically, we're trying to hit a moving target here. Synthesizers are not the same today as they were ten years ago, or twenty, or thirty. Those fiendishly clever manufacturers keep coming up with new variations on familiar themes, hybrids that combine elements of disparate technologies, and (once in a while) radically new approaches to sound production. My advice: Relax and enjoy the ride.

What is software?

All of the instruments mentioned above had one thing in common: They were discrete, free-standing pieces of hardware. In the beginning, analog electronics were the norm, but as time went on, more and more hardware synthesizers had digital circuitry inside — essentially, miniature computers dedicated to performing one particular task. Most digital synths produced from the early '80s onward used custom-engineered digital chips. At the time, the general-purpose chips in home computers simply weren't fast enough to do much in the way of digital synthesis.

Mercy, how times have changed.

The instruments discussed in this book have no physical existence as hardware. They consist entirely of software — essentially, long series of instructions that tell a computer how to make sounds, and what to show on the screen while doing so. The code that makes up a software synthesizer is not so very different from the code that tells your computer how to be a word processor, a Web browser, or a video game.

The software for a softsynth arrives in your computer, typically, in one of two ways. Either you install it from a CD-ROM or you download it over the Internet. In either case, the softsynth usually has to be *installed.* During installation, one or more files are stored on your computer's hard drive. If you look at the hard drive's directory, you'll find them in a folder named after the program or the company that distributes it.

Once the software is installed, you may be able to run it pretty much the way you would any other program, by double-clicking on the appropriate desktop icon or (on a Windows PC) selecting it from the Start menu. If it's a plug-in, however, you'll need to *instantiate* it (jargon for "create an instance of it" — in other words, tell the computer that you'd like to use it now) from within a host program. In either case, when you do this the software is loaded from the hard drive into your computer's RAM, and you're ready to jam.

Or almost ready. In order to make music with your new softsynth, you need at least one and preferably two additional components. First, you need a way to get audio out of the computer and into a pair of speakers. Usually this means some sort of soundcard. Helpful but not always required: a MIDI keyboard with which to play the synth. We'll have more to say below about both of these components.

How can they put a synthesizer inside a computer?

Believe it or not, computers are not magic. (Nor, occasional appearances to the contrary notwithstanding, are they malevolent entities out to destroy your happiness and turn you into a quivering wreck.) Everything that happens in a computer is ultimately just strings of numbers. The computer appears to be doing other things besides numbers because it handles the numbers very, very, very quickly, and because peripheral devices are attached to the computer that translate the numbers into a form we humans can more readily deal with — letters of the alphabet, for instance, or pictures, or sounds.

A synthesizer is no different. In order for a sound to exist inside the computer, it has to be described as a string of numbers. This is not the place for an in-depth discussion of digital audio, but in order to feel at home in the world of software synthesis you'll need to wrap your brains around a few basics, so let's take a closer look before we move on.

Let's start at the very beginning; that's a very good place to start.

You probably already knew this, but we live at the bottom of a thick blanket of air. This blanket, which is called the atmosphere, extends many miles upward from the surface of the Earth, growing thinner mile by mile, until it merges with the vacuum of space. If it weren't for gravity, the atmosphere would have dissipated into space billions of years ago, and life never would have emerged on Earth. Gravity is what holds the atmosphere in place — and while air may seem pretty flimsy stuff, like everything else that's subject to gravity, it has a measurable weight. What's more, there's a lot of it over our heads. At sea level, there's so much air pressing down on us that it exerts a pressure of about 14.7 pounds per square inch. (That's over a ton per square foot.) Except when the wind is blowing, we don't usually notice air pressure, but it's always there. The reason it doesn't squash us all flat is that our innards are pushing outward against our skin with exactly the same amount of pressure. We only notice it when driving up or down a mountain — those awkward moments when our ears pop because the pressure inside is no longer the same as the pressure outside.

Sound consists of rapid (and relatively small) fluctuations in air pressure. These fluctuations originate at some point — let's say, on the stretched skin of a drumhead when a conga player smacks it with his or her hand — and spread out in all directions through the air. When first struck, the drumhead moves downward, creating a low-pressure zone on the upper surface. As air molecules rush in from the surrounding area to fill the low pressure zone, the pressure in the surrounding area drops. In effect, the low-pressure zone propagates outward in all directions. A moment later, the drumhead rebounds upward, pushing the air molecules together and creating a zone of higher than normal pressure. Now the same thing happens again, in reverse. The molecules in the high-pressure zone spread out into the sur-

Figure 1-2.

Sound waves are conventionally illustrated with graphs that look more or less like this display, which is an audio editing window in Sonic Foundry's Sound Forge software. The X-axis (horizontal) represents time. Time runs from left to right. The Y-axis (vertical) represents air pressure, or the equivalent in some other medium, such as the electrical signal coming from a microphone. A higher point in the waveshape represents a moment when there's more pressure; a lower point represents a moment when there's less pressure. The horizontal line down the center of the graph represents the "rest state," or the normal background of air pressure in the environment, which would exist even in the absence of sound. If the waveshape never moves up or down from the center line, the graph is a diagram of silence.

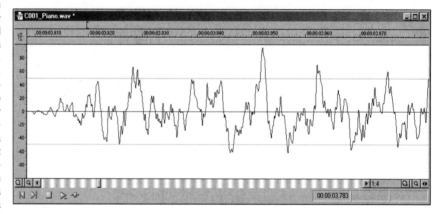

rounding area, which increases the pressure there. In effect, the high-pressure zone propagates outward, following the low-pressure zone. As the drumhead wobbles in and out, the process continues. Until the drumhead comes to rest, the air pressure at the surface keeps changing. That's how sound is created.

If you spend any time reading about digital audio, before long you'll run into a diagram that looks more or less like **Figure 1-2**. This shows more or less what sound would look like if we could see it.

The zones of higher and lower pressure are not stationary. They travel through the air, radiating in all directions from the sound source, at about 1,000 feet per second at sea level. When they reach a human ear, the ear senses them and reports to the brain on the exact shape and intensity of the pressure gradient. That's how we hear the conga drum, or anything else.

We can replace the ear with a scientific instrument equipped to track changes in air pressure — in other words, a microphone. A microphone is a type of *transducer*. That is, it transforms energy from one form to another. In this case, the physical energy of changes in air pressure is transformed into a fluctuating electrical voltage. The voltage fluctuations — which again would look very much like Figure 1-2 if we could see them — flow down the cable attached to the microphone.

It's essential to understand that the pattern of voltage fluctuations is virtually identical in shape to the pattern of changes in air pressure. A voltage increase corresponds to each increase in air pressure, and vice-versa. I said "virtually identical" because there will always be subtle differences, which depend on the engineering limitations of the microphone we're using. But assuming the microphone is reasonably good, we can ignore the differences for purposes of discussion.

The signal coming from the microphone is called an *analog* electrical signal, or "analogue" if you're in Britain, because the pattern of changes in voltage is directly *analogous* to the pattern of changes in air pressure.

If we plug the mic cable into an amplifier and plug the amp into a speaker, we have our old friend the public address (P.A.) system. The back-and-forth motions of the speaker (another transducer) will produce fluctuations in air pressure that will closely resemble the original fluctuations, only louder. If we plug the mic into a tape deck, we can record the electrical signal and play it back through a P.A. months or years from now.

As interesting as this process is from a technical standpoint, this isn't a book about mics, or speakers, or tape decks. It's about software. So we're going to do something more apropos: We're going to plug the mic into a computer. (Hah! You thought we'd never get here.)

Trouble is, the computer can't understand or make use of the voltage fluctuations coming down the wire. Computers only understand numbers. In order to get the mic's signal into the computer, we'll have to transform it into a string of numbers.

This neat trick is accomplished with a device called an *analog-to-digital converter* (ADC or A/D for short). The A/D converter, which is typically built into a soundcard, measures the incoming voltage over and over and stores each measurement as a number. Over and over, it sends the most recent number down the line to the computer, takes another measurement, sends it to the computer, and so on.

Once inside the computer, the stream of numbers representing the sound can be processed in an almost infinite variety of ways. In order to listen to it, though, we'll have to send the numbers back to the soundcard. Here, the process is run in reverse. The soundcard translates the numbers into a continuously varying electrical voltage using a *digital-to-analog converter* (DAC or D/A). The voltage is then sent to an amp and speakers, and we hear it as sound.

If all goes well, and if the person operating the computer software hasn't been too creative about processing the numbers, we'll recognize the sound coming from the computer as being identical to the sound — be it a conga drum, a human voice, or an entire orchestra concert — that first entered the microphone. But the results are not guaranteed. Any number of problems can get in the way, causing the sound to be distorted and mangled — perhaps subtly, perhaps so radically that it's rendered unrecognizable. In order to insure that the computer

FLOATING — WHAT'S THE POINT?

Music software companies sometimes toss the term "floating point" into their technical specs. In theory – and often in practice – digital audio that uses floating-point calculations sounds better. Without getting too technical, since this isn't a book on computer programming, let's just say that with floating-point math, it's a bit easier to handle large numbers, especially when you don't know in advance how large they're going to be. The opposite of floating-point is fixed-point. Whether, or in what circumstances, 64-bit fixed-point audio sounds superior to 24-bit floating-point audio is a bit like the question of how many angels can dance on the head of a pin, so we'll leave it for the Medieval theologians in the crowd to ponder.

produces the desired sounds, the ADC and DAC (to say nothing of the mic and speakers) have to represent the sound waves in an accurate way.

The key question, then, is this: How accurate does the computer representation of a sound have to be in order for human listeners to find it acceptable or even enjoyable?

Now we're ready to talk specs. The most important factors in producing good-quality digital audio are *bit resolution* and *sampling rate*. These terms both refer to the accuracy with which the audio is represented in the form of numbers.

You probably know that a movie or a TV picture doesn't actually consist of moving images. It consists of a sequence of still photos. The photos are projected on the screen one by one, but because they succeed one another so rapidly, our brains blend them together into the illusion of a single moving image. A similar process is used to represent a continuous stream of audio as a stream of discrete numbers.

A typical movie runs at a rate of 24 or 25 images (called "frames") per second. But the ear is a lot more discriminating than the eye. In order to create a good-sounding digital representation of a sound, we have to take "snapshots" of the fluctuating voltage at least 40,000 times per second. Each snapshot is referred to as a *sample* or *sample word*. (The word "sample" has two separate but related meanings, as explained in Chapter 5. In the discussion below, it's used exclusively to refer to a single number, not to a complete digital sound recording.) The rate at which samples are taken is known as the *sampling rate*.

The sampling rate used in music CDs is 44,100 sample words per second. This rate is used by many digital audio programs, including softsynths. These days it's a minimum standard: Many programs run at higher rates, such as 48,000, 96,000, or even 192,000 samples per second. Some older soundcards offer you the option of running at a lower sampling rate, such as 22,050 or even 11,025 samples per second. With a lower sampling rate, the fidelity of the sound will be somewhat degraded.

Forget about the microphone for a minute. A softsynth generates its tones from scratch, as strings of numbers, and sends the numbers to the DAC so we can listen to the results. Each and every second, then, a softsynth has to generate 44,100 discrete sample words (if not more). Oh, and that's *per note*. Play a five-note chord, and the poor softsynth has to generate and process 220,500 samples every second. If that sounds like a lot of number-crunching to you, you're right. That's why computer-based software synths have only become a realistic possibility during the past five years or so. Until computer chips got up into the 200MHz range, software-based synthesis just wasn't practical — at least not as a real-time proposition, and not if the goal was musically pleasing sounds. On a slower computer, a softsynth can render its audio output to a disk file, in which case it can take as long as it needs to crunch the numbers. But while rendering is a powerful technique that works fine even on a slow computer, you can't play a renderer from a keyboard and hear the music. That's what "real-time" means.

Let's go back to what happens at the ADC, when the signal from the mic is first being turned into numbers. We're measuring the signal 44,100 times per second — but how accurate are those individual measurements?

When you're measuring how tall your children are, you probably use a yardstick. The yardstick is most likely marked off in 16ths of an inch. In the backwoods USA, that is. In most of the modern world, it's a meter stick, not a yardstick, and it's marked off in millimeters, but we'll go with the yardstick. If your yardstick were marked off only into feet, with no marks in between, you'd have to record your children as all being two feet tall, three feet tall, four feet tall, and so on. A child whose actual height was between three feet and four feet would have to be recorded as being either three feet or four feet tall, because your measuring system would provide no information more accurate than that.

Being human, you're a lot smarter than a computer, so if you were using such a stupid yardstick you'd probably record Suzy's height as "a little more than three feet" or "not quite four feet." But a computer can't do that. For a computer, those in-between measurements *don't exist.* The computer can only record whole, exact numbers. So it needs to use a yardstick that's as accurate as possible — a yardstick marked off into a lot of tiny increments.

The yardstick for measuring sound is described in terms of the number of *bits* that can be used to store each sample word. The more bits, the more accurate the measurement.

It turns out that eight bits are just about the minimum you need to represent sound acceptably. With an 8-bit ADC, the sound "yardstick" is marked off with 256 small increments. The first-generation samplers I mentioned earlier, the Emulator and the Mirage, recorded and played back sound as streams of eight-bit numbers (bytes, in other words). Eight-bit sound is noticeably harsh and grainy, because the measurements of the sound pressure level are noticeably inaccurate. When inaccuracy creeps into the system, we perceive it as added noise.

Sound is stored on music CDs as 16-bit numbers. Sixteen-bit audio has a much cleaner sound (less inherent noise), because the sound waves can be represented much more accurately. In fact, the 16-bit "yardstick" is marked off into 65,536 tiny increments. But why stop there? If 16-bit sound is good, why not use 24-bit sound, or 32-bit sound, or 64-bit?

Modern digital audio software, running on a fast computer, often uses 24-bit or 32-bit numbers to represent sound waves. But the computer has to work harder to process larger numbers. When the computer is forced to work too hard, one of two things happens: Either the softsynth says, "Sorry, I can only play seven notes at a time," and flat-out refuses to add any new notes until it finishes with one of the notes it's already playing, or the audio output abruptly fills up with

Figure 1-3.

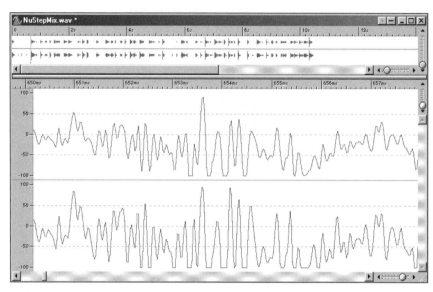

This close-up of a stereo soundfile (in Steinberg's Wavelab audio editing program) shows what clipping looks like. Note the plateau-like flat places at the bottoms of the waves near the center of the window. The file was recorded at such a high level that the numbers in this part of the file exceeded the maximum possible range. When that happens, your audio software will simply record the maximum possible value (or in this case, the minimum possible value) over and over. On playback, clipping has an unpleasantly harsh, buzzy quality.

very ugly pops, clicks, and stuttering noises. The audio output might even shut down entirely.

When the audio engine in your computer stutters or chokes because it can't spit out enough numbers quickly enough, we say you're hearing *dropouts*. Asking a softsynth to play too many notes at once is only one possible source of audio dropouts; there are others. On a PC, for instance, your soundcard may be sharing an IRQ (interrupt request) with too many other devices. To prevent dropouts, you may need to move the soundcard physically to a different slot in the computer. (This operation requires some care, however. If you're encountering dropouts, don't just start fooling around in the guts of the machine. Phone your soundcard manufacturer's technical support hotline and ask for their help.)

Each time the software developer improves the audio quality by boosting the sampling rate or bit resolution, the audio software can accomplish less before it uses up all of the available bandwidth in the CPU. "Bandwidth," in this case, refers to how many distinct arithmetic operations the CPU can perform per second. Basically, an 800MHz chip can perform twice as many operations per second as a 400MHz chip. Another term that's often used to describe CPU bandwidth is "machine cycles." The more machine cycles a softsynth uses per second, the fewer cycles are left over for the computer to do anything else, such as redraw the screen.

Sooner or later, we reach a point of diminishing returns: Improving the audio quality further isn't useful, because the difference to human ears will be very, very subtle, while the degradation in computer performance caused by the amount of arithmetic the software has to execute in real time becomes overwhelming.

If the sampling rate is too low, the high frequencies in the sound will get lost. If the bit resolution (also called word length, because each sample is stored as an 8-bit, 16-bit, or 24-bit numerical "word") is too low, the sound will be noisy. That's pretty much all you need to know.

It's highly unlikely that your softsynth won't support at least a 16-bit, 44.1kHz data stream, so if you're hearing a poor-quality signal, the source of your problems will probably lie elsewhere. Other forms of digital audio nastiness include:

■ *Clipping.* There's an absolute limit on how large the numbers in a digital audio system can be. (With floating-point math, this isn't precisely true, but the floating-point numbers will have to be converted back to integers before being sent to your soundcard, so clipping can still become a problem.) If your audio software tries to make a number that's too big, the waveform will reach the maximum possible level and then "clip." In an audio editing program, clipping looks like **Figure 1-3**. If it's brief, clipping sounds like a pop or click. If it goes on for more than a few milliseconds, it sounds as if the audio is being mangled with a buzz saw.

■ *Aliasing.* If the softsynth tries to make a sound that's too high in frequency, new overtones will be introduced. A detailed discussion of aliasing would take several pages and several diagrams. Suffice it to say that if a high-pitched sustained tone sounds bell-like when you don't expect it to, or if a tone with vibrato has an

Figure 1-4.
A USB Midisport 2x2 MIDI interface from Midiman/M-Audio is a simple, affordable way to get MIDI signals in and out of your computer.

unexpected up-and-down whooshing quality, you've got aliasing. The usual solution is to lower the cutoff frequency of the synth's filter, or choose a waveform that has fewer overtones (such as a triangle wave instead of a sawtooth).

A word or two about MIDI

Playing a software synthesizer from your computer's QWERTY keyboard is possible (depending on the software), but not much fun, except for testing the software or goofing around. Most softsynths are played using MIDI keyboards.

Some MIDI keyboards attach directly to the computer with a USB cable. Older ones may use a serial or parallel cable. If your keyboard isn't equipped with one of these connectors, you'll need to attach a *MIDI interface* to your computer (see **Figure 1-4**), and connect the keyboard's MIDI out jack to the computer's MIDI in jack using a MIDI cable.

MIDI (the Musical Instrument Digital Interface) is a communications standard used for transmitting musical performance information. Whole books have been written about MIDI. Fortunately, you can get up and running with software synthesis without worrying too much about the details. Here's what you need to know:

When you press a key on a MIDI keyboard, the keyboard sends out a message containing four essential items of information. First, it's a type of message called a *note-on,* which tells any receiving device that a note has just started. Second, the message contains a *channel number.* MIDI defines 16 different channels, all of which can be active on the same cable at the same time. Third, the message contains a *note number,* which tells the receiving device which note was played. Finally, the message contains a *velocity* value, which indicates how quickly the key was moving when it struck the keybed.

When you lift your finger from the keyboard, more or less the same thing happens: The keyboard transmits a *note-off* message, which contains a channel number, a key number, and a note-off velocity. (The note-off velocity value is rarely used.)

It's important to understand that MIDI note-on and note-off messages contain no information about the actual sound that you'll hear. If the synth on the receiving end is set to make a flute sound, that's what it will do. If it's set to make a drum sound, a drum sound is what you'll get. The transmitting keyboard neither knows nor cares what happens after it sends the note-on. The receiving synth could even be switched off or malfunctioning. That makes no difference to the keyboard, because MIDI — unlike, for example, the data flying back and forth in a printer cable — is a one-directional protocol. If the printer is out of paper, it can let your computer know. MIDI isn't quite that sophisticated.

An even more basic point that's sometimes misunderstood by folks who are just getting started: Because MIDI cables can't carry actual sounds, you can't record the sound coming from an external hardware synthesizer into your recorder software by connecting the synth to the computer via MIDI. All you can do with MIDI is record and play back performance information. To record any sound into the computer, you have to use its audio I/O facilities, whatever they may be.

Your keyboard will probably contain other types of performance controllers — pitchbend and modulation wheels, for instance, or knobs and sliders on the front panel. Each of these will send its own type of MIDI message. But here again, it's up to the receiving synthesizer what to do with the messages. It may even ignore them entirely.

Most of the software synths discussed in these pages can respond to MIDI controller data in various ways. Some can also generate controller data from their on-screen knobs and sliders. Assuming the synth is operating as a plug-in, you may be able to record this data into the host sequencer. MIDI controllers are an unbeatable way to make your synthesizer performances sound more interesting and expressive.

Plug-ins vs. stand-alones

Software synthesizers come in two basic flavors. Some are *stand-alone* applications, and some run as *plug-ins* within a host application. What's more, there are several plug-in formats, which are not mutually compatible with one another. If you're planning to run a softsynth as a plug-in, you need to check with the manufacturer before you purchase and make sure that the format used by your host app is supported. Some softsynths are available in several formats. The softsynth may be conveniently installed on your computer in all of its available formats when you run the software installer once, after which you can run the synth stand-alone or as a plug-in, whatever you need at the moment.

There are two common plug-in formats in the Windows world — VST and DirectX (also called DXi, which is short for "DirectX instrument"). VST, which stands for "Virtual Studio Technology," is a protocol developed by a company called Steinberg. It's used in Steinberg products, but has also been made available to other manufacturers. DirectX was developed by Microsoft. A softsynth that uses VST is sometimes referred to as a VSTi (for "VST instrument"). At this writing, the current version of VST is 2.0. All of the softsynths I'm aware of that use VST are compatible with version 2.0.

If your host application (a sequencer or multitrack audio recorder) uses only DirectX, you can run VST plug-ins by purchasing and using a *wrapper* program, as shown in **Figure 1-5**. The two leading wrappers are VST-DX Adapter, from FXpansion (www.fxpansion.com, currently $60), and DirectiXer (www.tonewise.com/DirectiXer, currently $49). Both wrappers can make VST instruments available within a DirectX host. There's no comparable technology for instantiating a DXi (DirectX instrument) in a VST host, but since most of the good softsynths are available in VST format, this is not a major problem.

Figure 1-5.
DirectiXer is a wrapper
program with which you can
create DirectX-compatible
versions of VST plug-ins.
When you run DirectiXer,
you'll be able to choose various options for each plug-
in. (In this screenshot I'm
wrapping the Waldorf
Attack percussion synth,
which is covered in
Chapter 7.)

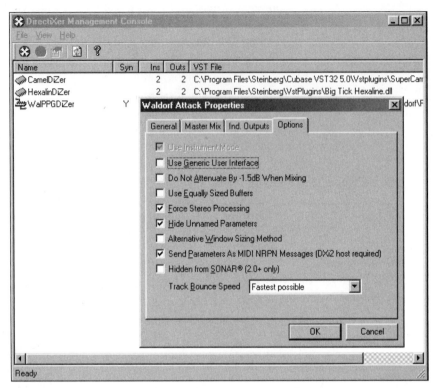

On the Macintosh side, the major plug-in formats are VST, MAS (used in Mark of the Unicorn's Digital Performer), RTAS (Real Time Audio Suite, used in Digidesign Pro Tools), and TDM (also used in Pro Tools, but requiring Digidesign hardware). Again, you can buy a wrapper program that will let a VSTi run in a MAS host. If you're a Digital Performer user, check with Mark of the Unicorn for their recommendations on wrappers.

When a synth is operating in stand-alone mode, you can use the computer pretty much the way you'd use a hardware MIDI tone module: Just start the synth software and then play your MIDI keyboard. The main advantages you'll gain over using a hardware module are the size of the screen and the affordability of the synth itself. The term "affordability" is somewhat puffy, though: If you've already purchased a computer and the necessary peripheral hardware, a softsynth is indeed affordable compared to a hardware instrument with similar capabilities. But if you also factor in the cost of the computer and hardware (including a MIDI keyboard), a softsynth will cost as much as or more than its hardware counterpart. On the other hand, you only have to buy the computer once, and you can run a dozen softsynths on it — not possible in the hardware world.

When using a softsynth, it's a good idea to quit any other software that might be running in the background, especially screensavers and Internet connections, as these can interrupt the audio output, causing dropouts. Many stand-alone softsynths have "capture to disk" modes, with which you'll be able to record your performance as a high-quality audio file. This file can later be converted to an mp3 (using a different piece of software), so you can share your ecstatic noodlings with the world on your website.

Running a softsynth within a host sequencer/recorder offers far more flexibility and musical power, so I'd recommend using plug-in mode when possible.

First, you can record your MIDI keyboard performance in a sequencer MIDI track, after which it can be edited. You can fix wrong notes, add or remove accents by adjusting the velocities of certain notes, change the timing of notes you played a little early or a little late, overdub knob sweeps, and so on. See your sequencer's manual for information on how to do all this.

Second, provided your computer is reasonably fast, you'll be able to run several different softsynths at the same time. For instance, you might lay down a drum track with Waldorf Attack (see page 240), some chords with the Native Instruments FM7 (see page 55), and a bass line and lead line with VirSyn Tera (see page 75). Since each synth has, to a greater or lesser extent, its own sound palette, your ensemble will sound richer and more satisfying than if you used the same synth for all of the parts. Also, running three stand-alone softsynths side by side is likely to be impossible. If nothing else, they'll fight over who gets to use the soundcard.

Third, you'll be able to process the sounds coming from your softsynths with plug-in effects. The sonic power of plug-in effects is not to be underestimated: These puppies *rock*. Whether you want to do some subtle tone shaping with EQ (equalization) or rip the face off the sound with a distortion effect, effects will add a lot to the timbral palette of any softsynth. Some softsynths have very capable built-in effects, but specialized effects will always take you further. Your sequencer/recorder software probably comes with its own suite of bundled effects — but again, you can accomplish even more with specialized third-party effects. (For more on effects, see Chapter 8.)

Your sequencer may come with a few basic softsynths built in. These are handy for laying down a bass line or a chord part, and with the aid of some plug-in effects they can sound surprisingly robust, but none of the built-ins has the deep features found in third-party synths you can buy separately.

What do you need to get started?

The first necessity, if you want to use a software synthesizer, is a decently fast computer — the faster the better. The synth developer's website will list the minimum and/or recommended system requirements, but I wouldn't suggest settling for a minimum system. If you do, you may be limited to as little as three notes of polyphony and no effects — pretty much a musical disaster if you're planning to do any serious work. Get the fastest machine you can afford. On the PC side, nothing under

800MHz is even worth talking about. If you're a professional or aspiring professional, 1.5GHz is probably a reasonable minimum. On a Macintosh, you'll get equivalent power with numbers that are somewhat lower.

Don't skimp on RAM, either. Even if the website says you can get away with 64MB of RAM, get at least 256MB. (Note: These figures are reasonable in the autumn of 2002 — if you're reading this book in 2007, you'll need to do your own research to learn what's currently in the ballpark.)

What computer operating system should you go for? The Mac/Windows choice is still largely a tossup. It seems to me Windows offers some small advantages in terms of the amount of software available, but possibly I'm prejudiced. There's some great music software that's Mac-only.

The question of which flavor of Windows or Mac OS to choose is slightly more awkward. Most Windows developers are supporting XP these days. Support for Mac OS X has been slower to arrive, but seems to be picking up momentum as I write this (in October 2002). If I were buying a Mac today, I'd insist on a machine equipped with both OS 9 and OS X. Six months from now, that precaution may no longer be necessary. In every case, though, the time to check with the software manufacturer and find out what OS variations they support is *before* you buy the computer. This caveat applies just as strongly to OS upgrades. If you upgrade from Windows 98 to Windows XP, for instance, you might easily find that one of your favorite music applications no longer runs — or that the application runs, but the manufacturer of your audio interface is not supporting the interface with a driver for that OS. List all of the components in your computer music system and check with *all* of the manufacturers before upgrading your OS.

Note, also, that in some cases the OS requirements listed in the reviews in this book were current *at the time when the review was originally written.* I've updated the information as well as I could, but some bad data may have flown in under the radar, so check the review date, then check with the manufacturer. If you want to run the synth under a newer OS, you may be able to, even though it isn't listed.

For reasons mentioned above, I recommend using plug-in softsynths with a sequencer/multitrack recorder as the host application. (If you're using one of the virtual rack systems discussed in Chapter 4, this advice is less applicable.) Some multitrack recorders, such as Digidesign Pro Tools, Syntrillium Cool Edit Pro, and Magix Samplitude, provide MIDI support (which you'll need in order to use a softsynth) only grudgingly, if at all. A better bet would be a full-featured sequencer/recorder, such as Steinberg Cubase (on either Mac or PC), Mark of the Unicorn Digital Performer (on the Mac), or Cakewalk Sonar (on the PC). You don't necessarily need to purchase the high-end version: An entry-level version, such as Cubasis VST, will be more affordable, and will most likely support softsynths. Before you buy any host application, though, check to make sure it's compatible with the software instrument(s) you're planning to use.

Next, you'll need some type of MIDI keyboard. For a desktop music setup, a compact unit like the Midiman Oxygen 8 from M-Audio (see **Figure 1-6**) would be hard to beat, but any MIDI keyboard at all will work. You may be able to pick up a used synth for a few bucks that's still perfectly good as a MIDI master keyboard, even though its sound-producing side is lame by today's standards.

If you're just getting started, you may be tempted to make do with your computer's off-the-shelf audio output (a consumer soundcard on the PC side, or the

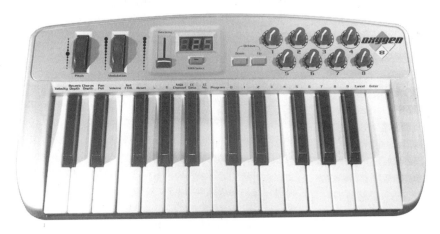

Figure 1-6.
The M-Audio Oxygen 8 keyboard (www.midiman.net) hooks to your computer via USB, and the two-octave keyboard makes it a good choice in computer installations where desktop space is limited.

built-in minijack on a Mac), but there are reasons why you probably won't be satisfied for very long. Here's why:

Computers typically spend some time doing lots of different "housekeeping" tasks. Though these are invisible to you when you're writing an email or whatever, they're going on in the background every second. But as we noted earlier, in order for audio to sound good, it has to be output smoothly, with no interruptions. The way software developers get around this is with *output buffering*. Essentially, the softsynth sends a chunk of audio data to the soundcard a little ahead of time. The soundcard then pulls this data out of the buffer as needed and sends it to the DAC. Before the buffer is empty (one hopes), the CPU will get around to sending another chunk of data to fill it up again.

If this doesn't make sense, think of the audio output as a bucket with a little hole in the bottom. The bucket leaks water at a constant rate. Every once in a while, a guy comes along with a pitcher and pours some water into the bucket. Then the guy wanders away to do something else. If he comes back with the pitcher before the bucket is empty, all is well — but if he doesn't show up, the bucket empties out, and water stops flowing out of the hole.

If the guy only shows up once every four or five minutes, you need a pretty big bucket to make sure the water keeps flowing without any interruptions. But if he shows up every four or five seconds, you can use a much smaller bucket.

In first-generation computers, the bucket had to be pretty big, because the guy couldn't walk very fast. Translation: The soundcard needed a big audio buffer in order to prevent dropouts, because the OS couldn't be relied on to fill the buffer in a timely manner.

When you play a note on the MIDI keyboard, the softsynth starts generating a note almost immediately — but the sound doesn't go directly to the audio output. It goes into the output audio buffer. If the buffer contains a full second of audio (176,400 bytes of 16-bit stereo at 44,100 samples per second), you won't hear the note you've just played until a full second has passed.

The time lag between when you play a note and when you hear it is called *latency.*

Latency is less of an issue today in software synthesis than it was a couple of years ago, but it's not an issue you can afford to ignore. With an acoustic instrument — a piano, guitar, or flute — there's essentially no latency. You play a note, you hear it. Musicians rely on that instantaneous aural feedback in order to shape their performances in an expressive manner. Playing an instrument in which there is significant latency is possible, but it's very difficult and unsatisfying. (An organist playing a pipe organ in a large cathedral may have to deal with more than ¼ second of latency. But the rich echoes will blur the sound, masking any unevenness in the performance.)

The built-in soundcard in your computer probably has significant latency. In order to use a softsynth in performance, or even to record with it and not get intensely frustrated by the sluggish response, you need a low-latency soundcard.

Various manufacturers have developed ways of getting low-latency performance out of soundcards. The most widely used protocol is called ASIO. If both your soundcard and your softsynth (or its host application) are ASIO-compatible, you're good to go. In Windows, Microsoft's WDM protocol also provides very low latency. And beginning in the newer releases of OS X, the Macintosh offers low-latency audio as part of the system, eliminating the need for an ASIO audio interface.

Figure 1-7.
The Creamware Minimax, which runs on the Creamware Pulsar hardware accelerator board, recreates the classic sound and features of the Minimoog digitally.

Another way around the latency logjam is to use a softsynth that runs on its own dedicated PCI board, which is tucked into a slot inside the computer. The synths available for the Creamware Pulsar card, for instance (see **Figure 1-7**), are inherently low latency, because the Pulsar hardware is not part of the computer's operating system, and is not subject to OS-type interruptions. Hardware-dependent softsynths are not covered in this book, however.

If you hear dropouts when using your softsynth, check to see whether the sound-card's buffer setting can be increased. Many cards let you adjust the buffer size and other settings. Conversely, if you're hearing an unacceptable amount of delay (latency), try decreasing the buffer size. When you reach a point where the audio starts to break up, increase it again just slightly, and the latency characteristics of your system should be optimized.

Finally, let's not ignore the characteristics of the amp and speakers through which you're listening to your computer. Consumer multimedia speakers (or even headphones) will do in a pinch — but you can make a violin out of a cigar box too, in a pinch. If you want to hear the full-bodied lows and crisp highs your synthesizer is pumping out, set aside enough in your budget for a decent pair of monitor speakers. Studio-quality nearfield monitors are available from Event, Fostex, Mackie, Roland, Yamaha, and many other companies. Having said that, "studio quality" is a marketing term (that is, it's all but meaningless). Quite often, it's the cheap gear that's advertised as "studio quality." Speakers that are advertised as "studio reference monitors" have at least some pretensions of being decent. If someone tried to advertise a cheap speaker as a studio reference monitor, their friends would throw scraps of food at them and put deceased rodents in their mailbox. Or at least we can hope.

If at all possible, avoid using your home stereo for monitoring. Home stereos often enhance the highs and lows in order to make music sound better. For music production, you want a monitor system whose frequency response is "flat" (that is, the input is essentially the same as the output, with no artificial enhancements). "Reference monitors," assuming they come from a reputable company, will usually have a more or less flat frequency response.

Copy protection

Most music software is copy-protected. Nobody likes copy protection — neither the manufacturers nor the users. It's a hassle. So why not get rid of it, then?

The way I look at it is, copy protection is necessary because musicians tend not to be wealthy. Also, they like to share with one another, because you can't have too many friends, right? When programs aren't copy-protected, musicians tend to pass them around like candy.

This is a problem because most music software companies are not in the megabucks league. Most have no more than 20 or 30 employees (or maybe only five or six). The employees are — you guessed it — musicians. They're trying to make a living too. Every pirated copy of a program takes money straight out of their pockets.

Another thing: Every time a music software company goes out of business because they don't have enough cash coming in, we all lose. First, we lose out on the cool products the company would have unveiled next year, which now will never see the light of day. Later on, we lose because the old software they created won't work under a new computer operating system. If you don't believe this is a real issue, talk to someone who used Opcode Studio Vision as their main recorder. When Opcode closed its doors, these folks lost years of creative work — files on their hard drives that they could no longer open or edit once they had upgraded to the next-generation Macintosh.

Even *with* copy protection, I've heard estimates that six out of seven people using a certain well-known music program whose name begins with "R" are using a cracked version, not a copy that they bought. Manufacturers are fighting an uphill battle. This is why I don't answer emails asking for advice on how to use specific programs. I have a standard reply: Contact the manufacturer's technical support department about that. True, calling tech support is a pain. You may have to wait on hold for 15 minutes, and you may not get the right answer the first time you call. But folks who have unregistered copies *can't* use tech support. (They probably don't have a manual, either.) They're up a creek without a paddle, and that's not my problem.

Copy protection comes in several flavors. Some programs ask for a serial number when installed, and that's the end of the story. Some use hardware copy-protection devices, often called "dongles." A dongle will attach to your USB or parallel port. If it isn't in the port, the program won't run. In order to run several USB-protected programs at once, you'll probably need a USB hub, but that's not a big deal.

Hardware copy protection is a pretty effective system. If you regularly use two different computers, you can physically carry the dongle from one to the other. As long as you're only using one computer at a time, your work flow won't be hampered. One word of warning, though: Don't lose the dongle! It's what you paid all that money for.

Other manufacturers use a *challenge-response* system, in which the installed program issues a "challenge" (often a string of nonsense words). You email the challenge to the manufacturer or fill it in on the registration page of their website, and they provide a response. When you enter the response into the program, you have an authorized copy. Challenge-response copy protection is vulnerable to hard drive crashes, and the software can't be transferred to a different computer (or even to a different physical hard drive within the same computer). But most manufacturers who use challenge-response will issue you a new response if you explain politely why you need it.

A few manufacturers use a system that asks for the original CD-ROM to be inserted in the computer's CD drive. This can happen each time you start the program, or only once in a while. The CD itself will probably be copy-protected in some manner, so that you can't duplicate it.

Downloading demos

Most of the synths in this book are available in demo form as free downloads. This is one of the cooler aspects of living in the Information Age: How many automobile dealers would let you drive the car for a month to see whether you like it?

Downloadable demos are usually crippled in some way, so as to encourage you to purchase a fully functional copy. After making the purchase online, you may be able to authorize your existing demo, which will unlock the crippled features.

Demos are commonly crippled in several different ways:

■ The demo may emit an intermittent beep, or the audio output may have a gap every 20 or 30 seconds.

■ It may not be able to save and load files.

■ You may be able to run it for a certain time period, or boot it a certain number of times, after which it will stop working.

To save you the trouble of downloading, we've stuffed as many demo programs as we possibly could into the CD-ROM that comes with this book. To learn what's included, see page 281.

What to do when disaster strikes

Here and there in this book, you'll read brief mentions of installation problems, system conflicts, and even bugs. Mostly, though, the tone of Chapters 2 through 7 is upbeat. Make a joyful noise and all that.

Sad to say, your experience with softsynths may not be quite such a bed of roses. Software is written by humans, and humans make mistakes (a.k.a. bugs). They also make choices (such as whether to create a VSTi or a DXi synth) that aren't mistakes from their point of view, but that may cause you problems. Since most music software runs in an environment where it has to work with software from other companies, there's plenty of room for system conflicts. And then there's the seemingly endless stream of problems created by user ineptitude, also known as "failing to read the manual." Truly, the list of things that can go wrong in a music computer is long and gruesome. Bugs are just the beginning.

When your softsynth doesn't make a peep, try running through the checklist below. I can't guarantee you'll find a solution to your problem, but if nothing in the list does the trick, when you call tech support they'll be impressed with your thoroughness, and they'll probably put forth a premium effort on your behalf.

■ Have you downloaded and installed the latest version of the softsynth?

DO I NEED TO KNOW PROGRAMMING?

Here and there in this book, you'll read references to synthesizer programming and synthesizer programs. As used in this context, the word "program" has very little to do with computer programs and computer programming.

A synthesizer programmer is a person who uses the controls provided in the synth to create new sounds. These sounds are then stored in the synth's memory, at which point they're called programs, presets, or patches. (These terms are pretty much interchangeable.) You can be a synth programmer without knowing a solitary thing about computer programming: Familiarity with computer code is not required. For that matter, you can make great music with software synthesizers by using the sound programs provided by the manufacturer. You don't need to program your own sounds.

Check the manufacturer's website to find out if there's an update with a newer version number. An update with a bugfix will often solve the problem.

■ Have you downloaded and installed the latest version of the host application in which the softsynth is running?

■ Have you downloaded and installed the latest version of the driver software for your audio interface (soundcard)?

■ If you're hearing undesirable noise: First, turn down the softsynth's output somewhat. If the noise persists, try increasing the buffer settings for your audio output device. If that doesn't help, check to make sure your audio output isn't overloading your speakers. Make sure you aren't running through a distortion effect (on an auxiliary send, perhaps).

■ If the application shuts down unexpectedly — if playback stops, or audio stops, or the audio starts stuttering — you may be overloading your CPU. If the application has a CPU meter (many of them do), keep an eye on it while recreating the conditions. If the CPU is maxed out, you'll need to simplify. One common way to do this is to create a *submix*, in which several softsynth outputs are rendered to the hard drive as a single stereo audio track. After rendering the softsynth performance, you can mute the softsynth tracks, which should free up some CPU time.

■ If the CPU meter is spiking for no discernible reason, try disabling your plug-ins one at a time in order to isolate which plug-in (or combination of plug-ins) is the root of the problem. If a given softsynth is fighting with a plug-in effect, for instance, you may be able to render the softsynth track as an audio track, remove the softsynth, and run the effect on the audio track.

■ If the softsynth responds sluggishly to your MIDI keyboard, try reducing the buffer settings for your audio output device. If that doesn't help, or if you can't get at the settings, check whether your audio device has a lower latency mode (such as ASIO or WDM) that you can switch to.

■ If the softsynth makes no sound, start by checking the MIDI input settings. Is MIDI actually reaching the synth at all? If so, is the synth assigned to the correct MIDI channel? Is your MIDI keyboard's MIDI out jack plugged into the computer's MIDI in jack? If so, is the MIDI port you're using selected in the host app? (Look in the Preferences or Options dialog box.)

■ Still no sound? Check to make sure your synth isn't on a mixer channel or MIDI track that has been muted. If the audio level meters show activity within the software, make sure your audio interface is powered up. (Some of them have to be plugged in and switched on.) Make sure your amp or powered speakers are switched on, and that the cable from the audio interface is plugged into the correct jacks in the hardware amp or mixer.

■ If MIDI seems to be routed correctly to the softsynth, and the audio output seems to be set up correctly, but you're still not hearing any sound, simplify the setup. Start the host app and create a new, empty song/document. First, try loading an audio file from your hard drive into an audio track, and play it back within the song. If you can hear it, you know the problem isn't with the audio routing. Try loading a different softsynth to check whether one synth works while another doesn't. If the problem is limited to one particular synth, take a look at how its parameters are set. The filter may be closed down, for instance, or all of the oscillators may be switched off.

■ If all else fails, then (to borrow a phrase from Firesign Theatre) maybe it's time to go live in a tree and learn to play the flute. There are worse fates.

When is a synthesizer not a synthesizer?

While this book covers several types of software instruments — electric piano simulations, drum modules, and samplers — that aren't strictly synthesizers, a number of types of sound-producing software are not covered.

To qualify as a software instrument for our purposes, a program has to be able to respond to realtime MIDI input by, at the very least, starting and stopping notes. This leaves out multitrack audio recorders, as well as groove-oriented sample playback programs like Sonic Foundry Acid.

Programs that create sound primarily by writing it to disk (renderers) and playing it when you click on the play button with the mouse are not included. U&I Software Metasynth, for example, is a very powerful program but not a realtime synthesizer.

I've also had to exclude programs that run on hardware accelerator boards plugged into the computer. The most powerful instruments in this class are those that run on the Creamware Pulsar and Scope systems, but synths burned onto soundcard chips (as in the Soundblaster line) are far more numerous. Neither type is included in these pages. There are also some instruments that use external hardware attached to the computer — Symbolic Sound Kyma and the Clavia Nord Modular, for instance — to make sound. You won't find them in this book, even though a computer is required for programming them.

Only software for Windows and the Macintosh is covered. There are some decent softsynths for Linux (if you're curious, a great site to poke around in is run by Dave Phillips at http://linux-sound.org), and I believe there are a couple for BeOS. None is covered here.

Finally, I've ignored the whole world of mod files and tracker software. The mod/tracker scene developed in the early days of computer audio, when computers weren't as fast as they are now. Mod files are compact, creating them is inexpensive, and they'll play on many different computer systems, including obsolete platforms like the Commodore Amiga. If you want to know more, go to Google (www.google.com) and search for "mod tracker."

Dedicated hardware
vs. computer-based instruments

Before we dive into our discussion of specific softsynths, you may be wondering — are software instruments the wave of the future? Are hardware synthesizers destined to go the way of the dodo and the great auk? Or does hardware still have a valid place in the world of high-tech music?

I don't think this is an either-or question. The scene is dynamic, and will continue to evolve — probably in ways we can't yet foresee. But I do think hardware instruments will continue to play a vital role — and not just because there are some great-sounding ones out there. Hardware instruments offer several solid (so to speak) advantages, none of which is to be sniffed at:

■ Other things being equal, the software in a hardware synth will be more stable and reliable than its computer-based counterpart. This is because the manufacturer "owns" the operating system and the chips on which the instrument runs. The manufacturer doesn't have to write code that can survive in the often hostile environment of a multitasking computer OS.

■ With a hardware synth, you get a guaranteed voice count. Synths that can play 24, 32, 64, or even 128 notes at once are common and affordable. Most of the computer synths discussed in this book choke at far fewer than 128 voices, even on a blazingly fast computer.

■ Hardware synths often have keyboards and/or front panels studded with knobs. In a single box you get both the tone-producing circuitry and a responsive and musical user interface. The mouse and the QWERTY keyboard just can't compete.

■ A hardware synth doesn't require a separate audio or MIDI interface, with all of the attendant installation hassles — all that stuff is built in. The convenience factor is hard to knock.

■ Computers are not notoriously easy to take on a gig. Granted, a hardware synth is fragile, too. It's not something you want to see a drunken roadie toss into the back of a van at 2:00 in the morning. But by and large, hardware synths are built to survive the normal rigors of the road. Most computers aren't.

Having said all that, software synths have some advantages too:

■ Because the manufacturing and shipping costs are far lower, softsynth developers have more freedom to innovate. This translates into more great-sounding instruments.

■ Softsynths can be updated with new features and bugfixes somewhat more easily than their hardware counterparts. (This is less true than it used to be. OS updates for many hardware synths can be downloaded and transmitted to the synth via MIDI. But it's still a factor.)

■ You can use an effect plug-in from a different manufacturer pretty easily with a softsynth. I don't know of any current hardware synth that allows third-party effects to be installed.

■ Assuming you already have a fast computer equipped with a decent audio interface, a softsynth will be considerably cheaper than its hardware counterpart.

■ A hardware synth has a fixed amount of memory. You may be able to store 128 of your own sounds, or 512, but no more. The hard drive on a computer can store gazillions of synthesizer patches.

■ The big screen. Need I say more?

Send In the Clones

2

There are two main reasons to use a software instrument. Some people are searching for sounds that have never been heard before. Others want precisely a sound that has been heard before. We associate certain sounds with certain moods, either because of some quality in the sound itself (the plaintiveness of an oboe, the nobility of a trombone) or because the sound has become associated with a certain musical style and thereby with a certain emotional climate (tremolo electric guitar with surfing, accordion with the casual urbanity of a sidewalk café).

In the realm of keyboards, the Rhodes electric piano evokes the jazz fusion and pop ballads of the 1970s and '80s, the Mellotron the expansive rock scene of the late '60s and early '70s. You can still buy most of these keyboards, if you don't mind hunting. But the real thing, be it a Hammond organ or a Minimoog, is likely to be expensive, and will be difficult to maintain in anything like playable condition. A computer simulation will be less expensive, less fragile, and less prone to mechanical breakdowns. In addition, the computer simulation may be tricked out with a host of features not found in the original — features purists will feel obliged to ignore, but that the rest of us can take advantage of whenever the whim strikes.

We begin our survey, then, with a close look at some of the leading software clones — imitations of the Hammond B-3 tonewheel organ, the Mellotron, the Rhodes electric piano, the Yamaha DX7, the Sequential Circuits Prophet-5, and other fabled instruments.

Modeling a real instrument in software is not a simple task. Ideally, the instrument designer should recreate not only the front panel and the type of synthesis but the sonic quirks for which the original instrument is prized. Perhaps the easiest instrument to clone in this roundup is the Mellotron: That's because the original made sounds by playing back tape recordings. To get their M-Tron to sound like the real thing, all Gmedia had to do was find and digitally record a good set of Mellotron tapes.

At the other extreme is the Hammond B-3. The original instrument produced sounds with a set of 96 tone wheels — physical disks that spun around. The motor that rotated them added its noise, as did the Leslie speaker cabinet through which the Hammond was (and is) generally played. Each aspect of the Hammond sound — percussion, key click, drawbar foldback, and so on — has to be meticulously modeled in software.

If you know a little about music technology, you may be thinking it would be a simple matter to recreate any instrument in software. All you have to do is capture its sound digitally, right? But the reality turns out to be a lot more complicated. If you listen to any single note, granted, a sample can sound perfect. Musicians, however, have a nasty habit of wanting to play dozens, hundreds, thousands of notes in quick succession. A sample, by its nature, is set in stone. Making a sample respond to a player's performance technique is not easy. Even coming close with a sampled instrument (as in The Grand, profiled below) requires some trickery. To achieve anything like the musical responsiveness found in the original instrument, software developers have to go further, using physical modeling algorithms to emulate things like the physical resonance of the instrument's body, the way the tone of tines changes (distorts) when they're struck hard, the character of an analog lowpass filter that was built with particular components, and so on.

Cloning a vintage instrument is a natural avenue for softsynth developers: There's a ready-made market, and you don't need to educate your customers about a lot of esoteric features. On the other hand, software clones tend to be somewhat more limited in their sonic palette than other types of designs.

Coming soon, expect to see more clones. Word is, GMedia is planning to clone the ARP Odyssey and Oxford Synthesizer Company OSCar (as the GMedia Oddity and impOSCar, respectively). Not profiled in this chapter but available as I write this:

■ Big Tick Audio EP-Station (an electric piano generated using FM), Cheeze Machine (a vintage string machine somewhat like the Crumar Performer or ARP Solina — available as freeware), and Ticky Clav (a Hohner Clavinet clone — also freeware).

■ Bitheadz Black & Whites, which models an acoustic piano.

■ Creamware Minimax, a Minimoog clone that runs on their Pulsar PCI card.

■ Steinberg VB-1, a bass synth that uses physical modeling technology to give you control over parameters such as pick position.

Steinberg Model-E

SOFTWARE MINIMOOG

Figure 2-1.
The classic look of the Minimoog is recreated along with the sound in the Steinberg Model-E. Oscillator 3 can be used for low-frequency or audio range modulation of filter and/or pitch for FM effects. The silver panel at the bottom introduces features not found in the Minimoog, like velocity control of cutoff frequency and amplitude, as well as spread (autopanning).

VST (Mac, Win)
$199

Pros: Excellent recreation of Minimoog sound. Filter with selectable slope. Filter can be set to self-oscillate. All parameters respond to sys-ex and controller automation.
Cons: Glide exhibits mild zippering at some settings. Somewhat limited modulation resources. No audio input. Can't sync LFO to MIDI clock.

The status of the Minimoog among synthesizers is rather like the status of Babe Ruth among baseball players. It was the first commercially successful synth, arriving on the scene only a couple of years after Wendy Carlos's groundbreaking *Switched-On Bach* introduced the public to the sound of the Moog synthesizer, becoming in the process the best-selling classical LP ever.

Switched-On Bach (or *S.O.B.*, as Wendy affectionately refers to it) was created with multitrack tape and a large modular Moog. In a modular instrument, the separate oscillators, filters, envelope generators, and other modules have to be interconnected with patch cords. What made the Minimoog a success was that it bundled a small but versatile set of Moog modules in a pre-configured array in a single box, complete with a keyboard. The price was less than for a modular Moog, and the convenience factor was through the roof.

In this short review from the October 2000 issue of *Keyboard*, Francis Preve compares the Steinberg Model-E to the original.

Since its release in 1970, the Minimoog has virtually defined the sound of analog synthesis. Its warmth was matched by its sheer testosterone, and for years every manufacturer scrambled to emulate its unique filters. Nowadays, it's difficult to find a used Moog in working condition, much less at an affordable price.

Steinberg deserves a high-five for the Model-E. They've come so close to nailing the classic Minimoog sound that the differences in nuance are more than offset by the polyphony, programmability, and ultra-stable tuning. This puppy rocks.

For those unfamiliar with the Minimoog architecture, here's the breakdown: three oscillators (one can be switched to LFO mode), pink/white noise generator, resonant lowpass filter, and two ADS envelopes. ADS envelopes? Back in the day, Moog cut corners by including a switch that added a release stage to the envelope. The release time, if present, would be the same as the decay time. While it's an odd approach in today's era of multistage time/level envelopes, the limitations help define the sound of the instrument. There's also a glide (portamento) function for those classic Keith Emerson patches.

How does it sound? If you're looking for warm, fat, classic analog sounds, they're all here in spades. Earthshaking basses are almost impossible to avoid, and lush pads are a breeze to program. I was even able to create fairly complex textures by using osc 3 to modulate filter cutoff, keeping the oscillator in the audio range for sideband effects. Analog FM, anyone?

Steinberg has made a few improvements on the original design. Velocity can control the volume and/or filter for added dynamic responsiveness. The filters now operate in 2-pole or 4-pole mode. There are some nifty autopanning functions.

Additionally, all parameters can be automated via either sys-ex or MIDI continuous controller data, so if you want to morph sounds while recording your performance it's a matter of creating a second track and twiddling away. While I would have liked the ability to map multiple parameters to a single controller within Model-E, this can be configured globally within your sequencer, so there is a workaround. Steinberg also includes a fair selection of commonly used parameter morphs as sys-ex arrangement/track files. If you want a two-bar filter wah-wah pattern, just cut and paste. Nice touch.

Model-E at a Glance

System requirements	VST 2.0-compatible host software
Polyphony	up to 64 voices per instance, up to 8 instances
# of multitimbral parts	16 per instance
Key modes	polyphonic, monophonic, both with portamento
Synthesis type	analog modeling
Oscillators	3 plus white/pink noise generator (osc 3 can be switched to LFO mode); triangle, triangle/sawtooth, forward and reverse sawtooth, square, pulse (x2)
Filters	1 lowpass with 12dB, 24dB selectable slope
LFOs	osc 3 and/or noise generator can be used as LFO or FM modulator
Syncable functions	none
Envelopes	amp ADS, filter ADS, both with release toggle
Modulation	envelope and osc 3 to filter, pitch, pan
Copy protection	CD
Downloadable demo	no

Downsides? Despite the Model-E's stunning simulation of the Moog sound, there are a few missed opportunities. Amplitude modulation is omitted entirely, and LFO amounts for pitch and filter cutoff are controlled exclusively by the mod wheel, so patches can't have modulation with base amounts. There's no way to sync osc 3 in LFO mode to MIDI clock data, either. Bummer. Lastly, there's a whisper of zippering artifacts in the glide function when used with wide intervals at certain settings. But in the context of a mix, this shouldn't be a major issue for most people.

I spent several weeks putting this plug-in through its paces, and the Model-E proved itself to be a dream come true. A polyphonic, multitimbral, programmable Minimoog for under $200? Pinch me. Hard. —*Francis Preve (Oct. '00)*

Native Instruments B4
VIRTUAL TONEWHEEL ORGAN

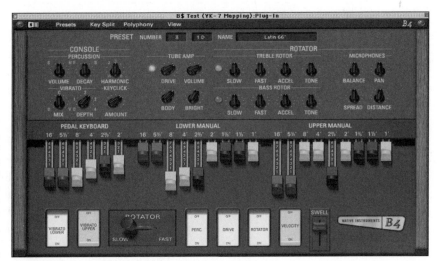

Figure 2-2.
Control view of the B4 (shown here) lays out all of the speaker and organ tone controls in an easy-to-read fashion. Keyboard view looks very much like a real Hammond organ, except there's only one set of drawbars per manual.

VST (Mac, Win)
$239

Pros: Ultra-realistic Hammond B-3 and Leslie speaker simulation. Choice of rotary or guitar amp speakers. Every parameter is accessible via MIDI. Dead-authentic Vox and Farfisa sounds to match its stellar Hammond emulation.
Cons: No leakage control. Upper and lower manual drawbars are reversed. Harmonium model is less accurate than other models.

The Hammond B-3 tonewheel organ was one of the most widely used electromechanical instruments. It's also one of the most widely imitated. Roland, Korg, and other companies have built hardware B-3 sound-alikes. For that matter, even Hammond (now a division of Suzuki) builds their own high-priced electronic B-3 emulator. The hardware clones are somewhat lighter and easier to cart around than the real thing, which was a notorious backbreaker, but none of them can compete with a laptop.

To a true B-3 player, of course, the idea of using a computer simulation is anathema. Even if the sound of the software were indistinguishable from the real thing, which is tricky since a real Hammond is played through a rotating Leslie speaker, there are tactile considerations: B-3 players push and pull the organ's drawbars in expressive ways while they play, and the organ's "waterfall" keys don't feel quite like those on a piano or a standard MIDI keyboard.

But as John Krogh and Ken Hughes report in the next pair of reviews (from *Keyboard's* Dec. '00 and Dec. '01 issues, respectively), the Native Instruments B4 plug-in comes remarkably close.

I fell in love with the sound of the Hammond B-3 the first time I heard Tower of Power's "What Is Hip" back in, well, let's just say it was years ago. Since then I've maintained my love affair, spending time practicing Jimmy Smith licks, picking "tones" off of classic records, and playing B-3 in bands and the studio. So when Native Instruments' B4 package appeared on my desk, I couldn't wait to get it out of the shrinkwrap and onto my G4.

Like other plug-in/stand-alone instruments in Native's stable, the B4 is designed to give you all the guts and glory of the real thing, right down to the look and feel, which even dyed-in-the-wool organ purists should appreciate. But looks aside, the B4 simply kicks ass. Besides being the most B-3 sounding instrument I've played (outside of a real Hammond), it can be used as an insert plug-in, so you can run guitar, vocals, or whatever through the Leslie and guitar tube amp simulators.

I tested the B4 as a plug-in with Emagic Logic and in stand-alone mode using OMS with MOTU Digital Performer. There were only a few unfavorable moments. DP froze up whenever I tried recording automation from the drawbars. Working with Logic was a bit of a chore since it automatically remaps certain controller messages on input. At first this prevented me from using my Roland VK-7's drawbars

B4 at a Glance

System requirements	Mac, Win; plug-in mode: VST 2.0-compatible host software; stand-alone or side by side with sequencer: DirectConnect, MAS, ASIO, SoundManager, DirectSound, or MME; OMS or FreeMIDI (Mac only)
Polyphony	up to 91 tonewheel voices
# of multitimbral parts	3: pedals, upper and lower manuals
Presets	120
Copy protection	CD-ROM on installation
Downloadable demo	yes

to control the B4, but I eventually I worked around this by reassigning specific drawbars to send different controller messages (ones that Logic wouldn't remap).

A great bunch of presets is included in the B4. These are available in ten banks of 12 programs each. I was particularly fond of "Latin 66" and "Soft Backing." You can create as many of your own as you like and store them. (I also spent some time writing down the registrations from my favorite B4 presets for future gigs with a real B.)

The B4 doesn't faithfully recreate every mechanical idiosyncrasy. Turning on percussion, for instance, doesn't disable the 1' drawbar as it does on a real B-3. And if you like, the B4 will respond to key velocity. To prevent overcrowding, the B4 provides only one set of nine drawbars for each manual and another set of six for the bass pedals.

A number of thoughtful MIDI features are on hand, including the ability to quickly and easily set up splits for single keyboard use. [*Editor's note: The B-3 was a dual-manual instrument.*] It can also receive on three MIDI channels simultaneously, so you can hook up two keyboards and a set of MIDI bass pedals, if you can find them. Every parameter is tied to a MIDI controller. (The mapping list is in the documentation.)

My only complaint? There isn't a leakage parameter. Native says this is planned for a future version.

Just for grins, I pitted the B4 against my Roland VK-7 in an informal comparison. I A/B'd the two by pulling one drawbar at a time for each instrument. I continued with various tests, and after about 30 minutes I was convinced: Hands down, the B4 sounded and responded more like a Hammond. It's doubtful I'll use the VK-7 for any of my projects again, except as a controller. —*John Krogh (Dec. '00)*

When Native Instruments' B4 first hit the scene, I was dubious. I didn't think a relatively inexpensive software product could best the pricey hardware B-3 simulators. Boy, was I wrong — B4 is awesome. Newly expanded in version 1.1 with models of the famous Vox Continental, Farfisa Compact, and harmonium, B4 now offers even more. It's not just for Hammond lovers anymore: It's a gotta-have if you need cheesy '60s organs in all their wheezy glory.

At first I was struck by how much the Vox and Farfisa sounds resembled the B-3 sound. Turns out the B4's Leslie simulation is so colorful that it makes even the thin, reedy sounds associated with combo organs sound big and beefy. Once I disabled the simu-Leslie, I heard the familiar organ tones from songs like "96 Tears" and nearly any Smash Mouth single.

Getting the most authentic sounds out of this update requires just a little imagination. On Vox organs, there are fewer than the nine drawbars present on a Hammond (and depicted in B4's beautiful UI). Farfisas have no drawbars; voice tabs select the harmonics. In these models, all the virtual drawbars are active, a feature that expands the palette beyond strictly authentic stops. By avoiding mostly the black drawbars, you get the familiar cutting tone of compact transistor organs. Add the black drawbars, and all sorts of psychedelic shades come forth.

B4's V1 vibrato setting yields the most historically accurate vibrato, but the other settings sound good too.

Three Vox models are offered: Continental Soft, Mixed, and Hard. With these, all of the classic moods are covered, from intimately cheesy to raucously cheesy. Two Farfisa models, Compact and Compact Boost, cover all the familiar Farfisa sounds too. Kudos to NI for what sounds like an adjustment to the overdrive — on the compact organs, the clipping sounds more ragged, spitty, and solid-statey than on the Hammond models. [*Editor's note: According to NI, the same overdrive is used on both types of sounds. The apparent difference is due to differences in the source signals.*]

A harmonium model brings the Maharishi-era Beatles vibe within easy reach. With a little overdrive, you can spot-on cop George Martin's part on "The Word." The attack characteristics of a real harmonium are softer, and there are subtle key clicks, too, which the genuine article wouldn't exhibit. All the same, it's appreciated because it adds more colors to the sonic paintbox.

Using B4 as a stand-alone instrument on a 450MHz blue-and-white G3 with Sound Manager and the software's default buffer setting, latency was way inside acceptable limits. Smears and glisses were smooth and natural-sounding. My only substantial complaint about this new version is that it makes me want to take it onstage all the more — now I have to buy a laptop so I can shrink my rig with B4 and Emagic's evp73. —*Ken Hughes (Dec. '00)*

Emagic EVP88
ELECTRIC PIANO MODELING PLUG-IN WITH EFFECTS

plug-in for Emagic Logic (Mac, Win)
$199

Pros: The best Rhodes and Wurly emulations to date. Very musical. Fun to play. Excellent effects. Great bang for the buck.
Cons: Audio smoothing not yet implemented with some automatable controls. Slight unrealistic click at the beginnings of notes on some models.

The venerable Rhodes electric piano, while much sought after by keyboard players, isn't nearly as heavy and bulky as a Hammond B-3 — but it's not a cell phone, either. Emagic's EVP88 is a respectable substitute, as Ernie Rideout reported in the Sept. '01 *Keyboard* review below. One bummer for fans of clone software: The EVP series is neither a stand-alone nor a standard (read: VSTi or DXi) plug-in. It can be hosted only by Emagic's Logic sequencer. Since Emagic was acquired by Apple Computer in the summer of 2002 and promptly abandoned the Windows platform, in the future the EVP is likely to be strictly a Macintosh instrument. That's not a bad thing, necessarily — some very good softsynths are Mac-only — but copies of EVP88 for Windows may someday be as sought-after as vintage hardware instruments. If you're not a Logic user, be sure to read the Lounge Lizard review that starts on page 46.

As exciting as my move to New York City has been, one of the downers of moving into a small apartment was having to sell my Rhodes Stage Mk1. It only made one sound, but I spent most of my practice time on it as well as nearly every rehearsal. Sure, the sampled Rhodes synth patches I have at my disposal now are perfectly usable; they sound great in a track, and they let me make music when I play live. But a sampled Rhodes just isn't the same as the real thing.

So when I drew Emagic's new EVP88 in the Keyboard Report Lottery, I could barely contain my enthusiasm: EVP stands for Emagic Vintage Piano. The EVP88 is the third in Emagic's line of Logic-only virtual instrument plug-ins, following in the steps of their ES1 virtual analog synthesizer and EXS24 virtual sampler. Unlike those versatile plug-ins, though, the EVP88 targets the sounds of Rhodes, Wurlitzer, and Hohner EPs, along with some of the classic pedals they were often run through.

Needless to say, the buzz about the EVP88 among keyboard-playing project studio recordists has been intense. Expectations are high: Will the EVP88 do for Rhodes emulations what the Native Instruments B4 did for software tonewheel organ and rotary speaker sounds, which is to say, nail 'em? For each player, the answer will depend on a few factors: what the real Rhodes or Wurly in their life plays and feels like, what their current MIDI keyboard feels like, and whether it has adjustable velocity.

Figure 2-3.
The Stage 73 had Fender knobs on its control panel, too, but they sure didn't do what the knobs on Emagic's EVP88 do. The big knob selects the electric piano model, and you can tweak such parameters as decay, release, bell and damper volume, stereo spread, and stretch tuning. The overdrive, phaser, and chorus are patterned after the classic stompbox varieties often used with Rhodes and Wurly sounds. The tremolo is right off the Rhodes Suitcase model, making it ideal for spacing out with headphones.

EVP88 at a Glance

System requirements	Logic 4.7 or higher (Mac, Win), any computer and OS that meet Logic's requirements
Synthesis type	modeling
Polyphony	88 voices
Models	Rhodes: Suitcase MkI, Stage MkI, Stage MkII, MkIV, Bright Stage MkII, Hard Stage MkII, Metal Piano, Attack Piano; Wurlitzer: 200A, Soft Wurlitzer, Funk Piano; Hohner Electra Piano
User-editable parameters	decay, release, bell volume, damper volume, stereo spread, stretch tuning, random detuning, fine tuning (±50 cents)
Effects	2-band EQ, overdrive, phaser, tremolo, chorus
Automation	knob motion
Copy protection	CD installation
Downloadable demo	no

I don't want to get ahead of myself, but I will say this: I can't stop playing the thing, it's such a gas. I've also solicited the input of *Keyboard* technical editor John Krogh, who with his pristine Suitcase MkII is a shoo-in for the Rhodes Fascist of the Year award. I also brought in New York jazz and funk phenom Adam Holzman, who, in the course of his work with Miles Davis, Wayne Shorter, Grover Washington, Jr., and Wallace Roney, has rarely been more than a few inches from his Wurlitzer 200. Among the three of us, you can bet we've got some opinions about electric pianos.

Overview. There is a VST version of the EVP88, appropriately and amusingly called the EVP73 ($99). With the exception of having fewer models, no phaser, and no chorus, everything described here pertains to it as well. Within Logic 4.7 or later, the EVP88 appears as a plug-in option in the Audio Instrument tracks. These tracks are objects that route MIDI to internal virtual instruments rather than to external MIDI modules. Setting up an EVP88 track is a piece of cake: Select an Audio Instrument track, and select the EVP88 from the Insert Effect menu in the mixer window. Play your controller at this point, and you'll hear a gorgeous Suitcase model. Double-click on the EVP88 name and the brushed-aluminum editor panel appears.

There's not much more to the EVP88 than what you see on the editor panel. The big knob selects the model from among several direct emulations and hybrid models. You can set the polyphony with the Voice control; up to 88 notes are available, if your CPU can handle it. If you're running the EVP88 with other CPU-intensive plug-ins, you can lighten the load by restricting the polyphony. You can also bounce your submixed EVP tracks to an audio file, freeing up horsepower for other plug-ins.

There aren't a lot of different electric piano models available in the EVP88, but what's here is high-quality. In the Rhodes family, you've got the Suitcase and Stage basics with Mk1, MkII, and MkIV variations, as well as a couple of models that take some of the Rhodes's tonal characteristics further than the real thing could. In the Wurlitzer department, the main model is of the classic model 200A, with a soft variation and a funked-out hybrid available as well. The last model is of a Hohner Electra Piano — not to be confused with the RMI Electra Piano. Having spent a fair chunk of my teenage years hauling around an RMI, I wish Emagic had included an RMI model, but perhaps that's just nostalgia talking.

You can change several of the model parameters to create your own sound variations, which you can save. The Decay control sets the length of time the initial attack lasts without changing the overall volume envelope decay; make it short and you get an electric harpsichord effect, make it long and you can turn a Rhodes into an organ. Setting the Release to a short value yields a truncated sound when you lift the keys, while a long value sounds as though the damper isn't quite doing its job.

You can increase or decrease the level of tine thwack and damper clunk with the Bell and Damper controls, respectively. The stereo spread can be set wide, with the lowest notes panned full left and the highest full right. Stretch tuning emulates the standard piano technician approach to tuning, in which the extreme low register is tuned a little bit flat and the extreme high is tuned high. The Warmth control adds a certain amount of detuning to particular notes up and down the keyboard, for that realistic road-weary Rhodes effect.

The effects Emagic included with the EVP88 are reminiscent of the kind of pedal effects that give the Rhodes and Wurly their classic sounds. The Phaser's controls for time, depth, and polarity let you dial in a really thick sound, *à la* Richard Tee. The tremolo works just the way it does on a Suitcase model, hard-panning the sound from right to left. Make sure the Stereo Intensity model parameter is set to its lowest setting when you use tremolo, as the tremolo pans to both sides only those sounds toward the center of the stereo field. The chorus is light and transparent, perfect for electric pianos. The overdrive provides a very believable tube overdrive sound, and it can really add gain to the sound. The two-band EQ is just about all you need to get your balance set.

If you don't like turning virtual knobs with your mouse or trackball, you'll appreciate the control view, which lets you type in values or dial them in with a slider. You can save your edited settings and recall them from the settings menu.

In Use. I ran the EVP88 using Logic 4.7.0 on an older Macintosh 266MHz G3 with an older operating system (MacOS 8.6), and a MOTU 2408 audio interface — not exactly a state-of-the-art computer system. But the machine met the minimum recommendations, so I figured I'd give it a go. Right off the bat I ran into some serious dropout and hideous popping problems. Thinking it must be my poor old processor, I tried everything I could to free up power for the EVP88, including switching to native Mac AV hardware, tweaking memory allocations, reducing buffer times, and so on. All to no avail. Then I discovered a Logic upgrade I hadn't been aware of (4.7.2) on the Emagic site. I downloaded it, ran the updater, and presto: No more dropouts, clicks, or pops, even with the sustain pedal down and the polyphony set in the 50- to 60-voice range.

Once I got it going, I thought the EVP88 sounded great but responded in a not-so-convincing manner. I wasn't expecting it to feel like a real instrument; how could it? The action of a real Wurly or Rhodes is such an integral part of the experience of playing it. But then I dialed in a velocity curve that made it easier for me to reach peak velocities from my weighted-action controller, and it transformed the experience.

When I played it alongside the Native Instruments B4 VST plug-in, though, I felt the EVP's output was a little wimpy. I had the outputs of the two virtual instruments set to the same level, yet the organ was overpowering the sound of the piano. So I engaged one of the compressors supplied with Logic, and I've been playing the EVP almost non-stop ever since, digging every minute of it. There are no velocity-switched sample jumps, no mismatched levels, and no overcompressed loud samples. The low end begins to bark naturally as you hit the keys harder. The sound of tines and dampers mingles in a very convincing and highly musical way. You can control the volume of each individual voice in a chord. It feels like you're playing a real musical instrument.

When I played the Stage MkI model, I couldn't believe how much it sounded and responded like my old Rhodes. The low end got rumbly, and the high end got thin and clear. When I engaged the stretch tuning and the Warmth parameter that introduces detuning, it felt like I was back in the body shop where my old band rehearsed, listening to my ever so slightly out of tune voicings bounce off Corvettes. Spot on. The Suitcase models knocked my socks off, too, as I ran through my Steely Dan and Joe Sample repertoire. The Hard and Bright models gave a very musical version of the compressed Dyno-My-Piano sound. The other Rhodes and Wurly models were no less playable, whether or not they seemed perfectly realistic to me.

A couple of things did bug me about even the best of the models. When the Bell sound is reduced, you can hear a slight click or pop at the beginning of each note you play, much like the key click on a Hammond organ, but not as pronounced. This occurs mostly within an octave or two on either side of Middle C, and is more noticeable when you play softly. Cranking up the Bell volume can cover it up, but it's possible to have too much tine sound that way. "There's an unnatural pluckiness to the attack to some of the Rhodes models, especially the Bright Stage MkII model," says John Krogh. "It's masked to a greater or lesser degree depending on the patch settings."

By and large, the sound of the damper is quite convincing, so much so that if you gently lay your arm across the lower half of the keyboard, you'll get the sound of a Rhodes Stage model being laid on its back for leg removal. One instance of the damper was less convincing to me: On the MkII model, below C3, the damper release began to sound more like a sampled jaw harp than a damper on a tine.

While it's possible to automate knob twists, I found that changing the effects settings in real time while playing would sometimes result in obvious stair-stepping and occasional pops. "The EVP's effects sound great," says John. "But you can't automate them at all without zippering and pronounced clicks, especially with the phaser." According to Emagic, smoothing will be added in the next release.

Overall, though, playing the models is a very musical experience. "I'm impressed with the Rhodes programs," said Adam Holzman after running through some blistering grooves. "They've got a little bit of the clunk and clang a real Rhodes has, without the shimmery DX/FM thing. The Wurly doesn't seem to have the punch on the attack that mine does, but it's much closer than most simulations."

John Krogh concurred. "The EVP88's built-in tremolo and phaser effects kick ass," he says. "They add significantly to the piano sound's realism. Shortcomings aside, the EVP88 sounds better than any electric piano patch I've played in a synth or sampler. The sound you get from a key-up is close to what a real Rhodes sounds like, which is one of the reasons why the EVP feels and sounds better than other imitations."

Conclusions. Depending on your experience with — and memories of — real Rhodes and Wurlitzers, as well as your current controller, your sense of how realistic this virtual instrument is may vary. If you tweak your velocity response, add some dynamic effects, and play with the control the EVP88 affords, though, you're bound to come under its spell.

This is hands-down the best Rhodes and Wurlitzer emulation available today. Playing its models is a musical joy, and it records in a very convincing and useful manner. It's not designed to replace the real thing, if you're smart enough to have held on to one. But if you wish you had one, the EVP88 will very likely satisfy that desire, and for a lot less bank drain and hassle than you'd have to go through otherwise. —*Ernie Rideout (Sept. '01)*

Native Instruments Pro-Five/52/53
SEQUENTIAL CIRCUITS PROPHET-5 EMULATION

stand-alone, VST (Mac, PC)
$199

Pros: Fat, warm sound. Smooth filters. Highly programmable. Tons of inspiring presets.
Cons: Parameter settings can't be typed in.

Let's set the record straight: The Sequential Circuits Prophet-5, which took the keyboard market by storm in 1978, was not actually the first polyphonic, programmable synthesizer. Oberheim beat Sequential to the punch on that score. But the Oberheim Four-Voice and Eight-Voice were somewhat awkward to use, because each synthesizer voice lived in its own module. Mount four of them side by side, add a keyboard and a microprocessor to store the knob settings, which is what Oberheim did, and you've got a programmable polyphonic synth.

The Prophet-5 was a big step forward, because its design was integrated. One bunch of knobs controlled all five voices. On top of which, it sounded fantastic. For several years, *every* keyboardist who aspired to being taken seriously had to have one. Sequential produced several more Prophet models, including the Prophet-600, which was the very first synth with MIDI. (They shipped two of them to *Keyboard* so we could test whether this newfangled MIDI stuff actually worked.) But none of the later incarnations ever achieved the success or notoriety of the original.

The Prophet-5's voice was a lot like the Minimoog's — two oscillators, an LFO, and a lowpass filter. And of course velocity-sensing keyboards were still years in the future. Ernie Rideout discusses some of its other features in the review below, which appeared in *Keyboard* in October 2000. Since then, Native Instruments has updated the software twice. The Pro-52 was never reviewed by *Keyboard*, but it added effects, an external audio input, and the ability to function as a stand-alone program. In September 2002 NI released the Pro-53. This new version (the price is now $199) adds a highpass filter, improved oscillator DSP, and an easier way to use the audio input to process external audio through the instrument. Also, a MIDI learn mode has been added to the knobs.

Figure 2-4.
True to the real Sequential Circuits Prophet-5 even down to the walnut veneer, the Native Instruments Pro-53 VST plug-in is completely programmable and controllable via MIDI. All of the original knobs and buttons are represented here, including the Prophet-5's signature Poly Mod section. Controls not on the real thing include the entire delay effect section, the filter highpass mode and envelope invert buttons, the filter's keyboard tracking knob (a button on the original), LFO tempo sync, audio input, a digital stability/analog drift selector, a keyboard velocity response button, a polyphony selector, and a retractable keyboard.

The Prophet-5, the synth that put Sequential Circuits on the map, was a groundbreaking instrument as well as simply being a gas to play and program. Native Instruments has recreated the Prophet-5 in a virtual instrument called the Pro-Five. On the surface, every knob, button, and function of the original instrument is represented. A handful of "modernized" items you won't find on the original include a retractable on-screen keyboard, selectable polyphony, LFO sync to

Pro-53 at a Glance

System requirements	VST 2.0-compatible host software
Polyphony	up to 32 voices
# of multitimbral parts	1 per instance (up to 8 instances)
Keyboard modes	unison, glide, polyphonic
Synthesis type	analog modeling
Oscillators	2; sawtooth, triangle, pulse
LFOs	1; sawtooth, triangle, pulse
Envelopes	2 ADSR; filter and amplitude
Modulation	2 sources; poly mod (filter envelope and osc B, selectable) and mod wheel to osc frequency, osc pulse width, and filter cutoff
Syncable functions	LFO and delay sync to MIDI clock
Copy protection	CD
Downloadable demo	yes

MIDI, and a keyboard velocity response selector. But other than that, it's the real . . . um, the virtual deal.

A lot of attention has been paid to what goes on under the hood. One of the Prophet-5's secrets of success was its mod routing — especially the ability to modulate oscillator A with the output of oscillator B. This is faithfully duplicated on the Pro-Five. The filter envelope could also be used as a mod source, with such sound-mangling destinations as waveform pulse width. In short, everything the Prophet-5 could do, the Pro-Five can do.

The plug-in comes with 512 preset programs, which you select via the file, bank, and program buttons. I haven't had so much fun scrolling through presets in a long time; there's hardly a dud in the bunch. I fired up Steinberg's ReBirth drum machine software, dialed in an energetic tempo, and let the beats fly as I tried out the generous portions of bass sounds, pads, leads, and effects.

I found the Pro-Five to be as warm and fat as you could want, with totally smooth filters. But the noisier and more aggressive aspects of the Prophet's sound are available, too. By manipulating the mod routing and noise generators on the Pro-Five, you can come up with some pretty bizarre sounds, from slowly percolating glissandos and Outer Limits radio bleeps to pitchless shrieks and menacing thumps.

The knob-packed interface invites twisting — that is, clicking and dragging — which if you're new to synth programming, can lead to a great new sound or total disaster. Fortunately, the manual comes with a useful tutorial that introduces the various control sections and shows how they're best employed.

Watch out, though, if you set the polyphony high and select a unison patch, which takes all of the voices available and layers them on a single note. Normally this makes a sound much fatter and more ballsy. If you've got the polyphony set high, say to 24 voices, and you switch to a unison patch, all 24 voices will be brought to bear on that one unfortunate note, quite likely overloading both the CPU and the audio outputs.

I was very happy with the results I got with a sequenced bass line as I applied a variety of controller data to the Pro-Five's programmable parameters. I only wish there were some way to specify knob settings numerically in addition to twirling them. But it sounds great, whether in a mix with other virtual instruments or with sampled drum loops, and it's really inspiring to play all by itself. —*Ernie Rideout (Oct. '00)*

Steinberg The Grand
MULTISAMPLED ACOUSTIC PIANO

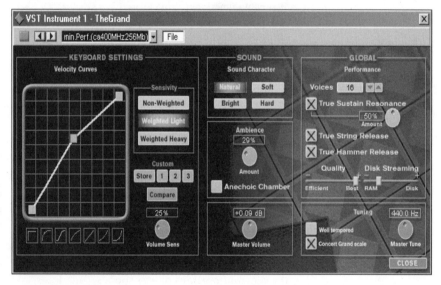

Figure 2-5.
You can change The Grand's velocity response using the editable graphic table to the left. The amount of room ambience is set with the knob in the center of the window. On a slower computer, you can reduce The Grand's polyphony with the parameter at upper right.

VST (Mac, Win)
$299

Pros: Full-length piano samples (no loops). Several subtle features, including damper pedal harp resonance, enhance the realism. Six-way velocity cross-switching.
Cons: Needs a high-powered computer. Highest velocity samples don't blend well with softer samples. One of the two preset tunings contains a few out-of-tune notes.

Since synthesizers are usually equipped with keyboards, it's only natural to expect that a synth will be able to sound like the world's most popular keyboard instrument, the piano. It turns out, though, that recreating the sound of a piano is one of the tougher things you can ask a computer to do. One sound developer called their sampled piano The Holy Grail for that very reason.

Most of the sampled pianos on the market, including The Holy Grail, come in the form of CD-ROMs whose presets have to be loaded into a general-purpose sampler for playback. Tascam GigaStudio, for instance, ships with its own sampled grand piano, as detailed in Chapter 5. Steinberg's The Grand, on the other hand, is a free-standing plug-in. You get both the sound of a piano and the software engine that plays the sound.

One factor that makes the piano so hard to duplicate is the sympathetic resonance of its strings. (This is referred to as "harp resonance" in the review below, because the strings are stretched across an iron frame shaped rather like a harp. Please don't confuse harp resonance with filter resonance. They're entirely different.) When you strike a key while the damper pedal is down, the strings actually struck by the hammer begin to vibrate — and so do all of the other strings whose frequencies are mathematically related. A good pianist can shape phrases, consciously or intuitively, by varying this resonance.

Another factor is the mechanism of the piano's action, which responds with great sensitivity to the speed with which the player strikes the keys. MIDI key velocity, which is limited to only 127 different values (or fewer, depending on what keyboard you're playing) can't compare.

An even bigger difficulty is that the tone of a single note on a piano changes constantly in subtle ways as the note dies away. To capture those subtle changes, a piano's individual notes have to be recorded as samples that are many seconds long. This takes up a lot of memory, at the very least. If the sampled notes are streamed from the computer's hard drive rather than being stored in RAM, it also affects the overall performance of your music computer system.

No, creating a playable digital piano isn't easy. And we haven't even started talking yet about which piano. A Bösendorfer? A Yamaha, perhaps? A Steinway? Would that be a Hamburg Steinway or a pre-CBS New York Steinway?

My advice (hinted at in this June 2002 review) is that if you want a piano, you may as well play a real piano, because the perfect digital piano has never existed, and probably never will. But that doesn't stop manufacturers from chasing after the Holy Grail.

Not a month passes that *Keyboard* editors don't receive several plaintive messages from readers asking us to help them find the best sampled piano. We always caution them that "the best" is a subjective term: The only way to really decide whether a sampled piano will work for your music is to try it — and preferably with an 88-note weighted-action keyboard.

The art and craft of piano sampling has matured, that's for sure. Even so, a piano is a difficult instrument to capture. The Grand is a serious attempt to create a sampled piano with as few compromises as possible — and while it's not perfect, it succeeds admirably on several levels.

First off, The Grand just plain sounds fantastic. Not only is it utterly playable, it includes some unusual features that enhance the realism. Best of all, the samples

The Grand at a Glance

System requirements	256MB RAM (512MB recommended), 1.3GB hard disk space, VST 2.0 compatible host application; PC: 400MHz PII or equivalent, Win95/98/ME/2000; Mac: 500MHz G3 w/100MHz bus, Mac OS 9.x
Features	velocity curve, room ambience, sustain resonance, string release, hammer release, selectable polyphony limit, master tune, 2 preset tunings, 4 preset "sound character" settings
Copy protection	serial number on installation
Downloadable demo	no

are unlooped: Each note decays naturally for its full length, with no weird transitions from the sampled dynamic envelope to an artificial envelope generator.

Steinberg gives no hint on the box or in the manual about what piano may have been sampled to create The Grand. According to developer Peter Gorges, "We want it to be judged for its sound, not for its connection to a known piano brand." The bass register is fuller and meatier than on my 6' Yamaha C-3, that's for sure, and the extreme highs are crisp, not thuddy. The lower midrange is a bit nasal for my taste, but the main melody range sings out beautifully. I never felt, as I do on some digital pianos, that I had to attack the keyboard to get the melody to rise above the left hand.

Thick chords were clearly voiced, not buried in mud. Playing softly was very satisfying (though I felt a bit hampered by the lack of responsiveness in the action of my venerable Korg 01/W ProX). [*Editor's note: The 01/W ProX is a synth with an 88-key weighted action.*] And when I slammed down both hands, The Grand truly roared. Its *fortissimo* layer is aggressive enough to please the rudest piano pounder.

For most of the instrument's range, six different samples are mapped to velocity zones for each key. I felt the velocity-switched samples were well-matched — except for the *fortissimo* layer. I found it strident and difficult to control, because the loudest samples are so much louder and brighter than those below them.

The Grand is not laid out with a separate set of samples on each key: When I programmed a constant-velocity chromatic scale into Cubase, I heard a new sample every two to four keys up the keyboard. The chromatic sample matching is good, but not flawless. Also, the slow beating between strings of a given note lends the tone a lively air, but it's a little more prominent in some samples than I'd prefer.

While The Grand is not programmable *per se*, you get some nice choices in the edit window. You can switch a separate "True Hammer Release" layer on or off; this replicates the sound of the action falling back to its rest position when the key is released. It falls back at a fixed, rapid rate, but in the absence of MIDI release velocity (which is defined in the MIDI spec but not widely implemented on today's keyboards), there's not much that could be done about that.

The Grand can be switched to a mode in which you'll hear a fairly realistic emulation of authentic harp resonance if you play a note when the damper pedal is down.

Even better, this harp resonance crossfades in smoothly if you press the pedal after the note is played. Other manufacturers who have tried to do harp resonance ended up with a dull roar when you played thick chords, but Steinberg has managed to tame the roar: The harp resonance sounds airy and full without being obtrusive.

You can program and store your own velocity response curves — a must for serious pianists. A bit of room ambience can also be added without using outboard effects.

You have four choices for sound quality: natural, bright, soft, and hard. Each seems to map the velocity layers in a different way. The bright and hard selections should work well for rock tracks. The soft selection is pleasant on first listening, but I'm not sure I'd use it even on a ballad, as it sounds a little muffled to me.

The Grand has two shortcomings you may want to be aware of. First, one of the two preset tunings has a couple of clinkers in it. "Concert Grand scale" is a stretch tuning, and I found it very satisfying. The "Well-Tempered" tuning, however, is unusable for any type of chordal playing, because a couple of the midrange samples are just plain out of tune. A couple of the octaves and some major thirds in the octave around Middle C are bad. This is an area where The Grand can't compete with a good GigaStudio piano: Tunings in the latter can be edited; those in The Grand can't. On the other hand, you can't instantiate GigaStudio as a VST instrument on a Mac!

The other issue is that The Grand is kind of a computer hog. It needs 1.3GB of hard drive space (it comes on three CD-ROMs). To be sure, that's not a lot by today's standards. The attack portions of all of the samples are loaded into RAM, so you'll need a lot of RAM — and long notes are streamed off the hard drive, so you'll need a fast computer and hard drive. For best results, Peter Gorges recommends storing The Grand's samples on a separate hard drive from your audio tracks — okay, now we're talking about a dual-drive machine.

I'm using a 1.5GHz PC with 1,024MB of RAM — a respectable machine by today's standards, and far better than the minimum system listed on the box. I found that I had to set my M-Audio Delta-66 to 18ms of latency to prevent clicky little dropouts in The Grand's playback, even when I pushed the latter's RAM-vs.-disk slider as far over to RAM as it would go. Peter reports 6ms latency with an RME Digi96/8 card, "even on a slower machine," so your mileage may vary. I feel an instrument with 18ms of latency is still playable, but when the instrument in question is supposed to be a piano, 18ms is borderline. And that was with no audio tracks playing in Cubase. All in all, let's just say The Grand takes full advantage of the latest in computer technology.

The Grand would be a good choice for several types of musicians, notably film score composers who need to rough out tracks and get director approval before booking a session in a studio, and indie pop and new age artists who want to get very close to the real thing without leaving their bedroom or basement. It's not a piano, but it's pretty darn close, and the price is right. If you find a real grand piano for $299, let me know. —*JA (June '02)*

Applied Acoustic Systems Lounge Lizard

ELECTRIC PIANO SIMULATION

Figure 2-6.
Leapin' lizards — dig the groovy analog VU meter! The upper row of controls in Lounge Lizard provides ways to shape the response of the physical modeling algorithm. The Mallet section allows precise control over the composition, action, and dynamics of Lounge Lizard's hammers. (Extreme settings of the Noise Color and Decay controls result in wild metallic textures.) The Fork section governs both the Tine and Tone Bar elements, allowing for hybrid instrument patches that go beyond the classic Rhodes and Wurly sounds. Instrument tuning can be stored as part of your preset. The Pick Up section adjusts the position and proximity of the model's electromagnetic pick-up emulation. The Amp controls can be gain-staged to deliver distortion and overdrive effects. The Wah section uses a two-pole resonant bandpass filter to recreate vintage pedal sounds like the Crybaby. The Phaser is optimized for classic electric piano effects. The Tremolo section features both sine and triangle LFO waveforms, and can be used in stereo for auto-panning effects. The Delay effect is designed to add depth and space to the Lizard's output. Controls for delay time and feedback amount can be adjusted independently per channel.

stand-alone, VST, DXi, DirectConnect, MAS (Mac, Win)
$199

Pros: Completely programmable electro-mechanical modeling allows for hybrid instruments. Accurate recreations of Rhodes and Wurlitzer pianos. Integrated effects.
Cons: Effect LFOs not syncable. Awkward requirements for stand-alone operation on Mac. Release characteristics not included in modeling engine.

The time was the late '60s and early '70s. The Rhodes (often called the Fender Rhodes, because for a time it was manufactured by a division of electric guitar manufacturer Fender) and Wurlitzer electric pianos were the first serious attempt to give keyboard players instruments with which they could compete with the steadily increasing volume of rock guitar players. Until the Rhodes and Wurly, as it's known, came along, keyboard players had to bang their fingers bloody on ordinary acoustic pianos.

Like electric guitars, the Rhodes and Wurly used electromagnetic pickups to capture the tones of physically vibrating elements, in this case tone bars or metal reeds, respectively. While smaller and lighter than acoustic pianos, the Rhodes and Wurly had real mechanical actions, in which hammers struck the tone bars or reeds.

This simple but effective method of tone production is an ideal candidate for physical modeling synthesis. In this review from the November 2002 issue of *Keyboard*, Francis Preve explains how Applied Acoustic Systems gives musicians control over the various parts of the physical model.

Nearly every form of popular music — from modern rock to downtempo to house — is laced with the classic sounds of real electro-mechanical pianos. I'm not talking about the cheesy '80s FM Rhodes patch that launched a thousand ballads, but the warm, thick, throbbing sound of hammers on tines — preferably with a dash of fuzzy overdrive on top. That's the flavor today's discriminating producers, keyboard players, and remixers are after.

With this in mind, Applied Acoustics (makers of the popular Tassman modular synth) steps up to the plate with their own take on this classic sound: Lounge Lizard.

Installation/Documentation. Authorization is of the online challenge/response variety. Not my favorite, but the process is largely automated, so it's not a huge hassle if your studio computer is online. Otherwise, it's snail mail or fax time.

The multi-lingual manual is in fully indexed PDF format, and fairly comprehensive to boot. A printed manual is also included. Unfortunately, certain configuration info can only be found in the ReadMe file. I discovered this when my system — a dual-processor PowerMac G4/500 — refused to recognize Lounge Lizard's stand-alone implementation, despite the fact that OMS was working beautifully for all of my other softsynths.

The reason? Lounge Lizard's stand-alone app requires that both OMS and MOTU's FreeMIDI drivers be installed and active on a Mac. This isn't merely awkward, it's downright annoying. Since other stand-alone instruments don't force this issue, it would be nice if Applied Acoustics took the time to address this shortcoming in a future update.

If you plan to use the Lizard exclusively within a sequencer, you won't have to jump through this hoop.

Parameters. Unlike other softsynths that rely on preset models of specific vintage pianos, Lounge Lizard offers precise control over the individual components that make up the overall sound of any electric piano. This offers the possibility of creating hybrid instruments that were never actually manufactured but sound utterly organic and, more importantly, real.

The user interface has a fun retro look, with big bakelite knobs, chrome flip-switches, red LEDs, and analog meters. Every parameter is clearly labeled and available on the front panel, with no digging through multiple pages and screens to get around.

Since Lounge Lizard's parameter array closely follows the inner workings of an electro-mechanical piano, creating new sounds can be an educational experience if you take the time to consider the physics of these instruments.

Lounge Lizard at a Glance

System requirements	Windows: PIII 500MHz processor, 32MB RAM, Win95/98/ME/2000/XP; Mac: G3 processor, 32MB RAM, OS 9.x
Version reviewed	1.0
Supported soundcard drivers	ASIO, DirectX, EASI, WDM
Supported formats	stand-alone, VST, DXi, DirectConnect, MAS
Synthesis type	modeling
Polyphony	32 notes
User-editable parameters	mallet force: strength, keyboard scaling, velocity; mallet stiffness: soft/hard, keyboard scaling, velocity; mallet noise: pitch, keyboard scaling, decay, amount; fork tine: keyboard scaling, decay, volume, tuning; fork tone bar: decay, volume; pickup position: symmetry, distance; amp: input, output
Effects	2-band EQ, phaser, wah-wah, tremolo
Automation	all parameters respond to MIDI CC information (configurable)
Copy protection	challenge-response
Downloadable demo	no

The Mallet section provides ample control over the dynamics and presence of the instrument's sound. The two primary sub-sections of this area are Force and Stiffness. The Strength knob governs the actual impact of the hammer against the fork/tine and the Soft/Hard knob determines the physical composition of the hammer. Softer hammers give that mellow sound, while harder hammers have a more aggressive quality. Both parameters include continuously variable keyboard scaling and velocity modifiers, so you can really tailor the response to your playing style. There's also a Noise section with keyboard scaling that defines the actual tone of the hammer impact against the fork, as well as decay time and noise amount for controlling the character of the impact. At extreme settings, these parameters introduced a harsh FM-like distortion to the sound.

The Fork section determines the overall personality of the instrument's sound. The two sub-sections here are Tine and Tone Bar. Tine refers to the small end of the fork and Tone Bar refers to the larger end. Adjustable Tine parameters include keyboard scaling, decay, and volume. The overall tuning for the instrument is controlled in this section, but that's kind of cool as it allows it to be stored as part of a preset.

In experimenting with the Fork settings, I discovered an underlying principle behind Lounge Lizard's approach to modeling. Tone Bar seems to govern the Rhodes vs. Wurlitzer character of the piano, whereas the Tine section modifies the characteristic bell-like sound that's commonly associated with the Rhodes. Fiddling with these parameters yielded some nifty and very usable hybrid patches that most other instruments don't offer.

The Pick Up (*sic*) section adjusts the placement and performance of the virtual pickups. The Symmetry parameter's behavior seems dependent on the settings in the Fork section. When in the center detent, the instrument has a bright, nasal quality. Turning the knob to either the left or the right mellows the sound in a pleasing manner. The Distance parameter brings the pickup closer to the tine, changing the presence and distortion of the signal.

The Pick Up section also includes Amplifier In and Out controls. High input values and low output values yield additional overdrive effects, whereas properly gain-staging this section gives a more natural sound. Applied Acoustics' implementation of these parameters is really musical, resulting in an organic, almost tube-like effect that I quite enjoyed.

Effects. As mentioned, the Lizard includes a full complement of processing tools for nailing those classic piano textures of yesteryear. The serial order of these effects is not included in the documentation, nor can it be reconfigured. My guess as to the arrangement is: overdrive, tremolo, wah, phaser, delay. It's a sensible configuration, so my urge to move things around was minimal. On the downside, LFO speed can't be synced to sequencer tempo for any of Lounge Lizard's modules, which tosses auto-rhythmic effects right out the window.

First up is the tremolo module. For the uninitiated, tremolo is amplitude modulation controlled by an LFO with variable rate and depth. Nearly every vintage electric piano included this effect, and it provides the signature volume undulation that characterizes many classic sounds. There's also a waveshape control that switches between sine and triangle waveforms, and a stereo/mono switch for autopanning.

Lounge Lizard's wah-wah processor uses a 12dB/oct resonant bandpass filter instead of the more common (and inaccurate) lowpass mode found on some wah plug-ins. While an LFO is available for auto-wah effects, the mod wheel is thoughtfully pre-assigned to control cutoff frequency. Huzzah!

The phaser is exceptional. Controls for frequency, feedback, and mix parameters are available, along with speed and depth. This module really nails the response characteristics of vintage units.

While the delay parameters look pretty standard — independent time and feedback for left and right channels — there's no way to determine the exact millisecond amounts, and there's no mix control either. That's okay by me: All too often, we find ourselves looking at numeric values instead of using our ears. The Lizard's delay is wonderfully musical and subtle, reminiscent of an analog delay (minus the noise). It truly seems optimized for enhancing the sound of electric pianos in a stylistically relevant manner. Besides, if you're using Lounge Lizard in a modern sequencing environment, you've likely got full-featured stereo delays in your arsenal.

Finally, there's a pair of high and low shelving EQs located near the overall volume knob. These are both tuned to 1kHz, with bass adjusting frequencies below and treble adjusting frequencies above. The choice of 1kHz as the center frequency is a nice touch as it imparts additional musicality to the response of the EQ.

MIDI Control. Every parameter in Lounge Lizard can be automated via standard MIDI continuous controller data, and the assignment of CC numbers to parameters can be reassigned globally for the instrument. The caveat is that reassigning CC parameters can only be accomplished when the instrument is in stand-alone mode. Not a huge issue, but something to be aware of, regardless.

In Use. I use electric pianos a lot in my music, so putting an instrument as flexible as Lounge Lizard though its paces was an enjoyable experience. As emulations go, the Lizard was superior to every sampled Rhodes or Wurly I've tried. With a sampled piano, you're usually limited to one or two velocity-switched samples, perhaps with a touch of velocity-controlled lowpass filtering, but that's about it. Modeling allows for enhanced realism. Lounge Lizard's models are well done, so the response and dynamics of each instrument match those of a real electric piano much more closely than a sample.

Comparing Lounge Lizard to other modeled electric pianos yielded slightly different results. When played side by side with Emagic's EVP88, the Lizard had a noticeably warmer and slightly more aggressive tone than the EVP88's models. But the EVP had the edge when it came to true accuracy, partly due to its note release characteristics and overall clarity. That said, the EVP88 is only compatible with Logic, so VST users are left in the cold. There is a VST version (EVP73), but it offers only one Rhodes model and doesn't include any processing or effects other than tremolo. Lounge Lizard has a distinct edge there, though it's $100 more than the EVP73.

In the context of a mix, the Lizard sounded terrific: organic, punchy, and very playable. Having effects built into the modeling engine made setting up the overall sound of each patch a breeze, since I didn't have to rifle through my plug-in collection in search of the right phaser, overdrive, or wah processors. And there was the added benefit of taxing my CPU a bit less than using three or four plug-ins to get the same sound. Purists may complain that the very nature of the Lizard's engine makes every instrument sound like a hybrid, but the end result is so convincing in context that this is splitting hairs.

Having control over the actual modeling components can also lead to some gnarly metallic textures. Setting the Mallet and Fork parameters to their most extreme values created sounds ranging from tinkly celestes to distorted industrial grunge worthy of KMFDM or Haujobb. While the overall palette is constrained by the modeling engine, there are definitely some synth patches in the Lizard that you'd be hard pressed to duplicate by other means. In just a few minutes of tinkering, I was able to create thundering tubular bells, a mutated xylophone-kalimba, and a few FM-like vibraphone patches. This Lizard is surprisingly limber.

Conclusions. If you're a Logic user, deciding between Emagic's EVP88 and Lounge Lizard is going to be a tough call. Lounge Lizard delivers precise control over every electro-mechanical element in a real electric piano, allowing the creation of hybrid pianos and synth sounds, whereas EVP88 focuses on recreations of existing vintage pianos. Both plug-ins feature flexible effects that sound great in context, and they're pretty evenly matched in terms of organic qualities, though Lounge Lizard has a bit more testosterone overall.

But if you're a VST, MAS, DirectConnect, or DXi user who craves more control and variety than Emagic's EVP73 offers, you need to take a long hard look at Lounge Lizard. It's quite the little beast. —*Francis Preve (Nov. '02)*

Steinberg Virtual Guitarist
GUITAR RHYTHM TRACK GENERATOR

Figure 2-7.
The user interface for Steinberg Virtual Guitarist may be trying a little too hard for authenticity, but it's an eye-catcher. Most soft-synths don't have Shuffle, Timing, and Dynamics knobs — they're useful here because Virtual Guitarist actually plays rhythm guitar parts.

VST (Mac, Win)
$249

Pros: Impressively realistic and convincing idiomatic guitar parts.
Cons: Surprising and needless installation hassles (reportedly on Mac only).

Lots of hardware synthesizers have arpeggiators or even more sophisticated pattern generators. In the software realm, the assumption seems to be that the musician will be using a sequencer to generate flurries of notes, so slick pattern generators are less common. True, synths like the Waldorf PPG Wave 2.V and VirSyn Tera have arpeggiators. But Virtual Guitarist is unique, as Ken Hughes points out in this review from the August 2002 issue of *Keyboard*.

Ask any guitarist, and they'll tell you the perfect digital simulation of a guitar has never been and probably never will be created. (Hmm — I'm sensing a theme here.) The aims of Virtual Guitarist are more modest — to let non-guitarists create convincing backing tracks. Just as I'd have no trouble using Steinberg's The Grand for a piano backing track or Native Instruments B4 for an organ backing track, I can see how Virtual Guitarist fills a real need.

Maybe you hate working with guitar players. They play too loud and too much, and they can't follow charts to save their lives. Maybe you play just enough guitar yourself to get painted into corners. Either way, Virtual Guitarist ought to be attractive. At the least, it promises a way to get an idea down so you can better communicate it to a guitarist you bring in later. At the most, it's a way to finish the project without calling a guitarist. You tell it the chords, and it plays idiomatic guitar riffs from its ingenious MIDI file- and sample-based engine.

After some installation issues (see below), I was off and strumming. Immediately impressive were the realistic articulation and solid tone of the virtual guitars. The acoustics are lovely and open, with lots of shimmery strummed parts and crystalline arpeggiated parts offered on a variety of six- and twelve-string models. The patterns automatically sync to the current tempo and track tempo changes as well.

The Strats, Les Pauls, and Teles are just as satisfying, if a touch less realistic. Switching virtual pickups gives you different tones, but it sounds more like drastic EQ curves than different pickups to me. The oily wah patterns are outstanding, and the heavy crunch riffs are cool as well.

Timing tightness can be adjusted, as can a host of other performance and tone parameters. With a little effort, you can easily get results that are completely convincing in a mix.

When I installed Virtual Guitarist on a brand-new 800MHz iMac, everything seemed at first to go as expected. The instrument was installed — but it couldn't find its content files. Maddening. Steinberg's website offers a downloadable app, VGSetContentFolder, to fix the problem. The site acknowledges that problems may occur when using VG with Logic. Understandable, but I was using Cubase, another program in Steinberg's stable. And I had to run the fix each time I instantiated VG. A new public beta installer was just going online at press time [Aug. '02]. Steinberg claims it eliminates the installation hiccups entirely.

It'd be unrealistic to expect the program to match the greaze of James Brown's rhythm pickers or the sweaty grunge of Blink 182, and it can't play lead at all. Nonetheless, it's marvelously clever. In many situations, it could save you the time and trouble of miking up a guitar or amp to capture a simple backing part. Virtual Guitarist is completely unique, groundbreaking, and fun. Keep an eye on this one. The takeoff is bumpy, but once airborne it soars.
—*Ken Hughes (Aug. '02)*

Waldorf PPG Wave 2.V
FAITHFUL RECREATION OF THE PPG WAVE 2.2

Figure 2-8.
The Waldorf PPG Wave 2.V models the original 1983 German instrument quite faithfully, right down to the panel graphics and the aliasing in the upper range of the keyboard. (In the software version, handily, you can switch the aliasing on or off.) In place of the original LCD data readout, the white buttons at right cause pop-up parameter displays to appear in the knob area.

VST (Mac, Win)
$199

Pros: Highly authentic recreation of a vintage synth. Knob moves can be recorded and played back via MIDI. Comes with hundreds of classic patches.
Cons: Velocity response controlled by two on/off switches. Not easy to program.

Using the PPG Wave 2.V, which I've done from time to time since penning the profile below for *Keyboard's* Oct. 2000 round-up of softsynths, is a guilty pleasure. It's not the fattest, richest, or most responsive synth on my hard drive; nor is it the easiest to make new sounds on; but darn it, nothing else sounds like it. It can be gritty or gurgly — the kind of sound that makes listeners sit up and say, "What's *that?*"

When the original PPG Wave 2.2 appeared in 1982 (shortly before the introduction of the DX7), the sound of digital waveshapes was a rarity. If memory serves, the PPG even had a computer program with which you could design your own waveshapes — tables of 64 (or maybe it was 256, but in those days memory was expensive) 8-bit numbers. Today, digital synthesis has branched out in a dozen directions. It would be a gross overstatement to say the PPG was where it all started. Digital synthesis experiments were going on in the 1960s, though none of them involved playing a keyboard in real time. And the Allen Organ Company was using digital oscillators in their electronic pipe organs in the 1970s. Even so, the PPG cheerfully evokes a simpler era.

PPG Wave 2.V at a Glance

System requirements	VST 2.0 compatible host software
Polyphony	up to 64 voices (system-dependent)
# of multitimbral parts	8 (MIDI channels 1 through 8 only)
Synthesis type	digital wavetable oscillators, analog filter emulation
Waveforms	about 1,988 (33 wavetables)
LFOs	1; triangle, square, positive and negative sawtooth
Filters	1 resonant lowpass
Envelopes	2 ADSR, 1 AD
Modulation	LFO, envelopes, and aftertouch to pitch, filter, amplitude, wavetable
Copy protection	CD-ROM installation
Downloadable demo	yes

Dominic Milano, who was part of the original *Keyboard* crew, would never let me near his precious PPG Wave 2.2. Considering how much it cost — in the $8,000 range — maybe that's understandable. But now it's my turn: I have a PPG in software. What made the original PPG special were its digital oscillators, which read their waveforms from any of 33 ROM wavetables. Each wavetable held 64 waves, each wave being half a cycle in length. By sweeping the oscillators through a wavetable, from one wave to another, under envelope or LFO control, you could create ear-catching tones that no other synth in the early '80s could touch. To be sure, the tones weren't hi-fi: The waveforms were 8-bit, and sweeping a wavetable tended to have a grungy, grainy sound.

The resonant lowpass filter (true analog in the original, now digitally modeled) had a unique whistling sound at high resonance settings. This has been faithfully copied in the plug-in — as have other idiosyncrasies. Eight-channel multitimbral operation is possible. Unlike the original, which would play only eight notes at a time, the plug-in can be up to 64-note polyphonic, and up to eight instances can be running at once if you have the CPU horsepower. Even with just one instance running, you can set up eight-voice layers in which each voice has a different tuning, for some nightmarish dissonant chords or rave-type minor 7th stabs.

The Wave 2.V has two oscillators. The second oscillator uses the same wavetable as the first one, but it can be detuned or play a different wave. Pitchbend can be applied to either oscillator, or to both. As in most synths of the era, both oscillators are processed by the same filter. New features not found in the original include graphic envelope and filter editing (very handy) and MIDI transmit/receive from the knobs.

When the 2.V is running in Steinberg Cubase VST and other fully VST 2.0 compatible sequencers, the knobs send and receive MIDI sys-ex data, which can be recorded into a sequencer track for expressive sweeps. You can also control them externally using MIDI controller data, which is far easier to edit. When I loaded the 2.V into Emagic Logic Audio Platinum 4.5, the 2.V's knob movements were translated by Logic into controller data — but because the controller assignments Logic used weren't correct, the 2.V didn't respond to this controller data when the track was played back. I also found that Logic can't yet [as of Oct. '00] transmit MIDI clock to VST plug-ins, which left me no way to sync the 2.V arpeggiator or LFO to my song. To make matters worse, the plug-in is designed so that the arpeggiator will take its tempo from the sequencer: It has no tempo parameter of its own, so in Logic the arpeggiator tempo is always 120 bpm.

As cool as this new PPG is, I can't help wishing Waldorf had given it a few modern touches. Velocity response, in particular, is minimal: Either the filter, the VCA, or both can be switched to respond to velocity, or not. Low velocities don't open up the VCA far enough for you to hear the notes, so some track editing may be required.

On the positive side, pitchbend, aftertouch, and the LFO can all sweep the wavetable, so there are lots of ways to make the sound growl or buzz. Keyboard loudness scaling is included as a parameter, which is helpful, as the instrument's high end can get a bit screechy. Also, the plug-in comes with several 128-program banks by different sound designers, including the 1984 factory patches. I had no trouble finding the right stuff for a quick four-track PPG arrangement — unless you count the amount of time I wasted doodling on various great-sounding patches.

I love this synth, and when Dominic dropped by to play it, he nodded several times and said, "That's the PPG sound, all right." It has a distinctive quality that will stand out in any techno, rock, or industrial track. It wouldn't be my first choice for sweeter styles, but no one synth can do everything. If you're looking for an unusual sound palette, the PPG Wave 2.V won't disappoint. —*JA (Oct '00)*

Native Instruments FM7
EMULATION (AND ENHANCEMENT) OF SOME CLASSIC YAMAHA FM SYNTHESIZERS

stand-alone, VST, DXi, DirectConnect, MAS (Mac, Win)
$299

Pros: Both authentic and cutting-edge sounds. Runs stand-alone or as a plug-in. Freely configurable algorithms. Thirty-stage looping, syncable envelopes. Compatible with existing DX/TX patch libraries. Audio input. Adds filtering, waveshaping, and 32 waveforms to the FM sonic palette.
Cons: No undo command. Microtuning tables aren't as good as in the DX7II series. Not multitimbral.

FM7 doesn't fit neatly in the "Clones" chapter, but it qualifies as a clone on steroids. While it emulates the Yamaha DX7, it's far more powerful, thanks to its filters, stereo output, and many other features. Still, if Native Instruments hadn't intended it to be perceived as a clone, they wouldn't have designed its main window (see page 56) to look so very much like the DX7's front panel.

Figure 2-9.

The cosmetics of the Native Instruments FM7 bear an eerie resemblance to the front panel of the original DX7. The "LCD" display at upper center is wider than the DX7 LCD, and this one is mainly for show. Information you enter about a patch will appear in the second line. The two displays to its right provide a bit of visual feedback about how the patch will sound, but again, they're not interactive. To select the operator you want to edit, or any of the other edit windows, use the row of buttons directly below the FM7 logo. Operators can be tuned in ratios or detuned by fixed Hz amounts using the Ratio and Offset parameters on the left. The ratio and fixed tunings can be used together for consistent beating rates or really ugly linear microtonal tunings. Modulation routings for the current operator are displayed on the lower left, just above the keyboard. Above the pitch and mod wheels (which can be operated with the mouse) is the waveform selector: You can choose any of 32 waveforms for the operator, including the vintage types found in Yamaha's TX81Z. Keyboard scaling curves (to the right above the keyboard) can have as many segments as you need. Click on any of the dots between the squares, and you can adjust an envelope or scaling curve segment to be concave or convex.

This review of version 1.00.004, which I wrote for *Keyboard's* March '02 issue, barely touches on the reasons for the success of FM synthesis, so maybe we should take a quick detour.

In a nutshell, when the DX7 hit the scene in 1983, most synthesizers (with the exception of the PPG, see above, which was built in Germany and fearfully expensive) could make only a few basic waveforms — the sine, triangle, sawtooth, and pulse/square waves beloved of analog purists. More complex tones were created by means of *subtractive synthesis*, which meant running a wave with a lot of overtones (a sawtooth or pulse) through a filter (usually a lowpass) so as to use only the overtones that were wanted at the moment. The DX7 turned this idea on its head. Complex tones were generated by means of *frequency modulation synthesis* (FM), a mathematical process developed by Dr. John Chowning at Stanford University in the 1970s, in which simple sine waves modulated one another. For a bit more on FM, see Chapter 8.

Creating your own sounds with FM was a tough nut to crack. The DX7's spartan user interface (one data slider and a two-line LCD) didn't help. But the DX7 had three things going for it, which combined to make it one of the best-selling synthesizers of all time:

■ The FM sound was amazingly versatile and detailed. Certain patches quickly became clichéd, but at the time, even that thin, thready DX7 harpsichord imitation set us back on our heels. Nobody had ever heard *anything* like that coming out of a synthesizer.

■ It had a velocity-sensitive keyboard, and the list price was $1,995. Most velocity-sensitive synths cost a whole lot more. Putting the detailed FM sound under velocity control brought both of them up to a whole new level.

■ The DX7 was one of the very first MIDI instruments, and appeared in the market at the beginning of an explosive period of expansion.

The original Yamaha DX7 was one of the most successful synthesizers ever built. Strangely enough, it eventually acquired a bad reputation — for several reasons, some deserved and some not. It was difficult to program, and its bell-like imitation of the Rhodes piano was used in way too many records. If you say "DX7," a lot of people still think of that particular sound. That's a shame, because the DX was capable of synthesizing quite a wide variety of sounds, from thick basses to snappy mallet percussion and truly bizarre special effects.

Yamaha themselves have continued to update the legacy of DX-style FM synthesis, most recently with the FS1R rack and DX200 groovebox. And of course any number of hardware and software synths sport a button or knob on the oscillator page with which you can do a little FM. But now that computer-based synthesis has come of age, there's a real need for a full-on virtual recreation of the DX7.

Native Instruments, who have emerged as a leader in software synthesis, have the tools to do the job. Their FM7 softsynth (which would appear to have Yamaha's blessing, inasmuch as a flyer for the DX200 is tucked into the FM7 manual) does 99% of what the original DX, the DX7II, the TX81Z, and other models would do, and a lot

FM7 at a Glance

System requirements	128MB RAM, 60MB free hard disk space; PC: Pentium 450MHz or better, Win98/ME/2000/XP; Mac: G3 400MHz or faster, MacOS 8.6 or higher, OMS or FreeMIDI
Compatibility	DirectX, MME, ASIO, Sound Manager; VST 2.0, DXi, DirectConnect, MAS
Synthesis types	FM, modeled analog, additive, waveshaping
Filter	dual resonant, series/parallel routing, continuously adjustable low/band/highpass response
Sample rate and bit depth	32-bit, rate is soundcard-dependent
Synthesis features	6-operator FM, dual multimode filters, dual LFOs, distortion, modulation matrix, unison mode, portamento
Effects	delay line with tone control, feedback, and diffusion
Other features	audio input, easy edit page
Arpeggiator	none
Synchronization	envelopes, LFOs, delay (MIDI clock, VST host clock in some sequencers)
Internal performance resampling	none
Copy protection	serial number on install
Downloadable demo	yes

Figure 2-10.
You can design your own FM algorithms in the FM7's matrix window. The nine blocks on the diagonal are the operators (including the distortion and filter operators and the audio input operator). By clicking and dragging on any vertical/horizontal intersection in the matrix, you can create and adjust a signal routing from one operator to another. The original DX7 algorithms are available from the drop-down menu at the top.

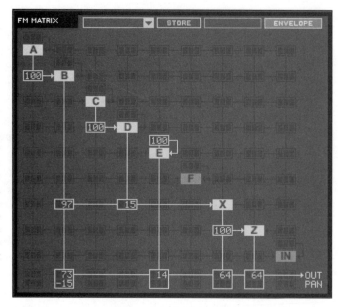

that they couldn't do. This is one kick-ass synthesizer. As the proud owner of two vintage Yamaha TX802 modules, I couldn't wait to install FM7 and put it through its paces.

Overview. The FM7 comes out of the box at warp speed: It's cross-platform (you can buy either the Mac or PC version) and capable of running either stand-alone or as a VST, DirectX, or MAS plug-in. I had no installation problems. On *Keyboard's* 1GHz AMD Athlon machine I was able to get 40 or more voices of polyphony in stand-alone mode without any glitching, with an audio buffer setting of 448 samples (which translates to about 10ms of latency). That's very decent performance, to say the least. On an older 400MHz Dell PC equipped with an Aardvark Direct Pro 24/96 ASIO interface, the latency when I played a MIDI keyboard was audible, but not bad enough to be annoying.

The voicing architecture, which we'll get into more fully below, goes significantly beyond what you'd expect if I said "a DX7 in software." You get dual multimode filters with adjustable series/parallel routing, plus distortion and a delay line. In place of the original 32 algorithms, the FM7 sports a fully configurable algorithm patching matrix (see **Figure 2-10**, above) — and each operator can be panned to its own position in the stereo field, which is very nice for setting up spacious layered sounds. The envelope generators, which can do surprisingly complex rhythm loops, are awesome.

Like the original (but unlike more recent Yamaha FM synths), the FM7 is not multitimbral. If you're running it as a plug-in, this is not an issue, as you can open multiple instances. For stand-alone use, though, being able to create keyboard split zones would have been nice.

Given the vast archive of old FM patches available for free on the Web, Native Instruments was wise to set up DX patch compatibility in the FM7. After scouring a few sites for downloads, I uncompressed and imported both DX7 and TX81Z banks. They worked perfectly. The quality of the free patches on the Web is not guaranteed to be uniformly high, but massaging the sounds once you've imported them is half the fun. I also did a few sys-ex dumps direct from a TX802 — again, with no hassles. In A/B listening tests, I didn't hear any differences between the original TX802 sounds and the imported versions (other than that the FM7 sounds cleaner).

I spotted a few loose ends that I hope will be addressed in the next revision. Most significant, there's no undo command. The program appears not to be entirely bug-free, either: A filter feedback routing magically appeared at one point when I was editing a different filter control. The pedal-steel pitchbend, while a welcome addition to the feature set (see below), sometimes failed to bend any pitches at all.

The most visible shortcoming of the FM7, in my book, is this: The microtuning implementation is inferior to the one on the DX7II and TX802. Those instruments allowed any key to be tuned anywhere in the instrument's range, but the FM7 gets by with a basic 12-note tuning table in which each key can be shifted up or down by only a half-step. To be fair, only about one musician in a thousand cares about this stuff — besides which, the FM7 is the first softsynth I can think of (other than NI's own Reaktor, which is covered on page 210) that will do user-programmable microtunings at all. So okay, the cup isn't ¾ empty, it's ¼ full. [*Editor's note: According to NI, the most recent release of FM7 will accept 128-note microtuning tables via MIDI system-exclusive.*]

The manual, written by frequent *Keyboard* contributor Craig Anderton, explains how to set up and run FM7 as a plug-in in various sequencers. The guide to the synthesis features is accurate, but doesn't go into as much detail as newcomers will likely need.

Sounds. The variety of patches shipped with this synth is pretty scary. All the classic types are out in abundance, as are more modern tones. In the former category you'll find Rhodes, Wurly, and Clav variations (of course), plenty of metallophones, decent plucked instruments such as lute and harp, analog-style pad/comps, and very serviceable pipe organ and French horn imitations.

It has to be said that the thin, tweezy FM7 trumpet is not going to be showing up at too many bullfights, but the strength of FM synthesis isn't really in emulating acoustic instruments. If you crave tubby synth basses, swirling crystalline pads, or wickedly pulsing dance drones, you won't be disappointed. The factory bank sports only a few lead sounds, which is surprising, as both luscious and rip-your-face-off leads are simple to create with this sound engine.

Patches can be saved and loaded in banks of 32 each, or in banks of 128. This makes it a doddle, as the Brits say, to mix and match your banks. In addition to 256 new sounds, the installation includes a 128-sound bank of vintage 1983 Yamaha presets. Other than providing a quick trip down Nostalgia Lane, these sounds may serve as a reminder of how far we've come in the last 20 years. Compared to the new stuff, many of them are pretty wimpy.

Random patch generation was a cool feature first found on some early DX7 editor/librarian software, so naturally NI included a Randomize button in the FM7. Don't start with an initialized patch and randomize it — you'll get nothing useful. By choosing an existing patch and setting not-too-large amounts of randomization for the various areas, I got some sounds that were intriguing enough to be worth editing further by hand.

Voice Architecture. Take a look at the screen on page 58, and you'll get some idea how flexible FM7's voice design is. In place of fixed algorithms, you can use any operator as a carrier, modulator, or both at once. Each operator can also modulate itself in a feedback loop, to create thicker overtones. (The DX7 had only a single fixed feedback loop per algorithm.)

On top of the standard six operators, FM7 includes a distortion operator and an operator with dual resonant filters. These two operators can be patched just like any other — for instance, you could send an operator's signal through a resonant lowpass filter and then feed the filter output back into the same operator as a modulator. At high amounts, this type of feedback quickly turns to noise, but with judicious settings it can give you some useful and unexpected tone colors.

The FM7 envelopes are similar to those in NI Absynth (see page 66). Each operator has its own amplitude envelope, and each envelope can have up to 30 points. Clicking on the tempo sync button in the envelope window creates a snap-to grid that makes alignment of envelope points quick and easy. The grid is strictly aligned to 32nd-note resolution, but you can edit individual points by hand without snapping them to the grid if you need triplets or swing. And because the envelopes will loop, setting up complex rhythm tones . . . well, I won't say it's easy, because both imagination and patience are required, but the musical results can be far-reaching. I'd recommend this synth in a heartbeat if what you crave are rhythmic pulsing drones.

Both velocity and key position envelope scaling are supported. An operator has only one slider for each, and the way they're implemented is not quite ideal: You ought to be able to set it up so high velocities would speed up the attack and slow down the release, as this would emulate acoustic instrument behavior — but you can't. (I'm told this has been fixed in the new version.)

I had no trouble syncing the envelopes to external MIDI clock coming from my Korg Karma. They locked up with the tempo in Cubase just as easily. In fact, individual envelopes can either sync or be left free-running, which can be handy if you've set up a long slow envelope sweep that you don't want disturbed by the sync. I did notice a significant time lag (up to half a second) between tempo changes

I made using the Karma's front-panel knob and the FM7's response, but since most of us don't write tunes with a lot of tempo changes, this may not be a big deal.

The two LFOs have all of the same waveforms as the oscillators, plus sample-and-hold. They can be synced to the tempo, naturally, and LFO rate can be modulated by velocity or key position. And each LFO has independent outputs for each operator.

If all this seems a bit intimidating, you may want to click on the "Easy" button. This opens up a panel of macro-type sliders with familiar names — brightness, ADSR envelopes for amplitude and timbre, and so on.

When the pedal steel pitchbend mode is activated, you can bend only the lowest — or highest, your choice — note in a held chord. I love this feature; all synthesizers should have it. One minor feature I did miss is dynamic panning. Each operator's pan position is programmable, but you can't sweep it in real time. (The DX7 had a monaural output — no panning there, either.)

The manual gives very little information about the audio input, but there's not much to it, other than the cool sounds you can create. Running an external signal through the filter is a standard trick, but here you can go further. The external audio can be used as either a modulator or a carrier in FM (or both at once). I tried running some drum loops from a CD into FM7, filtering them, and then using them as mod sources. The results were squiggly, scratchy, or nasty, depending on the filter settings.

The delay line (NI calls it a multitap delay, but you have no independent control over the taps) will do rhythmic echoes, chorusing, flanging, and even a metallic impression of room reverb. It will sync to incoming MIDI clock. When it's synced, the time slider settings include both duplet and triplet values. [*Editor's note: The most recent release also includes dotted values.*]

MIDI Implementation. Each FM7 patch can be programmed to respond to mod wheel, aftertouch, breath controller, and two (globally selected) MIDI controllers. As in the original instruments, these can either adjust the level of individual operators directly (this was called "EG Bias" on the DX7) or adjust the amount of LFO input to operator levels. Or both at once.

If that isn't enough expressive power for you, just click the Learn button, click any FM7 parameter (including points in the patching matrix), and wiggle a MIDI slider. It's that easy. These routings are global to the synth, not programmable per patch, so a bit of advance planning will help if you need to use the feature in various pieces of music at various times.

Insider tip: The DX7's keyboard only transmitted velocities up to about 100. In the FM7 preferences box, you can scale the incoming MIDI velocities so these patches will sound the way they did 20 years ago.

In Use. After booting Cubase VST 32 5.0, I instantiated a few FM7s as VST instruments and started developing a throbbing electronic mix. Aside from the kick drum (courtesy of Steinberg's LM9), FM7 provided all the basic sounds for my

MIDI tracks. Its factory banks gave me plenty of sonic variety. I laid down a couple of layers of pulsing drone sounds (envelopes synced to the Cubase tempo, naturally), a screaming lead, and a swirling pad.

After bouncing down my synth layers to a new stereo audio track, I instantiated FM7 as an effect and added some thick, warm distortion to the mix. Again, I was very impressed with the sound.

I was careful to set each instance of the plug-in to use only as many voices of polyphony as the part actually required. Even so, at a certain point (18 voices or so on a 1GHz system — and this was with no audio tracks playing), Cubase's audio output overloaded, freaked out, and shut down. This happened several times, even when the VST usage meter was hovering around 40%. I was able to get the sound output to wake up by saving the song, quitting Cubase, and reloading it. I ran into similar audio output meltdowns running FM7 as a stand-alone program when I set the polyphony too high. According to Native Instruments, this problem has been solved in the latest update, which is available for download.

Even with these little stumbles, my experience with FM7 was overwhelmingly positive: Both the sound and the user interface are everything I could ask for. This synth is going to become a regular part of my music setup.

Conclusions. The FM7 is a no-lose proposition. For fans of vintage DX synths, it offers more, better, and faster — more voicing options, better sound quality, and faster editing. For folks who just want a stack of sounds that go far beyond me-too virtual analog, a full-court-press FM implementation like this one may be a dream come true. The only issue I'm at all concerned about is that the audio output becomes unstable when FM7 is asked to play too many notes at once. This is not a catastrophic problem if you're careful, and in any case NI tells me they've corrected it in the new version.

I could list all the tight features again, but then the "Conclusions" would be as long as the rest of the review. For veteran FM programmers, the user interface alone (yes, it's even better than the one in your editor/librarian) may be worth the price of admission. Developing a new sound on this instrument takes about a tenth as long as it used to. If you don't care about programming, you may be more excited about the sound library compatibility. No matter how you slice it, FM7 is a winner. —JA (Mar. '02)

GMedia Music M-Tron
RECREATES THE SOUND OF THE MELLOTRON

VST (Mac, Win)
$69.95

Pros: Cheaper, lighter, and easier to maintain than a vintage Mellotron. Attack and release controls extend the utility of the soundset. True to the original, sounds are not looped. Inconsistent sound quality of Mellotron recordings is preserved.

Cons: Eats up lots of memory. No option to install only the engine and leave the sound bank on the CD-ROM.

Now about the Mellotron. In the final analysis, it was a junior Rube Goldberg device. At the time (the late '60s and early '70s) it filled a very definite need, but as soon as something better came along, the Mellotron was consigned to the dustbin of history. Yet here it is again, rising from the dead like a cobweb-covered Transylvanian nobleman.

The Mellotron is beloved of nostalgia buffs because its dreadful tones evoke the mood of certain famous recordings — the Beatles' "Strawberry Fields Forever," hits by Led Zeppelin and the Moody Blues, that sort of thing. It was a sample playback keyboard that had the bad luck to predate the birth of sampling. Its tones were stored on individual lengths of recording tape. When you pressed a key, a mechanism would drag the tape across a playback head, and whatever was on the tape (typically a violin section or a choir) would be heard. When you let the key up, a spring would whip the tape back to its starting position, ready for the next note.

Mellotrons were finicky beasts. The springs would break, or the tapes would break, or the tapes would get out of alignment with the heads. In order to change sounds, you had to open the case, remove one set of tapes, and install another set. It was a roadie's worst nightmare. Fortunately, the software version doesn't suffer from any of those problems, as Ken Hughes notes in this April 2001 profile. But if your nostalgia experience just wouldn't be complete without a big white box and racks of physical tapes, you may be interested to know that (according to an August 2002 feature in England's *Sound on Sound* magazine) new Mellotrons are once more being built.

I f you've ever heard the Beatles' "Strawberry Fields Forever," you've heard the sound of the Mellotron. One of its many sounds, that is. The 'Tron of legend was a big white box containing a tape playback mechanism for each of its 35 keys. All its sounds were quirky and lower than lo-fi, characterized by marked pitch and timbre inconsistencies.

M-Tron, a PC and Mac VST 2.0 instrument, offers a library of 28 classic

Figure 2-11.
The original Mellotron was just about as simple as the software version. Those aren't defects in the image: GMedia really did put coffee cup rings and cigarette burns on the front panel.

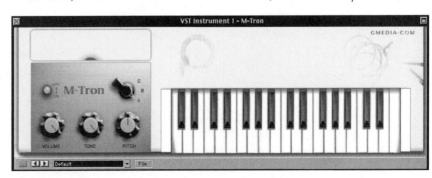

Mellotron sounds and some added features. Obviously, MIDI is now part of the package. Envelope attack and release controls, which the original machine didn't have, have also been added. [*Editor's note: GMedia now sells two additional "tape" banks at $49.95 each.*]

Other than the envelope sliders, the M-Tron's controls are about as spartan as the original's: 35 keys, a volume knob, and pitch and tone knobs. A toggle switch accesses the envelope controls and the sound selections. Encapsulating the Mellotron's original library of eight-second tapes uses a lot of memory: Some of the banks are around 27MB, and the software doesn't give you the option of leaving the sound bank on the CD-ROM the way Propellerhead Reason does. It has to be installed on your hard drive.

Yeah, yeah, but how does it sound? Every bit as charmingly lo-fi as a real Mellotron. Intonation is occasionally questionable, timbre is inconsistent, notes sometimes warble a bit. In a word, authentic. The "Strawberry Fields" flutes are here, as are the expected string, brass, and choir sounds. Rarely heard 'Tron vibes, accordion, mandolin tremolos, and oboe are also included. All have an elusive, scratchy black-and-white-movie sound to them. The rhythm banks are hilariously hokey and probably not all that useful, but in the interest of completeness they're appreciated.

Some soundware developers have missed the boat by cleaning up (and even — gasp! — looping) Mellotron sounds. Gmedia did a great job of preserving the idiosyncrasies of the original instrument (most importantly that eight-second note-length limit and the weird "gloop!" at its end) as well as extending its capabilities — the Mellotron didn't feature any kind of envelope controls, and MIDI was decades in the future. M-Tron puts volume, tone, pitch, attack, release, and pan under MIDI control.

If you have a jones for one of these old tape-tanglers but lack the cash, space, and/or patience necessary to acquire, house, and maintain one, consider M-Tron. I think you'll like it. —*Ken Hughes (Apr. '01)*

Analog Madness

3

The sound of an analog synthesizer has a mystique among musicians that may be a little tricky for outsiders to understand. It's all just electronic sound, right? And electronic sound is by definition cold and soulless, right? So what's all the fuss about analog sounding different or better?

Ignoring, for the moment, that crack about "cold and soulless," which may or may not be true depending on how you look at the process of making music, let's try to bracket what's special about the analog sound. Not that any of the synthesizers discussed in this chapter, or elsewhere in this book, are actually analog instruments. On the contrary. They're digital simulations that attempt, in some cases with a fair degree of success, to mimic the tone and response of analog circuits.

The analog sound is typically praised for its "warmth" and "fatness." This quality, which is hard to put your finger on, is due primarily to the behavior of the circuitry in the synth. When slightly overloaded, analog circuits tend to distort the signal in ways that the human ear perceives as pleasing. Unintended digital distortion, on the other hand, tends to be extremely nasty and undesirable. Even when not overloaded, analog circuits are always ever so slightly unstable, which makes the tone subliminally different from note to note. Digital algorithms (the mathematical structures that are the functional equivalent of analog circuits) are either perfectly stable or disastrously unstable. The apparent instability of a digital synth that's designed to sound analog is actually a clever and carefully controlled design feature. It's not instability at all.

True analog synthesis is also limited. Analog oscillators can typically produce only three or four extremely simple waveforms: sine, triangle, sawtooth, and pulse waves. More advanced analog synths overcome this limitation with waveshapers, ring modulators, and other devices that produce different types of waveshapes, but the fact remains — digital oscillators can produce far more varieties of tone than their analog counterparts. This is why "virtual analog" instruments (digital instruments that model their analog ancestors) generally include both the classic sine, triangle, saw, and pulse waveforms and numerous others.

Among analog aficionados, you'll hear a lot of talk about filters. In the original analog instruments, filtering was the main method by which the dreadful machine-like buzz of the oscillators was shaped into musically pleasing tones. While lowpass filters, which remove the upper overtones from the signal, were and are the most common type, multimode filters able to operate in highpass, bandpass, or band-reject mode were also found on genuine analog instruments. (For more on filters, see Chapter 8.) Modeling the frequency response and other characteristics of an analog filter in a digital synth is essential, but while it may be something of a black art, it's not an insurmountable hurdle. Most of the synths discussed below have very respectable analog-sounding filters.

Several important analog synths, including the Minimoog, had audio inputs. This made it possible to pass external signals through their filters. This is a desirable feature, and it's found on some, but not all, software-based "analog" instruments.

Two important modeled-analog instruments, Steinberg's Model-E Minimoog clone and Native Instruments' Pro-53 clone of the Prophet-5, are covered in Chapter 2. Other resources for modeled-analog synthesis are discussed in Chapters 4 and 6. In the following pages, you'll find profiles of instruments whose main claim to fame is their emulation of the techniques of analog synthesis.

Also included is one recent synth, Antares Kantos, that frankly doesn't fit very well in the analog category. I put it in this chapter because I couldn't figure out how to wedge it in anyplace else. It shares with early analog instruments the fact that it's monophonic (capable of making only one note at a time). If you need a better justification, sorry — I haven't got one.

Native Instruments Absynth
ANALOG/FM/WAVESHAPING SYNTH

stand-alone, VST (Mac, Win)
$299

Pros: Extraordinary sounds. Large set of timbral resources, including FM, ring modulation, waveshaping, and four multimode filters and three LFOs per voice. Retriggerable LFOs. Sixty-eight-segment envelopes. Envelope editing in absolute times and bpm.

Cons: No performance control of envelope times. No filter resonance modulation. No LFO or envelope sync to MIDI clock.

When I reviewed Absynth 1.2 for *Keyboard's* Oct. '01 issue, it was a Mac-only program. The Windows version is a more recent arrival. The most forward-looking feature of Absynth is its multi-stage envelope generators, which have shown up more recently in other synths from Native Instruments — but its most immediately striking aspect is its appearance, as the screenshot on page 69 attests. Arguably, "eye candy" ought to be irrelevant, but musicians are intuitive by nature, and easily swayed by gut reactions. As long as the user interface doesn't turn into a stumbling block, sez I, bring on the eye candy.

"**M**aybe we shouldn't review Absynth for a while," John Krogh said. There was an evil twinkle in his eye. "The fewer people who know about it, the more of an edge my music will have." John was kidding — he would never play games when scheduling Keyboard Reports. But the temptation was surely real. Absynth is one of the more awesome software synths either of us has seen yet. (And we've seen most of them.) With devastating tones, deep programming features, plenty of compatibility options, and a very sexy user interface, Absynth is the kind of program that's going to get talked about in a big way.

Overview. At heart, Absynth is part of the modeled analog school of synthesis. The waveforms used by its three oscillators are all single-cycle, with no sampled attack transients. Its multimode resonant filters (up to four per voice) and ring modulators would be right at home on an analog-style synth as well. But Absynth goes further in the digital direction, with waveshaping, basic six-operator FM synthesis, multi-segment envelopes suitable for drum pattern synthesis, and more.

Figure 3-1.
The main window for Absynth includes a mousable keyboard, a 128-preset bank list, and buttons for opening edit windows (upper right). The horizontal sliders above the keyboard are mousable as well, and when you add extra controller inputs to a patch, this area of the window will expand so they're all shown. Each patch has its own programmable volume slider, but there's no master volume.

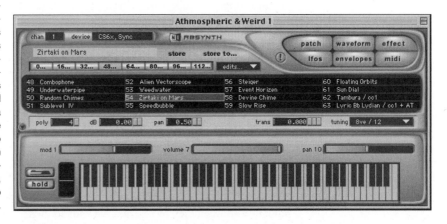

Absynth at a Glance

System requirements	Mac: 300MHz G3, MacOS 9 or higher, 128MB RAM; PC: Win98/2000/ME/XP, 500MHz PIII, 128MB RAM
Plug-in and audio streaming formats supported	VST 2.0, DXi, ASIO, DirectConnect, MAS, Sound Manager, FreeMIDI, OMS
Synthesis types	modeled analog, FM, waveshaping
Sample rate and bit depth	32-bit internal, 44.1/48kHz, records (stand-alone) at 16-bit, output resolution dependent on hardware
Synthesis features	6 oscillators, 4 filters, 3 LFOs, 3 ring modulators, 16 envelopes, and waveshaper for each voice; waveform editing
Effects	stereo delay
Other features	31 factory tuning tables; 8-part multitimbral in VST
Arpeggiator	none
Synchronization	manual parameter editing in bpm, external LFO retriggering
Internal performance resampling	to RAM
Copy protection	serial number and CD check during install
Downloadable demo	yes

After entering the serial number on installation, I was up and running with Absynth as a stand-alone app. Later I ran it as a VST plug-in, again without problems. The manual — printed in four languages — is short and sweet. If you're new to synthesizer programming, you may wish they had included a tutorial, but power users will find the interface a breeze to navigate.

Sounds. The factory presets in Absynth are keenly evocative. Rhythm patterns that sound step-sequenced (they're actually done with the envelope generators) abound — the big-bottomed analog of "RY-30++" and "Rotifiers 120 BPM," the tinkly Kraftwerkian beep of "135 Portamenthol," and the vaguely ethnic "Frame Drum 168 BPM" and "Vulcan Berimbau," for instance. The pads ("Space Pad," "Wave Pad," and "Solid Texture," for instance) tend to be in the Euro digital camp.

Surprisingly, the preset bank isn't filled with fat basses and screaming leads, though I spotted a few. You'll find some plucked instruments ("Asia") and exotic wind leads ("Sssnake") as well, but the biggest selection is in the in-your-face effects category: "Hendrix in the Manifold" serves up grinding digital distortion, "Steiger" tosses off some unusual pitch bleeps, and "The Mysterious Satellite" sends an indecipherable droning message.

On top of the 128-preset factory bank, Absynth ships with a number of partial banks with names like "Loops & Sequences," "Synth, Bass & Acoustic," and "Atmospheric & Weird." It has to be said, the flute and oboe presets are not especially realistic, and the acoustic bass has a strong FM flavor. But you'll probably be more interested in the weird pitch warbles of "LSD Hook," the machine keening of "Industrial Sector 1," or the ballsy electro "Long Rezo Kick Comb." Also of note: You can import patches from one bank into another, thereby rearranging your sounds as needed.

Figure 3-2.
The chrome-plated signal routing lines in Absynth's patch window make it look like something out of *Alien*. Each oscillator/filter/modulator group has its own vertical column, through which the signals flow downward. Oscillator balance is controlled with the three horizontal sliders at the bases of the columns. Modules that are inactive are dark; the fewer you need, the lower the CPU load. After being summed, the three signals travel from left to right through the row at the bottom (waveshaper, filter, effect processor). The two or three little buttons to the right of each number parameter are for coarse, fine, and ultra-fine editing, but you can type a number if you'd prefer. The Absynth oscillators can run in any of four modes — single, double, FM, or ring mod. A pop-up menu holds the waveform list. The main and sub oscillators in each pair can be individually tuned and modulated. The oscillator phase parameter can be used to add or subtract overtones.
Each oscillator feeds its own filter. Each filter has several modes, including lowpass and highpass with various slopes, plus bandpass, notch, and comb. One limitation: There's no modulation input for controlling the resonance amount during performance. The waveshaper (lower left) is great for adding controlled distortion, and can operate either monophonically or polyphonically. Its output feeds yet another filter.

Voicing. Earlier I called Absynth a three-oscillator synth. That description is too simple. Each oscillator is in fact two oscillators rolled into one. You can add the waves in each pair for six-oscillator tones, or modulate one with the other using either frequency modulation (FM) or ring modulation. Each oscillator pair then feeds its own multimode filter, and the output of each filter feeds another ring modulator with its own waveform and frequency controls. So in fact you can use both ring mod and FM on each oscillator. As a result, the fact that the oscillators have no hard sync or pulse width modulation is not much of an issue.

If the 41 single-cycle waveforms in the factory set aren't enough to keep you happy, you can generate your own using the wave edit window (see page 71). Wave edit windows are not a new idea (there's a very nice one in U&I MetaSynth, for example), but this one definitely goes the extra mile: You can blend waves, fractalize them, filter them, draw them by hand, normalize their gain, and much more. You can also import the first 1,024 sample words from an AIFF (Mac) or WAV (PC) file. And here's the kicker: Not only do your new waves show up in the oscillators' menu, they also show up, along with all of the factory waves, in the LFOs. When it comes to customizable modulation shapes, Absynth has got you covered — and that's before you even get to the envelopes. Note one limitation, though: The current version can't copy waves from one preset to another. [*Editor's note: According to Native Instruments, this feature has been added.*]

Moving along quickly (there's far too much in the guts of this machine for us to dissect it all), Absynth boasts three LFOs per voice. They're not limited to one per oscillator: You could use all three to drive the same filter cutoff, for example.

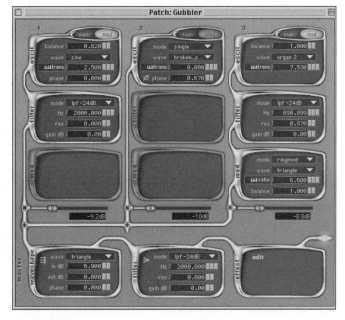

Figure 3-3.
Absynth's envelope
edit window is calibrated
in seconds — note the
ruler across the edit area
— and can be zoomed
both horizontally and vertically. Snap-to-grid point
dragging is provided, and
the grid is calibrated in
bpm. Using the transform
pop-up menu (upper
right), you can scale an
envelope up or down, set
its duration, or generate a
rhythmic pulse train at the
tempo of your choice.
The pulses can then be
edited to create rhythms
like the ones shown here.
The slope of envelope
segments can be con-
trolled individually, and
envelopes can loop, sus-
tain, or cycle through
without sustaining.

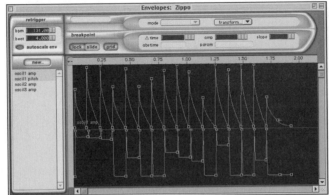

Each has upwards of a dozen possible destinations, including individual oscillator amplitude and the FM index/balance of the dual oscillators, plus effect time and panning. You can modulate LFO rate or amount from a control source, but LFO start delay is not implemented.

One small but cool feature I've never seen before is an LFO retrigger option. You could assign this to the sustain pedal, for instance, so as to trigger all of the LFOs in sync with one another. Oddly, the LFO "rate" parameter is actually a time parameter, which means that large numbers slow the LFO down. But it turns out that being able to dial in the time of an LFO wave can come in handy. It's a piece of cake to synchronize the LFOs with the envelopes, for instance.

The envelope generators (see **Figure 3-3**, above) are truly powerful — and you can have up to 16 or so per patch. Each envelope can have up to 68 segments, and they can be looped. A utility menu lets you create rhythmic loops easily.

Further tonal shaping is provided by the waveshaper, a controlled distortion device that can run either polyphonically, processing each voice separately, or monophonically, creating intermodulation among the voices in a chord. If the waveshaper is monophonic, the filter that follows it is also monophonic, but if the shaper is polyphonic the filter can be as well. The number of possibilities here is considerable — anything from dual filters in series to six crossfading oscillators being stepped on by a heavy waveshaper and then filtered into submission.

Last up is the effects processor. Always monophonic (but stereo), this is pretty simple, being nothing but a delay line with three modes — pipe, multicomb, and multitap. The multitap delay has three taps, each with its own level, pan, and modulation amount (the modulation sources are the same for all delay parameters). Times of up to ten seconds, coupled with a feedback setting, let you do rhythms or pseudo-reverb ambiences. The multicomb is more complex, offering six separate delays, each with its own time, gain, pan, lowpass, feedback, and modulation amount. The pipe delay is harder to describe, but an animated graphic gives a good idea what's going on. The "pipe" has a length, an input point, and two output points, which can be modulated to induce phase shift. Two cool things about the delay:

Time can be modulated by an LFO without nasty little glitching noises, and it gives Absynth a distinctive character that a more comprehensive processor (chorusing, hall reverb, and so on) might disguise.

MIDI Implementation. Absynth's MIDI reception is straightforward (there are no velocity response curves, for instance) but very versatile. Velocity gives you individual amplitude control over all three oscillators, all three FM amounts, and all three filter cutoffs. You can set the amount, and invert it. Missing: Velocity control of envelope times — important for traditional types of synthesis, but maybe not a big deal in more electronic styles.

Controller inputs can be routed to FM amount, filter cutoff, delay time, pan, and volume. Each input has a lag parameter, which is incredibly useful for smoothing out the response. Inverting the response is not possible, unfortunately, and the pitchbender can only bend pitch — it can't sweep a filter at the same time, for instance.

All of the filters, oscillator amplitudes, and FM amounts have their own keyboard scaling curves, which cover the entire MIDI note range and can be drawn with the mouse. Each note can be separately defined, making it easy to do keyboard splits and crossfades within a single patch. You don't find this kind of detail on a lot of synths, software or hardware.

In Use. Absynth didn't work properly under Emagic Logic Audio Platinum 4.5, so it was time to download the latest version. After I updated to Logic 4.7.3, Absynth instantiated and played just fine. Up to eight instances can run at once if your computer is fast enough, and I was able to lay down a very tasty multitrack groove with a fat Absynth beat, a pad, and a lead line. Absynth's built-

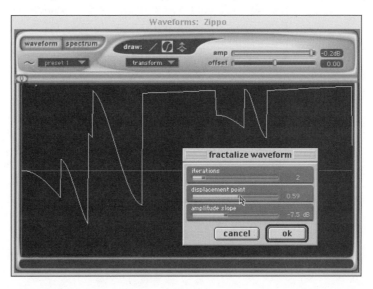

Figure 3-4.
Absynth's wave edit window offers a wealth of tools for creating your own single-cycle waves. Here, the "fractalize waveform" utility, visible in the pop-up box, is being used to add new overtones. In another mode, the wave edit window becomes an additive synthesis resource, complete with phase control over individual overtones.

in delay gave the tracks a crisp professional ambience even before I added plug-in effects. Logic's implementation of VST controller data (still rather crippled until 5.0 is released) created some minor problems in Absynth, but nothing I couldn't work around.

The envelopes and LFOs in Absynth don't actually sync to an external clock. I had to do a little envelope editing to get an Absynth percussion beat to line up with Logic's tempo, but a quick trip to the manual was all it took to get the "autoscale envelopes" command working like a charm.

Absynth crashed a couple of times when I was editing one of my patches, and several times on booting it I had to fiddle with its audio system settings in order to get some nasty distortion to go away. The problem disappeared very reliably when I switched to ASIO and back to Sound Manager. [*Editor's note: According to Native Instruments, "There is a good chance these problems have been resolved in version 1.34."*]

Running the freestanding version of Absynth, I used the built-in record utility (which has a handy wait-for-note button) to capture a few of the rhythm loops in the factory presets. This is an ideal way to export complex Absynth sounds to a computer where Absynth itself isn't running. Rumor has it that a couple of the more cutting-edge soundware CDs on the market — recorded by a developer whose name you'd recognize — were created using Absynth.

Conclusions. This is the kind of synth that makes me want to stay home and program new patches all week (and then devote a few months to composing music with them). Plug-in compatibility is important, and Absynth has that, but the voicing features are the main attraction. Oscillators, filters, rhythm-based envelopes, waveshaping, wave editing — it's all here. Yes, there's room for a few more parameters, notably LFO delay and envelope time modulation, but most of us won't miss them. Absynth is so hot, it's radioactive. *—JA (Oct. '01)*

LinPlug Delta 2.1
AFFORDABLE FOUR-OSCILLATOR ANALOG

VST (Mac, Win)
$99.90

Pros: Powerful synthesis/modulation capabilities. Gutsy sounds. Elegant multitimbrality. Two types of envelope generators. Dual filters.
Cons: No audio input.

Based on the review below and the information on LinPlug's website, Delta is one of the synths in this book that I wish I had time to try out myself. (Just today FedEx brought two *other* synths I'm still hoping to spend some quality time with before I have to send this manuscript off to the printer. Ah, the torture!) Julian Colbeck profiled Delta 2.1 in the Oct. '00 issue of *Keyboard*, but the current version is Delta III.

Among the new features not discussed below are four LFO modules, each with its own DAD (delay-attack-decay) envelope generator for LFO fade-ins and fade-outs; more sophisticated oscillators; improved envelope generators with a sustain "fade" stage, allowing for a rise or fall once the sustain level has been reached; a choice of three types of multimode filters, each with its own distinct sound; and a built-in effects section with chorus, delay, and reverb. Also, the most recent version ships with more than 500 presets.

I s it my imagination, or has Germany become the preeminent source of cool new software? Steinberg, Emagic, Creamware, Native Instruments . . . and now a welcome addition, LinPlug, whose curiously titled GakStoar Delta 2.1 [*Editor's note: LinPlug has since dropped the "GakStoar" name*] marshals immense resources with an impressively light touch. Hmm. A bit like Beethoven or Bach, in a way.

Delta is not modeled on any one real analog synth so far as I can tell, but its myriad modulation possibilities and multi-faceted range of tones and textures puts me in mind of an Oberheim Matrix-12.

This is a "hands-on" plug-in. Almost everything can be viewed and accessed from the main page; even its multitimbrality can be coordinated using a little 16-button keypad.

Figure 3-5.
Linplug Delta III offers numerous improvements over the 2.1 release. The four oscillators (two are shown at upper left) have continuously variable waveshapes, and three types of filters (upper right) are available. Selector switches on the left and right borders allow you to display various modules. Note the five-stage envelope in the left column and the two effects processors in the lower slots.

Delta III at a Glance

System requirements	Windows PC or Mac OS9/OSX, 300MHz, 1,024x768 screen resolution or better, 16MB available RAM, VST 2.0-compatible host software
Synthesis type	analog modeling
Oscillators	4 (dual waveform); sine (x4), triangle, sawtooth, square, pulse (x 4), stair-step, noise
Polyphony	up to 24 voices
# of multitimbral parts	8
Filters	3 resonant multimode types; low, high & bandpass, with 6–36dB selectable slope
Envelopes	8, with standard ADSR or 5-stage level/rate
LFOs	4; sine, triangle, sawtooth, square, S&H, noise
Modulation	8 x 8 matrix
Copy protection	serial number (via email on registration)
Downloadable demo	yes

Simple to view, but far from simplistic, Delta's engine room contains four oscillators, each able to harness two individual waveforms selectable from pulldown menus. The waveforms can operate at different broad pitch ranges and can be detuned fractionally (±100 cents) using one of Delta's distinctive big blue control knobs if you want to "get phat" as quickly as possible (i.e., without resorting to pulse-width modulation, though that's available as well).

I'm a sucker for using pitch envelopes, because you can define and redefine a sound's character so quickly and easily. The PE button on each oscillator panel activates the pitch envelope; too bad a single pitch envelope is shared among all four oscillators. That's a bit of a shame, given Delta's wide range of options elsewhere, but think of its unifying aspect as a bonus for taming otherwise over-complex silly patches, which Delta is extremely capable of producing once you dive into the multimode filters and multistage envelope generators.

Separate amplifier and filter envelope modulation is available per oscillator, though, and you can cross-modulate between oscillators 1 & 3 and 2 & 4 in terms of both frequency or amplitude for some distinctly non-traditional analog (more like FM) effects.

All eight of the envelope generators can operate in "enhanced" five-stage time/level-style, which is a powerful capability but frankly not everyone's cup of tea, or in the more fathomable ADSR mode. My eyes start to glaze over at about the decay level with time/level EGs, so the ADSR option gets a big thumbs-up from me.

Just off-center on the screen lies an exciting-looking modulation matrix where 16 mod sources and 16 destinations can be arranged. [*Editor's note: Only eight sources and eight destinations are provided in the most recent version.*] These are dead simple to activate. Sources include the LFOs: any of four to choose from in multiple waveforms, and syncable, too; plus pitch, velocity, aftertouch, pitch and mod wheels, and MIDI breath control. Destinations include any oscillator volume or pitch, master volume, either filter cutoff or resonance, oscillator pulse width, patch volume, and pan (filter or oscillator).

Delta 2.1 also sounds ace. In seconds I was producing, albeit unwittingly half the time, massive multi-attacked, diving, swooping extravaganzas that a Matrix-12 would be proud of. A flip through some of the presets revealed some devilish basses, and even the odd (and I use the word advisedly) piano.

GakStoar Delta 2.1 represents an incredible 75 bucks' worth. [*Editor's note: The current version is $99.90.*] Ten years ago you'd have paid 100 times that for such an instrument. Oh, and you can download a demo version for 90 days. Is life wonderful or what? —*Julian Colbeck (Oct. '00)*

VirSyn Tera
MULTI-FILTER SYNTH WITH EFFECTS AND STEP SEQUENCER

Figure 3-6.
Tera's elegantly designed main panel provides plenty of controls; too bad the window can't be resized. You can draw your own additive synthesis spectra for the spectrum oscillator (center) or use the three analog-style oscillators (upper left). Two of them have waveform modulation, two have FM. The two standard multimode filters (upper center) can operate in series or parallel. The three-band formant filter (upper right) can be used for EQ or moving vowel tones. Both the standard filters and the amplifier have built-in overdrive for fattening up the sound. Three insert effects (the row above the graphic envelopes) can be used in every patch. With the handy knob at the bottom in the center, you can make all of the envelopes longer or shorter without having to reprogram them one at a time.

stand-alone and VST (Mac, Win)
$249

Pros: Great-sounding, powerful synth with three resonant filters per voice, plus a spectrum oscillator. Sixteen-part multitimbral. A fresh approach to step sequencing. Innovative mouse control surface.

Cons: Step sequencer needs better editing commands. Not the easiest program to learn (could use a better manual).

As the screenshot on page 75 shows, Tera is a high-end analog instrument packed with tone-shaping features. Since I prefer to compose music in a linear way rather than by repeating patterns, I don't often use Tera's step sequencer. It embodies some fresh concepts, though, and goes further than the step sequencers in some other softsynths, so if you're into that sort of thing you may find it irresistible. For me, the main attractions in Tera are the spectrum oscillator, which can produce some gorgeous swirling timbres, and the flexible signal routing. I reviewed Tera 1.0 for the July '02 issue of *Keyboard*. New features in version 1.1 include multiple VST outputs (up to eight per Tera instance) and external synchronization of the sequencer from the VST host program.

There's never been a better time to have a fast computer. The power and sheer variety of the current generation of software synthesizers is truly inspiring. VirSyn Tera comes from a tiny start-up in Germany, but Tera's sound is ready for the big leagues, and it sports some fresh features too.

Overview. Tera is designed to work either as a stand-alone synth or as a VST plug-in. It's 16-part multitimbral, an important feature missing from some stand-alone softsynths. It also boasts an interactive 16-track step sequencer that doubles as a programmable arpeggiator.

While the basic synthesis type — analog-style oscillators and filters — is familiar, Tera serves up a couple of extras that add considerably to the timbral palette. First up is what VirSyn calls a spectrum oscillator. Calling this an additive synthesis tool for creating waves with up to 128 overtones doesn't really do it justice; its rich, swirling tones are quite ear-catching. (See the "Synthesis" section, below, for details.) Add three filters per voice, four LFOs, four envelopes, and a very open-ended signal routing setup, and the range of sounds you can make with this synth is truly vast.

Tera's user interface is a little unusual. The main window fills the screen, and can't be resized, for instance. Also, Windows' standard drop-down menus aren't used. For this and other reasons, it's not the easiest instrument to learn. If you're new to synthesizer programming, you might want to pick something more conventional to start out (Native Instruments Pro-52, for instance). Even as a certified synth programming hound, it took me a couple of minutes to figure out how the signal routings work. Also, Tera's owner's manual is not very good. But if the prospect of routing signals through a formant filter or a wave delay doesn't faze you, get ready for some fun.

That's not to say the interface is clumsy — if anything, just the opposite. When you click on an oscillator's WM (wave modulation) switch, the knob that controls WM amount fades into view on a blank section of the panel. Click the switch again, and the knob doesn't just disappear, it fades out smoothly. When the mouse is hovering over a knob or slider, the label below it changes from the parameter label (in gray) to a data readout (in yellow). And while Tera doesn't support skins per se, you can modify its appearance with numerous rather alarming color schemes. I'd like to be able to double-click on a data field and type in numbers, or scoot from field to field with the tab key, but many musicians prefer not to be bothered.

To economize on CPU resources, Tera automatically switches off any module whose output is not connected to anything. This is excellent. Inactive controls appear in a darker color, and don't respond to the mouse.

At this writing [July '02], Tera is Windows-only, but a Mac version has been announced; check the manufacturer's website for details. Speaking of which, currently VirSyn has no U.S. distributor, so the only way to purchase it is online. (It's not a download; the CD-ROM and paper manual are shipped to you from Germany when you order.)

Sounds. According to the manual, Tera ships with about 800 patches. I didn't count them, but that looks like a good ballpark figure. The sound memory is organized into 128 banks of 128 patches each. Some of the 23 banks that have been given names are full, some have only a couple of dozen patches, and some have only

Tera at a Glance

System requirements	PC: 400MHz Pentium, 64MB RAM, Windows 95/98/ME/2000/XP; Mac: OS 9/X, 128MB RAM; VST host (optional) for plug-in operation
Polyphony	up to 64 voices (system-dependent)
Sample rate/bit resolution	22.05/32/44.1/48/96kHz
Multitimbral parts	16
Splits/layers	16/16
Synthesis types	analog subtractive, additive (spectrum), FM
Oscillators	4 per voice: 3 analog-type (2 w/hard sync & FM, 2 w/waveshape mod), 64 waveforms each; dual spectrum osc w/up to 6 oscillators w/detuning
Filters	3 per voice; 2 multimode resonant (4 lowpass modes, 2 highpass, band, notch) w/adjustable slope, plus 3-band sweepable formant; fully controllable series/parallel routings
Envelopes	4 per voice; DADSR, single/multiple trigger, LFO triggering, modulation of individual stages
LFOs	4 per voice (sine, tri, square, ramp up & down, S&H, random); syncable
Included effects	per patch: distortion, stereo chorus, delay, wave delay; aux send from mix: reverb, chorus
Step sequencer	16 tracks, 512 patterns, 64 steps per pattern, 256 bars per song; chord steps, interactive controls
Arpeggiator	integrated with sequencer
MIDI control	notes, controllers, pitchbend, aftertouch
Copy protection	serial number on installation
Downloadable demo	yes

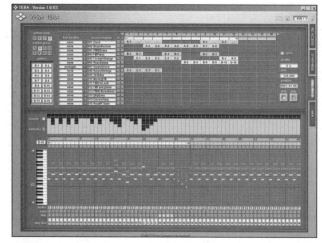

Figure 3-7.
The 16-track sequencer in Tera includes a song assembly area (top) and a pattern editing area (bottom). Sounds can be chosen for tracks in a column at upper left, but there's no provision for sending program changes during playback.

one or two. There's plenty to get you started, and also plenty of room to store your own creations.

As you'd expect, the factory set provides a generous helping of analog basses and pads, filter sweeps, and 808-style percussion. Glassy digital timbres and effects are also well represented. I'll leave it up to connoisseurs to decide whether Tera has a genuine analog flavor, but you can add overdrive distortion at several different spots in a patch, so getting a thick tone is not a problem. With a few knob-twists, I turned the "Lofi Handclap" patch into a rubbery monster that sounded like a kick drum being played through a broken speaker cone.

If you crave monstrous, cavern-filling tones, you'll be pleased to learn that Tera will do up to 16-way layering on one MIDI channel. It can also do 16-way keyboard splits. The layering helps make up for the fact that Tera's voice architecture doesn't allow individual oscillators or filters to be panned to different spots in the stereo field.

Synthesis. If you enjoy tweezing parameters and signal routings as much as I do, you'll be in hog heaven with Tera. Some of the sounds I came up with were more "interesting" than musically compelling, but there were always more ideas to try. Let's run through the features more or less in order — and please bear in mind, there are numerous minor parameters that didn't make it into this review due to lack of space.

■ *Oscillators.* The features of Tera's three analog-style oscillators will be familiar to just about any synthesizer programmer. The pulldown menu offers 64 waveforms, including some "negative slope" waves that only have the higher harmonics — a nice extra. Oscillators 1 and 2 provide waveform modulation, while 2 and 3 can be hard-synced to 1 for those classic sync sweeps.

FM inputs are also provided for 2 and 3. The cool thing here is that any audio signal in the synth can be used as the FM modulator. By routing an oscillator through a resonant filter and then FMing the oscillator with the filter's output, you can create some deliciously unstable tones. When you open up an FM input, the functions of the coarse and fine-tune parameters change. Watch out for this, as it's guaranteed to confuse the unwary.

■ *Spectrum oscillator.* I've never seen anything quite like this exotic beast before, and it's a powerful resource. Very digital-sounding, for the most part, and capable of both crystalline bell tones and wall-of-sound drones boiling over with animation. The closest comparison may be to the PPG: This sounds rather like what the PPG's designers may have been trying to accomplish, but couldn't because the technology of the early '80s wasn't powerful enough. [*Editor's note: This comparison may be too facile. The Malström synth in Propellerhead Reason 2.0, covered on page 99, is even more PPG-like. Then there's the PPG itself, or at least a digital emulation thereof, discussed on page 53.*]

The basic concept is not unlike additive synthesis: By drawing with the mouse, you create a curve containing up to 128 spectrum points, which define the relative loudness of the waveform's overtones. Actually, you create two curves. The morph knob (which, like anything else, can be modulated by an LFO, envelope, mod wheel, etc.) lets you crossfade between the two. Meanwhile, the spectrum knob operates like a sort of built-in lowpass filter, controlling how high in the overtone series the oscillator actually goes. The raster parameter interacts with the spectrum knob, cutting down on the number of overtones by skipping some of them.

Even if that's all the spectrum oscillator did, it would be cool. But there's more. You can have up to six oscillators playing the same spectrum at the same time, and detune them from one another. Small amounts of detuning produce a chorus effect, but you can crank the knob a lot further, creating a wildly atonal cluster chord.

■ *Filters.* Tera has both the standard modules — two independent multimode resonant filters — and a three-band formant filter. The latter can be used as a parametric EQ by setting the frequencies and bandwidths and then not modulating anything, or for modulation effects.

The standard filters both have input drive knobs, with which you can overdrive the filter circuit to fatten up the sound. The rolloff slope can be varied using the Shift knob, which offsets the cutoff frequencies of the separate stages within the filter. Be careful when you crank up the resonance and then pull the shift down to zero, because this filter will go into self-oscillation rather suddenly. (Safety note: Don't program any filter while wearing headphones.)

■ *Shaper, ring mod, and wave delay.* These modules will get used less often than filters, but they have a place in a full-featured synth. The waveshaper offers a number of preset shapes; it can get pretty uncontrollable if you feed it a sawtooth wave, but sine, triangle, and parabolic shapes can be shaped in colorful (if rather digital-sounding) ways.

The ring modulator does exactly what any ring modulator does — it multiplies two signals together to create sum and difference tones. The wave delay is a different kettle of fish. According to the manual, it's useful for physical modeling synthesis. It's a fast delay line; you feed it two inputs, one of which is normally its own output, and the feedback emphasizes certain overtones. If you switch off keyboard tracking, the resonances of the delay line will remain fixed, which can add a bit of harmonic shimmer to certain kinds of tones. When I sent pink noise through it, I got a thick and usable bowed/blown tone.

■ *Signal routing.* With a few exceptions, each audio module in Tera can receive an audio input from any other module, including itself. (The list of possible sources includes the ring modulator and waveshaper, but not the effects, as the latter are not applied individually to each voice.) Adding to the fun is a five-channel audio mixer. The mixer can be used as separate two-input and three-input mixers, while simultaneously sending all five channels to yet another destination.

With this setup, you can run two parallel oscillator/filter signal paths clear up to the output stage, pile all three filters up in series, run two filters through the ring modulator, or even use everything to FM one oscillator and then run it directly to the output. Speaking of which, there are actually two outputs; you can crossfade between them dynamically as well as modulating the voice's panpot. There's no way to pan one output left and the other right, however.

The modulation routings are even more flexible than the audio routings. Each knob and slider can pop up a little panel with two modulation inputs and associated bidirectional amount knobs — but if you need more than two inputs to a single parameter, all you have to do is hit the F5 key to pop up a larger panel that displays all 20 of your available routings.

Sources include not only the internal LFOs and envelopes but a few standard MIDI inputs (velocity, pitchbend, etc.). Any modulation source can be used to scale the depth of another modulation routing — velocity controlling the amount of envelope applied to a filter's cutoff, for instance, or an envelope controlling LFO amount.

■ *Envelopes.* It's great to have four envelope generators in a voice, and the overall time range available with these DADSRs (delay-attack-decay-sustain-release) is impressive — up to 91.1 seconds. The envelope diagrams can be edited graphically with the mouse, or numerically. Individual envelope times can respond to MIDI velocity, or to a continuous controller, an important feature for responsive keyboard performance, and one that's missing in many synths.

■ *LFOs.* Again, you get four to play with. They can be synced to MIDI clock, and the usual waveforms are available. Each LFO can free-run or be reset on each key-down, or all of the voices in a patch can share the same LFO 1 and so on, for coordinated pulsing rhythms. There's no way to adjust the starting phase of an LFO, unfortunately.

The manual indicates that the LFOs can sample one another's waveforms for staircase effects, but doesn't quite explain how to set this up. Turns out, LFO 2 samples

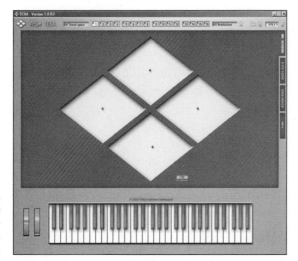

Figure 3-8.
Tera's innovative mouse-driven control surface provides four independent X/Y controllers.

the waveform of LFO 1 when set to S&H mode, LFO 3 samples LFO 2, and so on. The LFOs can run well up into the audio frequency range — handy if you need buzzing effects, but Tera offers more controllable ways to do FM.

■ *Effects.* Having a built-in distortion, stereo delay, and chorus/phaser/flanger for each patch adds a lot. Each effect has three or four algorithms — "tape" and "tube" distortion, for instance. They're wired in a fixed order, but this isn't a huge limitation. Global reverb and chorus are provided (with send and return level pots) in Tera's mixer.

Sequencer & Arpeggiator. VirSyn developer Harry Gohs has his own ideas about how a step sequencer ought to operate. This one starts with a huge bank of patterns — 512 of them. Each pattern can be up to 64 steps long, and each step can have any time value from a 32nd-note triplet up through a dotted whole-note. In other words, there's no requirement that a 64-step pattern be exactly four bars or eight bars long, or that you fill up a bar of music with an even number of steps.

You construct 16-track songs by dragging patterns into a song grid. The song grid itself is rigidly segmented into 4/4 bars, but the patterns themselves can contain polyrhythms. For instance, one track could be looping in 17/8 while another loops in 5/4, as long as both loops start and end on a bar line somewhere. A song can be up to 256 bars long. Shuffle rhythms are supported, but only eighth-notes can be shuffled, not sixteenths. Fortunately, the tempo can be set up to 300 bpm, so you can get sixteenth-note shuffle by doubling the tempo and all of the rhythm values.

In addition to having a rhythmic length, each step in a pattern can be muted or skipped, given a gate time (from 25% through 100%), or assigned to play a chord rather than a single note. Numerous chord voicings are available in a pop-up menu. Each step has its own velocity value, and also transmits a controller value, which can be used to modulate anything in the synth patch.

If you get a great pattern going, but find that its rhythm doesn't have the same bar line as some other pattern, you can rotate its active steps to the left or right — an essential editing tool. Patterns can be copied and pasted, and also randomized. Macro commands that would let you edit the time values of a bunch of steps at once would be a valuable addition. I'd like to see some block copying functions in the song editor, too: Clicking and dragging one pattern at a time is the only way to copy a section.

Pattern edits can be made while a song is playing, and won't cause the sequencer to hiccup. This is quite cool, as it makes the sequencer something of an interactive performance tool.

Still not satisfied? Each sequencer pattern can also be used as an arpeggiator template. This is hard to explain, so put on your propeller beanie for a minute. When you switch a track to arpeggiator mode instead of pattern play mode, it uses the current pattern data (which could change from bar to bar if the song is playing) to arpeggiate whatever chord you play. Each step in a pattern can be given an "arpkey" setting, which can be either a number (1–8) or "n" for next key. The number controls which note in the held chord will be triggered at that step.

The pitch of the pattern step is used as an offset from the key you're playing — for instance, if the step is set to D rather than C, the arpeggiator will transpose that note in the arpeggio (whatever note you're holding on the keyboard) up by a whole-step. Plus, all of the gate time, rhythm, and chord play functions still apply. Last but not least, you can run one sequencer track in arpeggiator mode while others are still playing normal patterns, which again adds to the possibilities for interactive performance.

I can think of several enhancements I'd like to see, starting with the ability to program embedded loops within a song and exit from the loop at a key command, which would be useful for live performance. Even without this, the sequencer is quite a fun utility — not as good at creating full songs as the sequencers in Reason and Storm [see Chapter 4], but very powerful in its own way. Since Tera will record its own output to disk, you can easily build up multi-layer loops using the sequencer and then import them into your favorite audio multitrack program.

Control Surface & MIDI. Tera's control surface (see page 81) is a souped-up version of the joystick on the old Sequential Prophet-VS and Yamaha TG22. The four diamonds are independent of one another; each responds to mouse moves by sending out X and Y axis control data. This data can then be used to modulate up to eight different synth parameters for each X or Y output. The range of control is independent for each destination parameter, and can be inverted for each, so you can set up complex crossfades easily.

As an added fillip, the mouse-controlled dots in the diamonds have "ballistics." When you drag with the mouse and then let go, they can slow down and stop gradually rather than abruptly. This allows for smoother modulation, and it's fun to watch, too. The control surface is still active when the sequencer is running.

Each X and Y axis in the control surface can be assigned to an external MIDI controller. MIDI controllers can also be assigned directly to single parameters without using the control surface, but this type of signal routing doesn't give you nearly as much flexibility: You can't scale or invert the controller data, and only one parameter at a time can be assigned to a given controller.

Also, you don't get to specify a controller number by typing it in: The "MIDI Learn" feature is the only way to assign a controller. The problem with this is, there's no way to check the assignment. To figure out whether a given controller is already assigned to a parameter, you have to wiggle the physical controller and see if anything moves.

Plug-In Operation. At first I had a couple of problems using Tera as a VST plug-in in Cubase VST 32, but when I notified VirSyn, they rushed me an update (version 1.0, R4) in which the bugs were fixed. Cubase's VST performance meter showed that I was getting quite a hefty CPU hit when I used Tera multitimbrally. Also, Cubase took twice as long to boot up when Tera was instantiated in the boot-up song. [*Editor's note: I'm told this problem has been fixed.*]

In R4, Tera's step sequencer both follows the Cubase tempo and lines up correctly with Cubase's bar lines. This is extremely cool, as it allows you to start development of a song in Tera and then bring it into Cubase for overdubs.

Tera responded correctly to MIDI controller data in Cubase tracks, but its panel won't transmit knob or slider moves to Cubase as controller data. They're transmitted as system-exclusive — harder to edit, but at least you can create automation moves.

In Use. I cooked up some incredible sounds in Tera (at least *I* think they're incredible): warm complex drones, startling nasal leads, wild cascades of beeps straight out of a sci-fi soundtrack, even a sweet, unobtrusive string patch or two. I just about couldn't tear myself away from programming long enough to work on any music.

When I started building a song in Cubase with several plug-in synths, including Tera, I found its multitimbral layering very useful. I laid down a beat in Waldorf Attack, then built up a massive pad sound in Tera, after which I laid down a melodic figure using a Native Instruments FM7 patch. Then, just to be nasty, I added Steinberg's The Grand and bit-crushed, compressed, and flanged it into a bad imitation of the world's largest toy piano. Once I downloaded and installed the R4 update, Tera played nice with others. Its 808-style percussion patches are far more editable than those in Attack, so Tera gave me more control over the sound of my beat.

Next, I switched over to stand-alone mode and tried building a song in Tera's sequencer. On a 1GHz computer with no other software running, 20 fairly complex Tera voices took up 90% of the available CPU power. I found the step sequencer's

Figure 3-9.
The design of the Kantos panel is so fresh as to be a little disorienting at first glance. The glowing spots on the horizontal and vertical "veins" are actually sliders. The Gate Generator (upper left) provides essential control over gate-on, gate-off, hold time, and signal floor. The multimode resonant filters (centered, near the top) offer both 2- and 4-pole slopes for highpass, lowpass, and bandpass modes. The oscillators (above the filters) have 38 waveforms and can import AIFF or WAV files. The Articulator (center) is capable of superimposing the input signal's formant content on the synthesized output, and includes a 3-band graphic EQ. The modulation matrix (lower left) allows nearly every parameter to be modulated by LFOs, envelopes, and even the pitch and/or harmonic content of the original signal. The two envelopes (center left) are graphically adjustable. With the mixer (lower right), volumes for synth, delay, and original input signal can be adjusted, panned, or muted. The submixer includes faders for an additional sine wave per oscillator, which can be added for additional oomph. The Tempo area (center right) allows the delay and LFOs to be synced to tempo by manually entering BPM or tapping the tempo with the mouse button.

method of entering and displaying rhythms less than intuitive: I was often reduced to counting on my fingers to figure out where the beats and barlines were. Even so, I was impressed at how full my song sounded.

Conclusions. I'd rather program a good synthesizer than eat, so working with VirSyn Tera was a real treat. Great filters, great oscillators, over-the-top timbral resources, versatile modulation routings — it has the right stuff. The only other way I know of to get this much power in a software synth would be to use something like Native Instruments Reaktor, which is more expensive and has a steeper learning curve. (And even Reaktor doesn't have Tera's spectrum oscillator.)

Tera's sequencer implements some cool concepts, but it needs a little more work to become a full-fledged composing/recording/performance system. Fortunately, the sequencer integrates well with any VST host that can send MIDI clock to plugins, and the integrated direct-to-disk recording lets non-VST users create Tera loops and textures to import into other programs. This synth is going to stay on my hard drive, that's for sure. —*JA (July '02)*

Antares Kantos
VOCAL TRACKING SYNTH

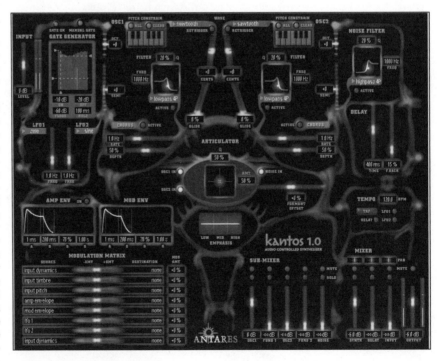

VST, MAS, RTAS (Mac)
$269

Pros: Extensive synthesis tools. Deep, lush, and quasi-organic synth textures that track nuances of original signal. Most parameters can be modulated in real time via characteristics of audio input (pitch, amplitude, timbre). Can import AIFF and WAV files for use as oscillators.

Cons: Parameters can't be directly controlled via MIDI CC or a MIDI keyboard. Pitch tracking is problematic with percussive source material. Consumes considerable CPU power. Envelope attacks lack a certain punchiness.

This just in: Among the several dozen softsynths discussed in this book, there are not several dozen synthesis methods in use. More like four or five. The same observation applies, *a fortiori*, to synthesizer control methodologies. Every softsynth that can be played in real time (if it can't, it isn't in the book) uses MIDI for performance control.

Every softsynth except Kantos, that is. Kantos is unique. To play it, you send it an audio input — preferably something monophonic, such as a vocal line or a sax solo. Its high-precision pitch tracker and other digital widgets extract the pitch, timbre, and amplitude information from the input. This information is then used to control the synth. Nothing else operates like Kantos, and nothing else sounds like it, as Francis Preve explains in this review from the Oct. '02 issue of *Keyboard*.

'm a sucker for exotic audio tools — the weirder and more powerful the better. Software such as U&I's MetaSynth and Waves' Enigma plug-in have become indispensable in my studio arsenal. They allow me to create sounds that are difficult (if not impossible) to realize using standard synthesis techniques.

That's why when Antares announced Kantos last spring, I was intrigued. Kantos has a serious buzz surrounding it. It's an audio-driven synthesizer that relies on the characteristics of an input signal to control and shape its output. One thing is certain, this plug-in is definitely something new under the sun.

With the well-deserved success of their ubiquitous Auto-Tune plug-in, Antares has proven they can deliver the goods when it comes to realtime pitch detection. So the idea of a synthesizer that detects the pitch of audio and uses this to generate sounds is tantalizing, to say the least.

Overview. Kantos is a full-featured dual-oscillator synthesizer, but it can't be controlled directly via MIDI continuous controller or note-entry methods. Instead, Kantos relies on live input or recorded audio to drive its synthesis engine. Any instrument — voice, guitar, saxophone, drums, even another synth — can provide the trigger and pitch information for Kantos.

If this sounds powerful and unique, that's because it is. Want to double a lead vocal with a gliding synth sweep? No sweat. Want to create ethereal drones and wave whispers that follow a guitar riff *à la* Bill Laswell? Go for it. Kantos can even handle

Kantos at a Glance

System requirements	Mac: G3 233MHz or better processor (G4 recommended) and OS as required by host application (System 8.6 to 9.X); PC: TB
Platform	Mac: VST, MAS, and RTAS; PC: DirectX, PC VST, and PC RTA
Synthesis type	modeled analog
Oscillators	4 total; 2 primary oscillators generate square, sawtooth, pulse, plus 34 sampled waves, 2 fundamental oscillators generate sine waves only; can also import AIFF or WAV format files
Oscillator sync	no
Filters	3 multimode filters (1 for each primary oscillator and 1 for the noise generator), 2- and 4-pole resonant lowpass, highpass, or bandpass; Articulator functions similarly to multi-band vocoding and includes 3-band graphic EQ
Envelopes	2 ADSR (assignable)
LFOs	2; sine, triangle, ramp up, ramp down, square, and random (sample & hold)
Polyphony	one stereo or mono voice
Multitimbral features	none
MIDI control	none
# of audio outputs	1 stereo pair
Built-in effects	global delay and 2 chorus modules (one per oscillator); delay time can be manually synced to tempo via BPM entry
Copy protection	challenge-response verification
Downloadable demo	yes

percussive material. Loops and beatboxes as sound sources yield impressive, otherworldly results, quite unlike anything you're used to in modern dance mixes. While it works best with cleanly recorded monophonic passages, Kantos can add spectral spice to nearly any type of source material, provided you're prepared to do a little tinkering. And there are loads of tinker-tools available within the program.

The included documentation is fantastic. Every feature is covered in detail, several times over, and there are a few tutorials that make use of different types of audio (loops, guitar, etc.). Antares is admirably forthright about what Kantos will and won't do, and the manual offers quite a few suggestions for real-world applications. Since Kantos is so unusual, these tips are a welcome addition.

User Interface. Kantos's luminous, H.R. Giger-inspired interface is captivating at first glance. Envelopes and filter curves are graphically adjustable, the gate functions provide a visual representation of the audio stream in real time, and quite a few elements glow and pulsate when adjusted. Most parameters can also be edited via direct numerical entry, for those who prefer that method. A lot of thought and creativity went into this UI, that's for sure.

Most interface elements are self-explanatory, but I still found myself scratching my head occasionally. For one thing, in this interface the signal flows from top to bottom instead of left to right. I've been programming sounds for decades, and Kantos is the first synth I've seen that uses this approach. Compounding matters slightly is the fact that the oscillators and filters flow downward in parallel — on opposite sides of the screen — into the Articulator (more on this below). While this is an accurate representation of the inner workings of this plug-in, it definitely takes a bit of getting used to.

Synthesis Overview. Because it's driven by audio rather than MIDI, Kantos needs to be instantiated as an insert or aux send effect. [*Editor's note: Even so, Kantos isn't an effect processor, it's a synthesizer.*] Audio first enters through a fairly complex gate, which can be optimized for a wide variety of signal types, both sustained and percussive. From there, the pitch-detection algorithms work their magic, controlling the pitch of the two oscillators. Each oscillator feeds its own multimode resonant filter, and the filter signals then feed the Articulator. Modulation sources include LFOs and ADSR envelopes, as well as a modulation matrix that includes realtime response to the amplitude, pitch, and timbral characteristics of the input signal. Also included are chorus algorithms for each oscillator, a noise generator, and a delay line. There's a lot of horsepower under the hood of this baby.

Since Kantos accepts any recorded sound as fodder for its engine, it's important to define the behavior of its detection algorithms, which include the gate generator, the pitch detector, and some sort of technology that extracts the harmonic content and formant characteristics for use elsewhere in the synth.

All of this begins with a gate that sports separate thresholds for both gate-on and gate-off, as well as a "floor" parameter (below which Kantos will ignore all incoming audio) and a hold parameter, which determines how long the gate will stay open before closing, regardless of the gate-off setting. It's crucial that these parameters be set up in a way that makes sense for the type of source material you're using. Otherwise, Kantos won't track the signal accurately. "Incorrect" settings can lead to spectacular accidents, but that's another story.

From there, Kantos's pitch detectors kick in, analyzing the signal's frequencies, extracting the pitch, and driving the oscillators. This is where it gets a little fadery. Percussive sounds — like xylophone, timbales, and marimbas — often contain a boatload of harmonic information in their attack, making it difficult for the pitch detectors to accurately analyze the signal. Additionally, the pitch duration needs to sustain long enough for Kantos to determine the fundamental frequency.

What this means in real-world terms is that sustained sounds with clean attacks and strong amplitudes work best, whereas plucky, staccato sounds (especially at fast tempos), sounds with processing (like chorus, reverb, delay, or even excessive distortion), and sounds with tons of enharmonic content can often confuse Kantos, regardless of the gate settings.

At first, this may seem like a major defect in the plug-in's functionality. In practice, I found that it often adds to the character and quirky usefulness of Kantos. Your mileage may vary. If you forgive Kantos for this failing, you'll be rewarded in other ways. It's simply a matter of your expectations.

Oscillators. Both oscillators have the customary selection of waveforms. Sawtooth, square, and pulse are accounted for, but Antares ups the ante with a fairly large array of sample-based waveforms, including voice, bass, strings, enharmonic loops evocative of classic '80s wavetable synths, industrial and synth effects, and even didgeridoo. The wave selection is well thought out and serves as terrific fodder for the synth engine. For additional fatness, each oscillator has its own chorus effect with independent rate and depth.

To help work around the inevitable limitations of Kantos's pitch-detection algorithm, oscillator pitch can also be quantized to any chromatic pitch — or group of pitches — via a click-and-go keyboard. Coarse and fine tuning are available, as well as independent glide for each oscillator. A retriggering function restarts a given sampled wave from each gate event. The combined power of these tools makes tuning Kantos to your track a total breeze. There's also a noise generator with its own filter for adding industrial grunge, nature effects, or even vocoderish whispering to your patches.

Kantos allows you to import AIFF and WAV files for use as oscillator waves. There's no size restriction on the size of these files, but the manual thoughtfully indicates that smaller (under 400K) looped files will work best. I experimented with this feature and had mixed results. A classic Fairlight voice sample worked beautifully. Short rhythmic loops worked after a bit of coaxing. But larger waves from sound effects discs weren't quite as flexible. If you have a well-crafted selection of pre-looped waves, you'll be all set. If not, don't sweat it, as Antares has you covered with a few extra bundled wavetables and a download area on their website for even more waveforms.

Filters & Articulator. Kantos is no slouch in the filter department either, featuring resonant lowpass, highpass, and bandpass mode for each of the three filters (one for each oscillator and one for the noise generator). Better still, each filter operates in 2- or 4-pole mode and is graphically adjustable. While I would have liked to see a notch or phaser mode included, it's not a heartbreaking omission.

The oscillator/filter combos feed the Articulator, which is where the serious sonic exotica occurs. Kantos's Articulator superimposes the formant and timbral characteristics of the input signal on the synthesized audio. Two parameters — amount and Q — are adjusted via a biaxial interface element (with yet another luminous orb indicating the parameters' position in the X/Y axis). A third parameter, formant offset, shifts the input's detected formants up or down for even more sonic mayhem.

Also included in this section is a 3-band (low, mid, high) graphic equalizer for emphasizing various frequency ranges. The actual ranges aren't indicated or separately adjustable, but the inclusion of this EQ helps shape the overall sound of the Articulator's output.

What does it sound like? Kinda like a vocoder. Sorta like a speech synthesizer. Different than both, but definitely useful and otherworldly. Setting the amount and Q parameters to their maximum values yielded the most dramatic results, but it can also be used subtly for adding a little something extra to patches, depending on your source input.

LFOs & Envelopes. Patch animation is covered nicely via two LFOs and two general-purpose envelopes. One of the latter can be used to modulate the amplitude of the synthesized tone.

The envelopes are of the standard ADSR-type, with time parameters adjustable in millisecond increments. Well not exactly millisecond, as 173ms was rounded to 171ms and 982ms rounded to 987ms, but that degree of resolution is more than adequate for most applications.

The LFO shapes include sine, triangle, ramp up, ramp down, square, and random waveforms with rates ranging from 0.1Hz to 20Hz. Both LFOs can be synced to tempo, but this value must be entered manually or tapped, as it's not detected automagically under VST. This isn't a major deal, but I would have liked to see the addition of various note values instead of strictly whole-note resolution (one cycle = one measure).

Delay. A simple delay algorithm provides everything from echoes to metallic static flange (comb filter) effects. Delay time and feedback parameters are included, and the time can be synchronized to tempo, again by directly entering BPM or by tapping the tempo with your mouse button. The tap-tempo function worked adequately, but I preferred simply to enter the BPM based on my sequence tempos.

As with the LFOs, tempo synchronization applies strictly to quarter-note values. If you want different rhythms, you'll need to get a calculator and do the math yourself. (You can download the free Music Production Calculator from www.hitsquad.com for this kind of work.)

Realtime Modulation. With all of the amplitude, pitch, and formant detection going on in Kantos, Antares decided to expose these features for use as modulation sources. Each of the three characteristics (and/or the envelopes and LFOs) can be used to modulate nearly every significant parameter available, including oscillator pitch, filter cutoff and Q (for each filter), articulation parameters, chorus rate/depth, delay time, delay feedback, LFO frequency . . . the list goes on.

It's quite something to have the overall amplitude or pitch of the input signal modulate the Articulator or delay feedback. When applied to acoustic or vocal articulations, the results have a strangely organic quality, despite their obviously electronic origins. This is truly inspiring stuff.

Mixers. Once processed (or mangled, as the case may be), the oscillator signals are sent to two mixer sections. First, the submixer accumulates the outputs from each oscillator and the noise generator, as well as a discrete sine wave generator for each oscillator that derives its pitch directly from the pitch-detection algorithms. The sine wave generator is a nifty touch, as it allows you to thicken the synth's output by reinforcing the fundamental frequencies of the input signal after pitch quantization has been applied via the oscillator settings.

The combined output of the submixer is then routed to the final mixer, which has one fader each for synth output, delay output, and direct input signal.

Every fader in each of the mixers also includes mute and solo controls with visual indication of their status. This is handy, as you can quickly isolate each characteristic of your sound for further tweaking.

In Use. During the time I worked with Kantos, I found myself encountering combinations of acoustic and electronic sounds that almost defied description. Had I heard them in other artists' tracks, I would definitely have wondered how they were created. Applying Kantos to melodic vocals definitely demonstrated the power and accuracy of Antares's pitch-detection expertise. Once the gates were set up correctly, Kantos did a terrific job of tracking even subtle nuances in the performances. I tried both male and female vocals with equal success. Using Kantos in this manner was perfect for supporting a vocal with a simple, slightly "vocoded" pad lead. Spoken-word material yielded a strange yet cool speech synthesis emulation. More ambitious sonic experiments led to interesting methods of replacing the lead vocal for breakdowns or psychedelic verses on dance tracks.

Other acoustic instruments produced mixed results. Sustained guitar solos, trumpet passages with clear tones, and saxophone samples were successfully tracked for the most part, with some lovely melodic ambiences being generated as a result. Marimba and kalimba loops didn't fare as well, though limiting the oscillators' pitch quantization to relevant keys went a long way toward helping Kantos deliver useful results.

Drum loops, on the other hand, proved to be fantastic fodder, despite my initial expectations about Kantos's ability to track the pitch. We're talking about a drum loop, after all! I explicitly chose pitches I wanted Kantos to generate (via the oscillators' keyboard interface) and let 'er rip. Everything from synchronized, percolating sweeps to ghostly syncopated undercurrents was possible. Creating rhythmic drones with this plug-in gave me hours of tranced-out pleasure. Down-tempo, up-tempo — it all worked, once the gates were set up.

Applying Kantos to synth parts was a bit different. Single-oscillator patches with medium decays worked fairly well, as long as the decays weren't too abrupt and the release times didn't cause notes to overlap. While Kantos sounded quite cool when layered with the original part, the inherent processing delays involved in analyzing the signal characteristics made it slightly problematic to get really punchy envelopes, regardless of Kantos's ADSR settings. The Kantos manual suggests several ways to replace bass synth parts on the fly by tracking the original bass line with a sine-wave patch, then processing the result with Kantos. I tried it. It worked okay, but it wasn't mind-blowingly accurate or in your face. Then again, if you think about it, this isn't a huge deal, since driving Kantos with another synth is a Mobius loop of redundancies. If you want to track a plucky arpeggio with a burbling ethereal drone, it's more than possible — just be sure to adjust the pitch quantization to match or complement the original part.

While Kantos definitely consumes more CPU power than the average plug-in, it worked quite well overall. I did encounter a few mysterious CPU spikes when running multiple instances of Kantos. The CPU meter was hovering around 50% on the dual G4, but Cubase's overload light came on unexpectedly, interrupting the sound. It was impossible to determine whether this was a bug or simply the side effect of a power-hungry plug-in, but it didn't crash either machine, so it's not really dangerous, *per se*.

Conclusions. Make no mistake — Kantos is capable of taking sounds to places you've never heard before. How you react to Kantos will depend on your overall approach to music and your needs from a synth plug-in. If you crave weirdness and possibilities from your instruments, you're gonna love Kantos. It's a happy-accident generator if there ever was one. Doubling instruments and vocals with textures that follow the nuances of the performance is a truly unique sound that isn't easily duplicated by other products, if at all.

On the other hand, if you expect Kantos to track everything you throw at it perfectly and behave like a well-tempered sonic servant, you'll be disappointed. The pitch detection and gate algorithms require certain kinds of content to function at their best. This is not a be-all do-all synth plug-in but a new way of approaching recorded material.

Kantos is a unique addition to the world of plug-ins. It's not for everyone, but for some musicians and producers, it will be a deep well of inspiration. —*Francis Preve (Oct. '02)*

BitHeadz Retro AS-1 VST
ANALOG SYNTH WITH MODULATION MATRIX

VST (Win)
$199

Pros: Powerful modulation matrix. Supports Retro AS-1 1.0 and 2.0 patches. Presets sound great. Up to 64 voices per instantiation. Saves setups of all 16 MIDI channels.
Cons: Difficult to page through patches in the editor. No undo. No audio input.

Sometimes your memory plays tricks on you. I could have sworn Retro AS-1 used to be a stand-alone synth for the Macintosh, but the first profile below (written by Angela Hill for the Oct. '00 *Keyboard*) discusses a VST plug-in that runs under Windows.

Figure 3-10.

Retro AS-1 VST's user interface is different than the stand-alone version of Retro, but contains much of the same functionality. All oscillators and filters are displayed simultaneously, and routings are configured via the Source and Destination pop-up menus. Note the CPU and Voices indicators — they provide feedback on how well the computer is performing.

Actually, my memory isn't at fault: Retro really did start out on the Mac. It was one of the first low-latency softsynths. Paging through the August 1998 issue of *Keyboard*, where Retro was first reviewed, I find that some of its contemporaries have fallen by the wayside. (Remember Mixman Studio? Great program. I'll tell you a story about that one sometime.) But Retro is still chugging along. I've chosen not to reprint the full text of Marty Cutler's 1998 review here, as it describes version 1.0 and is no longer entirely relevant. You'll find some still-breathing excerpts below.

Digging around on the BitHeadz site, I found a page where one can order either the Mac or Windows version of Retro AS-1 version 2.1 for a blowout price of $99 (regularly it's $259). This version is ReWire-compatible, by the way, as is version 3.0 for the Mac. The Windows version of 3.0 is due out early in 2003. BitHeadz also offers Retro Lite ($79), a Mac/Windows standalone program. "Lite" means you can't program your own sounds. To add to the confusion, I'm told Retro AS-1 has been renamed Unity AS-1. Unity DS-1 being BitHeadz' sample playback synth, the names are within one letter of being identical. Unity AS-1 is available by itself, or as part of BitHeadz' Unity Session package.

Even after poring over communications from BitHeadz, I can't quite figure out how many versions of this product there are, what formats they're in, or what their features are. You're on your own, kids. The feature list I received by way of a fact-check for the review below included things like MAS, RTAS, and DirectConnect support (probably not relevant for Windows users), selectable linear or exponential curves for envelopes, and an arpeggiator.

To be honest, there's been so much evolution in softsynths in the past few years that Retro wouldn't be my first recommendation for someone who wants to explore the still unfolding musical possibilities of analog-style synthesis. But since there's a downloadable Retro demo on the BitHeadz website, you don't have to trust my judgment: Try it out for yourself.

Retro AS-1 VST is a warm, clean analog modeling synth capable of emulating vintage analog synths. But don't be fooled — this is no one-trick pony. If you're looking for a synth that can quickly and easily create never-before-heard sounds, Retro is up to the challenge.

It comes with more than 1,300 presets to tickle your imagination. These sounds are well organized and usable. I especially liked the pads and sound effects. I had a blast starting out new arrangement ideas with the presets, but for a final mix, I felt a bit of tweaking was necessary to give them a "finished" quality.

The user interface is clear and efficient, making it easy to understand how patches are constructed. In fact, an initial run-through of the presets provided plenty of ideas for me to start tweaking and building new patches. Unfortunately, there's no easy way to flip through presets in Retro VST's editor; you have to use the Open File dialog every time.

Retro AS-1 VST at a Glance

System requirements	Windows 95/98/ME, VST 2.0-compatible host software
Polyphony	up to 64 voices per instantiation
# of multitimbral parts	8 instantiations, 16 MIDI channels per instantiation
Key modes	poly, mono, portamento
Synthesis type	analog modeling
Oscillators	3 per voice; sawtooth, triangle, pulse, sine wave (6 types), glottal, white/pink/red noise
LFOs	1; sine, triangle, square, sawtooth up/down, random
Filters	2 (serial or parallel) per voice; 16 filter types including 1/2/4-pole, low/high/all-pass (all resonant), comb, notch
Envelopes	2 ADSR
Modulation	8 simultaneous controllers per patch; envelope, LFO, note, velocity, release velocity, mono/poly aftertouch to pitch, volume, pan, oscillator parameters, filter parameters
Syncable parameters	LFO rate, delay
Effects	2 serial per voice; parametric EQ, shelf EQ, flange, chorus, phaser, delay, overdrive, distortion, ring modulator
Copy protection	challenge-response
Downloadable demo	yes

Oscillator waveforms and filter types are abundant [*Editor's note: There are 13 of the former and 16 of the latter in the current version, according to the BitHeadz website*], and all modulation routing is done via straightforward pop-up menus. While exploring the presets, I found a Theremin patch that used mod wheel as its main controller. Here's where I began to discover the power in Retro's modulation and routing system: Nearly anything can be routed to (and can control) nearly anything else, and up to eight sources and destinations can be assigned per patch. This synth has the flexibility of a yoga instructor!

Automation of Retro's parameters within Cubase works well, depending on which version you use. I was able to automate everything I wanted using sys-ex, including switching oscillators, sweeping filter cutoff frequency, and adjusting the amount of effects. However, while I was working on this review, Cubase 5 crashed several times. Sending bank select and program change messages from Cubase to Retro, for example, consistently caused a crash. BitHeadz recommends loading patches in the editor instead. Unfortunately, that means you have to hassle with the Open File dialog box when you want to hear a different patch. I also used Retro with Cubase 3.71 and found the older version to be more reliable.

Retro AS-1 VST doesn't have all of the functionality available with version 2.0 of Retro AS-1. [*Editor's note: According to BitHeadz, the stand-alone version has more effects, ships with more content, and allows patch splitting and layering.*] However, the VST version can load and play any patch since version 1. Retro AS-1 VST is a great investment — any musician could use and learn from it. —*Angela Hill (Oct. '00)*

Retro models a multitimbral analog synth. A Retro patch can use up to three oscillators, each of which can be set to the usual waveforms. A symmetry parameter can be used to change the shape of the sawtooth or pulse waves, and symmetry can be modulated to do pulse width modulation. There are two filters, which can be arranged in parallel or in series. Seven different filter types are available, including bandpass and resonant lowpass. The filters can be overdriven for distortion effects and will self-oscillate.

Additional sound-shaping tools include oscillator sync, filter modulation from an audio oscillator, and FM. All of this is controlled by an extremely flexible menu-style modulation matrix, which includes the usual realtime modulation sources — velocity, mono and poly aftertouch, note number, and four continuous controllers. Individual envelope segments can be modulated in real time, as can panning. One of the coolest features in the AS-1 is the ability to add more envelopes and LFOs to a patch as needed. On the wish list: It would be nice if more of the parameters were set in real-world values like milliseconds and Hertz rather than in an arbitrary 0–100 scale.

So how does Retro sound? It can sound as fat and beefy as a well-marbled sirloin steak. Rich evolving pads can be layered with nasal sync-swept lead sounds and resonant synth basses. The FM patches produce crisp bell-like timbres. Nasty digital-sounding overdriven timbres are also easy to achieve. There are two global effects (delay and reverb) and two insert effects: EQ, delay, chorus, flanging, overdrive, and distortion are selectable for the latter.

The user interface is clear and visually elegant. In the main patch editor window, the signal flow of the voicing parameters is shown as icons. These icons can't be moved or repatched, but they're pretty useful when you need to keep track of your programming. The parameters are edited with sliders.

For those who have the computer horsepower to achieve a reasonable amount of polyphony, Retro has a lot to offer. It's a great-sounding synth with a flexibility that will serve musicians well. —*Marty Cutler (Aug. '98)*

Muon Electron
AFFORDABLE THREE-OSCILLATOR

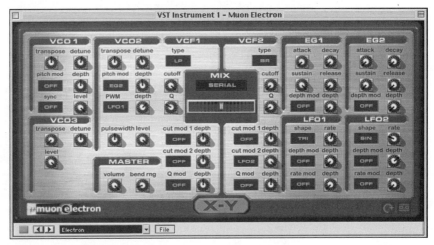

Figure 3-11.
The Muon Electron includes three oscillators and two filters. In a throwback to analog terminology, these are referred to as VCOs (voltage-controlled oscillators) and VCFs (voltage-controlled filters), even though computers don't use control voltages. The dual filter is a powerful feature.

VST (Mac, Win)
$75

Pros: Dual multimode resonant filters. Lots of modulation options.
Cons: Each oscillator has only one waveform. Not multitimbral. LFOs can't be synced to tempo. No mono mode for bass lines.

The ubiquitous and talented Francis Preve reviewed Electron for *Keyboard's* November 2001 issue. It's the flagship in a low-priced synth line that also includes the Tau Pro bass/lead monophonic synth ($30), the Atom Pro polyphonic ($20), and the Tau Bassline and Atom (both freeware). According to Muon Software, DXi versions of Electron and Tau Pro will be available by the time you read this.

Electron is one of those delightful software tools that sounds great, sports a comprehensive (if quirky) set of features, and is quite easy on the wallet. Boasting three oscillators, dual multimode filters, two envelopes, two LFOs, and a ton of modulation options, Electron can go head to head with the rest of the pack and hold its own quite nicely.

The oscillator section is a curious blend of power and quirkiness. With an internal 64-bit audio path and Muon's anti-aliasing algorithm, they sound great — bright like an ARP, yet fat like an old Oberheim. On the downside, each oscillator is dedicated to a single waveform. Oscillators 1, 2, and 3 create saw, variable pulse, and square waves respectively. Oscillator 1 can be hard-synced to either oscillator 2 or 3.

Two resonant filters — each with self-oscillating resonance and 2-pole (12dB/oct) slope — can operate in either lowpass, highpass, bandpass, or band-reject mode, and they sound excellent. I especially liked having band-reject mode, as it allows for some really nice phaser effects when each filter's cutoff is modulated via a different LFO.

The filters can be configured in one of five ways: serial, parallel, filter 1 only, filter 2 only, and linked (for 24 dB/oct operation). There are three modulation inputs for each filter (two for cutoff and one for resonance/Q), allowing LFOs, envelopes, and key tracking to further animate and refine the sound.

The LFOs feature sine, sawtooth, square, and triangle waveshapes, but unfortunately they can't be synced to tempo. LFO depth and rate can be modulated via several sources, including mod wheel and aftertouch. The envelopes are standard-issue ADSRs; envelope depth is controllable by velocity or the LFOs. You can't set Electron to monophonic mode, so there's no way to switch the envelopes to single-trigger for 303-style bass lines.

Other features include a graphic X/Y virtual controller that can be assigned to any two mod destinations and played in real time. The parameters are hardwired to MIDI continuous controllers 75–102, so you can sequence your twiddling. Electron is not multitimbral, which could conceivably become a problem if you're using it in Cubase, due to Cubase's eight-VSTi limit.

After online purchase, Electron arrives in your computer as an email attachment. After installing it, I booted Cubase VST 5.0 and got started. The four banks of factory patches showed me the power of this synth. The eponymous "Electron" patch is a dead-on recreation of the hard, thick sawtooth lead that has dominated epic trance mixes for the past couple of years. The pads are warm and lush, and the basses run the gamut from hard and thwippy to tubby and rich. The leads are a mixed bag, but serve as solid starting points for more radical experimentation.

For only $75, Electron covers a lot of analog ground. If you've got a VST 2.0 sequencer and a craving for hard and ballsy patches, you need to check this one out.
—*Francis Preve (Nov. '01)*

Virtual Rack Systems

4

At least as far back as the 1950s, music lovers could choose between modular and integrated hi-fi systems. (This was before the days of stereophonic recording, so it wasn't a stereo, it was a hi-fi.) If the prospect of stripping your own wires and matching electrical impedances made you nervous, you could get an integrated system, in which one manufacturer provided all the components, and the cabinet too. If you were feeling adventurous or wanted to impress the neighbors with the fact that you were an audiophile, you'd go for a mix-and-match modular setup — turntable from one manufacturer, tuner from another, speakers from yet a third.

The more things change, the more they remain the same. Musicians today can go integrated or mix-and-match when choosing a multitrack audio recorder, a keyboard, or even a software synthesizer. There are pluses and minuses on both sides, but the integrated "virtual rack system," a single piece of software that includes both sequencing and an assortment of softsynths and effects, has proven very popular. In this chapter we'll take a close look at the three leading programs.

For the most part, these programs don't do anything that you couldn't do with a standard sequencer/multitrack audio recorder and a batch of plug-ins. In fact, the sequencer and plug-ins can easily give you more power than Reason, Storm, or Fruityloops by itself — but the cost will almost certainly be higher, and getting the various software components to work smoothly together is not guaranteed to be easy. What a virtual rack system offers is a very considerable degree of musical power, at a reasonable cost and with fewer headaches than you'd have if you tried to assemble an equivalent system yourself, plus some specialized tools not found in the average sequencer. (Storm's automatic transposition of parts by reference to a chord progression is a good example.)

For that matter, the distinction between integrated and mix-and-match systems is not always clearcut. Two of the three virtual racks profiled here (Storm and Fruityloops) will host plug-in synths and effects. The third (Reason) can't host plug-ins, but it can run in tandem with your sequencer/recorder software using the ReWire software protocol. They can also be used in conjunction with MIDI hardware in various ways. One way or another, you can expand an "integrated" virtual rack system into a mix-and-match system.

Virtual rack systems tend to have one thing in common: Their sequencers are *pattern-based* rather than strictly linear. When using a pattern-based sequencer, you'll create individual patterns, which might be one, two, four, or eight bars long. To create a complete song, you string patterns one after another — for instance, repeating a two-bar verse pattern eight times to make a 16-bar verse section, and then switching to a different pattern for the chorus section. A pattern may contain only the performance information for a single instrument (a two-bar bass line, for instance), or it may contain many different tracks.

The pattern sequencer paradigm dates back to the earliest days of programmable music machines, when computer memory was a whole lot more expensive than it is today. While pattern-based recording is no longer necessary, it's still convenient, because pop music is so heavily based on repeating riffs and loops. If your music tends to use more complex structures with little repetition, I'm not sure I'd recommend a virtual rack system. In addition to segmenting the music in little one-measure and two-measure boxes, this type of software tends to make certain other assumptions, such as that your entire piece will have only one time signature and won't change tempo in midstream. Again, these are sensible assumptions for most pop music, but not for more experimental styles.

Not covered in this chapter: Orion Platinum from Synapse Audio ($199, www.orion-central.com, www.synapse-audio.com). When I installed it and took a quick look, I got the impression it wasn't as sophisticated as the other programs discussed below in certain areas. But don't forget — Fruityloops started out as shareware, and it has grown into a powerful, respectable program. By the time this book is published, Orion (which is not shareware; it lists for $199) may have gone through a major overhaul, and might be exactly what you're looking for.

These questions are never simple, though: As a fan of odd meters, I was gratified to see that Orion would let me line up a 3/4 pattern against a 5/4 pattern in its song playlist. Fruityloops won't do that. Orion will host plug-ins; Reason won't. And Orion has graphic controller editing; Storm doesn't. Wish we had a full review of Orion for this book, so you could get a more complete picture.

Propellerhead Reason
REALISTIC RACK WITH PATTERN AND
MULTITRACK SEQUENCING

Figure 4-1.
The main window in Reason. The "rack" containing the virtual "modules" is in the upper part of the window, while the lower area contains the sequencer tracks and controls. Each area can be resized vertically as needed. Here we see the mixer, two half-rack effects (reverb and delay), and the top portion of a Redrum percussion module. A few of the mixer controls have green lines around them, which indicates that automation data for them has been recorded into a sequence track. The track area shows four tracks, with a few track data groups (the shaded rectangles) visible. The sequencer control strip, which contains transport, tempo, sync, and loop controls, is along the bottom edge. Note also the handy CPU usage meter (lower left).

stand-alone (Mac, Win)
$399

Pros: Killer sound. Powerful synthesis and sequencing controls. Full automation for mixing and parameter changes. Versatile REX file player. Compact song file sharing via the Internet. ReWire support for interfacing with other software. Modules can control one another in real time. Rhythm patterns can be edited by shifting right or left.

Cons: No oscillator hard sync in Subtractor synth. Modules don't respond to program changes. Won't accept external plug-ins. No controller scaling in sequencer. Lacks programmable tempo and time signature changes.

As it happens, I wrote the reviews of both Reason 1.0 and Reason 2.0 for *Keyboard* (April 2001 and December 2002, respectively). The two reviews are presented separately in the following pages, since the review of 2.0 focuses mainly on the new features. I've taken the liberty of tidying up the 1.0 review slightly, since it discusses a few things that have been changed in 2.0. While Reason still suffers from one serious defect — it won't host plug-ins — it's not a fluke that it's the highest-priced of the virtual rack systems. Sure, we could have long, earnest debates about your favorite features in Fruityloops or Storm (or my favorite features, for that matter), but Reason's power and user-friendliness are hard to argue with.

Few music software releases in recent memory have been as hotly awaited as Reason. The runaway success of Propellerhead's ReBirth opened up a whole new paradigm: modeled analog synthesizer tones, percussion synthesis, and pattern-

Reason at a Glance

System requirements	PC: Windows 98/ME/2000/XP; Pentium II/233MHz or better; 64MB RAM; 16-bit soundcard, preferably with ASIO or DirectX driver; Mac: OS 9 or OS X; Power Macintosh with 604, 604e, G3, or G4, 166MHz or faster; 128MB RAM; both: CD-ROM drive, 256-color 800x600 monitor or better
Synthesis types	analog modeling, sample playback, granular
Sample rate and bit depth	11.025–96kHz, 16- or 24-bit (32-bit floating-point internal processing)
Polyphony	system-dependent
Synthesis modules	Malström "graintable" synth, Subtractor analog modeling, NN19 and NN-XT sample playback, Redrum sample-based percussion, Dr. Rex REX file loop player
Included soundware	Orkester orchestral multisamples (wind, brass, strings, percussion), 299 REX files, 293 multisample instrument patches (56 separate multisamples), 315 synth patches, 78 drum kits (625 individual drum sounds)
Effects	reverb, delay, chorus/flange, phaser, envelope-following filter, distortion, compressor, parametric EQ
Sequencers	Matrix analog-style monophonic module, Redrum pattern programming (32 presets each), multitrack linear song sequencer with graphic editing
Arpeggiator	none
Synchronization	MIDI clock, ReWire
Internal performance resampling	yes
File formats imported/exported	WAV, AIFF, Standard MIDI File; REX and SoundFont (import only)
Internal computer audio/sync I/O	ReWire in and out
Copy protection	serial number on installation
Downloadable demo	yes

based sequencing, all integrated in one piece of software. Everybody wondered: What would those clever Swedes come up with next? Reason was previewed, to considerable oohing and ahhing, at last year's NAMM show . . . and then we had to wait 11 long months for the product to ship.

When the press copies finally arrived at *Keyboard,* you can bet more than one editor dropped everything to install the program. A few weeks later, after coming up for a breath of air, I can testify that Reason is a knockout. It's impressive in almost every way — sonically, in terms of the feature list, and even cosmetically. Like ReBirth, it just looks cool.

But don't take my word for it. A free downloadable demo is available on the Propellerhead website (www.propellerheads.se). The demo won't save files or export audio, but all of the features work. For those of you who are relentlessly print-oriented, though, here's the full story.

Installation. Reason installed without a hitch on my beige G3 Mac. All I had to do was type the authorization code included on a slip in the box, and I was up and running. The program itself comes on one CD, and a second CD provides a healthy assortment of loops and other samples to get you started making music. You can transfer the latter to your hard drive if you have enough spare drive space, or leave everything on the CD. If you leave the soundware on the CD, Reason will want to see it in the drive each time the program is booted.

When I attempted to install Reason on my 400MHz Dell PC, which runs Windows 98SE, I hit a major snag. It turned out that Reason wasn't compatible with the ASIO driver for my Aardvark Direct Pro 24/96 audio interface. Eventually I got up and running with the Aardvark MME driver, which has a regrettably large timing latency (over 300ms). Propellerhead and Aardvark are working on the problem, so with any luck it will be resolved by the time you read this. On a second Windows PC (also running 98SE), Reason installed and played without a hitch using an Echo Mona audio interface.

The program comes with a printed Getting Started manual, but details on the modules are found only in PDF files, which are installed with the program. The documentation is very thorough.

Overview. When Reason booted up, I saw a screen more or less like **Figure 4-1**. Reason includes a number of software modules, so you can install just what you need for a given piece of music. The modules are presented on the screen as if they were pieces of rackmount hardware — instantly easy to understand and work with. But since this is a computer, you can "minimize" each module to make the most of your screen space.

The rackmount metaphor goes a step further. Press the tab key on your computer keyboard, and the "rack of modules" will flip around so you can see the "rear panels." Not only do the virtual patch cords dangle realistically between the "jacks" on the various modules, when the rear view first pops up the cords swing back and forth for a moment, as if the rack had been physically rotated. Cute.

Hold down the mouse button on any rear-panel jack, and a pop-up menu will appear giving you a list of all of the available connections for that jack. As the rack is quite tall and the tangle of cables can get pretty thick, using the menu is usually more convenient than actually dragging the cable into position by hand, though you can do that if you like.

Reason's modules can be played using step sequencers, as in ReBirth, and you can create songs by stringing together sequence patterns. If you're a more linear type of musician, you can use the modules as conventional sound sources instead, and either record MIDI data into Reason's own multitrack song sequencer or send MIDI from a conventional sequencer running on the same computer using ReWire.

Most of Reason's front-panel controls can be automated: Simply move them with the mouse while in record mode, and the data will be recorded to a track. Knobs, sliders, and buttons for which data has been recorded are outlined in green, and move visually while the music plays. One major difference between Reason and some other pattern-based devices should be noted: Controller data is recorded into song tracks, not into patterns. Copying and pasting individual controller moves to other locations is easy to do, and in fact offers more flexibility than if the data were recorded into the pattern, but if your music uses repeating filter sweeps, for example, you'll have to do a little extra work to match the sweeps with the patterns.

While we're on the subject of external control, Reason can map external MIDI controller data or the computer's QWERTY keys to its knobs and buttons. If you have a MIDI slider box, you'll be able to use Reason live and jam like a monster. Currently there isn't a way to copy a set of useful control mappings from one song to another, so I'd suggest creating a template and saving it as your default song.

If you're running Reason as part of a larger computer music environment, there are other ways to integrate your production tools. Reason has a ReWire input module, which allows you to import realtime audio from ReBirth to take advantage of Reason's effects or simply sync the two programs. ReWire can also be used to output Reason's audio to a compatible digital audio program. I had no trouble linking it to Cubase VST/24 on my Mac: The two programs' tempos were synced, and Reason's audio showed up in the Cubase mixer, where I was able to slap a few VST effects onto it.

Reason doesn't accept third-party plug-ins. If you want to use, say, Steinberg's PPG 2.V synth, you'll have to run it in a VST-compatible sequencer and sync the sequencer to Reason with ReWire. Even then, you won't be able to play patterns on the PPG using Reason's Matrix module, as Reason has no MIDI output.

Modules. Reason generates its noises with four different modules: a polyphonic analog-type synthesizer called Subtractor, a conventional drum module called Redrum, a REX file sample loop player called Dr. Rex, and a sample player called

NN19. [*Editor's note: Two more modules have been added in version 2.0. See below.*] But that's just the start of the fun.

Near the top of the Reason rack is a conventional-looking mixer module. The mixer has four aux sends per channel, which can be used for routing audio to Reason's effects processors, four stereo returns, and four extra mono inputs for routing signals directly to the sends. The effects themselves appear as "half-rack" modules (see the "Effects" section, below).

One small but considerate feature of the mixer, which may give an indication of the care that went into this program: When you instantiate a module, its name pops up in a pseudo-handwritten typeface on a little white "strip of sticky tape" positioned vertically next to the channel fader. Rename the module, and the name changes automatically, both on the mixer and in the sequencer track list. Very nice.

Above the mixer is an audio I/O module, which allows you to make connections to other ReWire-compatible software. Following the instructions in the manual, I booted Cubase first, activated a couple of ReWire audio inputs, and then booted Reason. At this point, the mixer's main outputs were automatically patched into Cubase. By activating more ReWire channels, it's possible to send individual Reason modules to Cubase for adding VST effects or whatever.

How many modules will you be able to run at once? That depends on your system, obviously. On my 300MHz beige G3 Mac, I loaded up a mixer, four effects, two Subtractors, two Matrices, a Dr. Rex, two Redrums, and two NN19s for a massive wall of ugliness. At this point, Reason's CPU usage meter showed that I was using about half the available horsepower.

The connectivity of the modules is a good deal more interesting than you might expect. Both Matrix and Subtractor have rear-panel outputs (see **Figure 4-2**) that send "control voltages" — not real voltages, as this is a digital device, but they function much the way old-fashioned patchable voltage-controlled synthesizers did. These "voltages" can be patched to various control inputs on Subtractor, the effects, or even the mixer. For instance, you could sweep the pan position of Redrum's audio output using a Subtractor LFO, or step the level of an effect return using a Matrix pattern. The voltage inputs even have trim pots!

Redrum has its own pattern sequencer, and Dr. Rex cycles through its loop automatically in time with the music. To sequence Subtractor or NN19, the tool of choice is the Matrix monophonic pattern sequencer. Some of the effects also have controllable inputs that can be hooked to the Matrix. Both Redrum and Matrix have alphanumeric keypad displays for selecting different patterns with mouse-clicks, and each of them stores 32 patterns, which you can select manually or using the song sequencer.

One item on my wish list is a polyphonic pattern sequencer for programming chords on Subtractor. [*Editor's note: There's still no polyphonic pattern sequencer in version 2.0. Both Storm and Fruityloops will do polyphonic patterns.*] There are two ways to input chords at present: You can play them on an external keyboard and record

Figure 4-2.
A portion of Reason's rear panel, showing the "patch cords" connecting various modules. Note also the fake power cords, air vents, and other decorative elements.

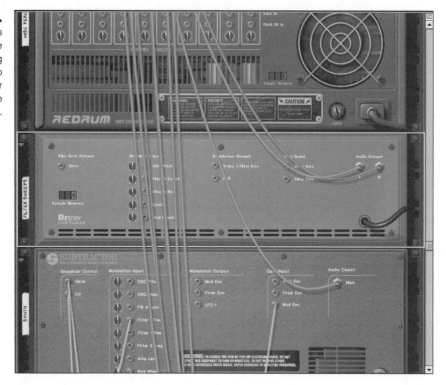

the MIDI data into Reason's sequencer, or enter it into the sequencer using a pencil tool. Either way, you're back in the land of linear rather than pattern-based sequencing. Another option is to hook up two or more Subtractors, each with its own Matrix. Subtractor is polyphonic, but it has inputs for only one Matrix.

All of the tone-generator modules respond to MIDI note input from external devices. Also pitchbend, mod wheel, and aftertouch. This data can also be recorded into the sequencer. On my G3, MIDI timing latency from key-down to sound output was short — only barely perceptible — and I was using Sound Manager, not ASIO. On a Win98 PC with a standard multimedia driver, latency was in the 300ms range, but Propellerhead tells us they can get as little as 40ms latency using a simple SoundBlaster card. Your mileage may vary.

Redrum. At first glance, Redrum may appear to be a typical pattern-based drum machine with ten slots for sounds. But there's more to it than that. For starters, each of the ten sounds has a tidy bank of nine or ten control knobs (see **Figure 4-3**). Thirty-two programmable patterns are available per Redrum per song. Each pattern can be up to 64 steps long. Since I like doing avant-garde cross-rhythms, I was pleased to find that patterns can be set to odd lengths, not just to 8, 16, 32, and so on.

On a more practical level, the steps can sync to Reason's clock at any of nine different rates, including a couple of triplet values. By setting up two Redrum modules and giving one a 12-step pattern synced to triplets, I was able to get two simultaneous patterns that synced at the bar line, but with one playing straight sixteenths while the other did a dub-style heartbeat kick in triplets.

Take a closer look and you'll discover that the ten sound channels don't all have identical features. Three allow velocity to control tone (lowpass filter cutoff, in other words), two have pitch envelopes, and the other five allow you to modulate sample start time from velocity. I developed some extremely cool beats by playing with these knobs, but it took some experimentation, as the results can be subtle. In particular, with short sounds, modulating the start time is quite likely to result in silence unless you move the knob just a slight amount.

One other essential feature: Channels 8 and 9 can be switched into hi-hat mode, so that each of them will cut off the other.

While flamming can be switched on or off for each drum sound on each step, the flam amount — that is, the length of the time delay between the first and second triggers in the flam — is global. Not just global to the drum or to the current pattern, but global to Redrum. Movements of the flam amount knob can be recorded into the sequencer, so if you're a demon for punishment you could edit the track data to change the flam amount from beat to beat, but I'm going to put per-drum, per-step flam control on my wish list. The good news is, shuffle rhythms can be switched on or off for each pattern. And if you need more control over your shuffle and flams, all you have to do is transfer the pattern data to the song sequencer for detailed editing.

One of the big limitations of some pattern-based sequencers occurs at the point where you've come up with a bodacious groove, only to find that the downbeat is in the wrong place compared to the rest of the instruments. Not to worry — Reason's edit menu contains "shift pattern left" and "shift pattern right" commands. In Redrum, you can also shift individual drums left and right. In Matrix (see below), the pattern's pitches can be shifted up or down.

Figure 4-3.
The Redrum drum machine. A different sample can be assigned to each of the ten sound slots. Each slot has its own solo and mute buttons (top), its own pair of send level knobs, and its own level, velocity response, and envelope length knobs. The other knobs have different functions depending on the slot. As in Reason's other panels, if you hold the mouse above a knob for a moment, a pop-up label will show its current setting. The buttons along the bottom light up, showing which beats will trigger for the currently selected drum. One switch above the row of buttons lets you select a hard, medium, or soft velocity for each button, and the other switches the button bank between steps 1–16, 17–32, 33–48, and 49–64. The numbered and lettered buttons to the left are used for selecting patterns.

Need more mixing flexibility? How's this? Each Redrum channel has its own audio outputs on the back panel. If you need to, you can patch each drum sound, in stereo, to its own mixer channel or its own effect. Naturally, when you use the individual audio outs for a drum, it disappears from Redrum's mix out.

How many Redrum sounds does Reason ship with? Hold on while I get out my calculator.

If you want to load a whole kit at once, you can choose from folders with names like Abstract HipHop, Chemical, Hardcore, RnB, and Electronic. (Some of the included sounds are excerpted from the soundware of well-known developers.) There are 13 folders and 78 kits in all. Since each drum slot has its own open-file button, however, you can mix and match your sounds to create (and save) your own kits. At this point, you've got 125 kicks, 121 snares, and 169 hi-hats to choose from, along with shorter lists of rimshots, toms, claps, cymbals, percussion, and effects. I make it a nice round 625 percussion sounds in all. But of course, that's only the sounds in the percussion folder. The NN19 sample-playback module (see below) has its own folders full of WAV files, which can just as easily be used in Redrum kits, assuming you don't feel like importing your own WAV files.

Figure 4-4.
Subtractor is Reason's virtual analog synth. There are no hidden controls (except for the trim pots on the rear-panel control inputs). The patch file selector is in the upper left corner; below it are voice control and modulation inputs. The oscillators and noise source are in the upper center of the panel, with the LFOs and modulation envelope below them. The mouse cursor is positioned over the rate knob for LFO 1, causing a pop-up window to show the current value of the parameter. The dual filters are at the upper right, with envelope sliders just below them and velocity control inputs in the lower right corner. Note the filter and mod envelope invert buttons, the oscillator phase knobs, and the fake pitch-bend and mod wheels. Not only can the wheels be played and recorded with the mouse, they cast a realistic shadow that moves along with them.

Subtractor. The science of emulating an analog synthesizer in software seems to have reached a mature state. Like most of the virtual analog instruments I've looked at in the past year or two, Subtractor sounds great. While not as powerful as, say, an Access Virus or Novation Supernova, it's fairly full-featured.

The lineup (see **Figure 4-4**) starts with two oscillators and a noise source. Each oscillator can play any of 32 different waveforms, including bell-like tones as well as the classic analog waves. When using any of these waves, be sure to play with the oscillator phase knob, as it can have a fairly drastic effect on the tone. With a square wave, this knob operates as a pulse-width control. Both ring mod and FM are included to broaden the palette still further, though oscillator sync is missing.

You get three ADSR envelopes, one each for filter and amplitude and a third for other types of modulation. What's cool is that each of the envelopes can be gated from an external "voltage gate" input if desired. This lets you do neat tricks like

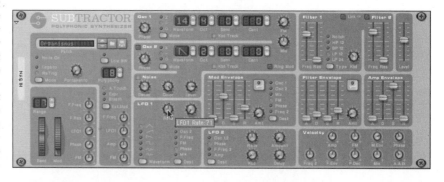

chopping up a continuous synth tone with a 32nd-note Matrix sequence. Amplitude envelope attack can be controlled from velocity, but if you want other types of expressive envelope changes you'll have to record the slider moves by hand.

Subtractor has two filters. Both are resonant, and the second can be switched off to conserve CPU power if you don't need it. The first filter is multimode, with highpass, bandpass, and notch modes plus 12dB and 24dB per octave lowpass. They're hardwired in series, so it's not possible to feed each oscillator to its own filter.

Two LFOs are included. Their features are slightly different: One has selectable waveforms, while the other has knobs for delay and keyboard tracking. Strangely, there's no way to sync the LFOs to the sequencer's beat — a standard design feature for this type of instrument, and a fairly boggling omission from such a feature-rich, rhythm-oriented product. [*Editor's note: In version 2.0, the LFOs can sync to Reason's tempo.*]

Take a close look at Subtractor's back panel and you'll find it has a powerful assortment of "control voltage" inputs and outputs, as well as the external envelope gate inputs I mentioned above. If you're inclined to go for over-the-top sequencing effects, you could patch up a couple of Matrix sequencers (see below) to one Subtractor and use the second Matrix to control filter cutoff or resonance, oscillator pitch, FM amount, or mod wheel amount. What's more, Subtractor has three "voltage" outputs, one each for mod envelope, filter envelope, and LFO 1. These can be patched to the control inputs of effects devices, individual drums in Redrum, or even mixer channels.

Subtractor ships with a healthy assortment of patches in six different folders — bass (46 patches), FX (18 patches), MonoSynths (40), Pads (56), Percussion (41), and PolySynths (114). Every patch I tried was supremely usable, and many were inspiring. The metallic grind of "Malfunction Lead," the eerie keening of "Dead Soul," the tubby "DeepBass," the clean chimes of "BrightEPiano," the eloquent sawtooth buzz of "AnalogBrass" — yum!

One minor issue deserves note: Subtractor doesn't respond to MIDI program changes. If you need to use three Subtractor sounds in the course of a song, the only way to do it is to instantiate three separate Subtractor modules and dedicate one to each sound. If Subtractor could buffer 128 patches in RAM rather than having to load them from disk, program changes would work.

Matrix. To play Subtractor, the tool of choice is the Matrix monophonic step sequencer. Like Redrum, this sequencer stores 32 patterns; each can be up to 32 steps long. Matrix has three outputs: note, gate/velocity, and one controller value. These can be patched to quite a variety of inputs on other modules, as discussed elsewhere in this review. A handy knob (see **Figure 4-5**) lets you select any of nine different time bases for the step, from half-notes through 128th-notes.

Matrix's controls are pretty simple — pattern selector buttons, an octave select switch for moving the display area up and down. One feature I'd like to see added

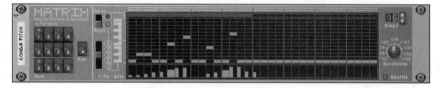

is a gate length control, either global for the entire pattern or (better still) adjustable per step. If you want to control gate length, the way to do it is to copy the Matrix pattern into a song sequencer track and then edit individual notes graphically. This will take a little more time and effort, but it's very doable.

Another missing item: You can't save Matrix patterns to disk by themselves. They're saved with your song, so it's easy enough to load up the song that has the pattern(s) you need and then use the Copy Pattern command to transfer them from one song to another. Pattern copying is supported for Redrum as well.

If you're using a Matrix to drive a Subtractor or NN19 module, the module becomes essentially monophonic. It's not possible to patch two Matrices into the same module at the same time. Reason could really use a polyphonic step sequencer for chord patterns. Chords can be recorded into the song sequencer from an external MIDI keyboard (or entered with the pencil tool), but if your audio interface doesn't support ASIO, you'll find it tricky to get the timing of your MIDI performance to sync to the song.

Dr. Rex. If you've ever played with drum loops that had been chopped apart using Propellerhead ReCycle, you know how many musical possibilities, from groovacious to bizarre, can be unfolded out of a seemingly simple beat. Even so, transmitting the ReCycled loop to your sampler can be a chore, and editing the individual slices (each containing a single drum hit from the loop) is an even bigger headache. The REX file format simplifies the process by allowing you to import ReCycled loops directly into a REX-compatible sequencer.

Dr. Rex goes even further. This module imports REX files and exports their MIDI note rhythms directly to the Reason sequencer. Most of the factory loops are two bars long, but I loaded up some soundware from AMG and found that one-bar and four-bar loops both import perfectly.

Once a REX loop is loaded, you can do several things. Filter, envelope, and LFO modulation can be applied. You can retune, pan, or adjust the level and decay time of individual slices. Then you can go into the sequencer and requantize the groove or jumble up the notes to create entirely new rhythms.

Dr. Rex is not as full-featured as Subtractor, being limited to one multimode resonant filter, two envelopes, and one LFO. It does have its own pitch and mod wheels, however, and a small but useful set of velocity controls.

Reason ships with 299 loops for Dr. Rex, in nine folders including Dub, House, Techno, Abstract HipHop, and so on. Given how many possibilities this module gives you for playing just one loop, 299 should keep you busy for a while. I especially liked having some great-feeling loops with just hi-hat and tambourine or conga and claps, which allowed me to add my own kick patterns using Redrum. The acoustic beats are excellent as well, and the Hardcore folder serves up some wickedly distorted drums.

Note that Reason won't create new REX files. For that, you need ReCycle.

NN19. Sometimes you don't want to fire a sampled sound as if it were a drum; you want to play chords and melodies with it. Or maybe you have some unREXed loops in WAV format. That's where NN19 comes in. This module puts keyboard-type sample playback at your fingertips. While it lacks the features found in high-end samplers (including the ability to record new samples), it definitely gets the job done.

To start with, you can lay out a group of samples across the keyboard and give each its own root key, tuning, loudness, and loop type (forward, forward/backward, or no loop). Multiple velocity layers and that sort of thing are not supported, and you can't edit the loop points of the samples.

At the level of the instrument as a whole, you can edit the filter, the envelopes, an LFO, velocity and controller response, sample start point, and a few other things. Velocity can modulate sample start point, which is very helpful for certain kinds of articulations. As with Dr. Rex, the LFO can have only one destination — filter cutoff, pitch, or panning. On the plus side, the filter is just like most of Reason's other filters (resonant multimode, in other words).

According to the manual, NN19 is supposed to be able to look at the root key data included in the header of individual samples, so that when you use the Automap Samples command, they will be spread out across the keyboard ready to play chords and melodies. When I tested this command with the factory-provided samples, however, it didn't work. Fortunately, it isn't needed with the factory sounds, as they're also provided in the form of ready-to-play multisampled instruments.

The sampled instruments included with Reason are in nine folders: Bass (20 multisample patches), Brass & Woodwind (48), Guitar (30), Mallet & Ethnic (24), Organ (25), Piano (37), Strings (35), Synth & Keyboard (50), and Voice (24). Since some of the sounds are duplicate multisamples with different filter settings and so on, it's a little hard to figure out exactly how many truly unique sounds you're getting, but the fact that certain files have names in capital letters may be a clue. In the bass folder, for example, there seem to be five separate multisamples: acoustic, fingerpicked, fretless, picked, and slap.

I liked just about every sound I tried, from the gutty, authentic didgeridoo to the rich, breathy choirs. While the Rhodes samples may not be as big or sweet as those on expensive hardware synths, they're authentic, with plenty of presence. The Grand Piano multisample is a little tinny in the upper midrange, making it more suitable for dance styles than for pop ballads.

Effects. Reason's effects cabinet contains all of the basics — reverb, stereo delay, distortion, an envelope-controlled filter, chorus/flange, a phaser, a compressor, and an EQ. All but the compressor have at least one "control voltage" input (the filter has three), which can be driven from the Matrix sequencer or, if you dare, from one of the Subtractor's three rear-panel outputs. All of the units also feature input level LEDs and on/off/bypass switches on the front panel. This type of switch is much better than just a bypass switch, as it lets you mute the effect without creating phase problems.

The reverb can produce anything from realistic cavernous spaces and tight, controlled drum booth ambience to endless sub-bass rumbles and long metallic ringing tones. It does this with four controls — room type, size, decay time, and high-frequency damping. If you want more predelay than is offered by the large hall algorithm, you'll need to patch a delay line in series with the reverb.

The delay line's time parameter can be set either in number of sequence steps (either sixteenths or eighth triplets) or in milliseconds. The time maxes out at a generous 2,000ms (two seconds). The output can be panned left or right, but alternate-side ping-pong panning and multiple delay taps are not supported.

I wasn't too impressed with the distortion module. It adds some buzzy high end to the synth tone, but lacks the kind of drive and roundness I'm used to hearing from distortion algorithms. I got much more aggressive results using ReWire and pumping Reason through the stock Fuzz effect that ships with Cubase.

The chorus/flange and phaser do the job; no surprises. The compressor has amount, threshold, attack, and release knobs, but again, no frills. The amount of makeup gain is automatic, not user-adjustable. I tried pumping a number of Dr. Rex loops through it, and never heard quite the amount of squashed-down body I was looking for. It came alive, though, when I patched its output into a filter effect and then swept the filter cutoff from Dr. Rex's LFO.

Sequencer. Whenever you add a module (other than an effect) to your Reason rack, the sequencer automatically acquires a new track with a matching name. This track can be used for three things: automating your knob moves, switching patterns in Matrix and Redrum, or triggering notes in Subtractor, Dr. Rex, and NN19. Reason has no MIDI output, so it's not possible to use its sequencer to play external devices.

Once you've recorded some data, you can edit it graphically, dragging notes around on the screen, inserting new ones with the pencil tool, and copying and pasting to your heart's delight. Like other aspects of Reason, the user interface here is close to transparent: Everything works just the way you'd expect it to.

The position of the sequencer area at the bottom of Reason's main window is less than ideal. This is because the main window has a fixed "rack module" width. Because I have a large monitor, I found myself wishing I could stretch the sequencer track display so as to be able to take advantage of my full screen width. [*Editor's note: In version 2.0, the sequencer display is detachable.*]

Note data in the sequencer tracks can be quantized to the usual rhythm values, and a strength parameter is included in case you want a little looser performance. Sixteenth-note swing/shuffle quantizing is also supported, as are user-definable grooves. Excellent! For example, you could extract the rhythm from a REX file and apply it as a groove to a riff you've sequenced for Subtractor or NN19. Applying it to a Redrum pattern is only slightly trickier: You have to start by using the Copy Pattern to Track command, in order to give the sequencer's quantize function some Redrum data to work with.

Reason's track view includes a slick "groups" feature. You can select a block of data and turn it into a group, after which it can be selected, duplicated, and so on as a unit. Identical groups in the same track will all be given the same color by Reason, which makes it easy to see the structure of your song. If you edit the data in a group so that it's no longer identical to its neighbors, it will show up in a different color — again, making it easy to see where your fills and break-downs are.

Reason can be set to any tempo from 1 to 999.999 bpm, and to any time signa-ture from 1/2 to 16/16. However, there's no way to change either the time signature or the tempo in mid-song. Most users won't miss these features, but if you're a diehard prog rocker, don't say I didn't warn you.

If you're planning to record external MIDI data into the sequencer, you'll need to think a bit about your MIDI routing. Each module can be assigned a MIDI chan-nel, as can the sequencer. In some circumstances, it's possible to get doubled notes because the module is receiving each note-on twice — once directly and once via the sequencer.

Controller curves can be edited graphically with a pencil tool, and if you zoom in far enough vertically and horizontally this will give you plenty of control. Punch-in re-recording of knob moves is also supported. There's no way to squash or stretch controller data up or down; there's another item for my wish list. I'm not going to put event editing on the list, though, because Reason isn't really oriented toward this type of fiddly process.

When you record pattern changes into a Reason song sequence track, they're posi-tioned automatically at the next bar line — just what you'd want for dance music. If you're weird like me, you can drag them to other points in the bar, which will cause a new pattern to cue up on a different beat.

In Use. Reason is the kind of program that regularly rewards your experiments by cooking up incredibly cool grooves. While learning Dr. Rex, for instance, I instantiated two Dr. Rex modules, assigned a techno beat to one and a distorted hard-core beat to the other, and then started fooling around. I bandpass-filtered the hard-core beat directly in Dr. Rex. I then sent its output through three effects — an enve-lope-controlled filter, a delay line, and a reverb. Judging that something more was needed, I added a Matrix pattern sequence module and used it to drive the cutoff and resonance of the filter effect. The techno beat supplied a strong pulse, while the hardcore beat filled in the mix with a halo of disturbing echoes.

Okay, gotta save that one before the power goes down. Now, let's see, what shall I do for a bass line? How about the factory "Fretless" patch? I'll tighten up the attack, add some filter envelope, and then use the Matrix's control output to add FM to selected notes. Now combine that with the beat and see what we've got. Hey, not bad!

By the way, saving your creation in audio form is as simple as choosing "Export Loop as Audio File" from Reason's file menu. While Reason doesn't save mp3 files directly, it offers a variety of export options, including sample rates from 11.025kHz to 96kHz, and either 16- or 24-bit.

I discovered I could drag modules up and down in the rack to put musically related tone generators closer together. This didn't disturb the rear-panel connections. As I added new effects, though, I found that Reason would arbitrarily change my signal routings in an attempt to patch the effect in what it thought was a sensible place. The program really ought to have a "don't touch my cables, damn it!" option in the Preferences box.

I added automated sweeps to a Subtractor oscillator phase knob, filter changes to an NN19, and effect send level changes to the mixer. I was able to extend my song very quickly by block-copying in the song sequencer. And when I was finished, I emailed the song file from my home PC to the Mac at the office. From beginning to end, Reason behaved exactly as I expected it to: Not only did it not crash, it didn't even hiccup once. Such thorough beta-testing is very rare in the music industry.

I did find myself wishing for a "nudge time forward/backward" knob in the Redrum sound slots. The factory samples I loaded into a couple of custom kits, even though they were well truncated, didn't always line up with one another quite the way I wanted them to. Also on my wish list: Being able to name Redrum and Matrix patterns would make the song development process less confusing.

Conclusions. I've seen a lot of great music software over the years, but I can only think of two programs that impressed me as much as Reason. (No, I'm not going to tell you which ones they were. You'll have to use your imagination.) This is one slick piece of work.

If you're doing any type of riff-based music — which means just about any style of pop, dance, R&B, or electronica — Reason will open up whole new worlds of music possibilities for you. Its built-in sounds are first-class all the way, and the integration of sound modules, sequencing, and control signals is close to seamless. Sound designers will find a wealth of resources for developing loop libraries: The program is easy to use, yet extraordinarily deep. And as long as you use the generous set of factory sounds, you'll be able to share song files with your friends or Internet buddies in a very efficient file format.

Yes, I'm hoping to see enhancements in a few specific areas. But don't let a few limitations scare you: There's plenty in the 1.0 version to keep you busy until the next version is released. Assuming you have a modicum of musical vision and a powerful enough computer to run Reason, don't even think twice. This thing is so cool, only a fool would sit around waiting for it to get better. —*JA (Apr. '01)*

When Reason first appeared two years ago, it caused quite a stir. It wasn't the first program that bundled a selection of virtual synths and effects with a pattern sequencer, but the success of Propellerhead's ReBirth and ReCycle software guaranteed that Reason would be noticed. And it was well worth noticing. In *Keyboard's* April '01 issue I probed Reason's features in depth. This time around, I'll focus mainly on the new features in Reason 2.0.

Not to keep you in suspense . . . Two new tone modules have been added to the Reason arsenal. Malström, described as a "graintable synthesizer," sounds jaw-droppingly wicked, and its programming features are more than a bit different. The NN-XT multisample playback module goes quite a bit further than Reason's original NN-19 in terms of control over individual samples, but it's not a conceptual breakthrough. LFO sync to tempo, sorely missing from the 1.0 release, has been added. Also added: Support for Mac OS X, Windows XP, high-resolution samples, and SoundFonts. The sequencer window is now detachable from the main "rack" window, a feature often requested by Reason users. In order to take advantage of the power of NN-XT, Reason 2.0 ships with a full CD of orchestral samples.

Owners of 1.0, by the way, can upgrade for $99. Whether you've been Reasoning all along or are still getting by on intuition and guesswork (joke), I know you can't wait to learn about those new modules — but first let's do a quick recap, for the benefit of those who were standing in the popcorn line when the movie started.

Overview. Reason uses a "virtual rack" metaphor. As you add tone modules and other devices, they appear one above another in a cunningly designed graphic "rack" window. This eliminates the multi-window clutter found in some other programs. For the most part, the various devices operate entirely from their "front panels," with a minimum of dialog boxes and pop-up menus. And from their "rear panels," I might add. Hit the computer's tab key and the rack will flip around, allowing you to repatch both audio and modulation routings in surprisingly flexible ways using graphic patch cords.

Reason's tone modules include:

■ Subtractor, a virtual analog synth.

■ Redrum, a ten-channel sample playback drum machine with its own pattern programming.

■ Dr. Rex, a sample playback module optimized to play loop files in Propellerhead's variable-tempo REX format.

■ NN-19, a more conventional sample playback module.

■ NN-XT, an NN-19 on steroids.

■ Malström, a dual-filter synth capable of a wide range of animated tones.

The outputs of these modules can be processed by a suite of effects, including reverb, delay, chorus/flange, phaser, distortion, compression, an envelope-controlled filter, and two-band parametric EQ. Effects can be routed in series or parallel, and their knobs can be freely automated.

Also on the menu is the Matrix pattern sequencer, which can be used to play any module. A conventional linear multitrack sequencer is provided as well, allowing for more complex compositions than could easily be created with just Matrix and Redrum. And of course there's a 14-channel mixer module, whose channel gain and pan can be modulated for various purposes.

From the beginning, Reason shipped with a full CD of soundware, which contained both samples and presets for the various modules (in a proprietary format that makes it tricky to export samples and loops). The 2.0 release includes a second soundware CD called Orkester, which features multisampled orchestral instruments.

Reason can work in tandem with a sequencer/multitrack recorder using ReWire. Not only do the two transports sync, but you can send audio streams back and forth. This makes it possible to process Reason synth sounds with plug-in effects. It would be more convenient to be able to instantiate VST plug-ins — or even VST softsynths — directly in Reason. I can't quite figure out why Propellerhead hasn't added VST support. The other pattern-based virtual rack systems I've been using lately all have it.

In the Reason 2.0 ReadMe file is a warning that installing multiple ReWire applications in the same computer with Cubase VST 5.x can cause Cubase to corrupt its own files. I spent a couple of weeks trying to nail down the facts, but I never quite managed it. According to Steinberg, Cubase VST files can become corrupt only if you attempt to use more than 128 ReWire audio channels. But Propellerhead maintains that simply installing multiple ReWire apps, whether or not they're actually used, can trigger the problem. Possibly they're even talking about two different problems. In any event, I didn't experience any difficulties using Reason and Cubase VST together.

Malström. So — you think you know what a synthesizer sounds like, eh? You haven't met Malström. Described as a "graintable synthesizer," this synth (see **Figure 4-6**) serves up some unique tools. It's going to be the secret sauce in my next project, that's for sure. I'm a synth addict from way back, and I'm hooked.

A list of the main modules may not reveal how unusual or powerful Malström is. You get a couple of oscillators, a couple of LFOs (which double as one-shot modulation sources), a couple of filters, a waveshaper, and three ADSR envelopes. What's unusual is how they're configured. A full description of all of the parameters and modulation routings would take pages, so I'm going to hit the high spots.

Figure 4-6.
Malström boasts a huge array of animated timbres thanks to its unusual oscillators. The motion, index, and shift parameters control how the oscillator uses its wavetable. Each oscillator has its own ADSR envelope generator. The two identical filters (lower right) have five modes, including comb+, comb–, and amplitude (ring) modulation from an internal sine wave. The filter ADSR (upper right) is shared by the two filters. The two modulation generators (top center) can function either as LFOs or (in one-shot mode) as transient generators. Each module has its own on/off switch (the button in the upper left corner of the module). Signal routings are controlled with the pushbuttons in the filter/shaper area, which glow orange when active. The A/B switches in Mod A, Mod B, and the velocity and modulation areas at lower left select the destinations for the signals coming from these sources.

■ *Oscillators.* The oscillators combine granular synthesis and wavetable synthesis in a way that isn't well explained in the manual. Fortunately, it's easy to get an intuitive picture of what's going on, simply by listening. Hint: Don't just listen to one or two waveforms and assume you know what the index and shift parameters do. Their effect sometimes changes depending on the waveform.

With some waveforms, cranking up the shift is rather like raising the pitch of a conventional oscillator that's hard-synced: You get progressively higher overtones without affecting the base frequency. With waves based on wind instruments, on the other hand, moving the shift apparently causes the instrument to overblow, so that it plays higher in its overtone series. The index slider controls what segment of a longish wavetable will be scanned by the oscillator: As with the shift, the only way to hear what it will do to a given waveform is to grab it and move it.

Naturally, both the shift and index can be modulated in various ways, so a rich, animated tone is almost impossible to avoid. Within minutes after starting to fool around with Malström, I accidentally stumbled on a recognizable didgeridoo sound using one oscillator and some modulation — no filters, no waveshaping, nothing else. (And that was before I discovered the didgeridoo waveform.)

The oscillators have some other functions, such as built-in LFOs, their own ADSR amplitude envelopes, and linear cents detuning, but let's move on.

■ *Modulation generators.* These devices (called Mod A and Mod B) can function either as LFOs or in one-shot trigger mode. Each has its own set of output knobs (three for Mod A, four for Mod B). But there's no overlap in the list, so Mod A can sweep oscillator pitch, but Mod B can't, while only Mod B can modulate filter cutoff. This is a significant limitation. For instance, a patch whose sound starts with a quick pitch envelope "blip" can't have vibrato.

Each modulation generator can be switched so its output feeds oscillator A, B, or both. (In fact, the A/B/both output switch of Mod B also applies to filters A and B.) And they have a surprising array of waveforms — not only the expected saw, sine, triangle, and several flavors of random, but stairstep rhythms, shaped bursts suitable for adding attack transients, and so on. Mod B can control the amount of Mod A but not its rate.

Figure 4-7.
The NN-XT sample player's main panel contains only a pitch wheel, two mod wheels, and a few global knobs. The "remote editor" panel below it can be opened up or hidden to save screen space. The assignment of samples to keyzones is displayed in the central display area. You can drag samples left or right. Looping and tuning parameters for each sample are handled with the row of knobs just below the display area. A single LFO 1 (lower left) can be used with all samples, or each can have its own. Each of the mod wheels can be assigned to any of six destinations in the knob matrix at center left. The filter offers six different modes, including three lowpass selections with different rolloff slopes.

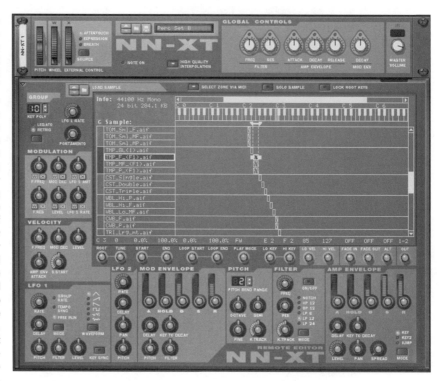

Six amount knobs are provided for velocity response (three of them with A/B/both switching), and four for mod wheel response (with the same switching). This is a useful complement of controls. You can do things like crossfade between Oscillator A and Oscillator B under velocity control, drive index, shift, and filter cutoff from the mod wheel, and so on. Being able to control shift from velocity is especially useful for adding new overtones smoothly at high velocities, and driving the index from the mod wheel can produce some startling animated sweeps.

■ *Filters.* The Malström filter section is way powerful. Each of the two filters can operate in lowpass, bandpass, comb, or ring modulator mode. They can be routed in series or paraellel, among other possibilities. Both oscillators can feed Filter B, or you can feed one oscillator through each filter. The Shaper module offers several types of waveshaping and an amount knob (but no modulation inputs), and it can process the input of Filter A, the output of Filter B, or both if the filters are in series. Really, the only way to understand all the routing possibilities is to squint at the front panel for a minute.

Even then, you won't have learned everything. Reason's back panel has direct audio inputs for Filter B and Shaper/Filter A. The manual gives three examples of cool ways to use these inputs.

The two filters share an ADSR envelope, unfortunately, with its associated amount knob and invert button. All is not lost, because it's possible to give one filter a decay sweep from modulation generator B while the other is being controlled by the envelope. Another odd limitation: Keyboard tracking is an on/off switch for each filter. Heck, the Minimoog had better keyboard tracking options than that! Here again, Malström is surprisingly flexible and surprisingly constricted at the same time.

■ *Sounds.* Like the other Reason synths, Malström ships with a good selection of presets. These are organized into seven folders: Bass (36 patches), FX (38), MonoSynths (40), Pads (58), Percussion (16), PolySynths (74), and Rhythmic (34). I'd guess the sound designers were told not to duplicate any of the analog types of sounds available in Subtractor, because most of them could be better described as "interesting" than as "fat."

I especially liked the bass called "Suspenders," which sounds like a bridge cable being hit with a hammer. The gurgling atmosphere of "Sweeepy" would work well in the scene in the movie when the explorers brave the entrance to the cave. "Paranoid" combines several different metallic machine noises in a slow rhythm. "LegatoSeqBass" layers a pulsing rhythm over a rich round sub-octave — try this one at 125 bpm. And the mod wheel adds an understated scream to the thick "Whirlgroans" lead.

I found myself wanting to edit many of the factory patches, if only because Malström so thoroughly invites experimentation. The awkward bit is that you can't save your edited versions back into the same folder as the factory patches. You have to use a separate folder. Thereafter, you'll need to jump back and forth in the disk directory depending on whether you're loading a factory patch or one of your own. Either that, or save the factory sounds out to your new folder one at a time. (They can't be copied from the desktop.) This is not a very user-friendly way to approach patch storage.

NN-XT. Reason's original sample playback module, the NN-19, did the basics, but Propellerhead wisely decided that more was needed. NN-XT (see **Figure 4-7**) allows you to create keymaps with layers and velocity switches and crossfades. Layering samples, incidentally, is a great way to import audio tracks from another piece of software. As a workaround for the fact that Reason lacks audio tracks, it's serviceable.

Each sample can have its own full set of parameter settings (filter, LFO, and so on). On the back panel are eight stereo output pairs, allowing you to route individual samples through their own effects.

At the top level, the NN-XT's panel gives you global controls for filter cutoff and resonance, attack, decay, and release time of the amplitude envelope, and decay time of the modulator envelope. These knobs are handy as macros for quick editing, but they're the *only* knobs in the NN-XT that can be assigned to controllers, either external MIDI or the controller data in Reason's own sequencer. In this respect, NN-XT is actually less capable than NN-19.

By opening up the NN-XT's "remote editor panel" (nothing remote about it — it's not detachable), you can fiddle with the parameters for individual keyzones. At the very beginning of the section of the manual that describes how to use the panel, Propellerhead makes a distinction between *selected zones* and *the zone with the edit focus*. A given edit operation may apply to all selected zones, or only to the zone with the focus, and a zone can be selected without having the edit focus or vice-versa. Eventually I figured it all out, but from an ergonomic standpoint I feel the editor panel could use a little more work.

Each sample has a good basic set of controls, including root key, start and end offsets, loop start and loop end, and velocity and key zones. By adding velocity cross-fading, I was able to make the orchestral snare in "Perc Set A" much more playable and responsive.

Orkester Soundbank. The idea of providing a CD-ROM of orchestral samples with a groove-oriented product struck me, when I first heard of it, as a bit odd. Propellerhead may be right in observing that dance, hip-hop, and techno musicians aren't the only ones who use Reason — but if the company is serious about supporting mainstream pop and film composers, they're going to have to do better than the sounds on the Orkester CD.

To be fair, let's note that Reason costs $399, and the Orkester soundbank accounts for, at most, no more than 10% of the total functionality of the software. That being the case, this is a $39.95 orchestral library. Hey, for that price it's pretty darn good.

The bass clarinet and oboe are definitely usable, as is the orchestral percussion. (Hint: Try loading some of the orchestral percussion samples into Redrum.) I liked the cello and violin sections; the violins are a bit abrasive, but they can be tamed with the filter knob. Curiously, while the violin legatos were sampled at three dynamic levels, no velocity cross-switched preset was created in which these samples are combined. It's a do-it-yourself job. There are some layered presets that use, for example, cellos and violins to create a full-keyboard layout. Most of them sound quite decent, considering.

The tenor trombone seems to have been played by someone with very limited embouchure or breath control: The tone lacks brass body, and wobbles in a seasick way. The solo trumpet is better, but not a lot better. Here again, you have a choice of *fortissimo, mezzo-forte,* or *mezzo-piano* trumpet multisamples, but there's no cross-switched preset.

I could find some other things in this soundbank to gripe about, but what's the point? In the context of Reason as a whole, it's a minor extra, not worth quibbling over.

Sequencer. In addition to being detachable from the main rack (a definite plus, especially if you have a decent-sized monitor, as it's no longer necessary to scroll up and down quite so much among the rack's front panels), Reason's built-in sequencer has been enhanced with some new tools, including an eraser and a line drawing tool. Other than that, it's pretty much the same as in 1.0 — perfectly usable, but not as powerful as a full-function sequencer.

You can cut and paste blocks of data, edit individual notes on a piano roll, use shuffle and groove quantizing, and so on. For devices with rhythm pattern memories (Redrum and the Matrix step sequencer), you can record and edit pattern change commands. I was disappointed, though, to find that controller scaling hasn't been added. You can record controller data by moving an on-screen knob with the mouse, and later edit it with a pencil tool, but you can't select a range of controller data and squash or boost its range. Nor, for that matter, can you drive external MIDI devices such as hardware synthesizers from the Reason sequencer. MIDI checks in, but it doesn't check out.

Here's a sequencer tip, before we move on: Turn on quantizing to sixteenth-notes, draw some controller events (envelope attack, for instance) with the pencil tool, and then drag-copy your controller rhythm into a number of adjacent bars. This is a quick way to make a repeating pattern that's in sync with the song, and it can be applied to parameters that don't have rear-panel inputs suitable for use with Matrix.

MIDI Implementation. Right-clicking on a Reason knob or slider opens up a little dialog box, in which you can assign any MIDI controller, so as to use Reason with a slider box, for example. Only one knob can be assigned to each MIDI controller, which is a bummer, but since Reason lacks scaling and processing for the controller data (a feature very effectively implemented in Fruityloops, by the way), assigning several knobs to one controller would be less useful.

Reason's MIDI Implementation document also lists a fixed set of controller assignments, with which you can control the knobs and sliders. Trouble is, this list is riddled with errors. The first two assignments I tried were listed as applying to Malström's Oscillator A, but in fact those controllers manipulated the parameters in Oscillator B.

Another issue for those of us who like using MIDI hardware is that Malström devices don't respond to program change messages. This is because they don't have RAM buffers containing 128 patches. Patches are always loaded from disk when needed. If you're hoping to use Malström or Subtractor live, this is a significant limitation.

One cool feature you don't see every day: Reason's switches (the mixer track mutes, for instance) can be remote-controlled by MIDI notes. The switches toggle back and forth, activating when they receive the first note-on and deactivating when they receive a second one. This makes it child's play to mute and unmute channels while doing a live remix. You still can't save and load MIDI remote setups and apply them to an existing song, though. Either create a default song that has the setup you want and always use it when starting a new piece of music, or recreate your favorite setup by hand, one controller at a time, in an existing song.

In Use. Up to now, I haven't used ReWire much, so I decided it was time to jump in. I booted Cubase VST 5.1, then booted Reason, and I was off to the races. Before long I'd sketched in a wicked synth bass line in Cubase with Steinberg's simple JX16 synth, which I processed through my new favorite plug-in, SuperCamelPhat 2, to make it thick and nasty. Reason's Redrum module laid down a tasty electro beat, and Malström provided a hair-raising pad. I ran Malström through a Waves reverb plug-in in Cubase to give it more space, and routed the Redrum kick to a separate ReWire channel so I could process it with Cubase's simulated tube compressor.

By this time the Cubase VST Performance meter (CPU usage, in other words) was hovering around 55%. This is a 1.5GHz machine, not a Model T Ford, and I was beginning to wonder how I'd be able to do a more complete arrangement without resorting to hardware synthesizers. The culprit turned out to be the Waves reverb. When I replaced it with Cubase's own Reverb32, the meter dropped below 30%, and in the context of a full mix, I wasn't taking too much of a hit sonically.

Next I added a screaming lead courtesy of Reason's Subtractor synth, processing it through a simple delay line (a DirectX effect from Sonic Foundry). I played both Malström and Subtractor from Cubase MIDI tracks rather than using Reason's sequencer, mainly because editing a song in one track window is a heck of a lot easier than trying to coordinate two. This approach also bypasses an awkward MIDI issue, which is that Reason routes incoming MIDI data based on its channel, while Cubase ignores the actual channel and routes MIDI based on the currently selected track. In order to avoid undesired synth layers, I would have had to switch channels on my master keyboard, select an unassigned Cubase track in order to play a Reason instrument, or both. Getting Reason's direct MIDI input out of the picture and using ReWire's MIDI pipeline solved the problem.

Redrum exhibited some dropped notes while I was recording Cubase tracks, but once I finished recording and listened to the playback, everything was fine. I also discovered that Redrum can't be used as a MIDI metronome in Cubase while recording, as Cubase's metronome preferences box doesn't list ReWire devices as possible outputs. And when I reopened Cubase after saving and quitting, the Reason synth tracks were reassigned to the default MIDI output. This is a side effect of the fact that ReWire applications have to be booted in a certain order. When Cubase starts, it doesn't know there are any ReWire MIDI channels available. Reloading the Cubase song file *after* Reason is started solves the problem in about five seconds.

These fiddly little issues are normal when two complex applications are being asked to work together, and certainly not a big deal. Overall, I was more than pleased by how smoothly my ReWire work went, and excited by the combined sounds of Reason synths and drums with external softsynths and plug-in effects. I'm sure I'll be working this way again in the near future.

Conclusions. Reason is an elegant and powerful program. It sounds fantastic, and for the most part it's very user-friendly. As long as you don't need to lay down vocals or acoustic instrument tracks, you really can produce complete mixes and rock your listeners with this one program. The enhancements in 2.0 are welcome — especially the Malström graintable synth, which is so good it's scary. Aside from Malström, though, version 2.0 is more an incremental advance than a great leap forward. NN-XT is useful but not groundbreaking, and the Orkester sound CD is nice as a freebie but hardly worth getting excited about. At the same time, features that would have lifted Reason to a whole new level, notably the ability to play audio tracks and support for plug-in synths and effects, still require that you use ReWire and a second expensive application such as Cubase or Sonar.

Assuming you're set up to do that, Reason will definitely rock your world. It's one of the leading software instruments on the planet, and there's a — ahem — reason for that. They're not getting this one off of my hard drive anytime soon. —*JA (Dec. '02)*

Arturia Storm
DANCE-ORIENTED RACK WITH CHORD SEQUENCING

Figure 4-8.
The main composition/playback screen in Storm 1.0. The song recorder is at the upper left. The upper right corner contains the Kepler chord module. Up to four sound modules can be installed in the "rack" to the left; here, I'm using Tsunami, Arsenic, H3OPlus, and Scratch. The narrower rack on the right can contain up to three effects processors. Shown are Distorsion [*sic*], Seq Filter, and Dual Delays. Each module's output levels are handled by the knobs immediately to its right. The output mixer is in the lower right corner.

stand-alone, VST (Win, Mac)
$99

Pros: Seriously addictive. Great analog-style drum and bass sounds. Functions as a ReWire host, slave, or mixer. Can record and import WAV, AIFF, and MP3 files. MIDI control options and playable over MIDI. Realtime tempo and pitch shifting of samples. Automatic smoothing of automated control moves. Cool mouse-driven graphic interface.

Cons: No redo, only undo (albeit with several levels). Undo doesn't affect all operations. No pitchbend for synths. Poor documentation. Patterns in most modules are one 4/4 bar long. Insufficient editing of control/automation moves. Only four instruments at one time in the rack. Fairly processor-hungry. Drum machines can't load other samples.

Storm, which I reviewed for *Keyboard* back in November 2000, was my first experience of a virtual rack system. While not as high-profile in the United States as Reason, it has a competitive edge in a couple of areas. You can program chord progressions for your songs, for instance, after which the bass and chord synths will follow the progression automatically. Neither Reason nor Fruityloops has any equivalent. Storm also has some limitations, such as only allowing four softsynths to be instantiated at a time. In the new version, there's a workaround (less than elegant, I must say) for this problem: You can run two Storm instances on the same computer at the same time, and sync them to one another. It's also significant that Storm's drum modules are limited to four different note loudness levels. This gives drum tracks a rigidity that I don't much care for.

In Craig Anderton's review of version 2.0 (first published in December 2002), he documents some new goodies, including the ability for Storm to operate as a VST plug-in. He also points out a boggling limitation that I missed: Storm doesn't respond to MIDI pitchbend data. Storm's price has been reduced, by the way: Version 1.0 originally cost $149, but 2.0 is only $99.

There's some redundancy between my review and Craig's, but maybe there's some educational value in seeing how two seasoned reviewers approach the same product. Or maybe I'm just too lazy to scissor them together. You be the judge.

Somebody save me — I'm having too much fun. If I don't stop soon, not only will I miss my deadline but I'll be rolling out a major drum 'n' bass recording project, thanks to Arturia Storm. This program takes PC-based synthesis to new heights of interactivity. And you don't need to be a pocket-protector-wearing geek to get into it. Storm doesn't give you a million parameters to tweak, just the ones that will produce stylish results quickly.

In *Keyboard's* April 2000 issue, we spotlighted Storm as one of the 25 hits of the January NAMM show, while poking a little fun at the fractured English of the press release. Storm's distinctive, brightly colored graphic style may have influenced our

Storm at a Glance

System requirements	Win95/98/2000/XP, Pentium II 400MHz or higher, 128MB RAM; Mac OS 8.6 or higher (incl. OS X 10.1.4) with OMS 2.3.7, G3 400MHz (192MB, 500MHz required with OS X); 200MB free disk space
Synthesis types	sample playback, analog modeled
Sample rate and bit depth	24-bit, 44.1kHz
Polyphony	system-dependent
Synthesis modules	Arsenic monophonic bass synth, Bass 52 bass guitar synth, Equinoxe 3-osc mono synth, H3OPlus sample sequencer, Hork drum machine with acoustic percussion samples, Meteor drum machine with electronic percussion, Orpheus 16-voice polyphonic synth, Psion drum machine with "electro" samples, Puma drum machine with world percussion, Scratch module for "scratching" samples, Shadow chord synth, Tsunami virtual analog drum machine
Included soundware	495MB of samples in 10 different genres
Effects	chorus, compressor, distortion, dual delay, flanger, LP resonant filter, reverb, ring modulation, step filter, vocoder
Sequencer	20-400 bpm; pattern/song, 16-step patterns, up to 400 bars; 64 pattern presets per module
Recording methods	pattern programming of events, digital audio sequencing, audio recording with EZtrack, realtime MIDI data recording into Orpheus and Shadow
Arpeggiator	no
Synchronization	MIDI clock (send, receive), ReWire, VST
Internal performance resampling	yes
File formats imported/exported	16/24-bit WAV, 16/24-bit AIFF, MP3 (exports 8 different bit rates)
Copy protection	serial number on installation, then registration to cancel 20-session limitation
Downloadable demo	yes

tongue-in-cheek comments as well. Arturia is a small French company with, at press time, no U.S. distribution, which may account for their sometimes funky phraseology, but their software is for real. [*Editor's note: As of late 2002, half a dozen U.S. retail outlets are listed on Arturia's web page.*]

Overview. Like many of the newer softsynths, Storm is designed to look more like hardware than software. To make music, you start by selecting up to four tone modules and three effects devices from a toolbox, and drag them into your "rack" with the mouse. The toolbox features ten synth or drum modules and seven effects. Two more synth modules were released while I was learning the program, but they arrived too late for me to do a thorough review.

Once you've selected your modules, you switch over to the Composition window (which takes a few seconds as Storm "builds" the rack). Here you can program up to 64 different patterns for each module, record automation moves using onscreen knobs, and program a song of up to 400 bars. Even the effects sends and returns can be automated. Your song can include chord progressions with a new root every two beats: The pitch-oriented synths and samples will follow the progression automatically.

You can record Storm's output as a stereo WAV, AIFF, or mp3 file. If you need to, you can even re-import this mix (it shows up onscreen as a "tape cassette") back into one of Storm's sample playback modules as a submix so as to add more tracks. Your set of patterns and imported samples can be saved in a song file.

There are several features I'd like to see added to Storm. Near the top of my list would be some type of controller editing environment. [*Editor's note: Version 2.0 still lacks controller editing, which puts it one down on the other virtual rack systems. You can run Storm as a VST instrument inside a sequencer and do the controller editing there, however.*] If you don't like the knob move you've recorded, your only option is to keep redoing it until you get it right. MIDI output for the drum and synth modules wouldn't be a bad feature to see added, as there might be times when you'd like to incorporate an external synth in a Storm song. Dance producers will doubtless wish they could program snare fills in 32nd-note triplets rather than being restricted to sixteenths. And how about allowing folks with faster CPUs to put extra modules into their rack?

Doubtless other users will have their own wish lists — but overall, Storm has what it needs to produce full-sounding music in the dance/trance vein.

Synthesizers. Version 1.1 of Storm arrived with two pitch-oriented synthesis modules — a monophonic bass/lead module called Arsenic and a three-note-polyphonic chord module called Equinoxe. While I was working on the review, Arturia released a mondo polysynth module called Morpheus and a physically modeled bass synth called Bass 52.

Each module except Morpheus stores 64 one-bar patterns consisting of 16 sixteenth-notes; the Morpheus patterns can be up to eight bars in length. In Arsenic, note patterns are programmed using a two-octave keyboard display. You can choose any of four volume levels, or silence, for each step. The method for programming a rest in Arsenic is explained incorrectly in the manual. Here's the trick: After selecting a step, click on the lighted keyboard note so it unlights.

The synth module knobs are automated at the song level (see below) rather than being recorded into individual patterns, as the drum module knobs are. The rationale for this seems to be that it makes it much easier to program a four-bar filter sweep for a bass line. The controls are basic — don't look for LFOs, multimode filters, or ADSR envelopes except in Morpheus. Arsenic (see **Figure 4-8**) can glide, TB-303-style, between adjacent steps if you like, but the glide time is fixed.

Figure 4-9.
Three more Storm modules (top to bottom): Morpheus (polyphonic synth), Bass 52 (physically modeled bass synth), and Equinoxe (three-voice chords). Morpheus is the only Storm module that occupies two rack spaces. Its piano-roll pattern editor can contain patterns up to eight bars long, and the square area in the lower left corner can record two-dimensional mouse movements for waveform modulation. Note the pattern selector "keypad" on the left side of each module.

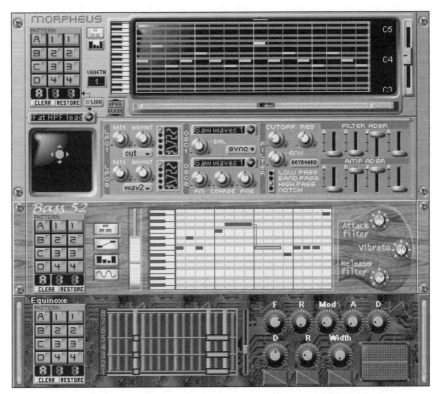

You can choose either a sawtooth wave or a pulse wave, and the waveform width knob works with both of them.

Equinoxe (see **Figure 4-9**) is good at adding basic rhythm comps, but it isn't the most inspiring module in the box. Even ignoring the feature set, the sound of the filter is on the thin side. For each step, you can program a three-note chord on a simple scale grid with scale degrees 1 through 8. The 3rd and 6th steps will play back as major or minor depending on the chord chosen for the Kepler module (see "Song Recording," below). The 7th is always lowered; major 7ths are not allowed, sorry.

Morpheus is a dual-oscillator polyphonic synth. It features a multimode filter, multiple waveforms, FM, dual ADSRs, dual LFOs, and a sweet two-dimensional joystick-like control surface for oscillator mixing. Two of your four rack spaces will be used by this module. Bass 52 does monophonic physically modeled bass sounds. Its controls are simple, but you can add vibrato to any note, and its timbre is crisp but well rounded. Both Morpheus and Bass 52 give you a dozen or so velocity levels per note, as opposed to the four in the other modules.

Drum Machines. Storm specializes in beatbox timbres. There are no fewer than five rhythm synths to choose from: Meteor, Tsunami, Puma, Psion, and Hork. Each has a slightly different set of features and/or sounds, but they all use an identical grid for programming rhythms. The eight drum sounds are listed in a column at the left edge of the grid: To place a drum sound on a particular beat, you click in the corresponding cell in the grid, which lights up a dot in that cell. Click again, and the dot gets brighter, which makes the sound louder. Four different volume levels are available per event, in addition to silence.

Unlike the synths, the drum boxes record knob moves into individual patterns. This is a great feature, as it allows you to program some seriously disturbed beats. The modules are always in record mode, so if you move a knob during playback, you'll see your move repeated each time the pattern plays. If you want to change the knob position and leave it in one spot, you'll have to hold onto it for a full bar.

Meteor, Hork, and Puma use sampled drum sounds, Meteor and Hork being somewhat vintage-sounding trap kits and Puma a Latin percussion battery. For each sound you're given knobs for pitch and decay. Psion operates in the same manner, but it has 808-style electro percussion sounds.

Curiously, a few of the sounds in these boxes don't simply get louder when you program a higher level, but switch to entirely different samples. In Hork, for example, you get the snare rim tap at the lower two levels and a handclap at the upper two. I suppose this is an economical way to provide a few extra sounds within a fixed grid, but it leaves you with only two possible volume levels for those samples.

Tsunami is a powerful synthesis-oriented drumbox. The eight lines on the grid correspond to four noise oscillators and four pitched oscillators. Each oscillator has its own bank of seven knobs. For the noise oscillators, you can control attack and decay, as well as the cutoff frequency, width, and resonance of the filter. Whip a few of these puppies around and you're almost sure to get something tasty.

The parameters associated with Tsunami's pitched oscillators are a little more mysterious, but don't worry about the details. Just mess with the knobs until you get something great. It won't take long. Tsunami will do anything from solid sub-bass kicks and factory steam blasts to Simmons toms and hilarious hiccuping noises.

Sample Players. When it comes to importing audio from other sources and integrating it into your song, Storm offers three options. H3OPlus is a four-track loop-based sample player with independent control over pitch and tempo. In other words, you can change the tempo without affecting the pitch, or vice-versa. EZtrack is for adding a lengthwise track (such as a vocal) over the top of the song. And Scratch gives you a dual-turntable emulator for mouse-operated scratching.

Unlike most of Storm's modules, H3OPlus (see **Figure 4-8**) uses four-bar patterns. This makes a lot of sense, as you may want to import two-bar and four-bar loops. Each H3OPlus module will play up to four stereo WAV, AIFF, or mp3 files at a time — and I had no trouble running four H3OPlus modules at once on my 650MHz PIII PC, for 16 stereo tracks. Samples are imported into the tracks using drag-and-drop from a floating disk file window. What could be simpler?

A sample can start on any sixteenth-note for syncopation and stuttering effects, and can be shortened by dragging on its right end (though not shortened from the left end so as to play only the latter part of the sample). You can also drag up or down to reduce or increase its volume. And as with other Storm modules, you have 64 presets to work with, so it's easy to build up complex sample playback arrangements. The main limitation is that no sample can overlap the end of the four-bar pattern.

H3OPlus tracks tempo changes and the chord changes programmed in the Kepler module. Its time and pitch changes are kind of lo-fi, but no special encoding is required, which is convenient. To tell Storm the original key and tempo, just right-click on the sample and fill in the information. If you don't want a loop to change pitch with the chord changes, leave the information box blank.

The Scratch module is never going to offer any competition for a real turntable, but it's fun. You can load two samples, crossfade between them by whipping the mouse from left to right, and scratch either turntable by dragging the mouse up and down. Your moves can be recorded as song automation. The other control is a number-of-bars parameter for each turntable. This keeps your sampled "vinyl" looping along with the rest of the song.

EZtrack holds a single stereo sample, its size being limited only by the available RAM in your computer. The module includes a handy graphic waveform display, complete with a bar/eighth-note grid, with which you can cut and paste sections of the file. Other samples can be imported into the EZtrack file by dragging, and EZtrack will time-stretch the audio if you alter the tempo.

EZtrack is supposed to be able to record new external audio, but I was unable to coax it into seeing the audio input of my Echo Mona interface. The manual and online help give no troubleshooting hints, and Arturia's attempts to troubleshoot the problem by email were unsuccessful.

Effects. The raw sound of the Storm modules is quite good, but adding (and automating) a few effects to your song can put the mix over the top. The effects toolbox includes chorus, flange, distortion, ring modulation, a stereo delay line, a resonant lowpass filter, and another filter with its own 16-step sequencer. Send any of these effects a stereo input, and you'll be pleased to discover that their output is still stereo.

The signal routing scheme for effects is ideal. Each tone module has four output level knobs — a dry level and three effect sends. Each effect also has an output knob (confusingly labeled "dry") that feeds the mixer directly, plus knobs to control the level of the feed to the other two effects. Using these knobs, you can set up parallel and series processing in any combination, or even create a controllable feedback loop between effects.

The effects parameters are simple, but useful. One nice touch is that where appropriate, they sync automatically with the song's tempo. This is true of the flanger, whose sweep can be set from four to 64 beats, and of the delay line. In fact, these

Figure 4-10.

The new version of Storm has a lighter, less imposing look. In this screenshot, it's running on a Macintosh (version 1.0 was Windows-only). The sequencer, which occupies the upper left corner, arranges patterns in a graphical, playlist-type format. The bottom track records automation and mix data. Equinoxe's Filter Cutoff is in MIDI learn mode. Here, controller 9 coming in over channel 1 will provide remote control of the cutoff. The dual delays (at the top of the effects rack) are not only tempo-synced, but can cross-delay into each other. The effects can send to other effects — and yes, all these send controls are automatable. Note the X-Y control surface on the vocoder effect. It can control multiple parameter pairs.

parameters can only be set to rhythmically meaningful values. The delay's left and right parameters can be set to any value from 1 to 32, but above 12 the delay times are no longer calibrated in sixteenths; instead, you get smaller subdivisions of some sort. This is an undocumented feature, though, and I couldn't figure out exactly what the rhythmic values were.

The ring mod can be cranked up to give major metallic noises. The delay line will put you in deep dub or trance territory. The distortion sounded crunchy and brittle; I got fatter results when I followed it with the lowpass filter. The sequenced filter is an especially cool tool. It has its own bank of 16 sliders for controlling the cutoff (plus a resonance knob). These sliders will impose a filter rhythm on top of anything else — the output of the distortion or delay effect, for example. Sadly, changes in these sliders' positions can't be automated.

Song Recording. Once you've developed some patterns, you're ready to click on the record button at the top of the screen and start sequencing your masterpiece. The five-track song sequencer records automation moves for each rack synth separately; a fifth track is for all of the effects and mix data. Most switching — of synth presets and tempo changes, for example — is at bar lines, but knob moves are recorded smoothly.

You can loop a range of bars and then overdub automation data until you get it perfected. Even so, there may be times when you'll wish for a controller editing window. Groups of bars can be cut and pasted, but since all of the effects and mix automation is stored in one track, there's no way to block-copy, for example, just the changes in the ring modulator knobs or mixer sliders by themselves.

The track display is segmented visually into tidy four-bar phrases. Sections of the display can be given different colors during recording, which makes it easier to see where you are in the structure, but if you forget to switch colors before going into record mode, there's no way to change the color afterward.

Preset changes in the Kepler chord module can also be recorded into the song. Patterns in this module are four bars long, and consist of eight major or minor chords of two beats each. For smoother voice-leading, you can also click on an octave-transpose button beside any chord symbol.

At first I thought Storm was capable of playing only in straight rhythms, which would have been a huge negative. But one of the controls that pop up when you control-click on the song transport bar is a slider confusingly labeled "Quantize." This slider adds a variable amount of sixteenth-note swing to your song. Not quite as flexible as adding swing to individual drum sounds, but still very useful. Somewhat more esoteric: Selected bars can be shortened one sixteenth-note at a time. Whether you want to compose a waltz or simply insert a few bars of 13/16 so the dancers will fall down, Storm is happy to oblige.

User Interface. Storm's use of graphic elements, such as icons that glow when the mouse passes over them, gives it a distinctive feel. For me, the absence of standard Windows menus makes it harder to find things. Hidden right-click and control-click options are present in a few places. In the plus column, standard keyboard commands are used for cut/copy/paste, which helps make up for the absence of menus.

You can copy a pattern containing both notes and controller data from one memory slot in a module to a different slot, so as to create a series of variations. Copying a rhythm pattern from one module to another doesn't work, however.

Since I have tendinitis issues, I'm always delighted to see a music program that provides keyboard equivalents that I can use instead of mousing. Storm lets you move many of the knobs by pressing and holding computer keys. You still have to use the mouse for turning drum notes on and off, but every little bit helps.

One control I'd like to see added to Storm would be a "rhythm reframe" button that would slide the pattern note data within a module one sixteenth-note at a time to the left or right so as to allow you to redefine the downbeat.

In Use. Assembling a song in Storm turned out to be trickier than I expected. Since I was already working on a song with a strong techno influence, I thought I'd try doing a Storm-only arrangement of the rhythm tracks. My first task: Assemble an eight-bar intro. I wanted a two-bar phrase, so I created the patterns for bars 1 and 2 in Psion (electro drums) and Arsenic (bass) and laid down an eight-bar loop in song record mode that switched, in every bar, between pattern A11 and pattern A12. This wasn't too tricky, although it would have been a lot easier to play the bass line on a keyboard rather than poking at it with the mouse, one sixteenth-note at a time. I found myself hoping the next version of Storm will do up to four-bar phrases in all of the modules.

Next I added a couple of simple chord patterns in Equinoxe. At this point I heard a bit of distortion in the output, so I decided to lower the output mix level. This was when I discovered that there isn't any way to lower the level as a static parameter change. I had to click and hold on the sliders while the entire intro looped to prevent them from popping back up to their previous level.

The same thing happened when I needed to adjust the filter resonance in Equinoxe. Every time I let go of the knob, it popped back to where it had been before, because Storm assumed I had recorded that knob's original position into every bar, even though I hadn't.

I wanted to add a fill at the end of bar 8, to lead into the first verse. This meant copying pattern A12 into A13 in each of my modules, and editing the A13 data. Not hard to do, but I could see I was going to have to break out the pencil and paper in order to keep track of which patterns were used where. If Storm had pattern names, I could have skipped the record-keeping.

In the end, I found that the best way to use Storm in my song was not to sequence the song in Storm (even though this particular song has, for me, an embarrassingly simple structure). Instead, I improvised in Storm at the correct tempo while recording its output as audio. I then imported the audio into my real sequencer and cut and pasted the best bits to build up an arrangement. I was extremely pleased with the extra energy these loops added to the production. Groove variations with and without echo were a snap, and the ring modulator gave me an eerie rhythmic pulse for a break.

Conclusions. If you're making any type of dance, techno, or drum 'n' bass, and if you have a reasonably fast computer, you'll love Storm. It has the tools to give your songs a ton of fresh attitude — some excellent percussion and synth sounds, automated knob moves, versatile effects, audio export/import, and more. Plus, it just looks cool on the screen.

I could come up with a fairly long list of features I'd like to see added, but this is because Storm is inspiring enough that I keep thinking of musical possibilities I want to explore. For now, I'm going to use it mainly to create audio loops (and whole sections) that I can export into a more powerful sequencing environment, as I'm not satisfied with its song recording functions. But then, when it comes to songwriting I'm an old-fashioned guy. If your music leans toward hypnotically repeating one-bar riffs, Storm's song recording may do you just fine. No matter how you slice it, the software synthesizer wars are heating up. We computer musicians are going to be busy and happy for years to come. —*JA (Nov. '00)* sually the In Use section comes toward the end of the review, but I was already in "In Use" mode within seconds of booting up Storm. Let me explain. . . .

Storm 2.0 is a virtual studio, with tone generators and effects, for Mac and PC. To start the review, I popped the distribution CD into the computer, entered a license number (provided with the CD) to get up and running, and expected to spend a while with help files and the printed manual.

But then a screen called Wizard Choice popped up. "Welcome to the Storm Composition Wizard," it said. "Choose the style of music that you want and let yourself be guided."

Hmmm . . . okay. I could choose from Hip Hop, Dance, Dub, Jazz Funk, and House. I clicked on Dub, and a series of screens showed up, each of which specified a particular step, often including comments about what I was doing. For each step, a pulsing border appeared in the area or around the control where editing was to occur. A few steps into the process, I'd already pulled up a sample for the introduction, chained together some drum, bass, and keyboard patterns, and added deep, synced delay to some sounds for that classic dub vibe.

Things got even more interesting when I added realtime control over a synth's filter cutoff and resonance. The Wizard moved the process along — and even before I opened the manual, a pretty cool reggae tune was churning away. Yes, it was a "paint by numbers" process. But it was fun, and provided a superb introduction to the elements that make up the program and the techniques involved in using them.

However, Storm isn't just about instant gratification. It's a very capable virtual studio with MIDI input, ReWire compatibility, and the ability to work as a VST instrument. Storm can also record digital audio in a few different ways — there's a lot going on underneath that colorful, somewhat whimsical interface.

Building a Studio. Storm provides a total studio environment. You can drag-and-drop up to four instruments and up to three bus effects into the Studio Builder screen's rack. When you click on a device prior to dragging it over, a short text description appears (a few are in French, as Storm comes from France — the online help is in four languages, and they get crossed a couple of times).

After creating your studio, Storm takes a few seconds to compile it and goes to the main screen. Unless specified otherwise, a demo tune using the instruments starts playing to get you in the mood. You can clear this to insert your own sounds and patterns, as well as change the rack's makeup while creating a tune.

Each rack position has a corresponding mixer level control and mute switch, as well as four send controls with automatable levels. The Dry send dumps the straight signal into the mixer's master output bus, but sends A, B, and C feed the three effects units.

Furthermore, each effect also feeds four send controls, identical to the instrument sends, although the control that could create feedback is deleted. This allows for some nifty routings. Send drums to the ring modulator, automate its center frequency and width, then send the ring mod out to a lowpass filter with cutoff/resonance automation — and automate the send feeding the filter. Want more? Send the filter output to, for example, the reverb.

Drum Time. Of the five drum machines, four have eight sounds with individual pitch and decay controls, a 16-step sequencer, 64 programmable patterns, and clear/restore pattern buttons. The main differences among these drums are the sounds (see Storm at a Glance, page 123). Each step has four velocities (click on the step to cycle through them), and you can mute individual drums. By the way, the clear/restore function is a great breakbeat technique. Hit clear to drop out for a few beats, then hit restore to have the pattern come crashing back in.

The standout drum functions are the realtime pitch/decay controls. These act on a per-note basis (if a signal has a long decay and you sweep pitch, the pitch won't change, but a new note will grab the current pitch value at the moment the sound starts). When looping, you simply grab and move until you're happy with the way it sounds — no automation recording required. If the loop repeats and you're still messing with the controls, new moves overwrite old ones.

Although you can't create patterns longer than one measure, you can record a pattern to a sequencer track (we'll cover the sequencer below), then add a different pattern in the same track, and so on, building up a longer composite pattern.

The Tsunami drumbox differs from the others by using four oscillators and four noise sources. You can program one noise source and one oscillator at a time. Controls include level, pan, and envelope parameters; noise also includes resonance, while the oscillators offer pitch. This quickly became one of my favorite drum modules, as it's perfect for getting vintage analog drum sounds.

On the downside, the drum boxes can't load new samples — the roster of sounds is fixed. But that also means you can get going immediately, and the controls add enough options to get a lot of mileage out of the sounds.

If Storm stopped here, it would be a bitchin' drum loop generator. After making the pattern(s), you can export as many measures as you want as a WAV, AIFF, or MP3 file, which of course contains the results of any automation (this doesn't just apply to drums — with Storm, if you can hear something, you can export it). Talk about lively, animated drum tracks — all those automation and control options allow for drum parts that really move and breathe.

The Kepler Module. This doesn't generate sound, but is a "key change" sequencer for any melodic modules set to react to Kepler changes. There are two steps per measure, with eight steps total; each step can be any note, major or minor. For example, if the first step is C major and the second is A minor, a module's notes — which might normally be programmed in a single key — modulate accordingly.

Back to Bassics. Arsenic is a basic TB-303-type acid bass line generator. It has a resonant filter and VCA (with automatable attack, decay, cutoff, resonance, etc.),

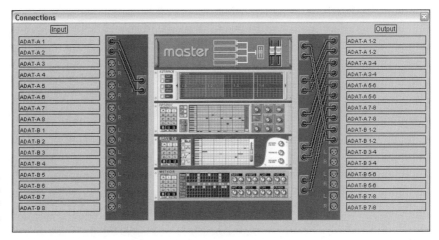

Figure 4-11.
In this screen, Storm's inputs and outputs are being conneced to a MOTU 2408 interface.

the ability to "tie" notes, octave switching, and editable velocity for each step. Like the drums, it has 16 steps and 64 patterns. It also offers sawtooth and pulse waves, each with continuously variable waveform shape control. Note that the automation with instruments, unlike drums, needs to be recorded into the sequencer or external host, as described below.

Bass 52 is a physically modeled bass module. It has fewer controls than Arsenic, but gets some wonderful, well-articulated bass sounds. A small strip along the bottom lets you edit volume and vibrato amount on a per-note basis.

Synthesizers. First, the bad news: None of the Storm synths responds to pitch-bend control. That's a major drag, but there are compensations.

Equinoxe is a 3-osc version of Arsenic with an additional decay and release control for the VCA (called Amp). It's pattern-based, allowing you to place three-note chords as desired. These can follow the Kepler module, so you don't place a minor or major third — you place a third, and the Kepler determines whether it's minor or major. This limitation doesn't exist when Equinoxe is played via MIDI, where it makes a pretty decent polysynth.

Orpheus is a polyphonic wavetable synth with 64 factory and 64 user presets (annoyingly, the user ones can't be named or exported; they're saved with the song). While pattern-based, the loop can be one to eight bars, or an indefinite length for playing along with a track. There are two multi-waveform oscillators (which can do FM), a four-mode resonant filter, two LFOs, ADSR envelopes for the filter and VCA, and an X-Y controller for sweeping through oscillator waveforms. While not as powerful as the X-Y envelopes in the Prophet-VS [*Editor's note: The Prophet-VS was a hardware synth produced by a now-defunct company called Sequential Circuits*], this feature can produce animated timbral effects. Another useful feature is an editing strip that allows step-by-step level, filter, and oscillator balance adjustment.

Shadow is a chord generator, also with 64 factory and 64 user presets. It's more sophisticated than Equinoxe, and is also a good polysynth when played via MIDI. You can create any type of chord (it's not dependent on the Kepler module, although it can be). The engine uses two oscillators, a noise source, two LFOs, and two envelope generators; there's also an X-Y controller with six pages, each of which controls a pair of synth parameters. As with Orpheus, this is the ticket to animated sounds.

Scratch. Scratch offers two virtual turntables and a crossfader, each of which can be MIDI-controlled. You drag samples onto the turntables, and use the mouse to grab a hand over the turntable. Moving the mouse vertically "scratches" the sample, while horizontal motion changes the crossfader. You can even stop the turntable so the sample starts from a specific point. This is a fun module.

Samplers. Storm can record digital audio in a couple different ways.

H3OPlus is an interesting four-track sample playback module. You can drag-and-drop samples onto these tracks, from individual drum hits to complete phrases — think "four-measure digital audio sequencer." What's more, the 64 patterns can contain different samples. This module is great for adding synced effects, creating drum kits based on samples, and so on. Furthermore, it can time-stretch imported loops so they'll match the tempo, and can base pitch transposition on the Kepler module. Just don't expect super-quality pitch stretching — it's funky.

One caution: Don't drag-and-drop over any MP3 files into H3O. Although you're supposed to be able to do this, the program crashed when I hit play.

EZtrack is a basic recording device. It listens to what's at the selected audio input (a patching window lets you connect your soundcard's various ins and outs to Storm's ins and outs) and records it — but that's not all. You can split the file, chop out pieces and drag them over to H3O, overlap audio, or chop the file to little pieces, drag them around to create an entirely new "arrangement," then drag it over to H3O.

The third way to record digital audio involves the sequencer, so let's go there.

Sequencing & Recording. The sequencer is relatively primitive. Four tracks store pattern changes for the four instruments, and a fifth track stores mix and effects changes. The tracks are calibrated with measure markers, and groups of four measures. Maximum song length is 400 measures. Neither notes nor audio is recorded in the sequencer; they're recorded in the individual instruments, either as patterns or bits of audio, and triggered by the sequencer.

There are two recording modes. In realtime mode, pattern changes are recorded in the instrument's corresponding track, while controller changes (mixer levels, FX sends, and instrument and effects parameters) go into the control track. In static mode, you select a particular sequencer region, and select a pattern or any control setting. The section will play that pattern with the selected control setting.

Even though there are only four tracks, you can easily build up more complex compositions by exporting some or all of your composition as an audio track, then bringing that into a sample player or recorder, thus freeing up the original tracks.

Except for the drum machines, whose parameter changes are stored in their respective patterns as mentioned previously, the automation control track frees automation from any pattern-related constraints. If Storm is set to loop, your fader movements will repeat with the loop. If you didn't like what you did during an iteration of the loop, just do it again — Storm will retain whatever you did for the most recent iteration. If you don't set a loop, then you can just keep tweaking away, even as the pattern repeats.

The sequencer offers a third way to record audio: a general-purpose record window where you can record any or all of the four tracks and/or the master, and specify a range over which recording will take place. It will basically record anything that appears over the tracks, whether programmed in the track or played in real time via MIDI (described next).

MIDI Control. You can tie Storm's knobs to MIDI controllers (mod wheel, footpedal, etc.) through a learn function, or just enter the channel and controller number if you already know it, and do realtime variations. Unlike automation data created from the front panel, previously recorded MIDI automation moves are overwritten only when a controller is changing — if you stop moving the wheel (or whatever), the old controller data takes over. So, if you want to redo the moves in a loop completely from scratch, it's best to use the Undo option and start over.

Also note that because all the control data is lumped into one track, you can't erase, for example, just the cutoff frequency control while leaving the decay control alone. However, these limitations become moot when using Storm as a VST device (described later).

All the instruments and drums can be played in real time via MIDI, but only Orpheus and Shadow let you record directly into the pattern window. For the other instruments, there's a workaround: Right-click on the sequencer to bring up the general-purpose recording module. Enable the track you want to record and play the part. When you stop, a "library" window opens up with the segment you've recorded. Drag what you recorded over to EZtrack or the H3O, and voilà — digital audio can be sequencer-triggered.

The Effects. These work as expected, although the automatable parameters are a big plus. The most unusual effects are the step filter sequencer, essentially a sample-and-hold filter effect where each step changes the frequency of a bandpass filter while an additional control alters resonance, and the vocoder. An instrument (*e.g.,* drums) or a voice recorded in EZtrack modulates the vocoder's onboard synthesizer, where you specify, and can choose from, eight sets of chords. An X-Y controller affects several parameter pairs. It's not a showstopper, but it's fun.

In Use. I decided to set up Storm as a VST instrument (using Arsenic, Orpheus, Puma, and Scratch) with Cubase SX, but had no luck. Then I tried it with Sonar using Fxpansion's VST-DX adapter: same results. It turned out Storm defaults to being a ReWire mixer when launched. I unchecked the preference, and it was ready to rock with both apps.

Storm automatically grabbed five Sonar audio channels — one for each instrument and one for the master out. But turning up both the instrument outs and the master caused comb filtering. [*Editor's note: Comb filtering is a hollow sound quality caused by mixing a signal with a slightly delayed version of the same signal.*] I got the best results using the individual instruments, but then there were no effects. However, when I turned down the synth's dry send, the master carried the effects only, which I could mix in with the instruments, *sans* comb filtering.

The host automatically created a MIDI track for driving Storm, so I selected Arsenic as a MIDI out and played a part in real time. Latency was negligible, and it played back as expected. I set up a pattern in Puma and let that run, although I could have played the drum sounds from the keyboard.

I recorded MIDI data into the Orpheus track, then wanted to add some X-Y waveform animation. Even when Storm was running as a VST instrument, two "learn" menus came up — I twiddled two controllers, and was good to go. Storm can of course play back the host's recorded note and controller data, but the audio can also be bounced to a hard disk track, as with any normal instrument. However, you can't record Storm knob motions directly into the VST host — they need to go in the Storm automation track.

I then decided to try ReWire, which works best when you have a tune already recorded in Storm and want to mix it in with some other music tracks running in the host, as recording data in the host's MIDI tracks doesn't trigger the program in this mode. I thought perhaps this was a function of using the wrapper with Sonar, but ReWiring Storm into Cubase SX produced no corresponding MIDI outs, thus indicating Storm is a ReWire 1 app, not ReWire 2.

Storm is processor-hungry, but the fact that you can access the various softsynths in a DAW program is cool indeed.

The Hall. I don't use my music computer for net surfing, but I did check out the Hall. This is Arturia's version of Napster, where users can share files and samples. They can also chat, check out tips, download new modules as they appear, and check on the latest Storm-related news. There wasn't much activity when I checked in, but the Hall has the potential to be a decent community as more people get up and running with Storm.

Storm in a Virtual Studio World. There's stiff competition for Storm, such as Reason, Fruityloops, and Orion. Fortunately, all have demos available, so you can do a leisurely comparison to see what works for you.

Reason is the most sophisticated in terms of sounds, patching, mixing, and sequencing, as befits its price. But it can't record audio, host plug-ins or soft synths, insert tempo changes in the sequencer, or serve as a VST instrument — although the ReWire 2 implementation is superb. Orion and Fruityloops are highly credible and cost-effective soft studios, even though their sequencing capabilities pale next to Reason's.

Price-wise, Storm competes directly with Orion and Fruityloops. Storm's biggest point of differentiation is that it can appeal to hobbyists who know virtually nothing about music and want instant musical gratification, but thanks to its VST (and ReWire) capabilities, Storm is viable for professional applications as well. If you're using Storm as a VST device with a host sequencer, do the math: 12 instruments + 10 effects = $4.50 per plug-in. (I don't include EZtrack, because your host will have more sophisticated recording capabilities.) What's more, the lack of pitchbend notwithstanding, Storm's synths and drum machines offer some options (such as X-Y controllers and the Scratch module) not found elsewhere.

When I started working with Storm, I thought it was ideal for the musically challenged. By the time I finished this review, I was sold on Storm as a fun instrument rack to go along with my DAW software . . . and I still use the "instant gratification" aspect to throw together quickie loops. At $99, you can't help but get your money's worth — this program is one of the best bangs for the buck in software-land.
—*Craig Anderton (Dec. '02)*

Image-Line Fruityloops
PATTERN SEQUENCING WITH
AUTOMATION AND PLUG-IN HOSTING

stand-alone (Win)
$149 boxed (incl. samples), $99 online

Pros: Cost-effective. Imaginative approach to music creation. Accepts VST and DX instruments and plug-ins. Comes bundled with a ton o' stuff, including synths and a sample library. Nifty onboard effects. Painless automation. Renders to WAV or MP3. Allows external MIDI control. High fun factor.
Cons: Only one level of undo, and not all operations can be undone. Insufficient explanations of some of the more esoteric features. Automation for non-Fruity VST instruments is hit-or-miss. Stereo outs only.

Maybe it was the name that put me off — I mean, "Fruityloops"?? Come on. But when I got around to trying out this program, I was very pleasantly surprised. It's deeper and more powerful than any $99 program has a right to be. Craig Anderton's May 2002 review in *Keyboard* covers version 3.4; new features in 3.5 include the ability to run Fruityloops as a VSTi inside a host application, a speech engine that can output robotic-sounding text phrases, more flexible quantizing options in the piano-roll editor, a new drum synth, the ability to copy and paste automation data, variable envelope segment slopes, step recording, new plug-ins, and much more. The aggressive manner in which Image-Line continues to add features to Fruityloops is impressive.

Fruityloops is huge in Europe, where it has provided an instrumental foundation for many dance-oriented tracks. It started out as shareware, but has since moved into the commercial domain, and is now distributed in the U.S. by Cakewalk.

Fruityloops is a loop/groove sequencer. It starts with drum machine–style programming, but there's a lot more to it than that. After creating a looped pattern with multiple tracks, using either the Roland drum machine–style step sequencer or a piano-roll view, you can string patterns together to create a song. You can render patterns and songs as WAV or MP3 files, or export the MIDI data driving the sounds as Standard MIDI Files. Track sounds can come from samples (WAV, SimSynth, or DrumSynth files) or "generators" — basically, software synths included with Fruityloops, or VSTi/DXi instruments. The program also supports plug-in effects (DX, VST, or Fruity proprietary format), and allows realtime MIDI controller input for parameter tweaking.

Although it's inexpensive and the manual seems aimed at entry-level users, this program has an awe-inspiring amount of power. It supports ASIO and

Figure 4-12.
Normally you wouldn't have all these windows open at once while working in Fruityloops — but this screenshot should give an impression of the amount of power the program offers. The grid of buttons at upper left is the heart of Fruityloops. This is where you create patterns using the instruments listed in the left column. For more control over how a pattern sounds, you can open the piano-roll editor (upper center). Almost anything that can be automated — which is a lot — can also be event-edited for pinpoint control over things like filter sweeps; the event editor window is at lower right. All the toolbars across the top — pattern selectors, transport, etc. — are dockable and movable. The TS404 (center right) is one of many included softsynths; it specializes in bass lines. The DX10, an FM synth, is one of Fruityloops' demo synths (center left). You can add effects to channels with the effects tracks (the almost entirely obscured window in the lower center). Fruityloops is loaded with plug-in effects, including a very capable flanger (lower right, overlapping the effects track window). The PanOMatic (lower center) is a volume/pan X/Y panner.

Fruityloops at a Glance

System requirements	Windows 95/98/Me/2000, Pentium 200MHz processor, 32MB RAM, 800 X 600 video display, ASIO or DirectSound-compatible audio hardware
Import formats	WAV, SYN, MID, RBS (ReBirth), ZIP (zipped Fruity file and samples), ZGR (BeatSlicer), and DrumSynth, XI (FastTracker Extended Instrument)
Export formats	16- or 32-bit WAV, Cool Edit 32-bit WAV, Acidized WAV, MP3, MID, ZIP (contains Fruity file and samples)
Effects plug-in formats	VST, VST 2, DX, Fruity
Instrument plug-in format	VSTi, DXi, Fruity
Supported audio resolution	16-bit, 44.1kHz stereo
Internal resolution	32-bit floating-point
Effects	7-Band Graphic EQ, Balance, Bass Boost, Overdrive, Center, Compressor, two delays, Fast LP, SV Filter, Flanger, Freq Filter, Mute, PanOMatic, Multi-Band Parametric EQ, Phase Inverter, Phaser, Reverb, Scratcher, Stereo Enhancer
Utility plug-ins	Big Clock, dB Meter, Formula Controller, HTML Notebook, LSD GM/GS synth, Notepad, Peak Controller, Send, Spectroman, X/Y Controller
Included softsynths	TS404, 3xOsc, BeepMap, Plucked, Granulizer, LSD General MIDI synth
Included demo synths	SimSynth, Wasp, SoundFont Player, DX10
Automation	for Fruity effects and instruments, as well as most program parameters
Synchronization	transmits MIDI clock
Copy protection	yes
Downloadable demo	yes

DirectSound, uses 32-bit floating-point internal resolution, and sounds great. It may seem like a toy, but the deeper you dig, the more gold you strike.

Installation. No online authorization or other weirdness: Just insert the CD, enter the serial number, then dive in. The program requires 73MB of hard disk space; adding in samples and other goodies ends up taking about 260MB.

In the list of audio output drivers, everything was marked as "emulated" except for the Primary Sound Driver, my GuitarPort USB interface, and ASIO. ASIO and the GuitarPort gave latencies around 11ms; don't even bother using emulated interfaces, whose latency is measured in hours (just kidding, but they are pretty much unusable).

Overview. Fruityloops' multitrack step sequencer has the usual 16 buttons per track, and each button represents a sixteenth-note. [*Editor's note: Sixteen steps are the default, but for a given song you can set the pattern length to more steps, or fewer.*]

Okay, you've seen that before — but you haven't seen the way this program edits. For each track, you can call up a programming window with 16 slider-like vertical graphic controllers and pages for pan, volume, filter cutoff, filter resonance, pitch, and shift (delays the note). It's quite something to be able to apply a change to each sixteenth-note rather than operating globally on the track — the interface for this is quite clever, and the variations you can add to loops make them far more interesting.

You can also call up a window that shows a little keyboard for each button. This allows the pitch of notes to be set easily for samples such as bass parts. (You can also play this in from a MIDI keyboard, or use the QWERTY keyboard to play notes.)

Channel editing options depend on what's loaded in the track. For samples, a channel settings dialog box processes the samples themselves with four additional edit pages. They're easy to access and view: You just move a scrollbar to switch from page to page.

In addition to the usual volume and pan, adjustable sample parameters include distortion (it's tasty, too!), reverb, pseudo-ring modulation, sample pitch (changes the duration), attack, decay, gain, stereo delay, filter cutoff, filter resonance, volume and pan, reverse, stretch (lengthens the sound while adding a metallic effect), and DC offset adjust. Many of these changes are reflected in a cool-looking waveform view. Another page provides echo, a great little arpeggiator, note gate time, and keyboard tracking (assignable to pan, filter cutoff, and filter resonance).

Editing a track containing an instrument brings up the instrument's front panel, where you can tweak knobs, move switches, etc. It gets even more interesting when you automate the controls, which we'll get to below.

In addition to generators and samples, you can load a channel with a "layer." This doesn't make sounds, but instead acts as a master controller for tracks designated as its "children." Notes, automation changes, and so on in the layer channel affect all the children, thus allowing layered effects. If you lay down a part and after a while want to layer it with others, no problem: Copy the part in the piano roll, then paste it in the layer's piano roll. And speaking of the piano roll. . . .

Piano-Roll Editing. Fruity's piano-roll editing is like the editors in a zillion other programs, but with a few twists. You use mouse tools to draw, erase, move, copy, extend, and transpose notes in the main section of the window, and edit controllers (velocity, filter cutoff, filter resonance, pan, and pitch) in a lower control strip. Unlike other programs, Fruityloops lets you drop chords, not just single notes, into the piano roll from a menu of 64 chord types.

A (pitch) slide function places notes to which other notes slide, and as you can have four different, color-coded slide groups, slides can go in four different directions for four different notes. Finally, for controllers, you can draw lines or curves under which the controller values fit. The approach reminds me very much of Master Tracks Pro, probably the easiest-to-use sequencer ever invented.

The Generators. Quite a few soundmakers are tucked away in the program:

■ TS404 is a bassline-style synth for TB-303-type techno sounds.

■ 3xOsc gives you three oscillators, which can then be processed with a resonant filter and envelopes exactly as the sampled sounds are.

■ BeepMap loads images (BMP, JPG, etc.) and converts them into sounds. Fun stuff.

■ Plucked, a sound generator based on the Karplus-Strong plucked-string algorithm, has only two controls, decay and color (although as with other instruments, there's an additional page for echo and arpeggiation effects). But it's one of my favorites, as the sound is very useful for adding melodic and percussive accents.

■ Fruity Granulizer compresses and stretches waves, and produces generally fun and bizarre sounds.

■ Fruity Vibrator does, well, something if you have a Microsoft force feedback device. I don't, so I couldn't test this out. Perhaps it has something to do with erogenous zones.

The following "save-disabled" demo versions (any channels using these are deleted when you save) are supplied. You can purchase full versions at www.fruityloops.com; prices are shown in parentheses.

■ SimSynth ($35) is an "analog" synth with three multi-waveform oscillators, state-variable filter, LFO, and ADSR envelopes for filter and VCA.

■ Wasp ($29) is another analog synth with three oscillators, dual LFOs, VCF/VCA ADSR envelopes, ring modulator, FM, and distortion.

■ SoundFont Player ($35), based on the LiveSynth engine, loads SoundFont files into Fruityloops.

■ DX10 ($19) is a cool-sounding, basic FM synth.

User Interface. You can't discuss Fruityloops without touching on the interface. Graphic changes are snappy; the default color scheme uses shading and embossing effects, with muted gray, to create a very neutral — yet inviting — environment. The orange LEDs don't just light, they glow; colors fade instead of switching off; and the oscilloscope-type waveform displays are right out of a '50s science fiction movie.

One great UI feature is an unconventional use of scrollbars. If you right-click on a scrollbar in a window that has horizontal and vertical scrollbars, the mouse acts almost like a joystick, controlling both axes by moving left/right, up/down, or both simultaneously. Why Microsoft hasn't ripped off this feature to use in spreadsheet programs remains one of the world's unsolved mysteries.

MIDI. It takes MIDI in. It sends MIDI out. It can transmit MIDI clock, but not sync to incoming clock. The real news is that it supports parameter control via MIDI, so you can take something like a Peavey PC1600 or KeyFax Phat Boy and do real, hands-on tweaking. This isn't a new concept, of course, but it's great to have it included in Fruityloops. [*Editor's note: In fact, Fruityloops supports processing of controller* *data on input. You can even design complex equations that process three MIDI controller values at once. A knowledge of trigonometry may not be essential to getting meaningful results, but it wouldn't hurt to know what a sine function will do. It also wouldn't hurt to know that Fruityloops "normalizes" all of the incoming MIDI controller data to a 0-1 range.*]

Effects. Fruityloops is loaded with effects, but setting them up is somewhat nonstandard. There are 16 effects "tracks" (a better term would be channels), which can hold up to eight effects each. To process a channel, you assign it to one of effects tracks (more than one channel can feed a track). An additional master effects track processes the entire audio output.

There are also four effects send tracks, but again, these work differently from the norm. You set up effects in the send tracks; these are driven by the effect track outs via four send controls. For example, suppose one effects track has compression, and another distortion. If you insert reverb into effects send track 1, you can then use the send controls in the effects tracks to add, say, lots of reverb to the one with compression, and a little reverb to the one with distortion. This is actually easier to do than it sounds. According to the online help, you can't assign channels directly to the send tracks, but there is a way: Assign a channel to an effects track, but don't load any effects. Then use the send controls to feed the desired send effects.

Here's a partial list of the more interesting effects:

■ Bass Boost has frequency and amount controls.

■ Blood Overdrive includes filtering options to yield smooth, non-spiky distortion.

■ Delay offers inverted stereo, pingpong, and a lowpass filter.

■ Delay 2 is similar, but with a different interface and subtly different controls.

■ Fast LP is a lowpass filter made to be tweaked in real time.

■ Filter is a state-variable type (LP, HP, BP, notch) designed for realtime tweaking.

■ Flanger has ten parameters, including phase adjustments, feedback, and the like.

■ Mute records mutes into sequences.

■ PanOMatic is an X/Y controller (pan/volume) so you can do pseudo-surround panning effects — make the sound softer when centered so it seems it's coming from behind you, for example.

■ Parametric EQ has 5 fully parametric stages and high and low shelf.

■ 7 Band EQ offers low shelf, high shelf, and five fixed-frequency bandpass filters.

■ Reeverb [*sic*] has eight parameters, including room size, diffusion, color, and so on.

■ Scratcher loads a file, which you can then "scratch" with the virtual turntable. You can also play the file, and there's even start-up time, like a moderate-torque turntable . . . way cool, way fun.

■ Stereo Enhancer is phase-based, so I tend to avoid these sorts of things.

There are several plug-in "effects" that I'd consider more as utilities:

■ Big Clock gives a big bar/beat/tick and min/sec/100ths of a second readout.

■ dB meter is a stereo meter (−36 to +6dB).

■ HTML Notebook reads HTML files, and you can use it to browse online documents. You can't edit the files, though.

■ LSD is a Roland GM/GS software synthesizer with 16 MIDI instruments. So why isn't it a generator? Who knows? In any case, you plug it into an effects channel and send it MIDI data from a track.

■ Notebook has 100 completely editable pages, and can switch pages automatically while your song plays.

■ Peak Controller is like an envelope generator on steroids; it can map envelopes and more to various knobs and sliders.

■ Send allows picking off the send signal from anywhere within an effects track.

■ X/Y controller lets you link two knobs to its control surface and control both with a single mouse movement.

Fruityloops includes a demo version of BeatSlicer (full version $35), which provides a function similar to that of ReCycle — it chops up files into slices and places these on consecutive tracks. Thus, you can speed up or slow down tempo without affecting pitch. The astute among you might wonder how, with its sixteenth-note quantization, Fruityloops can accurately reproduce grooved nuances. Well, the program automatically uses the time shift edit function to move slice start points as needed — a clever workaround.

Automation. Most of the Fruity effect and instrument parameters can be automated. Finding out whether a control is automatable is simple: Move the mouse over it, and icons show up in the info bar that indicate either automation, MIDI remote control compatibility, or both.

The automation on the Fruity effects plug-ins worked like a champ. I didn't have any other VST 2.0 plug-ins handy to test in Fruityloops, but as the Fruityloops ones are VST 2.0–based, it's a good bet those from other manufacturers will work too. One of the "thank you very much!" aspects of the automation is that there's a separate event editor for automation — just right-click on a knob, and a screen shows up where you can edit existing data, or draw in new data.

Automation for Fruity-based instruments worked smoothly. VST and DXi instruments, however (even the DreamStation), use a wrapper to work with the program, and their automation functions aren't necessarily supported. There have been reports from other users of successful automation with certain VST instruments, but none of the ones I have worked.

However, there's an easy workaround: a MIDI control generator that provides MIDI control signals. Match the control generator's port to the DXi or VSTi instrument, and you can record MIDI data to automate the instruments. The control generator can also drive outboard instruments via MIDI; several presets are included for popular plug-ins, like the Native Instruments Pro-52 and Steinberg Model-E, as well as hardware synths like the E-mu Orbit, Korg Z1, Nord Lead 2, and Line 6 Pod 2 processor. As with other MIDI data, you can edit controller data in a graphic edit window.

The Playlist. The song playlist operates graphically — somewhat like "painting" parts into tracks in Acid. This is especially true for single-bar patterns, because each playlist step represents a bar. With patterns that last longer than a bar (as created, for example, with the piano roll), you need to place a dot on the first bar, then leave spaces for the remaining pattern bars; otherwise, the pattern will retrigger every time it sees a dot. As many patterns as your CPU can churn out will play simultaneously, so if you program simple parts (just bass, just drums, etc.), you can treat the playlist section more like a multitrack editor.

The playlist supports cut/copy/paste editing, insert/clone/delete patterns, and looping, either by selecting a number of rows or by moving a loop point indicator to set the loop beginning (unless specified otherwise, the loop end is always where the patterns end). Looping can change in real time without missing a beat, thus opening up live performance possibilities.

Import/Export. Fruityloops supports several formats. The native Fruityloops song file format doesn't incorporate samples or DrumSynth/SimSynth patches, but a zipped file option saves everything as one compressed file, using the *de facto* Windows standard ZIP data compression format. It can also open zipped Fruity files without a separate unzipping program.

When you're saving to WAV or MP3, there are a lot of options. Several relate to a tradeoff between sound quality and rendering time, but with today's fast processors the high-quality modes are worth the added time. There's also dithering to 16-bit files, 32-bit WAV export in Fruity or Cool Edit format, various MP3 rates, mono (for file size reduction), and saving in Acidized WAV format, which allows the loops you create to be loaded into Sonic Foundry Acid and Cakewalk Sonar for time-stretching. (Just to be clear, Fruityloops itself doesn't time-stretch sampled loops.)

In Use. One of the things I like to do is create loops, so the whole review process quickly turned into one big "in use" episode. Whenever I came up with something cool, I'd save it to disk.

When it's time to create some loops, I generally open up the program, which defaults to four tracks: kick, claps, closed hi-hat, and snare. I create a nice little groove, then start editing the steps for pitch, filter, etc. to add some interest — I don't want to go nuts from listening to it over and over again while I add other parts.

Next up come some instruments. I use Plucked a lot, but the TS404 bass line is important as well. Usually by this point, I want to import some different drum samples that go better with the new direction the loop is taking, then I start adding echo, distortion, reverb, and other effects from the instrument editing pages.

Frankly, it's just about impossible to make bad sounds with Fruityloops (unless of course you want bad sounds). This is not because Fruityloops limits your possibilities to things it considers "good," but because there are just so many cool options it's hard to go wrong. Just one twist of a knob can take a groove in an entirely different direction, and if you've taken the time to set up a MIDI control surface (talk about decadence — I use the MIDI layer from my Panasonic DA7 digital mixer) it's great to be able to tweak parameters in real time while you're recording them.

Conclusions. We haven't even gotten into the humanize and randomize functions, the Project Bones export function, the online community aspects — but if I'm not careful, this review could go on forever. By that time version 3.6 would come out, and I'd have to start all over again.

I had worked with an earlier version of the program over in Europe with some DJs and musicians, and back in those days it was more like a glorified drum machine. After a quick look through the manual for 3.4, I thought, "Piece of cake — it's grown into a nice little groove-generating program." But the manual covers about 5% of what Fruityloops is all about; getting intimate with the help file is really the only way to understand the rich feature set, and even then some of the descriptions are somewhat sketchy. You'll have to experiment with the parameters and see what happens.

The obvious comparison is to programs like Reason and Storm, both of which use the virtual studio concept. The biggest difference compared to Reason is that Reason is a closed system, whereas Fruityloops allows you to load plug-ins and VST and DXi instruments and effects, thus increasing the sonic palette considerably. While Fruityloops seems to cost considerably less than Reason, if you buy full versions of the softsynths, you need to tack on about $120 to the base price. Fruityloops still has a price advantage, but the extras narrow the margin.

It may sound like a copout to say you should download the demos to see which one you like best, but that's really the only option. These types of programs all take very different approaches. Reason is a more streamlined, focused experience. Fruityloops is more like a modular synth: You bring together a disconnected group of options into one big virtual studio. I'd place Storm somewhere in between. Fruityloops does show a bit of "add-on-itis," where you realize that a feature was tacked on to an existing structure, and had it been there from day 1, it might have been implemented a bit more elegantly. But that's a very minor complaint, especially because Fruityloops has a high mad scientist factor, the graphic look is inviting, and the sound quality is spot-on.

Frankly, Fruityloops 3.4 was a major, and very pleasant, surprise. I think the folks at *Keyboard* thought they were doing me a favor this month by assigning me a "simple" groove-generating program. Dozens of hours later, all I can say is — this thing rocks. It has more twists and turns than a spy novel, and it's fun, sophisticated, deep, open-ended, and addictive. I suspect it's going to exercise my hard drive a lot in the months ahead. Come to think of it, it already has. —*Craig Anderton (May '02)*

Sample Players

One of the stops on medieval pipe organs was called *vox humana* ("human voice"). Ever since then, it seems, keyboard players have been avidly trying to sound like anything but keyboard players. There may be several reasons for this. For one thing, the keyboard itself is not a very responsive performance interface compared to a violin, saxophone, electric guitar, or human voice. It's a row of damn levers, is what it is. So having a keyboard that sounds like itself (whatever "itself" happens to sound like) is not always an attractive proposition.

On a practical level, the keyboardist is called on to substitute for all sorts of instruments that don't happen to be available at the moment. In the 19th century, piano reductions of well-known symphonic works were widely used in drawing rooms across Europe and North America. The phonograph and the radio hadn't yet been invented, so if you wanted to hear Beethoven's *Fifth* (which God forbid — it's a second-rate piece, far inferior to the *Third, Fourth, Sixth,* and *Seventh*), you were probably going to hear it played on a piano. Fast-forwarding to the present day, keyboardists in clubs around the world are called on to fill in for string sections, brass sections, backup singers, bass players, almost anything you can name.

So maybe the the rise of digital sampling was inevitable. In a sample-based instrument (generally referred to as a sampler, though the term is not always accurate, as explained below),

WHAT'S A SAMPLE?

Just to make life a little more interesting, the word "sample," when used as a noun, has two entirely distinct but closely related meanings. In the sense used throughout this chapter, a sample is a digital recording of a complete sound. (At least, it's "complete" in the sense that it lasts for some period of time. The start or end of the original sound might not be included in the sample.)

The word "sample" is also used to refer to a single numerical value within the longer sample. It's preferable to use the term "sample word" in this case, as in, "A one-second monaural sample with a sampling rate of 44.1kHz contains 44,100 sample words." But writers are not always this fussy. In a discussion of clipping distortion, for instance, which is caused when a digital audio data stream is overloaded, you'll sometimes see a sentence like this: "In this one-second sample, 37 samples clipped." Here, the two usages of the word "sample" are used back to back.

one or more digital recordings are laid out across the keyboard, ready to play. The recordings will be magically transposed up or down in half-steps, depending on what MIDI note number the sampler receives. A keyboardist equipped with a sampler can, at the press of a button or two, sound like anything from an obscure tribal instrument like the didgeridoo to a full kit of stadium-rock drums or the London Philharmonic. The sampler doesn't simply imitate those other instruments, you understand — it plays actual recordings of them.

It would be a gross exaggeration, however, to say that the sampler *becomes* another instrument. As noted earlier, the keyboard is a row of levers. It doesn't respond to changes in embouchure (the shape and pressure of the lips) the way a trumpet does. It doesn't respond to bowing techniques the way a violin does. This is the Achilles' heel — or, if we're honest, the Achilles' heel, ankle, calf, knee, thigh, and hip — of sampling technology: A digital sample of an instrument just about can't respond to performance techniques the way the original instrument did. A sample is pretty much cast in concrete. It sounds like whatever it sounds like, and there's not a whole lot the sampler or the person using the sampler can do about that.

Before we go on to talk about how samplers work, let's clear up a question or two of nomenclature: Loosely speaking, the instruments discussed in this chapter are samplers. But the chapter is called "Sample Players." Technically (at least in my mind, and I'm the one writing the book), a sampler is a musical instrument that can sample. That is, it can record new audio arriving from the outside world and then play back what it has recorded. All hardware samplers can perform this trick — yet none of the software "samplers" can do so. This is because they're designed to operate as part of a computer music system in which some other component does the actual recording.

You'll also run into a lot of hardware synthesizers that use samples to make their sounds, but can't load new samples at all. The manufacturer will provide a set of samples that they hope will be useful; these will be stored in ROM. The instrument has no RAM for adding extra samples, though it may have some facility for adding more ROM samples (which you'll have to buy from the hardware manufacturer). The horrible neologism I've seen used for these instruments is "ROMplers." I'd prefer to call them sample-playback instruments, but trying to make a clear distinction between sample players and sample-playback instruments would be enough to give Merriam-Webster a headache. So let's call them ROMplers.

A few of the instruments in this book, such as Steinberg The Grand and the GMedia M-Tron (see Chapter 2) are ROMplers. Sort of. Technically, their sounds live in RAM rather than ROM, so maybe they're RAM ROMplers, or RAMplers. (There's probably a Tom Lehrer song in there somewhere, but I'm not going to touch it.) The Big Fish Audio PlugSound instruments and Spectrasonics' more expensive Stylus, Atmosphere, and Trilogy (none of which is reviewed in these pages simply because they're too new) are also RAMplers. When you buy a PlugSound or Spectrasonics instrument, you get a whole CD's worth of high-quality samples (at least, the manufacturer hopes you'll feel they're high-quality) and a software playback engine — but you can't load new samples into the engine.

I've worked a little with Stylus — enough to be able to report that its main strengths are a superlative library of sampled beats and the ability to time-stretch the beats seamlessly. Its synthesizer features are fairly rudimentary, though superior to those in IK Multimedia SampleTank (see below).

Bitshift Audio's pHATmatik Pro is musically similar to Stylus: It lets you time-stretch loops without degrading the sound. But functionally the two programs are polar opposites. Stylus comes with its own massive library of loops, and you can't add your own or move the split points around. pHATmatik isn't a RAMpler at all: It lets you import your own loops and then slice them apart, very much in the manner of Propellerhead ReCycle. You're in charge of where the slice points go, which makes it pretty easy to fix little glitches. With both programs you can shuffle the MIDI data around in your sequencer, altering the beat to taste. pHATmatik (www.bitshiftaudio.com) is a Mac/Windows-compatible VST instrument.

The Edirol division of Roland sells affordable RAMplers, including HyperCanvas and Super Quartet, but they're not covered in this book either — again, not for any reason having to do with their quality, but simply because I didn't have a review that could be included. Nor will you find a profile of Creamware Volkszämpler. Unlike most Creamware softsynths, which run within the computer on the Creamware Pulsar PCI board, Volkszämpler runs on the host CPU like the other instruments in this book. I've been told, however, that Creamware is considering whether to discontinue it.

Seer Systems Reality was one of the first software-based sample players. It also includes FM synthesis and several types of physical modeling. Reality's little brother, SurReal, uses the same technology, but plays only preset sounds. Since Reality was reviewed in *Keyboard* at such an early stage in the evolution of software synthesis, the review is seriously out of date, and I didn't feel it would be useful to include it in these pages. I've learned, however, that Reality is slated for a major overhaul, which will roll out in the spring of 2003. Keep an eye out for it. I'm told Seer Systems has licensed an acoustic instrument synthesis algorithm called SuperConductor, which is so powerful it won't run in real time: The output has to be rendered to the hard drive. It's only a matter of time, though, before computers get fast enough. . . .

Multisampling

An important technique used to get around the inherent musical rigidity of samples is *velocity layering* (also called *velocity cross-switching*). Since the only thing you can do with a MIDI key is hit it harder or softer, most samplers allow you to assign multiple samples to the same key, and to switch or crossfade among them depending on how hard the key is hit. For instance, a sound developer might record a xylophone mallet striking the xylophone at six different speeds, from a light tap to a healthy smack, and map these samples to MIDI velocity values so that they're triggered by MIDI notes in velocity ranges 1–32, 33–51, 52–70, 71–89, 90–108, and 109–127.

A sampled xylophone preset set up in this way can sound much more realistic than a preset that uses the same xylophone sample for all MIDI velocities and only makes it louder or softer in response to the velocity of the MIDI note-on message. How well velocity layering works, however, depends entirely on how well matched the various samples are. Bad velocity layering can easily make a sample-based instrument, if not technically unplayable, at least impossible to control from the keyboard.

Samplers can perform various other tricks to make the illusion that we're hearing some other instrument more convincing. Here's a basic concept: Very few instruments sound the same throughout their range. A low note on a bassoon, for instance, sounds rich and gutty. A high note on the same bassoon sounds thin and piercing. In creating a bassoon preset for a sampler, then, we'll want to record a number of samples of the bassoon playing single notes at different pitches, and then assign these samples to various ranges of the keyboard. This technique is called *multisampling,* and the layout of samples across the keyboard is sometimes called a *keymap* or a *multisample* (see **Figure 5-1**).

Another reason for multisampling is because samples tend not to sound very realistic when they're transposed up or down over too great a pitch range. That was how Alvin & The Chipmunks (a novelty pop group of the 1950s) produced their nutty little chipmunk voices — by singing a song in one key while recording it, and then speeding up the playback so that the voices were an octave or so higher than they started out. The tweezy quality heard in a sample that has been transposed up too far is called *munchkinization* (after the diminutive Munchkins in *The Wizard of Oz*) or "the chipmunk effect." Conversely, if a sample is transposed down too far, it starts to sound sludgy and floppy. This is sometimes called "the Darth Vader effect" after the improbably deep voice of the *Star Wars* villain.

Different types of sounds can be transposed by different amounts before they start to sound bad. A bass synthesizer sound can sometimes be transposed by as much as an octave and still be perfectly usable. As a rule of thumb, though, if you're designing a sampler preset, it's probably not a good idea to transpose a sound up or down more than three or four half-steps. Many sound developers prefer to use two samples for each octave (that is, a new sample every augmented fourth) in the central range of the instrument.

Why not record a fresh sample for every key, and avoid entirely the undesirable sonic changes caused by transposition? Good question — glad you asked. In a high-

Figure 5-1.
This multisample layout, created in Native Instruments Kontakt, uses both keyboard zones and velocity layers. Each sample occupies one of the rectangles. The keyboard across the bottom of the screen shows what MIDI note (or notes) will trigger each sample, and velocities are mapped on the Y axis, with low velocities at the bottom and high velocities at the top. The three-way velocity layer at left is not doing simple cross-switching; instead, the samples are programmed to crossfade depending on velocity. The overlapping crossfade zones are lighter in color.

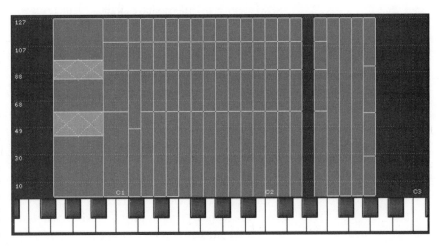

end sound library, you may find presets designed in exactly this way. The tradeoff is, the more samples are included in a preset, the more memory the preset will take up. In the first generation of hardware samplers (the E-mu Emulator, Ensoniq Mirage, and so on), it simply wasn't practical to design a preset using a different sample on each key, because memory was prohibitively expensive. These instruments averaged 64K (that's kilobytes, not megabytes) of memory. Today, with a software sampler running on a computer with 512MB of RAM, allocating a couple of hundred megabytes to the sampler's memory is not unreasonable at all — and you can pack a lot of samples into 200MB.

But musicians' need for more (and longer) samples is insatiable. With just about any modern sampler, for instance, we can combine multisampling and velocity layering in a single preset. Let's say we sample a dozen different bassoon notes, each of them five seconds long, at four different loudness levels each. We then set up the sampler so that it responds to the MIDI note number and MIDI velocity by playing back the appropriate sample from our multi-layered multisample. At this point (he mumbles, scratches his head, and then whips out a pocket calculator) we'll have 48 bassoon notes times 5 seconds, times 44.1kHz, times 2 bytes per sample word if it's a 16-bit sample, which makes a little over 21MB. That's not too bad. Assuming the bassoon player was able to produce a decent tone, and assuming the person creating the sampler preset (known as a sound designer) has done a decent job, a 21MB bassoon preset should sound reasonable and be playable.

Or maybe not. Most instruments can be played, you see, using many different performance techniques (sometimes called articulations). Short, sharp staccato notes don't necessarily sound the same as long, smooth legato notes, so recording a legato note and then shortening it in the sampler isn't likely to fool a critical listener. This is why the sound libraries for samplers often include presets with various performance techniques. Trying to load a dozen different bassoon multisamples into

RAM at once, in order to have all the articulations you may need at your fingertips, will take up just purely oodles and scads of memory.

Looping

In early samplers, the limited memory was stretched further using a technique called *looping*. Even though memory is less of an issue today than formerly, looping is such a fundamental aspect of sampler technology that I'm going to take a couple of paragraphs to explain it. That way, when you acquire your first software sample and open up the loop edit window, you'll have a better idea what you're looking at. Also, you may have heard about loops, as they've become nearly universal in pop music.

Let's go back to our bassoon preset. We recorded the bassoonist playing notes that were five seconds long. But what if the musician using the sampler happens to need a seven-second bassoon note? The way to stretch the sample is to take a section in the middle of it and play that section over and over and over and over and over, for as long as the MIDI key is held down. That's looping. Now our bassoonist can hold a note for half an hour, if we need her to. Good luck doing that with a real bassoon.

When instrument sounds are looped in this way, the loop generally starts *after* the first portion of the sample. This is because the tone quality of an instrument changes rapidly during the first few milliseconds after the player starts making the tone. These changes are called the *attack transients* of the note. If we snip off the attack transients and just listen to the loop, a looped instrument sample will sound pretty lifeless and artificial. But we don't want to include the attack transients themselves in the loop. If we do, we'll hear the bassoonist stuttering like a machine gun. The portion of the sound that's looped should be as smooth as possible.

In early samplers, the whole sample of a bassoon note might have been no more than 250 milliseconds (that's 1/4 second) long, including the loop. With more memory at our disposal, we have plenty of room for a long attack portion and a long loop. Long loops tend to sound smoother and more musical, for reasons that would take too long to explain.

In the case of a bassoon, looping works pretty well. But what if we want to sample a piano? The sound of a piano may seem simple, but in fact the tone of a piano note evolves constantly in a slow, smooth way as the note decays to silence. Looped piano notes tend not to sound very realistic, for that precise reason. Ideally, we'd like to sample the *entire* piano note and play it back from our sampler. Each sample will need to be 20 seconds long, or even longer in the bass register. Multiply 20-second samples by 88 keys by several velocity levels by stereo 24-bit recording, and all of a sudden we're talking about needing a couple of *gigabytes* of RAM. My computer doesn't have that much, and I'll bet yours doesn't either.

Oh, did I mention samples have to be loaded into RAM to be played? That's how samplers have traditionally worked. But a few years ago, a company called NemeSys introduced a software sampler called GigaSampler (now owned by Tascam and called

GigaStudio). GigaSampler did something revolutionary: It streamed long samples off the hard disk. For the first time, a grand piano in which each note was sampled at full length, with no looping, became a reality.

If you know anything about how audio is played from a hard drive — not a subject covered in this book — you'll be able to guess that the actual picture is a little more complicated than what I've just described. The first portion of each piano sample is held in RAM, just as in an ordinary sampler. That way, you can slam down both hands to play a ten-note piano chord, and you won't have to wait while the hard drive finds the ten samples. While the beginnings of the notes are being played from RAM, the hard drive (and you'll need a fast hard drive to do this trick) has time to go hunt for the long decay portions of whatever samples you're playing and load those decays into RAM.

At this writing, two of the samplers discussed in this chapter (GigaStudio and HALion) can stream long samples from the hard drive. This feature is slated to be added to Kontakt before the end of 2002.

Loops & libraries

The type of sample looping I've just been describing is where samplers started out. Today, though, samplers and sample players are far more likely to be used for playing rhythm loops — also called beats. One or two bars of a drumbeat, for example, can be sampled and looped, after which the drummer will tirelessly play the beat all night long if you want. If you're doing pop music, that's likely to be just what you'll want.

Once tucked away into the sampler, a loop can be sliced apart, filtered, or layered with other loops to create a thicker and more exciting beat. The possibilities for creative sound design and musical expression are immense, as are the possibilities for mind-numbing triviality. But this is not the place to air that debate.

If you're interested in using a software sampler for loop-based music, you'll be happy to learn that you don't have to hire a drummer and record your own loops. A couple of dozen *soundware* companies will be happy to sell you whole CD-ROMs full of beats in just about any style you can imagine, and some that you probably can't imagine. The big players in this game are East West (www.soundsonline.com) and Big Fish Audio (www.bigfishaudio.com), but smaller companies like Ilio (www.ilio.com) also offer high-quality soundware catalogs.

Soundware CDs are available in generic audio file formats suitable for computer use. If you're using a Windows PC, you'd buy a CD of WAV files. If you're using a Mac, the equivalent would be AIFF files. Most software samplers can load both AIFF and WAV files. You can also buy soundware in the form of audio CDs (the kind that will play in any CD player), but this is less convenient if you're using a computer.

You can also buy soundware CDs with files formatted for your specific sampler. The advantage of this is that the sound developer will probably have taken some extra programming steps. The sounds will quite likely be pre-looped, they'll be assigned to the keyboard in a way that will make them immediately playable, and the parameters of the individual presets (filter and envelope settings, and so on) will have been set to useful values. Because this work has been done for you, you'll have to pay extra for the CD.

Your sampler may be able to load files in the formats that are native to other samplers. Because Akai established an early lead as a manufacturer of hardware samplers, many samplers will load Akai-format files. It's by no means guaranteed, however, that the files will be loaded perfectly. You can probably count on the samples, loops, and keymaps arriving in your sampler in a playable form, but filter and envelope settings may be incorrect.

A word about copyright

Because a sample player can play any digitally recorded sound, you can very easily use it to play sounds *that you don't own.* For instance, you can rip amusing scraps of dialog out of old episodes of *Gilligan's Island* and include them in your next avant-country production.

Trouble is, that would be illegal. Or at least, it may be illegal, depending on what you do. Without going into a lot of legalistic hair-splitting (since in any case I'm not an attorney), here's the situation as I understand it: You can legally sample anything you want and use it (a) in the privacy of your own home or (b) in live performance. You cannot, however, legally distribute copies of any recording containing samples that you've lifted from outside sources unless you obtain written permission (called a *license*).

Don't believe anyone who tells you something like, "Oh, you can sample up to two bars. It's fair use." Yes, the law defines something called "fair use," but if you think your usage falls under the fair use umbrella, my advice is to consult a good copyright attorney, not your friends. There are a lot of myths and misinformation floating around on the subject of sampling, and there are a lot of musicians who would prefer to remain ignorant — because, after all, acquiring licenses for your samples is a huge pain and may cost you a lot of money.

Having said all that, when you purchase a soundware library, what you're really purchasing is a license that allows you to use the samples in your music. No further fees will be required, and most likely no paperwork either. But *read the fine print!* Some sample libraries are sold with restrictions on their usage.

Almost all soundware is sold with one basic restriction: You're not allowed to share the samples with your friends. If you're sharing a studio and a computer network with other musicians, you can't store the samples on a hard drive where others can access them. And above all, it's illegal to post them on the Internet.

What about downloading audio files posted on the Internet by others? You may be in violation of the law if you do this without the permission of the copyright owner, since you're making a copy on your hard drive. But it's unlikely the FBI or the RIAA will invade your home and search your hard drive for pirated audio. If you turn around and distribute (make copies of) audio that you don't have a license for, however, expect trouble.

All this may seem needlessly fussy and restrictive, but look: Somebody worked hard to create those samples. They're entitled to earn money for their hard work. That's what copyright law is for. If you wouldn't want someone stealing your song, don't steal other people's creative work. It's as simple as that.

Figure 5-2.
The main workspace in GigaStudio. The multi-timbral part display, which is one of a number of sets of controls that can appear in the large area on the upper right, has slots along the top for 16 instruments and control sliders (volume, pan, tune) for each instrument. By clicking on "Port 2," "Port 3," or "Port 4" in the upper left corner, you can switch to a view of a different set of MIDI channels (17–32, etc.). The small folder tabs below the large area bring up other useful displays — a list of instruments that have been loaded, a "MIDI Control Surface" for adding manual controller offsets to GS instruments, and a list of WAV files that can be triggered directly, without assigning them to an instrument. The lower area is taken up by the searchable database of instruments; here, I've searched for the string "tp," which brings up all of the trumpet sounds in the East West *Quantum Leap Brass* collection.

Tascam GigaStudio
THE ORIGINAL STREAM-FROM-DISK SAMPLER

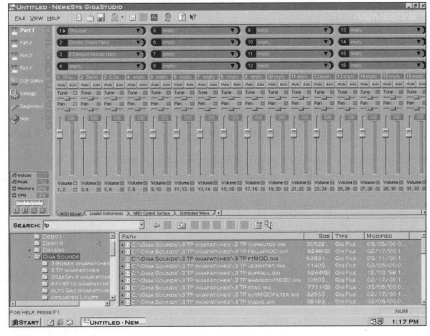

stand-alone (Win)
GS160 $699; GS96 $399

Pros: Size of playable samples limited only by hard disk size. Can access remote libraries via a Local Area Network. No audible timing latency. Up to 64-part multitimbral. Up to 32-way velocity splits and four-way crossfades. Sample switching and crossfading under MIDI control. Extremely fast load time for large files. Can import files from audio CDs. Performance resampling. Built-in effects. Database searching allows files to be found quickly.

Cons: Instrument editor is a separate, poorly integrated program. Audio editing requires third-party sample editor (not supplied). Effects plug-ins are in a proprietary format not yet supported by other manufacturers. No MIDI clock sync for LFOs or delay effects. Mixer sliders don't transmit MIDI data.

NemeSys GigaSampler — since renamed GigaStudio and acquired by Tascam — was not the first computer-based sample player. That distinction goes, if memory serves, to Seer Systems Reality. GigaSampler made quite a splash, though. It was the first sample player that could stream long sounds from the computer's hard drive. To emphasize the uniqueness of this feature, GS was shipped with a really, really large grand piano multisample. The review below, which I wrote for the September 2000 issue of *Keyboard*, covers version 2.01. Version 2.5, the latest as I write this, makes GigaStudio compatible with Windows 2000 and XP.

A s much as I like having real knobs and sliders to play with, I'm excited at the idea that I'm finally able to run a full-tilt music production studio in a computer. The technology is real; the only tricky bit is getting all of the components of the studio fully integrated so they run smoothly together.

NemeSys GigaStudio 2.0 is an ambitious attempt to provide a sample playback engine for such a studio. Running on a Windows PC, it provides as much as 160-note polyphony depending on your CPU speed, and has a standard array of syn-

GigaStudio at a Glance

System requirements	Windows 95/98, Pentium II 266MHz or AMD K6-2 or Athlon 400MHz or faster (for 64-voice polyphony); 600MHz recommended for concurrent use with audio sequencer; 64MB minimum RAM (256MB recommended), 6.4GB drive space, drive with less than 9ms access time, MIDI interface, 800 x 600 SVGA display, CD-ROM or DVD drive, soundcard with GSIF or Microsoft DirectSound compatible driver (must be native DirectSound, not emulated)
Synthesis type	sample playback/subtractive (filters)
Sample rate and bit depth	32, 44.1, 48, 88.2, 96kHz; 16- or 24-bit
Compatible sample formats	GigaSampler/GigaStudio, Akai S1000/3000, E-mu SoundFont 2, PCM mono/stereo WAV, audio CD
Internal performance resampling	yes
Synthesis parameters	multimode resonant filter, 3 envelopes, 3 LFOs, up to 32-way velocity cross-switching, 4-way multi-layer stereo crossfade
Polyphony	up to 160 voices (GS160), 96 voices (GS96), or 32 voices (GS32); system-dependent
Sequencers/ arpeggiator	none
Copy protection	password on installation
Downloadable demo	no

thesis functions (filters, LFOs, and so on). What sets GigaStudio apart, both from other computer-based samplers and from hardware samplers, is that individual samples can be of unlimited length, because they're not loaded into RAM. Instead, the audio is streamed from the hard disk. An 88-note sampled grand piano with full decay on each key — no loops, in other words — isn't just a theoretical possibility with GigaStudio. You can buy one and play it. Also, disk-based sampling also lets you load large sound files much, much faster than with a typical sampler.

While NemeSys contends that GigaStudio is an entirely different product line than its predecessor, NemeSys GigaSampler (reviewed in the Feb. '99 issue of *Keyboard*), there are strong similarities. [*Editor's note: While GigaSampler is no longer being developed or marketed, GigaSampler owners can upgrade to GigaStudio. See www.nemesysmusic.com for details.*] GigaStudio adds some important features and increases the ease-of-use factor, but certain limitations we noted in GigaSampler are still visible in the new program. Most significant, in my view, is the lack of integration within GigaStudio itself. Two main software components are provided — a multitimbral performance engine containing a mixer, effects, and other types of functionality, and a separate instrument editor. In order to do more than the most rudimentary editing at the sample level, yet a third program is needed. (GigaSampler used to ship with a copy of Sample Wrench from Dissidents, but with GigaStudio you have to supply your own sample editor.)

Overview. The GigaStudio performance engine (which I'll refer to simply as GS) is up to 64-part multitimbral: It has four 16-channel "ports" (see the main workspace screen on page 155), each of which can be separately addressed as a MIDI destination by a sequencer running on the same PC, or by a separate input on a multiport MIDI/computer interface. Each multitimbral slot has a fine-tune control, pan and volume settings, and mute and solo buttons. If the instrument you've loaded is programmed to respond to MIDI controllers, you can go even further by defining controller offsets separately for each channel and port. You can also link two or more ports to create multi-layer sounds. (By the way, "instrument" is GigaStudio-speak for a file that might be called a program or preset on some other sampler.)

GS is a superb tool for playing back memory-hogging multisamples of acoustic instruments, as witness the fact that more and more high-quality instrument libraries are being released in GS format. If creative sound design is your forté, however, you'll probably find yourself doing most of your sound sculpting in other programs and using GS mainly as a playback engine, as it doesn't have the kinds of advanced filtering and waveshaping found in some other samplers. GS comes with a copy of the GigaPiano, a 1GB piano in which each of the 88 notes is a separate sample with several velocity layers. Also included in the package are some drum sounds and three discs of soundware demos.

Across the bottom of the screen is a very slick database search engine that allows you to find the instrument files you need with an absolute minimum of fuss.

Figure 5-3.
GigaStudio includes a small but useful set of real-time effects. In the edit window for the reverb, shown here, you can control room size, pre-delay, damping, decay time, and diffusion using the horizontal sliders, the wet/dry balance using the sliders at lower left, and the EQ using the sliders at lower right. When the sliders have been set up to respond to MIDI controllers, you'll see them move when data is received.

Want to find all the WAV files on your hard drive? All the instruments with "viol" in their name? A couple of quick clicks, and you're staring at the list. If your computer is networked, GS will even find the appropriate files on any hard drive in the network — an enormous advantage for producers who work in large studios. According to NemeSys, you can even play files on remote drives without downloading them to the local drive. I didn't have a networked PC, so I couldn't test this feature: How well it works for you will depend on the speed of your network connection and the amount of network traffic, among other factors.

Along the left edge of the screen is a small utility section with readouts of free memory, CPU usage, and the number of voices playing at a given time. As well as I could tell by loading a stereo GM piano sound and grabbing some ten-note chords, the 600MHz AMD Athlon processor in the computer NemeSys loaned us for this review would probably max out somewhere around the advertised 160 voices. (No, I didn't try mashing down 161 MIDI keys at once and listening for dropouts. There *aren't* 161 MIDI keys.)

Adding effects and running an audio sequencer concurrently in the same machine will naturally reduce the polyphony. While NemeSys lists a 266MHz PII as the minimum system, don't scrimp if you're planning to run an audio sequencer alongside GS: Get the fastest computer you can afford. NemeSys recommends that if you're planning to run multitrack audio through the computer along with GS, you give each program its own physical hard drive, not just its own drive partition, in order to avoid conflicts in which both programs are trying to use the drive's read head at the same time.

What about needing memory, though? Isn't this a disk-based sampler? Yes and no. While long samples are played from disk, GS buffers the first part of each sample in RAM, so as to be able to start the sound instantly when you strike the key. This is a sensible and efficient system. I found myself wishing, though, that the onscreen listing of instrument files had a display of the amount of RAM each of them will take up when loaded. It's very possible to run out of RAM when loading a number of instruments, so the RAM required by a given file would be useful information to have.

You can add effects processing (see the reverb window on page 158 and Effects, below) to any multitimbral part — up to four plug-ins per mixer channel, in fact — or save on your CPU usage by sending several channels to the same aux bus. Both pre- and post-fader bussing are supported. Effects are one of the areas where GigaStudio is much improved over GigaSampler (which had none).

A third-party editor is required to turn GS into a sampler; on its own, it's strictly a sample playback instrument. Well, that's not quite true: It can resample its own audio output (an essential feature), but it can't record external audio. You can enter new numbers for the the loop start and end points of any sample in the GS Editor, but that's the only sample-level editing provided. When comparing the cost of GigaStudio *vs.* a hardware sampler (most of which will do waveform cutting and pasting, at the very least), don't forget to factor in the cost of this added component.

Once you get through the "Getting Started" guide (80 pages, no index), GS's documentation consists strictly of online help. You can click on a feature on the screen and be taken directly to a help page describing this feature, which is very cool. Even so, I can't help wishing that the help file had more cross-links and/or more thorough explanations of how to perform various operations. I often had to search in the help index because the page that opened up didn't have the information I needed — and a few important terms aren't in the index at all. Also, you can't scribble notes in the margin, and in the absence of a document that you can read through page by page, it's easy to miss cool features entirely. I'd prefer a printed manual, or even a PDF file that I could print out.

GS scores high on the user-friendliness scale thanks to its extensive use of drag-and-drop functionality. Right-clicking is often useful as well, so be sure to try it if you can't find the command you need. The screen layout is very clear, at least on a decent-sized monitor.

[*Editor's note: GigaStudio has had five updates since this review was published, so the information in the following paragraph is probably not relevant. It's included principally in the interest of journalistic integrity.*] During my two months with GigaStudio, I experienced a few crashes, some consistent, repeatable problems, and more than a few intermittent glitches. On one occasion, the editor software crashed three times in a row when I tried to use its undo command. Later the same day, the same command worked fine. Using version 2.0, I consistently had to quit the editor and restart it in order to edit a different instrument; this problem is fixed in version 2.01. I also created a situation with 2.0 in which a couple of disk files got corrupted somehow; I was unable to duplicate the problem later, but this kind of thing is fairly alarming. Since it was intermittent, I can't testify for certain that the

2.01 release fixes the problem, but NemeSys is working hard to polish the program, so chances are you won't run into it. (Besides, you always make backups of your files, right?)

Performances. I've already touched on many of the features of the Performances. Here are a few other items:

If you only need to trigger a bunch of samples from a MIDI keyboard, with no filtering, cross-switching, or other voice parameters, GS offers a handy shortcut called Distributed Waves. You can drag mono or stereo WAV files into a window area where they'll automatically be assigned to adjacent keys. The WAV files can then be triggered just like a real GS instrument, and will respond to velocity by getting louder. This part of the program is a terrific workspace for both Foley editors and dance producers.

WAV layouts can be saved and loaded. There's a button called "Sort" that closes up gaps in the keyboard layout if you've created any. Only one of these WAV layouts can be loaded into memory at a time, but that's okay — if you need more than one, just create them as standard GS instruments.

The GS audio mixer has 32 channels, conveniently configured as 16 stereo pairs. If you're using multi-channel audio hardware, each pair can be routed to any pair of outputs. I noted one minor problem here: If you've muted some channels and then click on the solo button for another channel, when you un-solo that channel all of the channels will be unmuted, even if they were muted before. The same thing happens with the mute and solo buttons in the MIDI multitimbral part setup.

The mixer sliders (including those in the effects) will respond to incoming MIDI data for automation purposes, but GS can't actually create the MIDI data and transmit it to an external sequencer — an odd and frustrating omission. Bizarrely, considering its name, the GS MIDI Control Surface doesn't transmit MIDI either, except within GS itself. The mixer sliders respond to MIDI, but I had to record it into Cakewalk using my trusty Peavey PC 1600 slider box.

Why would you want a MIDI Control Surface that can't transmit MIDI? Turns out there's a good reason. This utility is where you assign offsets (filter cutoff, LFO depth, etc.) to instruments that are loaded into your current GS setup. The offsets can then be saved as part of the GS file. The instrument you're using has to be programmed ahead of time to respond to the various MIDI controllers in an appropriate way — and you also have to tell your sequencer not to zero out the controllers each time you stop playback, as that will screw up the GS instrument offsets. Many sequencers do this by default, so check your owner's manual for details.

Editor. If you've loaded a sound into GS and find that you need to adjust the filter cutoff, LFO rate, or whatever, you'll need to launch GS Editor (see the Editor window on page 163), which is a separate program. This is a little less convenient than simply opening an edit window: After making certain types of edits, you have to click on a "reload" button to transmit the edits back to GS in order to hear them, or click on an "apply" button, or both. This non-realtime process slows down an editing session and leaves the door open for confusion. Even after working with the program for a while, I'm not 100% sure which edits have to be reloaded and which don't. And when you reload, your edits will be saved to the disk file — whether or not you want to save them. In most samplers, you can make any number of sound changes and then save the results only if you like what you're hearing. There are ways to give yourself this flexibility in GS, but they require a couple of extra steps.

The GS editor has a clean, sensible layout, and allows various kinds of graphic editing and drag-and-drop operations. The voicing parameters that it provides are useful, but not entirely state-of-the-art. There's no matrix modulation, for instance.

Like its predecessor, GigaStudio can assign up to five "dimensions" of cross-switching to each key. This works out to a maximum of 32 possible samples that can be active per key. You can switch or fade from one sample to another under the control of velocity or a MIDI controller message. With stereo samples, you're limited to four dimensions, but this still allows 16-way velocity cross-switching, which is a pretty luxurious high-end feature. The ability to do four-way crossfading between samples and edit the in and out points of the crossfade zones is a new feature not found in GigaSampler, and it adds quite a bit to the expressive possibilities. For instance, you could fade in some sampled room ambience under mod wheel control.

Each sample can have its own full set of parameters; you don't have to set up layers where a whole multisampled keyboard layout shares one set of envelopes, as on some samplers. Also, GS has multimode resonant filters and a pair of envelope generators that offer a couple of extra parameters beyond the basic ADSR design. Again, these are good features to see.

Pitch, filter, and amplitude each have their own LFO — but the LFOs have a fixed sine/triangle waveform suitable mainly for vibrato and tremolo. LFO depth can be modulated from the mod wheel, or from aftertouch (for the pitch LFO), breath controller (for the amplitude LFO), or foot controller (for the filter LFO), but not from any other MIDI controllers. LFO rate can't be modulated at all, except by switching to a different sample that has its own rate setting, and the LFOs can't be synced to MIDI clock.

Filter cutoff can be controlled by any one of ten different controllers, including aftertouch. (This is an additional filter modulation input beyond the velocity response.) Resonance can also be controlled via MIDI. The filter keyboard tracking is an on/off switch, but this is more an ergonomics issue than an actual limitation in voice programming, since it's easy enough to create a separate region on each key, using the same sample(s) for each region, and then give each region its own filter cutoff.

Velocity response within each area (filter and amplitude) gives you a choice of three curves and five settings from low to high. The documentation, however, gives not even an oblique hint about what the names of the response curves (linear, nonlinear, and special) might mean, so finding the right velocity response for a particular sound, even if you're a seasoned synthesizer programmer, is a matter of trial and error.

The editor lets you create macros for quick edits, and also has a setup wizard that makes it easy to create an entire multisampled instrument quickly. If you're creating a custom sampled Rhodes or alto sax, for instance, these features will be very welcome. And here's another cool bit: You can save your favorite instrument parameter settings without the samples, as an "articulation" file, and then load the settings into another instrument.

Even with all these features, though, it's clear that instrument definitions in GS are optimized for playing sampled versions of real instruments, not for the needs of remixers and experimental-minded musicians. You won't find Kurzweil-style waveshaping, E-mu's multiple filter types, or Yamaha's lo-fi effects here.

Effects. GigaStudio ships with three NFX-format plug-in effects — a reverb/chorus, a chorus/flange/phaser, and a multitap delay. A fourth plug-in, a parametric EQ, is emailed to you for free when you register your software.

The effects sound very good: The reverbs, in particular, are smooth and spacious. The sound quality is especially remarkable when you consider these are extremely low-latency effects and don't hog an excessive amount of CPU time. Each instance of the reverb/chorus, for instance, took about 6% of the CPU in my 600MHz machine. The "realtime" effects plug-ins in a typical computer-based audio recorder generally buffer a certain amount of audio ahead of time, while the NFX effects, like those in a hardware processor, are truly realtime.

Each of the three plug-ins offers a number of algorithms. For the reverb/chorus, for example, you can select various hall, plate, and room spaces, or an algorithm that adds a simple chorus in series with the reverb. Most algorithms have between five and seven parameters; the delay has five for each of four independent taps. Each effect also has a semi-parametric EQ stage.

The delay algorithms can be programmed in bpm or millisecond values, a helpful feature that goes a long way toward compensating for the absence of MIDI clock sync . . . or at least it would if it worked consistently. In practice, the plug-in tended to change my attempted data input in a drastic and unpredictable way. This bug was especially evident when the system audio clock was set to anything other than 44.1kHz. Even at 44.1, when I typed in "7" for the millisecond setting, the software changed it to 60ms. NemeSys tells us this bug has been found, and will be fixed in the next update. [*Editor's note: I'm told it has definitely been fixed.*]

More goodies: You can switch either the wet or dry signal to output on either the left or right channel rather than in stereo, for instant separation. Each effect has a

Figure 5-4.
The GigaStudio Instrument Editor has lists of presets and WAV files in the windowpanes at left, a graphic editing area (center), and a number of edit displays (lower right) that can be selected by clicking on the various tabs. Here, EG/LFO1 — the display containing the amplitude envelope generator and LFO parameters — has been selected. When you choose a parameter, the graphic display above automatically switches to show the settings of this parameter for all of the zones on the keyboard. A bunch of zones can then be edited at once by clicking and dragging. In the lower center is the "dimensions" editing area, where various samples within a single keyboard region can be assigned to cross-switch in response to velocity or a MIDI controller. Note the "loaded" and "reload" indicators near the upper left. When the reload light is lit, you need to click on the GS button just to the left of the indicators in order to transmit your edits to the performance engine in order to hear them.

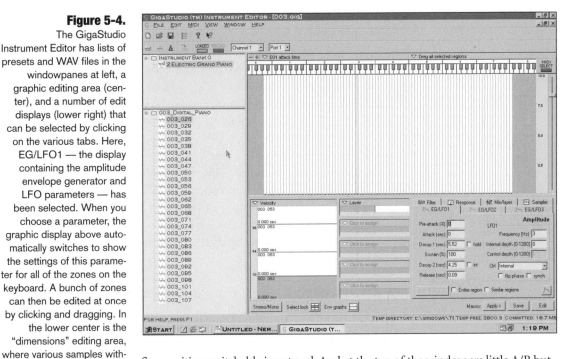

five-position switchable input pad. And at the top of the window are little A/B buttons, which let you undo and redo your most recent series of edits — very cool. Naturally, you can save your own effects presets, which will show up in the drop-down menu.

All of the effect parameters can be controlled in real time via MIDI. Because of the low-latency nature of the processing, though, some parameter changes will produce interesting glitches, such as temporary pitch changes in the wet output. Hey, think of it as a new type of modulation.

NemeSys tells us they're hoping to see other software developers release NFX plug-ins, but no announcements had been made at press time. [*Editor's note: Nor since then, as far as I'm aware.*] A decent compressor and some controllable distortion would add a lot to the GigaStudio sound palette. In case you're curious, NemeSys tells us that the need for extremely low latency makes it unlikely that they'll be able to add support for VST or DirectX plug-ins.

In Use. Playing a well-crafted multisample instrument in GigaStudio is a wonderful experience. The 1GB stereo grand piano shipped with the program is crisply recorded and has some of the best matched velocity cross-switch samples I've ever heard — not to mention the realistic note decays, which utterly outclass the decays on any other sampled grand because you're hearing the real decay of the string sound, not something done with a loop and an envelope. I was also knocked out by *Larry Seyer's Upright Acoustic Bass,* which has some amazingly gutty, realistic bass samples. Even the General MIDI bank NemeSys provided for the review sparkles. Plus, loading instruments is so much faster than on any other sampler, reshuffling my multitimbral setups and trying out new sounds was positively a joy.

But playing GS from a keyboard is only part of the story. Since most of us can't afford two computers running side by side, I figured a good real-world test would be to run it on the same computer with a digital audio sequencer. So I slapped together a laidback trip-hop groove, combining a few tracks of stereo audio in Cakewalk 9.0 with MIDI tracks that were playing GS instruments. The two programs worked seamlessly side by side, with nary a glitch.

The alto sax from the *Quantum Leap Brass* CD-ROM turned out to be noticeably flat compared to the other instruments. I was able to solve the problem using the tuning slider in GS. There are two fine-tune sliders, in fact: One adjusts the tuning in 5-cent increments, while the other has 1.5-cent resolution. (If that's not enough control, you can boot the editor and change the tuning of individual samples there in 1-cent increments.)

Next I imported a Roland-format drum groove into GS from Q Up Arts' *Streetbeats by Poogie Bell.* I did the import in two steps, using a program called CDExtract 3.2 to transfer the Roland file to SoundFont 2 format and then loading the SoundFont file into GS. That process worked without a hitch (except for the fact that I had to call NemeSys to learn how to do it, since neither "import" nor "soundfont" is listed in the GS online help index).

NemeSys recommends that you use separate hard drives for GS and your audio sequencer, but I was able to get away with running all of the audio off of one drive. Then again, I wasn't pushing the system by maxing out the number of voices or audio tracks in the arrangement. Your mileage may vary.

I had to direct the audio outputs from Cakewalk and Sound Forge to different pairs of physical outputs on the Midiman Delta 1010 audio interface, as two audio programs can't generally share outputs under Windows. Since I use a Mackie 1604 for mixing, this was not a problem; if you're hoping to run straight from your consumer soundcard into a cassette deck, you can still use your sequencer for MIDI, to trigger GS sounds, but concurrent audio playback won't be possible. Since you'll undoubtedly want to run an audio editor from time to time along with GS, I'd strongly suggest budgeting for a multiport audio interface.

Conclusions. If you're doing sessions — be they pop or film score — and if you've got the budget for a stack of GigaSampler-format CD-ROMs, you'll love GigaStudio. Its ability to find and load sounds quickly will save you endless hours of studio time, and the sound quality is wonderful. You can play it from a MIDI keyboard with no annoying latency, and then cruise the Internet or play video games without investing another nickel on hardware, all for less than the cost of a comparable hardware-based sampler. [*Editor's note: Tascam doesn't recommend using a GigaStudio computer for non-music-related activities.*] Or is there such a thing? No hardware sampler will put a couple of gigabytes of samples under your fingers at the same time.

Editing and customizing your own sounds in GS will prove less enjoyable than loading and playing other people's libraries, both because some useful parameters are missing and because the editor software isn't as well integrated as it ought to be with the performance engine. I won't complain too much about the absence of sample-level editing, because most of the people who will be buying GS already have a powerful audio editor on their hard drive. But it would be nice to at least be able to normalize new samples and truncate the dead space at the start of a sample without having to open up another program.

If you looked at GigaSampler when it came out but weren't convinced, take another look: You'll probably find that GigaStudio has the features you wanted. The redesign is clean and easy to use, the realtime effects, while basic, are ready and waiting to enhance the sound, and the realtime crossfading is bound to come in handy. Overall, GigaStudio is an excellent high-end musical instrument. —JA (Sept. '00)

Figure 5-5.

Kontakt's main window includes a dual-pane browser (left) and the main instrument rack (right) — and that's it: Pop-ups and dialog boxes are kept to an absolute minimum. Modules in the instrument rack can be opened up to perform various types of edits. Here, the Loop Editor has been opened, and we're looking at a kick drum sample. Up to eight loops can be assigned within each sample using the buttons to the left below the waveform display. The number of repetitions can be programmed for each loop. The waveform display can be zoomed in or out both vertically and horizontally. A loop end/start display helps in creating smooth loops. The modulation routing module (the narrow band near the bottom of the window) has pop-up menus for both source and destination. Need to get at your essential samples quickly? Add them to the Favorites menu (labeled "FAV.", upper left).

Native Instruments Kontakt
DRAG-AND-DROP SAMPLER WITH TIME-STRETCHING

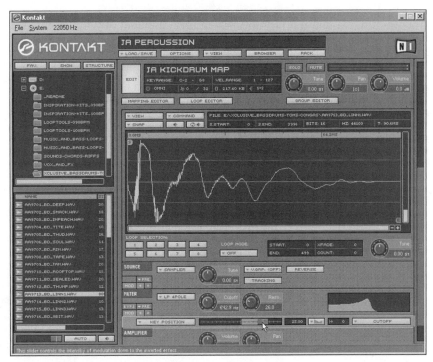

stand-alone, VST (Mac, Win)
$399

Pros: Velocity and key position crossfading. Built-in time-stretching and pitch-shifting. Excellent variety of filters and effects. Controller curve mapping and controller lag processing (smoothing). Thirty-two-stage looping envelope and step generator.
Cons: No undo. Can't stream samples from hard disk. Can't record output direct to disk when used as stand-alone app.

When I started working on this review of Kontakt (which appeared in the October 2002 issue of *Keyboard*), I was kind of hoping I wouldn't like it. You see, I've written rave reviews of several other Native Instruments synths, and I was starting to worry that people would think they're paying me off or something. I figured, maybe Kontakt would be the program that I could salvage my sagging credibility by slamming.

No such luck. It's another winner.

According to Native Instruments, the version 1.1 update adds support for more file types, including SDII. Dual-processor support is also a reality, and streaming playback from disk is scheduled for the 1.2 update.

For most musicians, a sampler is an ideal way to do realistic renderings of other sounds — string orchestra, drum loops, crowd noises, you name it. A few more adventurous souls, though, see it as a creative tool for mangling sounds beyond recognition. The first full-featured sampler that lived entirely in a computer, GigaSampler,

Kontakt at a Glance

System requirements	Mac: G3 350MHz or better; PC: Pentium II, 300MHz or better; both: 128MB RAM, 40MB free hard disk space, 3GB additional space for included soundware, audio and MIDI interfaces, VST 2.0 compatible host application for VST operation
File formats imported	Akai S1000 & S3000, Steinberg HALion, TASCAM GigaSampler/GigaStudio, Emagic EXS24/EXSP24, SoundFont 2, SND, LM4, Battery, WAV, SDII & AIFF
Multitimbrality	16 instruments (MIDI channels and/or layers)
Supported file bit resolutions	8, 16, 24, 32; sample rate is host hardware–dependent, up to 192kHz
Virtual outputs	hardware- or software-dependent, up to 32
Polyphony	system-dependent (up to 256 stereo voices per instance)
Voicing features	multimode filter, distortion and other voice effects, LFOs, envelopes, step generator; tone machine and time machine modes; velocity and key position crossfading; reverb and other mix effects
Automation	via MIDI
Syncable functions	envelopes, LFOs, delay effect, step sequencer, time machine, tone machine
Copy protection	CD plus serial number on install
Downloadable demo	yes

established itself firmly on the realistic-sounds side of the ledger, and didn't offer much in the creative sound design department. Native Instruments Kontakt lacks some of GigaSampler's realism-enhancing tricks, nor will the current version of Kontakt stream long samples from hard disk the way GS, Steinberg HALion, and Emagic EXS24 do. But Kontakt goes considerably further in the areas rabid sound designers drool over — filters, effects, envelopes, modulation routings, and MIDI control thereof. I also found Kontakt easier to use than GigaStudio, once I got familiar with its interface. And let's not forget, GigaStudio is strictly stand-alone on the PC. Kontakt is happy to run either stand-alone or as a VST plug-in, and is cross-platform for either Windows or the Mac.

In recent months, HALion and Emagic EXS24 have heated up the softsampler wars considerably. Programs such as IK Multimedia SampleTank offer other options. And E-mu is poised to enter the fray by switching to software for their next-generation Emulator, the E5. In Kontakt, they have a formidable foe.

Overview. At the top level, Kontakt supports up to 16 instruments at a time. Each can be on its own MIDI channel, or you can assign several to one channel for layered sounds. Each instrument contains a sample map, in which samples can be assigned freely to key and velocity zones. Samples are then grouped, and each group has its own filter and effects assignments. You can have the whole instrument be one group, put each sample in its own group, or mix and match.

Next, add velocity and key position crossfading to the picture. This is handy not just for conventional instrument sounds but for blending two loops with one another from the keyboard. The one thing Kontakt won't do is switch among sample groups in response to an external MIDI controller, the way GigaStudio will. [*Editor's note: According to Native Instruments, this feature will be included in version 1.2.*]

While Kontakt won't host other VST plug-ins, it has its own suite of excellent-sounding built-in effects, including reverb, chorus/flange/phase, and a few flavors of distortion. With a fast computer and some decent soundware, this might be the only instrument you'd need to do a complete production.

Kontakt's voice architecture is extremely cool, as we'll see. But the soundware shipped with the program is less impressive. For more on these topics, keep reading. I had no trouble assigning Kontakt to the ASIO audio outputs in my computer, nor any trouble with the MIDI inputs. When Kontakt is being used as a VST instrument, you can specify how many stereo and/or mono outputs you need, and route each instrument to any mono output or stereo pair. This is a powerful feature for sound design, because two Kontakt instruments can be assigned to the same MIDI channel, yet feed different outputs for external processing or crossfading.

Kontakt's browser windows, which occupy the left side of its main window, are simple and effective. The upper browser pane shows your disk organization, and the lower lists files. When instrument files are visible in the lower pane, you can drag-and-drop them into the main instrument area. When sample files are visible, you can open Kontakt's keymap window and drag them into position. The file size is shown for both instruments and samples, which is moderately helpful, but I couldn't find a display that showed how much RAM remained in Kontakt's allocation, so I was left guessing as to whether a particular instrument could be loaded successfully.

Alternatively, the browser can display the structure of your Kontakt instruments as if it were a file tree. With complex instruments, this is surprisingly handy: You can look at the whole layout of the instrument in miniature, and clicking on any module brings it front and center in the rack.

A few ergonomic niggles, and then we'll move on: Not only is there no undo command, but Kontakt allows you to quit the program without prompting you to save any unsaved files. [*Editor's note: This problem has been fixed in version 1.1.*] Also, each Kontakt instrument has its own solo and mute buttons, which is good — but if you've muted some instruments and then solo one, when you unsolo it, all of the muted instruments are unmuted. This is not the way unsoloing is supposed to work.

According to Native Instruments, Kontakt reads Akai S1000 and S3000, SoundFont 2, GigaStudio, HALion, EXS24, Steinberg LM4, and NI Battery files. I loaded programs from East West's *Quantum Leap: Rare Instruments* Giga package without trouble. Akai S1000 programs from Zero-G's *Pure R'n'B* loaded successfully, but the rhythm loop samples arrived without loop points. (I wasn't able to determine whether the problem was with Kontakt or with the files.)

NI is making it easier for users of other samplers to switch to Kontakt. They have a $199 cross-grade price for owners of HALion, EXS24, and GigaStudio. Users who sign up for the cross-grade offer will not lose their old sampler.

Voicing. Let's start with the stuff everybody wants to know: Kontakt is well endowed in the filter department. The filter modes include lowpass, highpass, bandpass, and notch with various rolloff slopes, plus a phaser, two sweepable vocal formant filters, and a 3-band filter with continuously adjustable low/band/high type for each band. Not only do you have lots of choices, but the filters sound great. Each voice can use only one filter, but this isn't usually a problem, especially with that 3-band filter to fill in the gap.

When I installed the initial release of Kontakt, I was taken aback to find no filter modulation — no envelope inputs, for instance. After a quick trip to NI's website to download version 1.02, the filter modulation was up and running.

In addition to a filter, each voice can use distortion, saturation, lo-fi, a compressor, and a stereo enhancer. These can be chained in any order. By adding lo-fi and distortion to a sampled reggae bass loop, for instance, I was able to turn what was essentially a sine wave into a much more aggressive fuzz bass.

I didn't find the compressor very useful. Instead of leveling out an overly percussive sound, which is what I wanted, it insisted on adding a snappy attack tran-

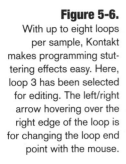

Figure 5-6.

With up to eight loops per sample, Kontakt makes programming stuttering effects easy. Here, loop 3 has been selected for editing. The left/right arrow hovering over the right edge of the loop is for changing the loop end point with the mouse.

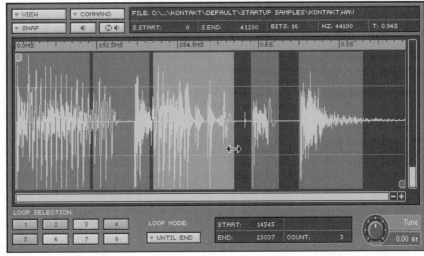

sient, because the minimum attack time is a nominal 1.0ms. (To my ears, it sounded somewhat longer.) If I set the threshold high enough to avoid this, the compressor basically did nothing.

Kontakt's envelopes are terrific. And here there's no limit on the number you can use. If your computer is fast enough, you can have a dozen per patch. Three types are on offer: a DBD (decay 1, breakpoint, decay 2) for pitch sweeps, an AHDSR, and a 32-stage rate/level envelope complete with looping. I'm not sure why the DBD can't be used for simple filter sweeps, but it can't.

The 32-stage envelopes, borrowed from NI's FM7, are a terrific resource. You can set up complex rhythms with them to turn a sustaining sound into a beat. Each slope in the envelope can be as convex or concave as you like, and envelope programming is done graphically.

Need more? Check out the step generator. This modulation source can be programmed with up to 32 steps, which it will cycle through as on an old-style analog sequencer. Program one for the pitch and one for the filter cutoff, and you have an instant groove.

At first I thought the step generator and LFOs didn't sync to an external clock. Sync is well implemented, as it turns out, but the sync parameter is not only undocumented but entirely hidden, due to an unfortunate design choice. (Tip: Click on the "Hz" label to bring up the menu.) The 32-stage envelopes can also be synced, so you can produce quite complex rhythms.

Normally, each Kontakt instrument is only one voice wide. If you want a classic two-oscillator sound, though, you can layer two instruments or overlap two samples within a single instrument using the Group features. (Overlapping samples can be velocity- or position-crossfaded as well as layered.) Copying Groups is easy. There's no command for copying an entire instrument, but saving it to disk and reloading

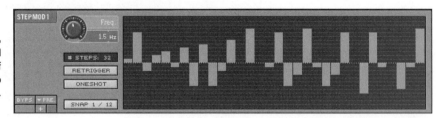

Figure 5-7.
For rhythmic filter and pitch effects, the tool of choice is Kontakt's step modulator.

it into a new slot is a simple workaround. In trying to detune one of my layers, I spotted a minor bug: Even though the Edit All button wasn't activated, all of the layers were being retuned when I moved the tuning knob. Clicking twice on the button solved the problem. [*Editor's note: Fixed in version 1.2, according to NI.*]

Now for the fun stuff: In addition to doing normal sample playback, a Kontakt group (a set of samples that all use the same filter, modulation, etc.) can be set to tone machine or time machine mode. More than anything else, these are reminiscent of the groundbreaking Roland VP-9000 hardware sampler, but without the VP's rather daunting price and other limitations.

Time machine mode lets you change the tempo of a drum loop or other sound without changing the pitch. You can do this by assigning the sample to a range of keys, in which case each key plays the sample at a different tempo, or using the fine-tune knob. The latter is calibrated in percent rather than bpm, but if you need the loop to lock up with your music, you can sync the time machine to MIDI clock.

I wanted to layer a couple of the factory Absynth-generated loops to create a composite rhythm bed, but they aren't tempo-matched. So I tried using the time machine to line them up. I didn't care much for the results: As I slowed down one of the loops, its groove got jerky, and some of the percussive elements acquired audible flams.

Tone machine is primarily for vocal material. It removes the pitch information from a sampled phrase while preserving the consonants and vowels. You can then play the phrase from the keyboard and impose a new melody, or play in-tune chords. In legato mode, the tone machine won't start the phrase from the top when you hit a new key, it will keep going.

As in the VP-9000, you can slow a phrase down to an absurd extreme in the tone machine. I tried this with a plucked Arabian instrument sample and found myself in possession of a rich, rolling bass tone: The granular synthesis process stretched out the natural transients of the plucked sound in a beautiful way, and the formant knob gave me pinpoint control over the timbre. With vocal material, tone machine sounds fairly robotic, but sometimes robotic is what you want.

As it happened, I started my Kontakt review with the computer MIDIed up to a standard five-octave keyboard. While auditioning the piano, I naturally wanted to check out the top and bottom registers. To my surprise, Kontakt doesn't have a transpose knob, only a tuning knob, which changes the pitch of the individual samples in the instrument. No worries, though: To transpose the incoming MIDI data, all I had to do was open the Mapping Editor, select all of the zones in the piano, and drag them up or down.

Sample Editing. Open the Mapping (keymap) Editor, click on a sample, and then open the Loop Editor. Here you can zoom in and out in the familiar-looking waveform display, but it's not actually a sample editor — to cut and paste audio, draw out clicks, and so on, you need to open an external audio editing program.

When it comes to editing loops, though, this display has the goods. Up to eight loops can be used per sample, and each can be given a number of repeats (or infinite repeat). You can drag the loop boundaries, or the entire loop, with the mouse. There's also a loop end/start display, a standard tool for making sure the loop point is smooth. It would be nice if the zoom in/out buttons worked in this display, but it's easy to get a smooth loop, and that's what counts.

It's great that the audition sample button in the wave display bypasses the filters and stuff — but it's not great that it also bypasses the instrument's volume knob. When I clicked on this button, the sample came blasting out of my speakers at full volume, and the only way to turn it down was at my hardware mixer. (NI is aware of this behavior, and tells me a fix is planned for the next update.)

After assigning Steinberg Wavelab 3.0 as my external audio editor, I told Kontakt to load one of its samples into Wavelab for editing. The sample showed up correctly in Wavelab, but when I edited it in Wavelab (and saved the file), the edited version didn't show up in Kontakt. (According to NI, this has been fixed in the 1.1 update.) Kontakt still had the original version in RAM — and there's no "reload sample" button. To hear the edits, I had to save the file to the correct directory and then reload the whole instrument.

To change the root key of any sample, which has the effect of tuning the sample up or down by half-steps, simply drag the orange root-key indicator left or right on the graphic keyboard. The fine-tune and amplitude offset parameters for individual samples, however, are well hidden: They're not in the Mapping Editor at all, they're in the browser's Structure display, which is a bit bizarre.

Being able to set up eight loops in the course of a sample is cooler than I expected. I was able to add some unusual stuttering rhythms to drum loops. Being able to modulate the loop start point or loop length from a MIDI controller or LFO will take you even further into the Twilight Zone. The only drag with this type of modulation is that Kontakt won't find zero-crossings when it's moving the loop around. A user-adjustable loop crossfade parameter is provided, but if you move the loop quickly in real time, some clicking will become audible.

Included Soundware. Kontakt ships with five CDs of soundware. That may sound like a major attraction, but there's less here than meets the eye. For starters, there

Figure 5-8.
First seen in Native Instruments' FM7 and Absynth, these flexible 32-step envelopes will loop rhythmically. Click on the Tempo-Sync button to turn on the snap-to grid, or drag on the circular dots to make each segment as concave or convex as desired.

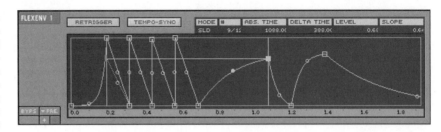

are some big holes in the sound list. A good hardware synth manages to pack a much wider sound palette, including some orchestral samples, choir, and synth waveforms, plus more meat-and-potatoes drums, into less than 50MB.

The best sounds are in a grab-bag disc called *NI — Best of Synth.* The samples here are recordings of NI's softsynths, including Absynth, B4, Battery, FM7, Pro-52, and Reaktor. The B4 folder has a couple of respectable Hammond tones in it — a muted setting with third-harmonic percussion, and a full-out grinding organ with fast Leslie. The Absynth folder is more stimulating: The wildly imaginative electro loops made me wish I had Absynth on my machine (the more so as these loops are not tempo-matched with one another, and the key signatures are undocumented).

The Absynth "Picked E-Bass" multisample has a nice gutty attitude, but unfortunately one of the loops is close to a half-step sharp. "KillerBass," in the Pro-52 folder, is just as problematical: The samples in the multisample are very different from one another in tone, so you'll need to do some remapping in order to play a coherent-sounding line. (Fortunately, this is easy to do.) There are also some very good sounds on this disc, don't get me wrong — but you'll have to hunt for them.

The other four discs were put together by a soundware company called Yellow Tools. One each is devoted to piano, drums and percussion, bass, and guitar. A 200MB acoustic piano is a nice perk, no doubt about it. This one doesn't have quite the richness or depth I'd like to hear, but it's pretty good. The $B\flat$ below Middle C is thin and harsh, while the $E\flat$ below it is tubby, but most of the key zones blend smoothly with one another. Unlike some other sampled grands (notably the GigaStudio and the Wizoo/Steinberg), the Kontakt grand has no mechanism for producing damper-up resonance or hammer fall-back noise. One layer of samples is all you get.

In addition to the acoustic grand, the piano CD serves up two FM electric pianos (i.e., DX7), which are very similar to one another in timbre. That's it, folks — no authentic Rhodes, no Wurlitzer, and no Clavinet. On top of which, the four-way velocity switching on "FM-E-Piano" is so abrupt that I couldn't play the instrument in a musical manner from the keyboard. Notes pop out or get swallowed in an uncontrollable way, because the differences in loudness and brightness from one velocity zone to the next are too extreme. They used up 278MB of disk space on this turkey, and the key to making it playable is to throw away all but the loud samples (easy to do in the Mapping Editor) and add a bit of lowpass filter controlled by velocity.

Next, I slid the Drums & Percussion CD into the drive. The Drums folder contains five kits — three "electro" and two "real." Most of the drums are velocity cross-switched, some with as many as 16 samples per key. With things like the acoustic snare drum, this adds a lot to the realism. Even so, with 138MB of drum samples on the disc, you get only three acoustic snares. None of the kits provides a complete 61-key drum layout, as you'd expect on a hardware synth with a much smaller set of samples. You get about 16 sounds in the electro kit and 22 in the acoustic kit. Far more inspiring than the rather flabby electro kits are the Battery kits on the first CD. These kits are very effective.

Next I delved into the Synth Bass folder in the Acoustic/Electric Bass CD. I found a total of four Minimoog-like synth basses. Each was laboriously multisampled with two-way velocity cross-switching, so that the smallest of them requires 20MB of memory. Yet after all that work, nobody bothered to add something as basic as mod wheel vibrato. None of the four even uses Kontakt's wonderful filters — the filter sweeps on the attacks are sampled in, so you can't adjust them. Not only that, but "Synth Bass 4" has a thump at the end of the attack in most of the samples. I could have programmed a better bank of basses in Kontakt using a raw sawtooth wave.

The "Fingered Long" electric bass is solid and very usable. The acoustic bass, however, is unpleasantly metallic, without much body. To my ears, it sounded more like a guitarron than a bass viol — and indeed, Native Instruments tells us it's a Martin B-1 acoustic bass guitar (a fact not mentioned in the documentation). Many of the samples have fretboard buzz. The buzz is undeniably authentic, and more is added at high velocities in a realistic way, but they should really have included a full-range acoustic bass with no buzzing. Also, the bottom *E* has a pitch wow: The sample starts a little sharp, but the end of the note is a little flat. The *F* directly above it doesn't have this problem, so you can remap it out of existence.

Since it's a sampler, Kontakt can be loaded with pretty much any sound you want, so there's no need to be dissuaded by the shortage of primo stuff in the included set. Kontakt's support for a variety of file types means there's no shortage of good soundware you can use.

MIDI Implementation. Any knob in Kontakt can be controlled by external MIDI data — and you can assign several knobs to the same controller, which some softsynths won't let you do. There are two ways to do this. If you use the shortcut (right-clicking on the knob and then using the MIDI learn input) you don't get to scale the amount of controller effect, but by assigning the controller as a normal modulation source, you can scale, smooth, or remap the controller data. Release velocity and poly aftertouch are selectable as controllers.

Even the individual rates and levels of the multisegment envelope can be controlled via MIDI — a useful feature some synth designers overlook.

In Use. Since I'm still using Windows 98 for most of my music, I tried running Kontakt inside Cubase VST 5.1 rather than jumping forward to Cubase SX. Kontakt performed as well there as it did stand-alone.

To test Kontakt's multitimbral prowess, I loaded a few of its better sounds and laid down a groove in Cubase with electronic drums, electric bass, and a pad. When I was satisfied with the sequence, I started enhancing it with Kontakt's own effects — chorus for the pad, reverb for the snare, and some distortion for the kick. Everything worked fine.

I hit a snag when I used Kontakt's step generator to add filter modulation to the hi-hat. I discovered that the step generator's pattern doesn't reset itself to the downbeat in this situation: My filter accents were different every time I started playback, depending on where I had stopped the time before. If I had been using a looped sample with a full bar of hi-hats, I could have solved the problem by clicking the Retrigger button, but retriggering won't line the pattern up with the bar line when each hi-hat hit is a separate MIDI note.

I ran into minor buglike weirdness in only a couple of spots — when I was editing envelopes graphically, and when I assigned different drums in a kit to different sample groups and then started editing the signal paths of the groups. Both problems tended to clear up after I clicked around for a minute. Other than that, Kontakt was remarkably stable.

Overall, I'm very pleased to have Kontakt on my hard drive. It sounded great and was easy to use, and I'm sure it will get a workout in future projects. If the included soundware were better, I'd have no hesitation using it as the main sound source for my next tune.

Conclusions. Kontakt's front panel is a little different, and a couple of parameters are tucked away in unlikely places — but once I got used to the Kontakt way of doing things, I was a happy camper. This is one powerful sampler. The filters and other voice effects are great for fattening up wimpy sounds, and the 32-stage envelopes and step modulation generator will let you do things no other software sampler can touch. The tone machine and time machine modes, while not pristine sonically, will be lifesavers in certain situations, and may suggest some creative possibilities too. I like the do-everything-in-one-window design, especially in a VST instrument.

True, I was looking at a 1.0 release, and one or two essential features are still to be added. An edit undo command would be useful. More important, Native Instruments needs to improve the quality of the included soundware. It's not a total loss by any means, but having to hunt through the badly programmed instruments in search of stuff I could use left me feeling a little grumpy.

Should the soundware or the inability to stream long samples from the hard drive disqualify Kontakt from serious consideration? Absolutely not. While it won't do everything, in the sound design department it blows most other samplers out

of the water. Fair is fair. You could make serious music with any of today's software samplers, but if you need to go the extra mile, Kontakt will take you there.
—JA (Oct. '02)

Steinberg HALion
FULL-FEATURED SAMPLER

Figure 5-9.
HALion's main panel resembles a hardware instrument. The filter (upper left) has cutoff and resonance controls, its own ADSR envelope, an envelope amount knob with inversion, and lowpass, bandpass, highpass, or notch response (the lowpass filter can use a 12db or 24 dB/octave rolloff slope). The DCA (upper right center) has another ADSR envelope and a control that ties envelope amount to MIDI velocity. The two LFOs (upper right) offer ten waveforms each. LFO frequency varies from 0 to 30Hz, and you can sync to the host application's tempo. Note that all front panel editing can be absolute (parameter changes force all samples to the front panel value) or relative (parameter changes add to, or subtract from, the individual samples' settings). The 10-½-octave keyboard lets you play notes with the mouse, and blue dots flash on the keys to show what's being played on the track. The closer you click to the front of a key, the higher the velocity. The MIDI and disk activity section (lower left) shows whether disk access is occurring, which MIDI channels are playing, the current program's channel, and the program output assignments for the multiple outs. The navigation strip (along the bottom) is your gateway to the other editing pages. The Macro button jumps back to the normal front panel.

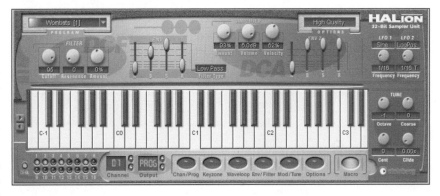

VST (Mac, Win)
$399.99

Pros: Not RAM-limited — can stream huge files from hard disk. Multitimbral. Easy to learn if you know samplers, deep enough to keep you amused long-term. Resonant multimode filter. Imports multiple file formats. Useful modulation options. Responds to MIDI controllers. Can be automated with suitable VST 2.0 host.
Cons: Can't import Roland, Kurzweil, or Ensoniq file formats. No dedicated filter keyboard tracking control (use the modulation section). Coupled with a hard disk recorder, can make heavy demands on your system.

Maybe it's just the fact that I'm an editor, but I always get a little irritated by cUTesy CAPitaliZation in proDUCt NaMeS. Other than that, there's not much I can say about HALion, since I haven't used it. Craig Anderton wrote this review for the Feb. '02 issue of *Keyboard*, so I'll let him give you the tip. Take it away, Craig!

S tand-alone samplers for the Mac (BitHeadz Unity) and PC (Tascam GigaSampler) have been around for a couple of years now, and GigaSampler upped the ante because of its ability to stream huge files from the hard drive while you play the keyboard. In HALion, Steinberg has adopted the stream-from-disk idea and stuffed it into a full-featured VST 2.0 plug-in sampler.

As in other samplers, you'll find an array of synth-type modules (filter, LFOs, envelopes) for sonic control and mutation. HALion also has several tricks up its sleeve that you'll appreciate only after you get intimate with it. And the program comes with four CD-ROMs of soundware to get you started.

Overview. In terms of its voice architecture, HALion has no surprises. Raw waveforms are tucked into samples, which are assigned to zones. Programs include multiple zones, and banks contain 128 programs. Like most virtual samplers, HALion doesn't actually sample. It loads and plays existing files from disk or CD. Since you'll be using it in a multitrack recorder that can grab incoming audio and store it for retrieval in HALion, this is an academic point at best.

Traditionally, a sampler holds no more sample data than can fit in available RAM. But like GigaSampler, HALion overcomes this limitation by streaming audio files from hard disk, so its samples have no significant length limitations. HALion can import Gigasampler-compatible libraries (though not perfectly, as we'll see). Want a multi-gigabyte piano or a collection of sound effects for Foley? Want to be able to fly in vocal phrases from a variety of performances? Done.

Steinberg recommends 512MB of RAM, because it takes time for a hard drive to start playing a file. So HALion stores each sample's attack in RAM. Trigger a note, and it flies out of RAM while the hard drive catches up. For optimum performance, the disk with your streaming HALion files should be defragmented, and preferably separate from the one where you've stored your audio tracks. Trying to do lots of audio tracks while several instances of HALion are also running is asking for trouble.

As with any plug-in soft synth, when HALion sounds are played back from a MIDI track there's no delay because the program addresses the instrument directly. When you play it from a keyboard, any delay between hitting the key and hearing the note (latency) depends on your soundcard's driver.

HALion at a Glance

Minimum system requirements (recommended system in parentheses)	VST 2.0 compatible host application; PC: Pentium 266 (400MHz), 128MB RAM (512MB), Windows 95/98/ME/2000; Mac: PowerMac 604e/266 MHz (G3), 128MB RAM (512MB), Mac OS 9.0 or higher
File import formats	Akai S1000/2000/3000; E-mu EIII/IIIX, ESI, E4/4K, E64/E6400, ESynth/Ultra; SoundFonts 2.x, Giga, LM4/LM9 drums, REX files (mono only)
Multitimbrality	16 channels
Supported file bit resolutions	8, 16, 24, 32
Virtual outputs	8 (4 stereo, 4 mono)
Polyphony	up to 256 voices (RAM/CPU-dependent)
Voicing features	2 LFOs, 2 eight-stage envelopes, high/low/bandpass/notch filter
Automation	within VST 2.0 hosts that support automation
Copy protection	unknown
Downloadable demo	no

To my eyes, the Macro page (main instrument panel) looks vaguely like an Alesis Andromeda hardware synth. This page serves up multiple global controls; you can change values by turning software knobs, or by typing in the numeric field (for some knobs this process is buggy — the typed value may change when you hit return or select another parameter).

From the Macro page, the filter controls affect all samples. You can drill down further to the Env/Filter page to make filter adjustments for individual samples, as well as increase the envelope to eight stages with variable slopes (continuously variable from concave to convex). In this page, the knobs get brighter with higher values, which is a nice extra bit of visual feedback.

Each page has a similar layout: An information strip along the top shows the current program and sample info, a column along the right displays the programs, and along the bottom there's a keyboard for playing notes, the navigation strip, and the MIDI/disk activity section. This makes it easy to jump around among the various pages and see the current MIDI status at any time.

The Channel/Program page is used for creating and editing multitimbral setups. For each of the 16 MIDI channels, you can choose one of the 128 programs in a bank, and also its output assignment. If you need to layer two programs, it's easy enough to copy the sequencer's MIDI track and assign it to a different HALion channel.

In the Keyzone window you assign samples to key positions via importing or graphically with drag-and-drop, set up keyboard or velocity crossfades, sort samples, mute or unmute them, sort by pitch or alphabetically, and so on.

One extremely cool feature in the Waveloop window is that you can detune either the sustain or the release loop. This is useful when you're doing a single-cycle loop and the loop goes just slightly sharp or flat relative to the attack. There's also a play button in this window, which makes it easy to play just the loop and verify that it sounds smooth. HALion doesn't support forward/backward looping, however.

The Mod/Tune page contains the modulation options (up to 12 routings, with 21 sources and five destinations in the list), as well as a MegaTrigg feature. This is similar to a "logical filter," or to GigaStudio's "dimensions" — it sets certain conditions (such as a particular combination of note-on and controller values) under which certain samples will play. For instance, you could program it to switch from dry drum sounds to drum sounds with sampled room ambience when you push down on a footpedal. This page is also the home of the LFOs, tuning, and voice grouping controls; these let you assign samples to one of 16 polyphony groups, with a fixed number of voices — the usual example is assigning open and closed hi-hat to a one-voice group so they cut each other off.

The Options page is where you set the sound quality and master tune, adjust master volume, determine how much memory to dedicate to sample pre-loading, and name your programs.

On all pages other than Macro, you can choose a sample for editing from a drop-down menu at the top of the page. The Options page also offers a "key activates sam-

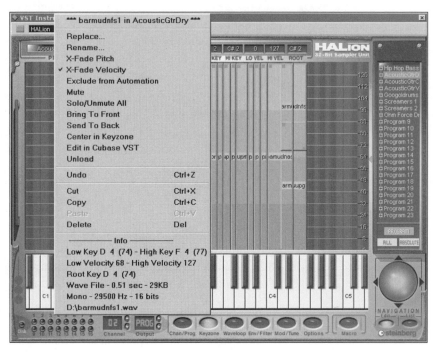

Figure 5-10.

In HALion's Keyzone window, I've right-clicked on a sample to bring up a context-sensitive menu. The two samples at the right side of the window are set for velocity crossfade; the sample to the left is pitch-crossfading with these samples. Clicking on the field behind the samples brings up an additional context-sensitive menu for global keyzone functions, such as importing and sorting samples.

ple" function, which lets you choose a sample for editing by playing its note on the virtual keyboard or an outboard MIDI controller.

Installation. My start with HALion was rocky. Steinberg recommends using Cubase 5.1, so I went to the Web to grab the update file for Cubase 5.0. It didn't work, so I called tech support; the problem was a spurious suffix that somehow got added to the updater file names. Removing the second suffix (changing .W02.W02 to.W02) solved the problem. It isn't actually necessary to download anything: The HALion CD includes a Cubase 5.0 rev 2 updater program, which insures HALion compatibility for 5.0 owners.

I then tried to install HALion 1.0. When it seemed finished, I clicked on the install window's close button, but an alert said I was interrupting the setup process. You need to click on the actual word "Exit" rather than the close button. Then I couldn't find a way to import GigaSampler files. A trip to the Steinberg website revealed a 1.1 HALion update, which includes that option.

So I updated HALion; the manual said to slip in Content CD 1 and load the .fxb bank, but there were no .fxb files. So I imported an instrument instead, loading up an .fxp file. Aha! Escape velocity had been achieved.

Compatibility. I tried importing various sample formats: Akai S1000, GigaSampler, WAV and AIFF files, and SoundFonts. All worked fine, with some cautions. The REX file import option doesn't take advantage of the REX MIDI information, but it maps each slice of the file to its own HALion key, after which you can create your own grooves using the REX file sounds.

I was particularly interested in Giga importing for the Mac; there was something magical about popping a Giga CD into my PowerBook's CD drive and watching HALion recognize it, then import the Giga instrument, even though my G3 PowerBook is underpowered for running HALion.

But translation is an inexact science. Giga's dimensions, which add a lot to the expressiveness and realism of some Giga libraries, don't have an exact equivalent in HALion, so you'll likely need to do some tweaking using MegaTrigg layouts or velocity-switched splits to approximate what they sound like in GigaStudio. But at least in my experience, the velocity and keymapping came across without a hitch, and Akai translation worked fine for the dozen or so CD-ROMs I tried.

I don't have any Giga libraries with multi-CD files, but I've been told it's necessary to save them to your hard drive (using GigaSampler itself) as one continuous .GIG file before HALion can load them. Also, compressed Giga files will present problems; they need to be saved from GigaSampler in uncompressed format before loading into HALion.

HALion worked reasonably well with Cakewalk's Sonar running FXpansion's VST-DX adapter. However, Sonar's DXi protocol won't recognize multiple outs, I couldn't persuade HALion to recognize the host's clock rate for LFO sync, and HALion seemed to want more RAM allocated than when it was running in Cubase.

I also cut pieces of audio from a long solo in Cubase, dragged them into the Keyzone section, and sequenced them to create a new phrase. Sure, I could have just done cut/paste/copy with the digital audio in a Cubase track, but that wouldn't have allowed for audio-warping filter and LFO effects.

Sounds. HALion ships with three sample CDs from Wizoo and one from eLab. There's also some demo material on the installation CD from Ilio (almost 200 files, with MIDI Groove Control files from the *Skippy Grooves* series) and Ueberschall (61 WAV files and some audio demos). The Wizoo sounds include two basses, two drum kits and percussion (with lots of velocity-switched samples), piano, piano with strings, nylon guitar, and nylon guitar with strings.

The third Wizoo CD has electronic drums, synth bass, electric guitar, strings, very tasty velocity-switched electric pianos, "oscillator toolbox" (Minimoog waveforms), clav, organ, polysynth pads, "digital decays," and weird metallic effects, most with several preset variations on the core samples.

Having worked with the Wizoo guys, I have to recuse myself from saying too much. But I think it's safe to say that anyone would find these files, both in terms of quality and selection, to be way beyond the call of duty for "free content."

The eLab samples are construction kit material, as opposed to Wizoo's instrument approach. The Drum Tools folder contains a bunch of electronic/acoustic drum samples, there are two folders of loops (not REX files) at a variety of tempos, two presets loaded with tons of effects-oriented samples, a folder of strange voices and vocal effects, and close to 700 WAV files (samples from other eLab products). Overall, I'd rate the included content as a significant incentive for buying HALion. It took me hours just to audition the sounds.

In Use. I needed a bass patch for a song I was working on, so I decided to import some of my own Chapman Stick samples and create an instrument. I went to the Keyzone window, right-clicked for Import Sample, selected the four samples, and imported them *en masse*. HALion placed them on the right root keys, although I'm not sure how it knew to do that — these were just standard WAV files. I selected them all, and from the context-sensitive menu chose Expand Selected. HALion automatically set up appropriate keyboard split points — great. The instrument sounded fine, but a little crossfading and filter keyboard tracking tweaked it to perfection. Total elapsed time: under three minutes.

Next, I thought I'd load several relatively long loops into the lower octave, then use Cubase to bring them in and out to create a remix.

The first task was to import and assign a bunch of WAV samples. I initially did this from the Options page, and typed in values for the low key, high key, low vel, high vel, and root note parameters. This was tedious, because you can't tab across the fields. It was much faster to drag-and-drop samples from the program list or desktop into the Keyzone page; dragging multiple samples drops them off on successive keys, starting where you clicked. Or you can right-click on the key and import a sample or samples directly from disk. Another method is to drag the samples into the program list, then drag from there into the Keyzone page. This is typical of HALion: There are usually several ways to do anything. If you try to do something intuitively, odds are you'll hit on one of the methods.

I wanted one percussion loop to decay from normal level to silence each time it played. I also wanted to adjust the filtering on some loops — a job for the Envelope/Filter page. This page also has a Fatness control for overdrive effects, which helped turn a bass arpeggio's personality from Marie Osmond to Skinny Puppy.

After assigning and tweaking the loops, it was time to play notes in Cubase to trigger the samples. To add an automated filter cutoff change for one of the drum loops, I first excluded all other samples from automation, selected the drum loop sample, enabled a track for recording the automation, went into record, and twisted the cutoff. It performed as expected. However, although the manual says you can apply automation to individual samples or groups of samples, I found that automation occurs on a channel basis. If you assign multiple loops to the same channel, automation data will affect all non-excluded samples. Placing each loop on a different channel allows you to automate each one individually.

Finally, I bopped back to Cubase and finished off the tune. Overall, I found using HALion straightforward and fun.

Figure 5-11.

In Live, the browser pane (upper left) shows files, while music is constructed in the spreadsheet-like area to the right. In Session mode, clips are loaded into these cells. Each track has its own column into which clips can be dragged. You can have any number of clips playing at the same time (depending on your CPU speed), but you can only have one clip playing per track, so if you want a fuller-sounding arrangement, you'll need to add more tracks. Each row of clips is one "scene." You can trigger all the clips in a scene simultaneously by pressing the scene's play button (in the column at right). A green triangle to the left of the clip means the clip is currently playing. Scenes let you organize groups of clips into sections of a song (e.g., all the clips that make up the verse groove, breakdowns, chorus, and whatever). To map a MIDI note to a clip, press the MIDI button (upper right), then click on the target clip and play your MIDI keyboard. Assigning continuous controllers is just as easy. You can turn trigger quantization on using a button in the upper left center row (the button says "1/16" here). This helps prevent you from triggering clips early or out of time. And here's another cool feature for live use (or Live use): Tracks can be routed to a separate

continued on next page

Conclusions. HALion has won me over, big-time. On my PC, it didn't crash once or exhibit any anti-social behavior, and its file import abilities opened my music up to new libraries of sounds. It has become a welcome addition to the studio, but I'm always careful to run it within the limits imposed by Cubase or Sonar, my computer, and HALion itself. That seems to be the key to a successful relationship.

HALion 1.1 was a significant improvement over 1.0. As with most modern software, you may need to do some tweaking to insure the best possible performance, especially if you're using a slower computer or one with less RAM. But when you consider the functions, the price, and the versatility, there's no question HALion is a winner. —*Craig Anderton (Feb. '02)*

Ableton Live
PERFORMANCE-ORIENTED LOOP PLAYBACK SAMPLER

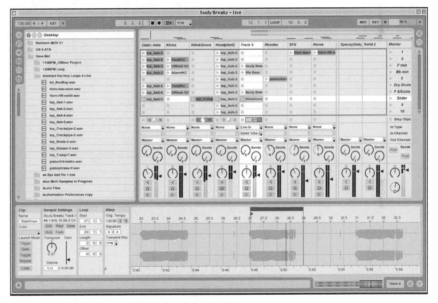

stand-alone (Mac, Win)
$399

Pros: Acid-like time-compression/expansion. Streamlined, easy-to-use interface. Extensive MIDI and QWERTY keyboard control. Samples can be loaded, triggered, and recorded on the fly without stopping the computer. Cool built-in effects. **Cons:** Audio transients aren't used in the automated placement of warp markers. No sample editor. No Solo command. No convenient way to bounce phrases to disk.

I had to wrestle a little with the question of whether Live belonged in this book. As John Krogh describes it below (in a review of Live version 1.03 from the headphone cue output using the row of headphone buttons near the bottom of the columns. This lets you audition samples privately before adding them to your mix for everyone to hear. The area along the bottom is for editing individual clips. The clip's audio waveform is shown here. The gray vertical lines on top of the waveform are warp markers, which tell Live where the beats and subdivisions are. A horizontal bar (in blue on screen) defines a loop. The music within the boundaries will be repeated until you turn off Loop.

February 2002 *Keyboard*), it's not exactly an instrument. In some respects, it's more like a sequencer/multitrack audio recorder. What sets Live apart from other sequencers, as John explains, are its interactive performance features. For practical purposes, then, it's an instrument, even if it doesn't entirely look or behave like one. If your main usage will be to build up studio arrangements using loops, which Live will certainly do, there are several other programs worth looking at, which aren't included in this book because they can't be played live. Almost any multitrack sequencer/recorder will do the job.

According to Ableton, version 1.1 of Live added 24-bit recording/playback and Mac OS X support. Version 1.5 added a render-to-disk command, full ReWire support (master or slave) on Windows and OS 9 (in OS X, Live must be the ReWire master), and a built-in reverb. Version 2 checks in with "selectable stretch modes to provide 'clean' time-stretching; the ability to set or tap the tempo at any time, before, during, or after recording; editing of tempo as a continuous curve; enhanced file management; a revised arrangement section; improved jamming capabilities; assignable MIDI control of the transport; and DJ mixer-like crossfading." The price has been upped from $299 to $399.

L et's face it: While conventional MIDI/audio sequencers are extremely powerful for studio work, most of the currently available programs don't have the interactive features musicians need for live performance. Simply playing back submixed background vocals, percussion loops, and whatever else is no problem with a computer, but if you want to use your computer as an instrument — that is, playing and manipulating audio in an improvisational way — most sequencers fall down.

Ableton's cross-platform program, Live, is an audio sequencer that does things a bit differently. Unlike most recording software, which is oriented toward studio production work, Live's prime target is the DJ/electronic musician community. As such, the interface is extremely well suited for live performance — there are no sub-

Live at a Glance

System requirements	PC: 400MHz CPU, 128MB RAM, Windows 95, 98, NT 4.0, 2000, or XP, soundcard; Mac: G3, 192MB RAM, OS 9, 10.1, or later; both: CD-ROM drive
Supported plug-in & audio interface formats	VST and DirectX; ASIO, DirectX, Sound Manager, ReWire
Sample rate & bit depth	44.1/48kHz, 16/24-bit
Mixer sends	4 stereo, pre/post fader switchable
Max. # of insert effects	limited only by CPU
Synchronization	MIDI clock and SMPTE, bpm-based effects
Built-in effects	4-band parametric EQ, compressor, delays (filter, grain, ping-pong, simple), chorus, auto filter, Erosion, vinyl distortion
Copy protection	serial number
Downloadable demo	yes

menus to get lost in, no overly complicated controls to figure out, and no automated punch-in/out. Heck, there isn't even a metronome.

There is, however, a lot to get excited about with Live, so let's jump in.

Overview. It may take a few minutes for anyone who's familiar with traditional MIDI/audio sequencers to get their head around Live. You can (sort of) record in linear fashion, as you would with other recorders, recording drums and overdubbing bass, synth comps, and so on, with as many overdubs as you'd like, but if you do you'll be missing the point.

In Live, audio is treated as building blocks — clips, in Live-speak — that get loaded into cells within Session view (see the main screen image on page 181). The program works rather like a pattern-based sequencer, in which you string together patterns to create an arrangement. Clips can be independently triggered via MIDI, QWERTY keyboard, or mouse, and will continually loop until you stop them. You can add effects and tweak them in real time, all without stopping playback. This means it's possible to create arrangements very quickly. This is one of Live's big advantages over traditional recording software.

Ableton calls their software a "sequencing instrument," and I'd have to agree with their description. You don't record music into Live so much as play it as an instrument. More on this in "Building Arrangements," below.

Here's a brief rundown of what you'll get with Live:

■ Automatic beat matching. Live detects tempo information from loops and automatically time-stretches them on the fly to match your song's tempo. This is similar to how Sonic Foundry Acid works, except that Live doesn't factor in pitch. If you work with harmonic material that was recorded in different keys, you'll have to manually transpose these clips to a common key from the Clip View window.

■ Unlimited undo. If you like, Live will record all your automation moves, clip triggering, and everything else associated with your session. After you've finished recording your moves, you can fine-tune them (along with other aspects of the track) until you're happy. And if you go too far with applying effects or editing automation data, Live's unlimited undo can get you back to where you started.

■ Compatibility. The program runs on Mac and PC, supports Sound Manager, ReWire, ASIO, and DirectX audio systems, and can record at 16- and 24-bit.

■ Effects. A set of ten effect plug-ins is included — some utilitarian (EQ and compression) and others truly inspiring. Filter Delay has separate syncable left and right delay lines, and Vinyl Distortion comes remarkably close to making tracks sound as if they came straight off of wax. These two are capable of lending heaps of attitude to just about any ho-hum sample.

Equally useful for "digital-sounding" delays and creating ambient washes of sound, Granular Delay combines elements of granular synthesis with a syncable stereo delay. Lots of cool sounds to be mined with this effect.

Even more good news: You can use VST plug-ins, too.

■ Sample editing. There's no built-in sample editor, which is a shame. Fortunately, you can link Live with the sample editor of your choice. When you want to edit a sample, Live will automatically open the audio file in the sample editor you've selected.

■ Documentation. The manual, like many others, tells users what can be done with the program, but rarely explains why or shows you how to perform certain operations. Luckily, Live isn't a terribly deep or complex program from a user standpoint.

■ Control features. What good would a program aimed at live performance be if you could only control it from a mouse? In Live, you can pretty much run everything, from launching individual clips and song sections to riding track faders and tweaking effect sends, via MIDI. If you want to run your session using a QWERTY keyboard, you can do that too.

Time Warping. One of the advantages of Live is its ability to beat-match loops on the fly, something many sequencers costing twice as much can't do. The way it works is, Live makes a guess as to the tempo of a loop based on the length of the audio file. Once it guesses the tempo, Live will place warp markers where it expects the downbeats and subdivisions to be. As the audio is streamed from the hard disk (samples aren't loaded into RAM), Live time-compresses or expands the audio, lining each region of audio between markers to match its tempo grid.

If a loop is precisely trimmed, Live does an excellent job at guessing the loop's tempo. But because the placement of markers is determined solely from a metronomic grid (attack transients aren't factored in), markers tend to be off just a bit for loops with any amount of swing (see **Figure 5-12**, page 185). "Straight" dance loops are no problem, but what do you do with a loop of a live drummer who plays with a lot of swing? You need to adjust the warp markers by hand to line up with the individual hits. This sounds worse than it is — I found that in most cases I could correct playback problems related to poor marker placement by lining up a few key hits of a groove. At times, though, adjusting the warp markers made the loop timing feel worse. Live would push and pull the tempo of the groove within the loop itself.

One benefit of Live's time-stretching is that audio transients don't get smeared or softened the way they do using the stretching features in some other audio recorders. Another advantage (or disadvantage, depending on how you look at it) is that by lining up markers with audio transients, you can make grooves with swing feel straighter. I know what you're thinking: "How can removing the feel from a loop be a good thing?" Because this allows you to tighten up loops with varied feels — a must for dance music.

Building Arrangements. The first thing you need to understand about Live is that audio is treated as clips. Clips can repeat (loop) or not, and can be triggered, or launched, according to the launch mode you select:

Figure 5-12.
This snare hit near 1.2 (beat 2) isn't exactly on the beat, so Live's warp marker doesn't line up. Sometimes you'll hear a flammed hit or stutter on playback when Live gets to a marker that's not lined up with an audio event. You can fix this by dragging the marker to line up with the attack. However, this will change the feel of the loop — it will become more "straight," which may or may not be what you want.

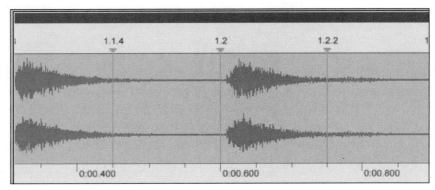

■ *Trigger.* Clips are played as one-shot samples starting and ending at user-definable points.

■ *Gate.* Audio plays only while a MIDI note, mouse button, or QWERTY key is held down. As soon as you lift up, the audio stops.

■ *Toggle.* Audio is triggered by a note, mouse button, or key-down, and will continue to repeat until you play that note or press that mouse button/key again.

■ *Repeat.* As long as the mouse button/MIDI note/QWERTY key is held down, the clip will be repeatedly triggered at the quantization resolution set in the transport control bar. A resolution of 32nd-notes, for example, will give you stutter playback — perfect for use with single-shot kick and snare samples.

The second thing to understand is that there are only two viewing/editing modes: Session and Arrangement. Clips are loaded in Session mode. You're free to trigger clips as you'd like, but if you want to capture your performance (the order in which clips were triggered, mixer moves, and all other aspects of a performance), you need to press the Record button, then start triggering clips. That's it. All your moves will get recorded as an arrangement that you can then edit and refine in, you guessed it, Arrangement mode.

A word about getting started: You could begin a song by grabbing a bunch of loops from the hard disk and plugging them into cells at random, but for a more musically rewarding experience, it pays to put some forethought into the samples you choose. In a typical live situation you wouldn't just show up for a gig without having learned the songs that you'd be performing or which instruments and patches you were going to play. The same thing is true with Live. I started my sessions by experimenting with different samples to find out which ones sounded best at the tempo I was working at, and how various samples might work together for different sections of my track.

After finding loops that work well, I suggest you organize them into some sort of structure. Clips that are in the same row can be played simultaneously as a scene; you can arrange clips for a verse in one row, pre-chorus clips in the next row, and so on. It's not a bad idea to name your clips as you go.

Figure 5-13.
VST effects show up like
this in Live. Parameters can
be shown/hidden by press-
ing the arrow (upper left).
Pressing the Edit button will
open the normal interface
for the plug-in.

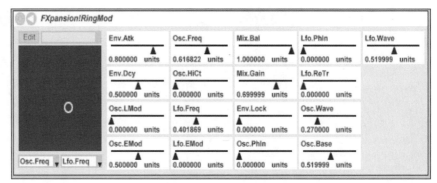

Once you've recorded yourself triggering different song sections, you can go over to Arrangement mode to fix any botched fader moves, effects tweaks, and missed triggers. I won't bore you with the details of this process, because the graphic edit procedures are pretty much the same as what you'd find in any linear audio recorder.

Now you're ready to make a stereo mix of your track. Since Live doesn't let you specify the number of bars you'd like to resample (the way many other programs do), the way to record your song is by record-enabling one of Live's tracks and setting its input to the Master output. Once again, press record and let Live record the track.

Additional audio tracks can be overdubbed in much the same way, except instead of setting the track input to Master out you'd choose one of the inputs on your audio interface.

In Use. I don't play out much these days — besides writing for *Keyboard,* I get my music fix mostly from composing and producing tracks for TV commercials. But my studio-centric viewpoint didn't stop me from putting Live through its paces as a performance tool.

Lately I've been experimenting with breakbeat-type programming at around 130 bpm, so I started by sifting through my sample library. Uptempo loops were obvious candidates to start my track, but because Live's time-stretching worked so well, I found I could take hip-hop and trip-hop loops in the 90–100 bpm range and crank them up to breakbeat speed with great-sounding results.

With several loops loaded into the Session window, I reorganized my material into separate song sections, and named these scenes accordingly (take a look at **Figure 5-11** to see what I mean). Now I was ready to set Live up for improvising.

Mapping MIDI notes and continuous controllers was a snap. My main controller keyboard doesn't have as many knobs as I'd like, and for my track I wanted to tweak effect sends, effect parameters, and so on. No problem, I'll just add a Phat Boy MIDI knob box to the mix. Wrong. Live can only accept MIDI data from one MIDI device at a time. Where was my MIDI merger box when I needed it? [*Editor's note: The current version supports multiple MIDI inputs if your computer provides them.*]

As I was practicing different song ideas I discovered a snag: I could trigger multiple clips at the same time without any playback problems, but when I tried to trigger a scene and a clip together simultaneously, the clip would get truncated — it wouldn't play through to the end of the sample. A call to Ableton resolved the issue: "That's what the Remove Slot Button command in the Edit menu is for," they told me. "Just select a bunch of slots, or a scene, and issue that command." Once I did this, the clip played back fine when I simultaneously triggered a scene. There was no visual feedback telling me that I had removed a slot's button, however. Nor was this feature covered in the Edit menu documentation.

There were a couple of other strange problems with mapping QWERTY keys to clips, but apparently this was due to stability problems with my machine's OS (version 9.1.2). When I ran Live with OS 9.0.4 I didn't experience this type of mapping weirdness.

After I had worked with Live for a couple of weeks, the light went on. Yes, Live is well suited for live performance, but it can be an incredibly effective tool for the studio too. I was able to beat-match loops for a commercial project with the greatest of ease, and the results sounded way better than what I could get with my main sequencer.

Live is also great for trying out song ideas, even if you plan on producing your final track in a different program. For example, I grabbed a couple of loops that inspired me, then set another track to record the input of my synth, and off I went. After recording several passes of a bass riff, I stopped the session to edit the newly recorded audio. I auditioned the new clip, zeroed in on two bars that felt the best, and repositioned the loop markers. Now I had a two-bar bass loop that I could use in my song. Building up an arrangement was that easy.

Conclusions. This is a 1.0 release, so naturally not every aspect of the program is going to be rock-solid and perfectly executed. That said, Live is solid in many ways, and its user interface succeeds where other programs fail. If you like the idea of using a computer as an instrument for live performance of loops and one-shot samples, Live is the best game in town. But to dismiss this program as software only for playing out would be a mistake. For those of you working in the studio by yourself or with other musicians, Live is a great tool for working out song arrangements. Or maybe you just need to beat-match a few loops and whip up a bunch of variations with different effects. Live is perfect for this kind of work.

And you get all of this for 300 bucks! [*Editor's note: The current version is $399, not $299.*] I know I'm sounding a bit like those overly hyped car lot salesmen on TV, but even though it's not a do-all audio recorder, Live is worth the excitement.
—*John Krogh (Feb. '02)*

Figure 5-14.
SampleTank's fire-
engine red panel. The left
side of the field shows
you the current multisam-
ple, and below that you
can see the four knobs
that let you tweak the current sound. The available
parameters vary accord-
ing to what sound you're
using. The right side of
the field contains the
search facility and the
file-path controls. Under
them are the effects edit
knobs and the effects
select drop-down lists.
Across the bottom left
are the buttons that
select the current MIDI
channel/multitimbral part,
with "LEDs" indicating
which parts have sounds
loaded. Next to the part
select buttons are the
output select buttons,
active only when
SampleTank is used in a
VST environment.

IK Multimedia SampleTank

BASIC SAMPLE PLAYBACK INSTRUMENT

VST, MAS, RTAS (Mac, Win)
L $279, XL $499

Pros: Huge, solid, musical soundset included, with more on the way. Dead-easy operation. Blink-of-an-eye loading of new samples. Very good effects.
Cons: Very limited sound programming. Requires a pretty heavy-duty machine to really get the most from it. Doesn't import WAV, AIFF, or SoundFont libraries.

The main attraction of SampleTank, it seems to me, is its ease of use. If you're mainly a pop songwriter and don't want to mess with a lot of fiddly con-trols or esoteric software features, this program might be well worth looking at, for reasons that Ken Hughes explains in the October 2001 review below. I'm a bit skeptical, but maybe that's because I'm a knob-twiddler at heart. Currently IK Multimedia offers a free "lite" version of SampleTank (available at www.sampletank.com, and included on the CD-ROM that comes with this book). This free version is only compatible with sample files provided by IK Multimedia, but they provide new content for it on a regular basis. The reg-ular version of SampleTank is compatible with Akai S1000 sample files, which are widely available in the music industry, but I couldn't find anything on the SampleTank website about WAV or AIFF compatibility — a huge limitation.

SampleTank. An intimidating assault vehicle that uses samples as ammuni-tion? Or a large container full of samples? Both images are apt. SampleTank is an assault vehicle in that it has fired an early salvo on what may become a crowded bat-tlefield of VST software sound modules. It's also a large container that stores and dis-penses an impressive number of very good sounds, and makes them available right quick.

It's easiest to think of SampleTank as a sound module — a 16-part multitimbral sample-playback unit with built-in effects and multiple outputs (a suitable ASIO card being required if you want more than stereo output).

Overview. Presenting a simple, uncluttered user interface, SampleTank is easy to get to know without studying the manual first.

The search feature is appreciated, since the SampleTank sound library is likely to get large. To take best advantage of the library, you'll want to have it all accessible at once. That makes for a sea of sounds, and the search feature makes it much easier to find the sound you're looking for. It's worth noting that the search doesn't just look at patch names; embedded within each patch are up to 32 keywords that the search engine can hook.

SampleTank allows its "tank" (the samples themselves) to be located in a different directory, or on a different drive, from its "pump" (the engine). This allows you to dedicate a separate drive to SampleTank if you like, leaving your audio recording/playback drive free to serve only that purpose.

Eight instantiations can run concurrently, for a total of 128 instrument parts, provided your CPU can bear the weight. On a 450MHz blue-and-white G3 with 256 MB of RAM, I was able to run only one Tank, with five instruments. A little disappointing, but I was able to make satisfying music that wasn't unduly compromised. Those of you with the fattest, fastest systems will get more utility from the instrument. Those of us without can always bounce SampleTank tracks to disk as audio and free up system resources for more MIDI virtual instrument tracks.

At press time, IK Multimedia had 12 additional SampleTank libraries in development. Sampleware cartels AMG, Masterbits, and Sonic Reality are developing SampleTank-native libraries of their own. There are versions of SampleTank to fit most budgets.

Installation. Parking the Tank on my computer was easy. The installer did all the work, and the registrar-bot on IK's email server shot me back an authorization code within minutes of my emailed request. I did my best to blunder through the process the way a rank newbie might, and came out unhassled and authorized in less than 15 minutes. I expect your experience would be the same.

It's possible to install just the engine and leave the library on the CD-ROMs, but I wouldn't recommend it unless it's your only option; you'll be giving up the quick loading time you'll enjoy if you install the samples on your hard drive. Nothing cools off the fever of creativity like the ice bath of a slow-loading sampler. Install the library.

Sounds. Sound editing is rudimentary; only four edit parameters are offered in each patch. While they differ from patch to patch, you most often get a filter cutoff or brightness control, attack and decay controls, and sometimes filter resonance. Other software sample-playback devices offer much, much more editing.

SampleTank at a Glance

Minimum system requirements (recommended system in parentheses)	Mac: 200MHz PowerPC 604 (Power Mac G3/G4), MacOS 8.5 or later, 64MB RAM; PC: 200MHz Pentium MMX (500MHz Pentium III), Windows 95/90/2000/ME/NT, 64MB RAM, soundcard; 240MB free HD space (128MB RAM, 2GB free HD space, ASIO soundcard); VST, MAS, or RTAS host program
Polyphony	up to 128 notes (CPU-dependent)
Oscillators	2; sample playback, with waveshaping
Envelopes	2; ADSR
Filter	1; multimode, variable slope
LFOs	2; multi-waveform
Effects	reverb, ambience, reverb delay, delay, lowpass filter, envelope filter, wah, chorus, multi chorus, AM & FM modulation, flanger, auto-pan, tremolo, rotary speaker, lo-fi (distortion and bandpass filter), distortion, phonograph, slicer
MIDI CC destinations	4 synth parameters, 5 effects parameters (preset-dependent)
Sample import	Akai S1000/S3000
Syncable functions	bpm-synced effects
Copy protection	registration code request
Downloadable demo	SampleTank Free (free, but limited)

When you offer as little sound editing as IK has on SampleTank, the thing is going to live or die by its factory samples. It lives. I was more than pleased with SampleTank's factory soundset.

The acoustic piano samples are quite nice, with well-masked split and loop points. Thankfully, IK Multimedia has eschewed the "empty concert hall" school of piano sampling and instead given us a smooth, bright piano relatively free of sampled-in ambience.

Every sound I tried was at least adequately musical: crisp, crystalline acoustic guitars, fat but focused basses, lush strings, choirs where you can almost pick out individual singers, decent organs that make use of the effects' pretty realistic rotary speaker effect, and on and on.

Synth sounds are out in force, a large number of the analog variety but quite a few that are less identifiable and still quite fresh. Several of the more digital textures inspired new ideas. It always bodes well when factory patches lead you beyond your standard tryout riffs. Throughout the factory soundset, sample loop points range from acceptable to imperceptible. Well done.

There are also a number of beat loops in the factory banks, grouped by tempo. I thought they were fresh and interesting, and I liked having maps of different elements spread out across the keys. The majority of loop content is rhythmic, with a few pitched or melodic loops sprinkled in.

Effects. Up to four effects can be applied to each SampleTank sound (up to the limit of your CPU's prowess), from a menu of 28 different flavors. The usual suspects all appear — reverb, delay, chorus, flanger, as well as a few less common effects like a simu-Leslie, an envelope filter, FM and AM modulation (which give results similar to a ring mod), tremolo, and a suite of audio mayhem tools.

Even the mundane effects sound really good. The delay in particular sounds subjectively warmer than most to my ear. The Leslie is pretty darn good, with a variation that puts its speed under mod wheel control. Bravo. I enjoyed using the lofi, distortion, and phonograph effects. I do wish the phonograph effect could be gated by note-ons and -offs; its pops, clicks, and noise begin as soon as you turn it on and end only when you turn it off.

Given that the VST environment offers outboard effects in spades, it might seem redundant to offer built-in effects. But this way, you don't have to use up more resources for effects. I found it convenient, and since my Mac was already at the brink with only five instruments loaded, the built-in effects let me add polish and sheen without stretching the machine's limits to the breaking point.

MIDI. Each sound's edit parameters can be placed under MIDI control. Continuous controllers 12, 13, 14, and 15 are assigned to knobs A, B, C, and D respectively. I automated the brightness of the CP80 piano during the course of my song, so I could brighten it up in the choruses and dull it down a bit during the verses. Like the four synth parameters, effects parameters are available for MIDI control too. The manual provides a list of available effects parameters and their default MIDI CC numbers.

Akai Conversion. While the drum kits included in the Tank are very good, Sonic Reality's *Interactive Drum Kits* contains some excellent sounds too. I have an Akai-formatted copy, so it was the perfect test CD to see how well SampleTank XL's Akai sample converter works. I'm happy to report that there's very little to say; after a minute or two of drive whirring and status bar movement, the converter finished its work. When I browsed SampleTank's file directory, there were the IDK samples. They were playable immediately, with the keymaps preserved. Love it — a complete no-brainer.

For another test, I reached randomly into a bin of Akai CD-ROMs in the *Keyboard* storage closet. What I grabbed was an antique Masterbits mixed-mode audio/Akai violin library. Fair enough — you might have a favorite old CD-ROM you'll want to convert and continue using. No dice. Only ISO-9660-formatted CD-ROMs will work in the converter. [*Editor's note: Apparently the CD drive in an Akai hardware sampler doesn't conform to the ISO-9660 format. Ken was using an actual Akai CD, rather than a computer-type CD with Akai files.*]

A guitar sample converted from Best Service's *Pure Guitars* played almost the way it did on my S3000; there were subtle differences in the amp envelope, and modwheel vibrato was a touch slower. If you've ever used Akai CD-ROMs in a "compatible" hardware sampler, you've run into these kinds of things before, and SampleTank's occasional misinterpretations are no worse (but no better, either) than those on other non-Akai samplers that read Akai libraries.

Curiously, SampleTank doesn't support WAV, AIFF, or SoundFont file imports. Maybe in a future revision, IK Multimedia will open the door to these formats as well.

In Use. I cracked open Cubase 5 and instantiated SampleTank as a VST plug-in. At first I had trouble with Cubase crashing and parts of the sample library refusing to load, but after I upped Cubase's memory allocation, the lockups, disobedience, and auto-quits ceased. This is potentially important, since the multisamples, when loaded, all reside in RAM. Many are quite large, and loading up all 16 of SampleTank's slots will casually devour lots of memory.

After dialing in acceptable memory settings, I had a great time working with it. Auditioning sounds with the help of the search feature and the quick load time made choosing them fun rather than tedious.

I chose a Fender P-Bass multisample with a little fret buzz on some notes. By itself it bordered on troublesome, but when the bass was placed properly in the track the buzz was deadly cool. It added an extra layer of believability to a carefully programmed bass riff. Drums are in good supply in the factory banks, and I chose a natural-sounding studio kit ("Studio Natural," actually). In the track the kit's ambience all but disappeared, but without that little bit of air around them the drums would have sounded dead. And I didn't have to use up CPU cycles adding ambience with SampleTank's effects.

I used a couple of 120 bpm loops in a 120 bpm song and had trouble keeping them synced. It's a shame, because many of them evolve over four bars and I could only use the first two before having to retrigger them to keep 'em in time. The workaround involves either adjusting the sequencer's tempo to match the loops or committing the SampleTank track to disk as audio and chopping it up.

Using the native audio hardware on my Mac, I noted a fair amount of latency when playing SampleTank. It required a little getting used to, but wasn't so bad that it hobbled my playing. Single notes or block chords, the slight sluggishness was about the same. It made programming the drum track a little more challenging than usual. If I'd had an ASIO audio interface in my Mac, latency would have been minimized.

Operating SampleTank itself was cake. The part select buttons are small, but no smaller than some controls on ReBirth and Reason. While it was no biggie for me, a visually impaired computer musician I know came to mind. He might have more trouble than usual with SampleTank for this reason; he complained about Reason's many micro-buttons.

Conclusions. I like SampleTank a lot. It's been great fun to be able to just boot up Cubase and then the Tank whenever I have a little inspiration and want to capture the kernel of an idea or even a complete groove. Its sounds are uniformly good (and in some cases inspiring), and I'm tantalized by the promise of SampleTank-native libraries from well-respected sampleware houses. Excellent VST instruments are nothing new. The list is already long and steadily getting longer. But SampleTank is new and different in that it's the first plug-in of its kind — a bulging boxcar full of widely varied, high-quality sounds available almost instantly. Instant access helps stoke the creative fire rather than pour water on it. —*Ken Hughes (Oct. '01)*

Digidesign Soft SampleCell
SOFTWARE UPDATE OF A CLASSIC COMPUTER-BASED SAMPLER

Figure 5-15.
SampleCell's bank window (left) is where individual instruments are assembled for multitimbral use. The sample instruments I've loaded here include a Rhodes, a Minimoog, and a sustained string section, each assigned to its own stereo output pair routed into Pro Tools (not shown). To the right are the Matrix window, where modulation assignments are made, and the Misc. Parameters window, where basic settings such as transposition, filter cutoff, pitchbend range, and so on are accessed.

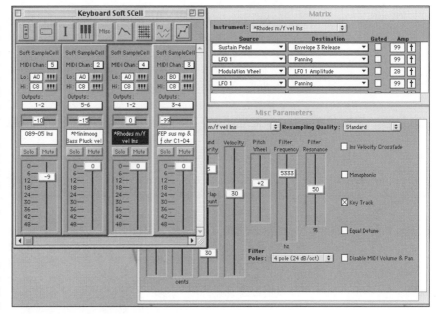

stand-alone (Mac)
$349

Pros: Easy to use. Four-pole resonant lowpass filter. Powerful modulation matrix. Supports up to 1GB of sample RAM. Banks are automatically recalled using DirectConnect.
Cons: Audio outputs can't be routed into ASIO or MAS audio systems. No syncable LFOs.

Return with me now to those thrilling days of yesteryear, when computers were too slow to do much of anything in the audio department. Digidesign became a music industry powerhouse by providing add-on NuBus boards that made it possible to use a Macintosh as a professional audio tool. They still do (though of course the boards are no longer NuBus). Along with their Pro Tools line of recorder hardware/software, they had, for a while, a product called SampleCell. SampleCell operated pretty much like any of the hardware samplers that were available at the time, but it lived on a card inside the Mac.

When computer CPUs became fast enough to handle audio, Digidesign decided to retool SampleCell as a software-only instrument. Hence, Soft SampleCell, discussed in John Krogh's Aug. '01 review, below. Beware, though: If you're not using Digidesign audio hardware, you won't be able to run Soft SampleCell in conjunction with your sequencer, though you can run it as a stand-alone application via Sound Manager.

With the power of today's computers, many musicians are ditching their hardware samplers in favor of virtual sample-playback instruments that offer better integration with MIDI/audio sequencers and the ability to use a computer's RAM for loading samples. Long before this trend, though, Digidesign's SampleCell provided musicians with the first affordable computer-based sample playback solution. It combined the guts of a sampler (eight audio outputs and sample RAM) with software that allowed musicians to build multitimbral banks of instruments whose raw samples were loaded onto the SampleCell hardware card. But that's ancient history.

The latest version of SampleCell no longer requires a dedicated card for loading samples and audio output. This is perhaps the biggest difference between it and previous versions, and it makes sense: Recent generations of Macs have fewer slots

Soft SampleCell at a Glance

System requirements	Digidesign-qualified Power Mac, 32MB of RAM (128MB recommended), OS 9.0.4 or later, OMS 2.3
Audio system compatibility	DirectConnect, SoundManager, DirectI/O
Max. polyphony	96 voices (system-dependent)
Max. sample RAM	up to 1GB (system-dependent)
Sample formats	SampleCell, SDI, SDII, WAV, AIFF
# of multitimbral parts	16 channels, # of parts dependent on system resources
Key modes	poly, mono
Sample rate & bit depth	up to 192kHz; 16/24-bit
Loop types	single, double, forward, backward
# of velocity layers	6
Filter	1-pole lowpass or 4-pole resonant lowpass
LFOs	3; sine, triangle, upward/downward sawtooth, square, random, noise
Syncable functions	none
Envelopes	3 assignable ADSRs, one hardwired to amplitude
Copy protection	floppy disk or iLok
Downloadable demo	yes

for installing special interface cards and processors for music applications. Of course, there are other changes with version 3.0 (which Digidesign calls "Soft SampleCell" in most of their literature, for those of you who might go to their website looking for information).

Overview. In many ways, version 3.0 is the same old SampleCell many of us have known and loved for years, except that sound is now routed out through Sound Manager or through DirectConnect- or DirectI/O-compatible hardware for 24-bit playback. A few minor additions have been made to the software, most notably a four-pole resonant lowpass filter. It sounds nice, and with the resonance jacked up you can create dramatic filter sweeps via any of a variety of MIDI controllers.

Up to 1GB of samples can be loaded at once, provided there's enough free RAM in your computer. This is a tremendous jump in functionality compared to the hardware version, which supported only 32MB of sample RAM per card.

Not new, but worth pointing out: There's a respectable amount of programmability in the modulation department. For example, there are 18 available mod sources (including two LFOs, three envelopes, and a random generator) and 26 destinations to choose from. For each instrument (patch) you can assign up to 20 modulation routings — impressive for any sampler, hardware or software. The only significant shortcoming here is that you can't sync the LFOs to MIDI clock.

You can use SampleCell as a stand-alone multitimbral sound source or within a MIDI/audio sequencer, provided your sequencer supports DirectConnect. This is Digidesign's protocol for routing audio outputs from software instruments into Digidesign TDM and 001 hardware interfaces, similar to Propellerhead's ReWire, which works with VST and MAS audio systems. With DirectConnect, you're able to route up to 32 audio outputs from SampleCell into the virtual inputs of your audio sequencer, allowing you to process the outputs with plug-ins. For many, this will be the deal-closer. But this functionality isn't entirely new: TDM users have had the option of piping audio from a SampleCell card into their Pro Tools software mixer for several years now.

Pro Tools is DirectConnect-compatible, and other non-Digi sequencers such as Logic and Digital Performer will work with DirectConnect, provided the host software is running on a system with Digidesign hardware installed. What does this mean for users with ASIO or MAS systems? Bad news: You won't be able to pipe SampleCell's outputs into your digital audio workstation. According to a Digi rep, there are no plans currently to support any other audio systems.

There are a few other shortcomings with version 3.0. For starters, there are no portamento/glide or legato key modes, which puts SampleCell behind the curve of the current crop of software samplers. In addition, only one authorization is allowed, and you have to authorize from a floppy disk, which is a drag for anyone who bought a Mac in the last couple of years. [*Editor's note: According to Digidesign, the current version, 3.1, can be authorized with a license card for the iLok system.*] (When you register your software, Digi will send you a backup floppy authorization disk.)

SampleCell has to run alongside a host app. It would be better if it would run as a plug-in within a host, because it would mean less jockeying back and forth between programs — all your work could be done within Pro Tools, and there'd be fewer tracks to manage.

SampleCell's user interface, while not the sexiest I've seen, is absolutely simple to grok. Want to tweak the envelopes? Press the button that looks like an envelope. A generous-sized window will appear, letting you get hold of the ADSR shapes by clicking with the mouse. Setting up keymaps with velocity ranges and so on is equally intuitive.

When it comes to sample editing features, all you're given is the ability to set loop points and trim audio regions. For more intensive work, you'll need a sample editor. This isn't a big deal, as most of us will be using SampleCell with some sort of digital audio workstation, so chores like normalization can be done there.

In Use. I used SampleCell as a multitimbral instrument within Logic and Pro Tools 5.0, both running on TDM, and to program custom sounds running SampleCell stand-alone routed through an ASIO SoundManager driver. Adding SampleCell to my OMS setup was the first thing I did. This went off without a hitch. However, I later discovered that Logic's built-in SampleCell driver wouldn't work with the software-only version. (This means Logic users will need to run OMS, even if they're directly interfacing with an Emagic Unitor8 interface.)

Once I had MIDI input happening, I jumped into my first session. Being a SampleCell user from way back in the NuBus days, I was in familiar territory when I first launched version 3.0. I immediately went to work configuring a multitimbral bank using instruments from a variety of libraries — drum loops and hits, synth basses, orchestral strings, and an assortment of vintage keyboards rounded out my palette. All the sounds from various SampleCell-format libraries loaded fine. The latency I experienced when playing these instruments was acceptable — around ten milliseconds, I'd guess.

During one programming session I tried to load more samples than the software had room for in RAM with its current settings, and was denied. I then opened up the preferences, allocated more sample RAM, and was able to load more sounds. I never had to reboot the software or computer, and the software never crashed. Having the ability to pig out (or not) on RAM is one of the big advantages of Soft SampleCell over the older card-based version.

With version 3.0, all SampleCell instruments and DirectConnect settings are recalled within Pro Tools. When I tested this, SampleCell was automatically launched when I opened a session with SampleCell tracks, but no sounds were loaded, nor were DC input assignments set the way they had been when the session was last closed. A call to Digi's tech support revealed that full session recall works only if you save the SampleCell bank and PT session in the correct order: Save the bank first and close it, then save the PT session and close it. Once I quit my sessions in that order, everything recalled properly. According to Digi, they're working to improve this behavior.

We recently received a few new TDM plug-ins, including Line 6's Echo Farm vintage delay, so I was anxious to spice up some vanilla SampleCell patches with these new plug-ins. This is where things started to get fun. It was a trip updating some of my old library sounds with lo-fi and vintage effects, giving these once-stale sounds a new lease on life. I piled on a number of plugs to eight sets of SampleCell output streams running alongside my digital audio tracks. I was curious to see whether this combination of native software instrument streams with TDM effects and mixing would choke or cause weirdness with the computer. It didn't. I never ran into a problem, and after building up my MIDI track count, I couldn't detect any lag or slop.

Conclusions. Soft SampleCell is a solid and very programmable sample-playback instrument that picks up where previous hardware versions left off, adding support for lots more sample RAM. Other than this, there's not much new to get excited about with version 3.0. Even though it supports 24-bit samples, it seems a bit behind the times compared to the current crop of native-based instruments that can be instantiated as plug-ins within a host app.

The fact that SampleCell can't be used in MIDI/audio sequencers running audio hardware other than Digi's is disappointing for those who use MAS or ASIO audio systems. These shortcomings aside, SampleCell remains one of the easiest software sample-playback instruments to use, and for Pro Tools users, it shines. The integration between the two programs is a beautiful thing. —*John Krogh (Aug. '01)*

Design It Yourself

6

I have a soft spot in my heart for modular synthesizers. My very first synth was a four-panel Serge Modular system. At the time — this was in 1980 — far more convenient instruments, such as the Sequential Prophet-5, were readily available, but I was interested in exploring the kinds of esoteric sounds that you could only get by physically plugging in patch cords to connect one module with another. Even before the Serge, I had learned synthesis on an ARP 2600, which was also patchable. So maybe it's not a surprise that I reviewed three of the four synths in this chapter myself.

Experimentation is the main appeal of modular synthesizers, both software and hardware. The musicians who get involved with modulars tend to be out on the fringe. If your main interest is in writing or recording pop tunes — or, for that matter, in composing TV soundtracks, dance remixes, new age instrumentals, or traditional classical music — you'll probably find that you can get the results you're seeking more quickly with other types of instruments.

Software-based modulars are a big improvement over their hardware counterparts in at least two respects — repeatability and expandability. Once you've created a great new sound with a hardware modular synth, the only way to be reasonably sure you can reproduce the sound later is to write down each and every front-panel connection and knob setting on a piece of paper. (Even then, there are no guarantees.) With a software modular, all you have to do is click the "save" button. In addition, each module you add to a hardware system costs money. Six oscillators cost precisely twice as much as three oscillators. With a software modular, adding more oscillators — assuming your CPU has enough unused horsepower — is as easy as clicking on a toolbar or parts box with the mouse.

The modular synths in this chapter provide two ways to produce unusual or unique sounds: by connecting conventional modules in unconventional ways, and by using the exotic modules provided in the software's toolbox of basic components. As an example of the first method, consider that a typical synthesizer gives you two or three oscillators with which to sound each note. In a modular system, you can easily use a dozen oscillators to make one note, detuning them from one another by various intervals to get a monstrous stacked chord. Using the second method means hooking up modules that do things like granular and physical modeling synthesis. To be sure, these processes are also available in a few non-modular instruments, but in a modular synth they tend to be more controllable, and to lend themselves more fully to unusual-sounding results.

Modular softsynths tend to resemble their hardware forebears in certain respects: The various modules are connected to one another using graphic "patch cords," which you drag from the output of one module to the input of another with the mouse. VAZ Modular, however, uses pulldown menus to do the patching. Computer users may find the menu system more convenient, but the true modular fanatic understands how useful it is to be able to see the signal flow at a glance. Also worth note: Modular synths can be used to process incoming audio. Software modulars typically include "external audio in" modules that can receive signals from the computer's audio interface, and some of them can also be used as plug-in effects within VST or DirectX host applications.

If you'd like to explore the depths of modular synthesis on your computer, but you have more time than money, I'd definitely recommend that you look into Csound (www.csounds.com). Csound is an extremely powerful music synthesis application, it runs on a wide variety of computer platforms, not just Windows and Macintosh — and it's available for free. That's the good news. The bad news is that Csound is not very user-friendly, even compared to a commercially developed software modular. Csound originated in the days before computers could perform real-time synthesis, and it was developed in an academic environment, where advanced functionality counts a whole lot more than ease of use. To make music in Csound, you have to create both your instruments and your score by typing computer code. When you're finished, Csound will render your creation to disk, and you'll open the newly rendered file in some other application to listen to it.

Today's computers are fast enough to run Csound in real time, either stand-alone or as a VST plug-in, and there are a couple of programs (also free) with which you can do this. Gabriel Maldonado's CsoundAV (http://csounds.com/maldonado), which runs on Windows machines, may be the most developed. I've had some problematic experiences with CsoundAV, but I haven't tested it rigorously. Since it's basically a one-person effort by an unpaid developer, Maldonado has to rely on his users to spot and report bugs. Running Csound in the old-fashioned way, I've become quite a fan of the software, but it's not for the faint of heart, nor for those in search of instant gratification.

If you're using Linux or Windows NT, you might want to check out another free do-it-yourself solution, Miller Puckette's Pd (http://crca.ucsd. edu/~msp/software.html). Pd is a lot like Cycling '74 Max (which is reviewed below). jMax (http://www.hanappe.org/jmax.html) is a free, open-source version of Max that runs on the Java Virtual Machine. To use jMax, you'll need to know how to use a compiler; if you're not a programmer already, this may not be the right instrument for you. Another free music software package that uses a highly user-programmable and somewhat friendlier modular paradigm is KeyKit for Windows (www.nosuch.com/keykit/). KeyKit has no business whatever being mentioned in this book, as it's strictly a MIDI generator and processor, but it's so cool that I can't resist letting you know about it.

Figure 6-1.
A more or less typical homegrown Max patch — this is an audio record/playback device I put together while going through the MSP tutorials. It records when you press the "r" key and plays back (at a variable speed) when you press the "p" key. The recording time can be specified (upper right), and the deathless results saved by clicking the Write button (center right). Clicking on the "write" message box (center right) opens up a standard file dialog, allowing you to save the contents of the buffer~ object. Comments (the floating text seen here and there) can be inserted anywhere in a Max patch. Each object's inlets and outlets show as black tabs. When you hover the mouse over an outlet, you'll see a brief description of what it sends. Audio patchcords (in the lower left and upper center areas) are normally yellow, but all objects can be colored if desired.

Cycling '74 Max/MSP
GRAPHIC-ORIENTED MUSIC PROGRAMMING LANGUAGE

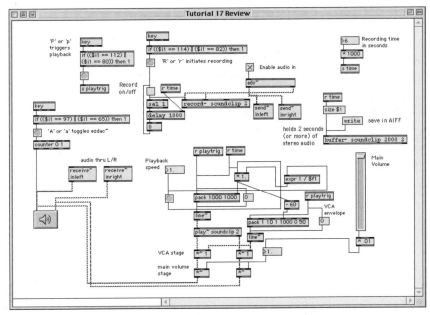

stand-alone (Mac)
Max/MSP: $495; Max only: $295

Pros: Powerful, extensible programming language. Many user-friendly amenities. Graphic "patchcord" orientation is easy for musicians and non-programmers to

understand. Excellent documentation and tutorials. Many free downloadable extensions are available. Can be used to create self-contained applications.
Cons: Requires dedication and effort to learn. Graphic programming opens the door to clutter and confusion.

I spent some time learning Max back in the late '80s, when it was strictly a MIDI processor. My computer at the time was a Mac SE30, which had a tiny black-and-white screen and a 40MB hard drive. At the time, the main appeal of Max was to experimental composers: It was an ideal environment in which to develop algorithms that would process your MIDI input in real time and spit it back out in some other form — transposed echoes, sweeping polyphonic arpeggios played from a knob or slider, and far more esoteric effects. Using Max to build a virtual machine that will generate endless streams of not-entirely-random music is a challenge, but it can be very rewarding.

The addition of MSP (Max Signal Processing) allows Max to do the same kinds of tricks with audio that it does with MIDI. Because of its background, though, calling Max/MSP a modular synthesizer is an oversimplification, if not an insult. As the review below, which I wrote for the August 2002 issue of *Keyboard*, makes clear, it's much more: It's a programming environment in which you can create your own synthesizers, effects, or whatever you can imagine. You can even package your Max/MSP creations and sell them commercially. Cycling '74 has recently released a Max/MSP extension called Jitter, which makes it possible to process video in real time.

At this writing, Max is only available for the Macintosh. OS X support has been announced, and should be out soon. A Windows version has been under development for several years, and I'm hoping fervently that the wait for its official release can be measured in weeks, as my studio is PC-based. But Cycling '74 is a small company, and patience is a virtue. If you're a Windows user and find that Max/MSP still isn't out, you may want to look into Sound Quest Infinity (www.squest.com). Infinity looks and operates very much the way Max/MSP does, though it's less fully developed in certain respects.

What would you like your computer to do today? Music software is getting more amazing every year — but even so, there are still challenges that no off-the-shelf program can handle. There are times when the best, or only, option is to do it yourself.

Write your own music software? Isn't life complicated enough without that? Depends on what you want to achieve. If you need a software version of a Prophet-5, DX7, or PPG, trying to create it from scratch would be foolish indeed; commercial programs have you covered. But maybe you're dreaming of an arpeggiator you can control with a bank of MIDI knobs and footswitches. Or a preset manager that will let you control an entire stage rig with one mouse-click. Or a sampler that will let you

Max/MSP at a Glance

System requirements	OS 8.1 or later (OS X not currently supported)
Audio streaming compatibility	ASIO, ReWire, VST 2.0, DirectConnect, Sound Manager
Audio file compatibility	AIFF, SDII, Next/Sun, WAV; imports any Quicktime-supported file format (mp3, etc.)
Copy protection	challenge-response
Downloadable demo	fully functional for 30 days

record your onstage raps and instantly put them up for scratching from a MIDI modulation wheel. Or an installation piece that can generate avant-garde tone clusters based on listeners' positions and movements in the room. Or possibly you're studying electronic music in college, and you'd like to learn more about what's involved in creating digital synthesizers and effects from the ground up.

If any of the above describes you, you'll want to know about Max/MSP.

First developed by Miller Puckette at IRCAM in the late '80s, Max started out as a realtime processor/generator for MIDI communications. Since 1989, David Zicarelli has been expanding and enhancing Max; it was distributed through Opcode until that company closed its doors, at which time Zicarelli's own Cycling '74 took over. In 1998, realtime audio was added to Max in the form of MSP (Max Signal Processing) extensions. The newest release, Max 4.0/MSP 2.0, brings Max/MSP up to a whole new level.

The downloadable demo is fully functional for 30 days — but be warned: That's barely enough time to get acquainted with the software. The learning curve is steep indeed. Student discounts are available (consult the Cycling '74 website for details). Also, if you're working mainly with MIDI hardware synths, you can purchase plain old Max 4.0 and skip the MSP side. I reviewed the full Max/MSP package, but since the two are fully integrated, from here on I'll simply refer to the whole thing simply as Max.

Overview. Rather than jump straight into a laundry list of cool features, let's zoom out and look at the big picture. What is Max? It's a graphic-based computer programming language for realtime processing of MIDI and audio. You can generate audio or MIDI entirely within the program, and process either or both in real time. You can build your own dream software synth, or your own multitrack audio recorder/editor. Max can use Sound Manager, ASIO, VST, or ReWire for input and output.

Once you've created your dream machine, you can save it in a runtime-only version. You're allowed to distribute or sell this commercially if you like; at present, no further licensing fees are charged by Cycling '74, and your customers don't have to own Max to use your software. (We're told a new policy on commercial distribution is being contemplated; if this feature is important to you, ask Cycling '74 for the latest details.) You may not get rich as a Max programmer, but the ability to create self-contained apps is the mark of a serious software development package. [*Editor's note: While researching this book, I spotted several shareware synths on the Web that were developed in Max/MSP.*]

The newer versions of Max include an array of graphic interface tools, including the ability to import graphics files, so your software doesn't have to look like a Max program — but if you're more concerned with functionality than cosmetics, you can easily use the assortment of buttons, knobs, sliders, meters, and other widgets that are provided. There's even a factory object that will store up to 128 presets for your custom patch.

You can use Max's simplest capabilities (changing the MIDI channels of messages, for instance) without worrying much about the nuts and bolts of computer programming, but as you venture beyond the basics you'll be plunged almost immediately into a world where you need to store variables, understand the difference between integers and floating-point numbers, use algebraic formulas, assemble lists of data, and so on.

Max's graphic programming style doesn't really eliminate the need to deal with this stuff. In fact, the graphic orientation imposes a second level of complexity. As in a hardware-based studio, Max objects are connected with "patch cords" on the screen. In theory, you can see at a glance exactly what's going on with your signal flow. In practice, a Max patch can quickly turn into a spaghetti nightmare. Plus, in a hardware studio, all of your patch cords can be carrying signals at once. Max operates within a computer, however — and while a computer operates at blinding speed, it can only do one thing at a time. Because of this, Max objects need to be hooked up to one another in specific ways in order to produce the desired result. If you try to "neaten up" your Max patch by dragging objects around on the screen, you can actually change the behavior of the patch by altering the order in which signals are processed. The patch may stop working entirely.

Having done a fair amount of hobbyist programming with both text-based and graphic programming languages, I can appreciate the advantages of both methods. But even though text-based programming may make musicians cringe, there are times when a text-based language is easier to deal with. In a text language, for instance, if I've created a variable called velThreshold, I can use it anywhere in my program simply by typing its name. You can't do this in Max. Instead, you have to insert a new graphic object called "value velThreshold" (which will contain the same data as any other value velThreshold object in your patch), connect its output to the input of the object where you want to use the number you've stored, and then send a signal called a bang to the value object anytime you want to use the number. If that's intuitive, my name is Popeye and I had spinach for lunch.

There are ways to structure your Max patches so they look neat and are easier to understand. For starters, selected objects can be hidden when you leave edit mode, leaving an uncluttered user interface with which you can interact during a performance. Beyond this, you can create an entire library of your own objects and insert them into your programs just as if they were standard Max objects. There are two ways to do this: You can create custom objects directly in Max, or write them in C. (The latter requires more programming chops, not to mention a C compiler, but is more efficient if you're creating a DSP-intensive object such as a custom filter. Needless to say, Max provides off-the-shelf filters, so you don't need to do this if you don't want to.)

The modular way of working pays big dividends, not only by preventing screen clutter but by letting you reuse code that you've polished to perfection. Max comes with a number of predefined user objects, ranging from a reverb and a compressor to some fairly esoteric synthesis patches. What you won't find are fully developed emulations of commercial synthesizers (as are found in Reaktor, for instance). Quite a lot of stuff is available as free downloads, however, and more is being developed all the time. Max has filters and oscillators in abundance. But even something as basic as syncing a Max "metro" (metronome) object to an external MIDI clock signal requires a bit of programming; it's not handled for you.

At first, the layout of Max patches may seem anti-intuitive, because everything happens in right-to-left order. There's a reason for this: Most Max objects are triggered (producing an output) when they receive an input in their left inlet. To use a "+" object, for instance, which is how you add two numbers, you first send a number to the object's right inlet. This number is stored in the object, but the object doesn't generate any output. When you then send a number to the left inlet, the + object adds the new number to the stored number and outputs the result.

Many Max objects, while appearing simple enough on the screen, can respond to dozens of different messages. The "coll" (for "collection") object, for instance, can receive messages like "assoc," "clear," "dump," "filetype," "insert," "max," "nstore," "prev," "refer," "swap," "subsym," and so on. It's up to you, the Max programmer, to figure out how to send each object the appropriate message at the appropriate moment, and then handle the output that it produces when it gets the message.

MSP objects are distinguished by the fact that their names end with a tilde symbol — chosen, one presumes, because it looks like a sine wave. The sfrecord~ object, for instance, captures a soundfile to your hard drive. The teeth~ object is a comb filter with feedback. Useful tools include scope~ (an oscilloscope) and meter~ (an audio level meter).

That's enough to give you a feel for Max programming. If you want to know more, download the 30-day trial version and check it out for yourself.

Tutorials & Help. The first step in learning Max is to go through the tutorials. There are more than 50, and they're excellent. They lead you step by step through the main objects in Max, showing what they do and how to connect them to other objects in useful ways.

Each tutorial comes with its own Max patch, all hooked up and ready to play with. As I went along, I modified many of these to do more complex things — a much

Figure 6-2.

Max provides an assortment of user interface objects for building your program. In this jumble (which exists purely for purposes of journalistic display and doesn't actually do anything), we see such objects as a matrixctrl (upper left), a filtergraph~ (mid/lower left), ezadc~ and ezdac~ on/off buttons (lower left), a pict-slider X/Y mouse controller (lower center), a general-purpose graphic object called lcd (lower right), a pop-up menu (center right), a function generator (upper right), and a variety of sliders and buttons.

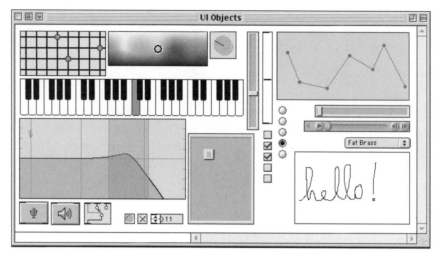

better way to learn than simply reading an endless recitation of facts and features. For instance, in Tutorial 22, "Delay Lines," I modified the MIDI in-to-out delay to produce three echoes at reduced velocities rather than a single echo. Then I got creative with the random output patch by randomizing the velocities as well as the notes and adding a second delay line so each random pitch was repeated once in a rhythmic way.

Going through the tutorials will introduce you to many of the concepts you'll need to grasp in order to write your own Max patches — using the expr (algebraic expression) object, for instance, to scale linear MIDI controller values so they'll work in exponential fashion.

Max's online help is unique, because the help windows are written in Max itself. They're interactive: You can click on the objects and they'll actually move (and display their output data or even send audio to your speakers). Plus, you can cut and paste working groups of objects from the help window into your own patch — a feature I've never seen in another program.

New in Max 4.0/MSP 2.0. The latest release of Max/MSP includes a mouth-watering array of enhancements. If you want to pore over the details, by all means download the PDF documentation and take a look.

Some of the new stuff is primarily ergonomic — ways to hide, show, and colorize objects, a context-sensitive pop-up menu, the ability to position user pop-up menus over your own graphics and have them look nice, and so on. Comments added to a patcher window can be given two-byte characters (useful in Japanese and other languages). You can even add pop-up "hints" to your program, which the user will see when the mouse is hovering over an invisible hint object. And because this is Max, the text contained in the hint can be changed while your program is running.

New math operators (cos, sin, pow, tan, and so on) have been added, and many

Max objects that previously needed an integer input can now accept floating-point numbers. There are some useful new tools for handling lists (lists in Max are one of the more powerful, and confusing, types of data). You can control the Apple DVD Player with the new appledvd object.

A new feature called scripting lets you interactively change the structure of a patch while it's running. Objects can be added, deleted, repatched, resized, or made visible or invisible using scripts. For instance, you might want a particular user button to be visible only when it can actually be used.

The timing resolution of the program has been improved. While it's still operating on a 1ms interrupt (which is fine for MIDI), you can schedule audio signal changes more often if you need smoother sound quality.

Support for third-party audio interfaces such as the Korg 1212 has been removed from MSP 2. Instead, MSP now uses ASIO. ReWire is also supported, which is a huge plus, as it lets you run Max/MSP in conjunction with ReWire-compatible sequencers. Going the other direction, there's a non-realtime audio driver, which is useful for creating and saving sounds so complex they couldn't be generated in real time.

Max can host VST 2.0 plug-ins using the vst~ object, which saves an enormous amount of time, as it's no longer necessary to put together your own overdrive effect or whatever. By double-clicking on the vst~ object, you can open an edit window that displays the plug-in's usual graphic knobs and sliders.

Some of the biggest news in MSP 2 is its improved handling of polyphonic synth voices, allowing dynamic voice allocation to be set up easily. Another biggie: Altivec optimization is implemented for most mathematical operations.

Spectral domain processing (*i.e.*, filtering) is handled by the new pfft~ object. Lo-fi addicts will appreciate the degrade~ object, which performs sample rate and bit reduction. Granular synthesis tools are provided by the stutter~ object.

A handy new filtergraph~ object lets you edit the filter characteristics of the biquad~ object graphically. There are several new filters as well. The waveform~ object not only displays the audio data in a buffer~ object but lets you do some graphic editing on it — changing the loop length with the mouse and so on. The waveform~ object isn't exactly a full-featured audio editor, but it provides tools with which you or your end-users can do several useful tasks, such as cropping and normalizing the audio data.

In Use. My first do-it-yourself Max project was to create a 16-note step sequencer. After a couple of hours of work and a couple of false starts, I had a very nice little sequencer: pitch and velocity sliders, a tempo slider, a note duration (gate time) slider, a swing percentage slider, velocity compression and cut/boost, and play/rest buttons for the 16 steps. I wouldn't go so far as to say my sequencer was actually good for anything musically, but I had a feeling of pride at having reached my goal.

One of the first things I noticed when I hooked up a synth (a Korg Karma) to Max was that the Karma's MIDI performance sensors are not as hi-res as they could be. The Karma's keyboard outputs only about 32 different velocity values between 7 (the lowest possible output) and 127. Its modulation paddle can't output all possible CC1 values: No matter how slowly I moved the paddle, successive outputs were always 2 or 3 values apart. If you're planning to use Max to control delicate musical processes, I'd suggest checking the sensors on your hardware to make sure they have the resolution you need.

The next challenge I set for myself was to create an audio patch that would play slow, dreamy FM tones with random pitches and rhythms for an Eno-style ambient environment. Generating random numbers and playing sine waves posed no problems, but when I heard each sine wave cutting off the previous one, I figured I needed to know more about how MSP handles polyphony. Rather than read the tutorials, I jumped ahead and slapped a poly~ object into my patch — at which point Max crashed my computer. Guess it's time to go back and read the tutorials.

It turned out my patch was monophonic not because I needed to use poly~, but rather because I was sending each voice module more messages than I thought I was. After a bit of debugging, I had my dreamy drones playing in the background while I worked on other things. I then edited the patch so it chose pitches from a table of just intonation values rather than playing them entirely at random. My patch sounds pretty good, but already I've thought of six or eight ways I want to enhance it.

By this time I was getting a little tired of those nice clean FM tones, so I decided to make a waveshaper. The pong~ object gave me what I needed. Hooked to a couple of LFOs with suitable scaling of their outputs, it turned a sine wave into a rich, rolling tone, which I then filtered with a lores~ object. Browsing through the manual, I learned about the kink~ object, which does a different kind of waveshaping. With kink~ patched in, I had a truly fat bassline synth up and running.

Expert Forum. In order to get a well-rounded view of Max, I talked with several artists who have used it for years. They brought out some points I had missed — not surprising, with such a complex program.

Kurt Ralske has worked in pop music and film composition, but his primary creative outlet at present is as a video artist. He runs Max on a G3 laptop, and uses a set of Max extensions called nato.0+55 (www.eusocial.com) for interactive video processing. His patches can control the audio by analyzing the video or vice-versa. According to Kurt, the company that makes nato.0+55 is not always super-easy to deal with, but their software is being used by numerous video artists. [*Editor's note: Since this review was published, Cycling '74 has released Jitter, a package of video objects for Max.*]

"You get this incredible freedom with Max," Kurt pointed out, "but with freedom comes responsibility. You're responsible for everything, including the user interface. It's a chore to get everything to work the way you want, and then it's a second chore to create an interface that will be the most useful to you."

Tim Place is a doctoral student at the University of Missouri. He uses Max for live performance pieces in which the computer records, loops, and mangles audio from acoustic instruments, and also for museum installation pieces. Tim's library of custom Max/MSP objects, called Tap.Tools, is available at www.sp-interme-dia.com/software/tap tools.html.

Because he first encountered Max as an undergraduate, I asked him what aspects of the software are the most difficult for students to grasp.

"When people encounter it for the first time," he said, "I think the toughest part is understanding structure. In a traditional sequencer, the timeline is straightfor-ward. You can use that kind of timeline in Max, but if you do, you'll be missing a boatload of the excitement. Max frees you to move through musical events in nonlinear ways." This possibility creates two challenges — envisioning how you want the music to unfold structurally, and then creating a Max patch that will do what you have in mind.

"The other aspect of structure that's difficult," Tim added, "is the programming and processing structure: keeping track of all of the sub-patches within the patches." Even when you understand the structure of your patch, he added, getting the preset object to store its current state can be tricky, because the preset object doesn't store the state of sub-patches. Also, "If you copy and paste a patch with a preset in it," he noted, "the copy doesn't contain the presets."

On the plus side, Tim has been impressed with how responsive Cycling '74 is. "In the past there have been issues that I've had, and within a couple of months the issues have been addressed with an update." He's also enthusiastic about being able to cus-tomize his software: "With software like [Propellerhead] Reason, you get these great black boxes, but you can't take them apart. With Max, if you download a patch from someone's website and it doesn't do quite what you want, you can take it apart, see what they did, and adapt it or add to it."

Bob Ostertag (www.detritus.net/ostertag) came to Max as "a diehard non-pro-grammer. I was adamant that programming computers and making music were different things." For ten years, Bob made his experimental pop CDs using an Ensoniq sampler, but when he was ready to move up to a more powerful instru-ment, "I found that the new instruments were tailored to the dance music mar-ket. In theory, you can do more with them, but I couldn't find anything to buy that I was interested in."

So Bob took the bull by the horns and created his own general-purpose sam-pler in Max. The hardest part of the process, he reports, was "the sheer amount of time it took. I don't know how many records I could have made in the same amount of time. To make a general-purpose instrument in Max is serious computer programming. When I was about halfway through the process, I realized I was doing something that would typically involve a team of programmers at a commercial software company — and they would all have degrees! But now I have my own sam-pler that's built for my own taste and ideas." Thanks to the extensive tutorials in Max, Bob says, he had no trouble learning the programming side.

Bob's sampler lets him change loop start and end points on the fly, layer loops, and resample either the audio input or the audio output during a performance. He controls it with a drawing tablet. "Five variables come out of the tablet — the x and y positions of the pen, the pressure of the pen, and the vertical and horizontal tilt of the pen. With my other hand on the computer keyboard, I can reassign those variables instantly to control whatever I want to."

If I had talked to five more Max users, I'm sure I would have picked up unique insights from each of them. Everyone who uses Max, it seems, does it in his or her own way.

Conclusions. If you want a definitive verdict on Max/MSP, get back to me in about a year. While I've spent a big chunk of time with it over the past couple of months, I'm still only scratching the surface. It's safe to say that whether you're working with MIDI or audio, Max/MSP will do anything you can imagine, and hundreds of things you've never imagined. But getting from the idea to a finished musical production is not guaranteed to be quick or painless.

Working with Max/MSP is a form of computer programming, with all that that entails — algorithm design, careful step-by-step logic, and debugging. Great documentation and a friendly graphical programming environment, both of which Max has, will only take you so far. Being able to download and customize other people's Max objects and patches will help solve technical problems and provide fresh inspiration, but ultimately Max is a do-it-yourselfer's paradise; it's not about instant gratification.

If your musical needs go beyond standard MIDI, synthesis, and effects — and especially if you want to explore the world of realtime interactive computer-aided performance — you'll be short-changing yourself if you don't give Max/MSP a serious look. It's an extraordinary and exciting tool. —JA (Aug. '02)

Native Instruments Reaktor & Dynamo
DO-IT-YOURSELF SYNTHESIZER TOOLKIT

stand-alone, VST, DXi, DirectConnect, MAS (Mac, Win)
$599

Pros: Extremely powerful sound programming environment, capable of an enormous range of sounds and effects. Comes with dozens of ready-to-play synths and effects that can be fully customized. Runs stand-alone or as a plug-in. Each synth stores up to 128 user presets.
Cons: Little or no documentation on preconfigured synths. No runtime version available for third-party synth developers.

Compared to Max/MSP (see above), Reaktor almost qualifies as easy and fun

Figure 6-3.

Reaktor synths and effects are controlled in performance with knobs, sliders, and buttons, as seen here in the upper left panel. You can arrange the panel layout however you like, and assign MIDI controllers to everything. You can name and store your own presets for each synth by clicking on the camera icon in the toolbar. Presets are listed in the pop-up menu. The convenient arrow button is used to revert to a preset's stored settings. Reaktor's global controls (also in the toolbar) let you set the sampling rate, clock tempo, the polyphony and MIDI receive channel of each instrument in the Ensemble, and more. The nuts and bolts of Reaktor programming can be seen in the lower window. Single-function modules and multi-function macro modules are connected with one another using graphic patch cords. The modules in the row across the top, for instance (two inverters and an exponentiator), perform math operations. You can create many types of Reaktor instruments without worrying about math, but the deeper you get, the more important it will become. Note the convenient ToolTip (lower right), which pops up whenever the mouse hovers over a module. When the mouse is over a patch cord, the ToolTip displays the data values flowing through the cord — very handy when you're trying to figure out why a patch isn't making any sound! In the floating Properties box at right, you can change the name, appearance, and control range of your modules.

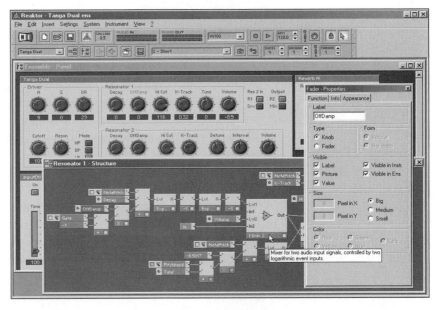

to use. Almost. Reaktor has been a synthesizer since it was first introduced, and creating a synth with it that you can play from a MIDI keyboard is undeniably easier than in Max. On the downside, Reaktor's user interface objects have far less flexibility than Max's, Reaktor doesn't handle inter-module patching or complex algebraic processes as elegantly as Max, and you can't make a runtime-only synth with Reaktor: If you want to distribute your Reaktor creations to other musicians, they have to own a copy of Reaktor.

For the record, in my recent usage of the Windows version of Reaktor 3.0.5 I've encountered more minor bugs than I did with the Mac version of Max/MSP. I've also learned (just this morning, in fact) that each time you click one of Reaktor's front panel switches, it triggers unrelated events in other modules. In my view, this behavior is unhygienic in a conceptual sense. I'm sure the Native Instruments programmers had reasons for designing the program this way, but whether or not it's conceptually sound, it can lead to serious practical difficulties.

I've reviewed Reaktor twice for *Keyboard*, most recently in the November 2001 issue. In between, Native Instruments released a bundle of pre-built synths called Dynamo. Dynamo is included in this chapter (see "Joe Gore on Dynamo," page 218) not because it's a modular synth *per se*, but because the Dynamo synths were developed in Reaktor. Joe's October 2000 review gives a good sense of what you can do with Reaktor — and where else was I going to put it?

T he quest for fresh sounds is never-ending. If you're in a hurry, a soundware CD or a hardware synth with hundreds of finely honed factory presets may be the way to go. But if you're the type who likes to roll your own — if you prefer to take a little extra time, explore fresh horizons, and build fascinating gadgets you can interact with in unheard-of ways onstage or in the studio — you'd be hard-pressed to make a better software choice than Reaktor. [*Editor's note: In the context of this book, the preceding statement should not be taken as an indication that Reaktor is superior to Max/MSP. They're simply different.*] This program is the ultimate do-it-yourself synthesizer kit. But there's more to the story than that: Reaktor comes bundled with dozens of preconfigured synths and effects. Even if you don't have the time or patience to design instruments from scratch, when you start using Reaktor you'll be smiling.

Overview. Where to start? This is a big, complex piece of software. Maybe a quick checklist:

■ Compatibility: Most of the major bases are covered here. Reaktor runs on a Mac or in Windows, is happy to talk directly to your soundcard's ASIO drivers or to a DirectConnect or MAS program, and can operate as either a synth or effects plug-in in a VST or DirectX host program.

■ Installation: Painless. There's a USB dongle in the box, but you can request a dongle with a different hardware connector if you need it.

■ Sounds: Incredible. More below on this crucial topic. Reaktor ships with

Reaktor at a Glance

System requirements	PC: PIII 500MHz or AMD Athlon or Duron, Windows 95/98/ME/2000, soundcard; Mac: 400MHz G4, OMS or FreeMIDI compatible MIDI interface; both: 256MB RAM, 50MB hard disk space (300MB recommended for full install), free USB port
Plug-in and audio streaming formats supported	VST, DirectX, DirectConnect, MAS; ASIO, Sound Manager
Synthesis types	modeled analog, sample playback, additive, FM, granular, wavetable lookup
Preconfigured effects	too many to list; can be used to process internal synth sounds or external audio
Available modules, macros, and preconfigured synths	too many to list
Arpeggiator and sequencer	numerous factory synths include step sequencers; arpeggiator can be created by hand
Sample rate and bit depth	1/4 to 4x soundcard sample rate (typically 22.05 to 384kHz); 32-bit internal; output resolution dependent on hardware
Synchronization	MIDI clock
Internal performance resampling	to RAM and hard disk
Copy protection	USB hardware key and serial number
Downloadable demo	yes

numerous synthesizers already programmed and ready to play — everything from simple bassline generators to turbocharged loop manglers. Several modules that do controlled waveform distortion let you dial in warm, thick, or disturbing tones, your choice.

■ Learning curve: The manual includes a 48-page introductory tutorial, which is very helpful, and 150 pages of reference material on the many modules. Even with all this, I occasionally had trouble figuring out why a patch wasn't working as I'd intended. Novice Reaktor users would probably appreciate a more thorough set of tutorials — but since all of the internal "wiring" of a Reaktor patch is easy to display and edit, learn-by-doing mode works well. Also, Reaktor has a user community on the NI website where you can post questions and download other people's patches.

Unlike a traditional modular synth ("traditional" meaning hardware), Reaktor separates the patching layer from the front panel. The screen shot in **Figure 6-3** should make the concept clear. This approach takes a little getting used to, but it offers some real advantages: You can create a tidy panel that contains only the controls you actually need for performance; the messy cables are hidden from view.

As you get deeper into programming, though, you'll need to think about various technical issues. What should the range of a knob be, for instance, in order to give you a meaningful control sweep? This level of detail, which some modular instruments hide from you, can be either a blessing or a curse (or both at the same time).

When I reviewed Reaktor 2.0 (*Keyboard,* Feb. '00), I was only lukewarm about the program. Some of the issues I noted at that time, such as the fact that it's difficult to program knobs to display "real world" values, are still visible in the new release. Several things have happened, however, to peg my personal VU meter. First, the new version includes a ton of macro modules and pre-programmed instruments, which makes creating your own synths much easier. (See "What's New in 3.0?," page 216.) Second, the growing enthusiasm for Reaktor among the experimental music community hinted I should have been paying a little more attention to functionality and less to user-friendliness. Third, the deeper I get into the program, the more I like it. It definitely grows on you!

I still feel there's room for improvement, mainly in the user interface area. The structure window, in which base-level programming takes place, would benefit from a way to route patch cords on a rectangular grid, as in Max/MSP. Complex patches can get to be quite a tangle. When you add a new knob or slider to your panel, it's usually tossed into the upper left corner rather than being put near the other controls in the same block; having to edit your panel layout over and over as you add new components gets pretty tedious. Assigning a MIDI controller to several knobs at once, or limiting the range with which the MIDI controller data affects a knob, requires an extra programming step. And while you can move all of the graphic objects around in the panel to create a sensible display,

Reaktor makes some basic graphic decisions that you can't change, such as the type-face of object labels and which controls will be grouped inside of rectangular group border lines.

Factory Ensembles & Sounds. Reaktor ships with analog-style synths, FM synths, sample players, rhythm step sequencers, and other devices that are not so easy to describe, plus reverbs, phasers, flangers, delays, and so on. The term "Ensemble" refers to the top-level Reaktor file: An Ensemble can be multitimbral, and can contain instruments, effects, and even an output recorder for capturing your performance to disk.

The "New in Reaktor 3" folder has half a dozen powerful Ensembles (a Reaktor term for a finished, ready-to-use instrument). The first one I opened was called GrainState. This amazing device can turn any sample into a constantly evolving cloud

THE REAKTOR MODULES

Far too many modules are included in Reaktor for us to even list them all, much less explain what they do. A strong selection of preconfigured macros (higher-level modules) is also on tap. You can also make your own macros and load them from the pop-up menus. Here's a quick overview of the basic module list.

■ Panel controls (faders, knobs, buttons, and switches) come in several sizes. Knobs and faders can be given whatever range and resolution of output values you need. There's also an X/Y mouse control surface.

■ The MIDI in and out objects handle all the basic data types. Using the MIDI out objects, you could build an algo-rithmic note generator or control other instruments from a Reaktor step sequencer. One limitation: MIDI in objects have no channel parameter, so each instrument in an Ensemble can only receive on one MIDI channel. The Ensemble as a whole can be multitimbral.

■ Arithmetic objects – a dull but important category. Adders, multipliers, inverters, logic gates, counters, accumula-tors, comparators, and so on.

■ Mixers, panners, and amplifiers.

■ Reaktor's oscillator lineup is fairly comprehensive. All of

the standard analog waveforms are covered, as are parabolic and impulse waves, multi-sine oscillators for additive synthesis, and so on. Dedicated LFOs are provided, but any oscillator can function as an LFO. Hard sync, pulse width, and FM all come in the factory toolkit, as does sample playback with multisample keymap handling and Akai S1000 format file loading. Then there's sample resynthesis and granular synthesis . . . let's move on.

■ Step sequencers and control sources for them.

■ Assorted envelope generators, ranging from HR (hold/release) to DBDR, ADSR, ADBDSR, and multi-stage ramps.

■ Filters. Again, all of the expected types show up in the menu, along with some less common items. You can select 1-pole, 2-pole, or 4-pole multimode filters, most with inputs to control resonance. Modeled filters include NI's own Pro-52 (modeled on the Prophet-5 filter) and a ladder filter modeled on a circuit patented by Bob Moog.

■ While you can use the factory effects or build your own, the basic effect modules (building blocks) include delays, wave-shapers, clippers, a quantizer, a frequency divider, and so on.

■ Mono and stereo "tape deck" record/playback devices.

Figure 6-4.
Envelope generators
can be displayed with a
graphic that shows the
envelope shape. (Sorry, but
you can't click and drag on
the graphic.)

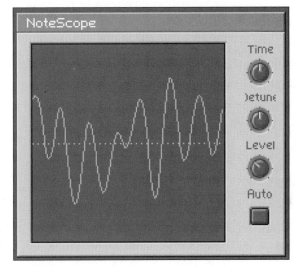

Figure 6-5.
Reaktor's factory Mood4
synth includes this handy pre-
programmed widget, a
NoteScope that displays
the waveform.

of exotic sound grains. Be warned: The two eight-step sequencers operate in a sort of sideways-and-inside-out manner compared to most step sequencers. I spent 15 frustrated minutes tinkering with them before the light dawned.

Travellizer takes a completely different approach to granular processing, with several X/Y control surfaces you can operate with the mouse. Also in this folder are the ReBirth-inspired Obvious101, a two-oscillator synth called Sonix in which you can draw your own waveforms (and hear the results in real time), and the Virtuator, a three-oscillator synth with an unusually versatile dual filter that produces an incredible variety of squelchy tones. I was having so much fun with these Ensembles I forgot to take a break for lunch.

Not new in 3.0, but cool: BiMachine is a simple eight-step sequencer with two sound sources — a sine wave for pitched lines and a filtered noise generator for percussion. I decided to add an LFO to sweep the noise filter a little; this modification took only minutes.

Wondering whether you should upgrade an earlier version of Reaktor? If you purchased Reaktor 2.3 in 2001, the upgrade is free [as of Nov. 2001 – please check with Native Instruments for their current upgrade policy]. If you've had it longer, or are still working with an older version, the upgrade is $135.

Among the enhancements in 3.0:

■ A more efficient audio engine, which translates to more polyphony and/or more modules running on the same CPU.

■ Structures can now be edited in the VST environment, which speeds up song development.

■ New audio and Event Table objects, which can act as oscillators, event sequencers, or triggerable memory banks. Other new modules include analog modeled filters, scanning mixers, and so on.

■ Direct-to-disk recording and direct-from-disk streaming.

■ User interface tweaks, including drag-and-drop audio file loading, more control over panel object sizes, and a floating properties box.

■ In 3.04, you can change the colors of your instrument panels.

The Ensemble called Phrazer (no relation to the BitHeadz program of the same name) allows you to mangle the pitch and timing of sampled loops in avant-garde ways. A garden-variety two-bar drum loop can turn into a stuttering, cheeping, lurching monstrosity with the greatest of ease, thanks to a 16-step sequencer that operates from five rows of knobs.

The Tabulator synth does some rich, crisp wavetable sweeps — cutting, yet somehow vintage at the same time. Both [*Keyboard* associate editor] Ken Hughes and I started having spontaneous *Dr. Who* flashbacks when we heard it. The FatOverdriveFB Ensemble produces some defiantly tubby tones. At the other extreme, FM-Shaker+4TapDelay does a variety of plucked and brushed sounds, both tuned and untuned.

A few of the Ensembles are pretty inexplicable. I got some rude noise bursts out of Rez, but the purposes of and interactions among the controls remained largely opaque to me. The Tanga Dual Ensemble is constructed along similar lines, with resonant delay lines providing the tone, but it proved easier to use. I got some nice brushed string sounds from it. The strangely named Take On Reloop – ModByFXR Ensemble mangled a loop with some rhythmic filter modulation, but the lack of documentation left me wondering what else I might do with it. None of the factory Ensembles is documented, other than with ToolTip text, and the ToolTips are not always used: Sometimes they just say "No Info."

The folder called "Synth – Analog" has more than a dozen different Ensembles, some simple and some not so simple. They all sound good. Mood4 is a three-oscillator synth with a resonant lowpass filter and two ADSR envelopes. The output is processed by a four-voice chorus to add fatness — but if you want LFOs, you'll have to add them yourself. The benefit of this is that it's pretty easy to learn Reaktor programming by modifying the factory Ensembles. Also, folks with slower computers will appreciate the fact that they can lay down a simple bass line or whatever by loading a synth that requires less CPU power. (Speaking of bass lines, try out Frumbo. It's a simple but beefy 3-op FM synth designed specifically for bass. Attack and body tone can be controlled in various ways.)

The most complex synth in this folder is BTS–Dream. This is a three-oscillator, four-envelope monster with two filters, a full matrix modulation switching panel, a granular synthesis module in the effects section, and various other bells and whistles.

In Use. I used Reaktor both as a stand-alone synth and as a VST plug-in in Cubase. It was easy to capture sonic experiments in stand-alone mode — all I had to do was hook a recorder module to the output of the Reaktor instrument.

I found the Clipper and Mirror 2 Levels modules very useful for creating an analog-type synth with a fat sound. I had to do a bit of fiddling with my patch, both

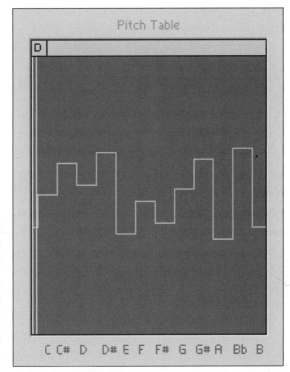

Pitch Table

D

C C# D D# E F F# G G#A Bb B

Figure 6-6.
Using Reaktor's Event Table object, I installed this tuning table so I could play in just intonation. My table is interactive: Click and drag on any of the bars in the graph while playing the corresponding note, and you'll hear the pitch move up or down.

to find the right signal routings and to give my knobs a useful range of values. Once that was done, I had controllable distortion and could dial in a few extra overtones to taste. Later I discovered that the factory Wave Fold macro has this type of processing already set up.

The Resynth module proved extremely interesting as a source for twisted sounds. It uses granular synthesis, which among other tricks can give you independent control over the speed and pitch offset of a drum loop (or any other sample). After an hour or so of tinkering, I had eight knobs hooked up, and people were wandering into my office to ask what was making those noises. I especially appreciated the fact that Resynth has a waveform display. This allowed me to dial in the loop start and loop length to an interesting part of the waveform.

Since I have a long-standing interest in alternate tunings, I decided I'd like to use Reaktor to play in just intonation. The Event Table module gave me the tool for the job. It has an onscreen display where I was able to edit every note in the scale with the mouse. The table object is more versatile than I needed — it will interpolate between adjacent values, load new values in real time using internal signals rather than the mouse, and so on. After spending several hours on my project, I discovered a microtuning macro in the factory set that provides a more elegant approach to scale tuning. At press time I'm still working on my full-featured microtonal synth, but it already sounds totally stunning (to me, at least). I can only get four or five notes of polyphony on the 400MHz machine in my home studio, though; looks like it's time for a new computer.

In order to test Reaktor in a VST sequencer environment, I loaded up *Keyboard's* 1GHz AMD Athlon PC with the latest version of Cubase VST/32 5.0. I instantiated several different Reaktor synths and processed them through assorted VST effects to create a sort of industrial groove. I could have used Reaktor as an effects plug-in just as easily. The manual doesn't give clear instructions on how to record Reaktor's knob moves into the sequencer — the information is there, but in order to find it you have to know already where the feature is located. All

JOE GORE ON DYNAMO

My name is Joe, and I'm a Reaktor addict. No joke. Native Instruments' ultra-powerful modular synth/sampling environment has become an obsession. For my money, it rivals Pro Tools in its "change the way you make music" potential. Dynamo, Reaktor's baby brother, is less powerful, but equally habit-forming.

Basically, Reaktor lets you build virtual instruments from scratch; Dynamo only lets you play the 25 instruments that come with the program, or additional ones you download from the Native Instruments website. That may sound limiting, but each of these instruments is extremely deep. They include clones of such vintage synths as the Minimoog, SH-01, PPG, and DX7; fat analog-sounding drum-box sequencers; ear-bending granular synth applications; and awesome sample-manipulation programs capable of such tricks as generating random variations from rhythm loops, or individually adjusting the pitch, dynamics, filtering, and effects for, say, each sixteenth-note value within a loop. Best of all, some instruments combine synthesis and sample-playback in thrilling new ways. It's difficult not to generate unprecedented sounds within minutes.

The sound quality is excellent, though it inclines more toward digital-era aggression than analog warmth – these are hard-edged sounds with lots of slice. At times, it feels as if the tones are from 30 years in the past or 30 years in the future. You can get rude burbles straight out of the Columbia-Princeton lab, or frighten-

ingly futuristic morphs and mutations. You can instantly route any MIDI controller to any onscreen pot or slider. (Dynamo + Keyfax PhatBoy = maximum audio carnage.) And don't forget to check out some of the amazing instruments from the online library.

I've gravitated toward two ways of using Dynamo: Sometimes I open it as a Pro Tools or Cubase instrument, sync to MIDI clock, and dial through sequenced patterns or sample-playback synths in search of nice surprises. At other times, I run it as a stand-alone application on my laptop and go spelunking for song-starter ideas. When something attracts me, I snare it in Dynamo's built-in recorder and save the results as an audio file. You can also save settings as snapshots. There's a handy help-balloon function – and you'll need it on some of these crowded front panels.

There are shortcomings: Dynamo's graphics are merely serviceable. I did experience some software glitches, especially within Pro Tools. You can only open one instrument at a time using DirectConnect. (Multiple instances are possible with VST 2.0–compatible software.) And Dynamo is not a good choice for those seeking fast, predictable results. If you simply want to, say, scroll through bass presets, you should probably look elsewhere.

If you crave startling new sounds, your only excuse not to get Dynamo is that you're saving up for Reaktor. Dynamo's inspiration factor is astronomical – if you can trust the word of an addict.
–Joe Gore (Oct. '00)

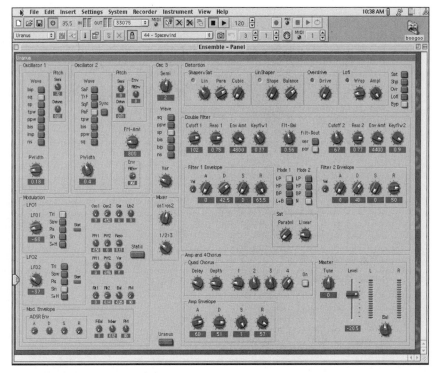

Figure 6-7.
Uranus, a powerful subtractive synth, is one of 25 Reaktor-based instruments included with Dynamo. Note exceptional features like the choice of eight waveforms, four-stage chorusing, dual filters, and the havoc-wreaking distortion/saturation section.

it took was a click in the correct check-box for each knob, and I was happily twiddling away.

Reaktor installs with its undo command disabled. I just assumed the undo feature was not implemented — annoying, to say the least. Only weeks later did I learn the Preferences box would let me enable as many levels of undo as I needed.

While working with Reaktor, I ran into a few situations where it seemed to have become a little unstable — oscillators that wouldn't sound no matter what I did with their output level controls, a button in an overdrive module that changed the LFO rate in a different module, that type of thing. I also spotted a definite bug in one rather obscure module. While Reaktor isn't 100% bulletproof, it never exhibited any major weirdnesses, and crashed only once (most likely due to DSP overload; I was running it on the 400MHz machine at the time). I'd rate its stability very high.

Conclusions. Most synthesizer software appeals to a fairly narrow segment of the market — folks who want a faithful recreation of a Prophet-5 or PPG, for example. Reaktor is unique in that it provides major resources for both experimental-minded musicians and those who want to just load up a bassline synth and get on with the mix. You can start by exploring the many great-sounding factory-supplied synths and then get as deep into customizing them as you dare.

Assuming you have a reasonably fast computer and a fast audio interface, Reaktor has an unbeatable price/performance ratio as a stand-alone program. Add the fact that you can create your own synth and effects plug-ins in two major formats, and I'm in awe. —*JA (Nov. '01)*

Applied Acoustic Systems Tassman
MODULAR SYNTHESIZER

stand-alone, VST, DXi (Win)
$399

Pros: Includes unusual physical modeling processes that greatly expand the sonic palette. Sub-patches can be created to speed programming. Will run as a plug-in under VST 2.0 or DXi.

Cons: No modulation inputs (other than external MIDI continuous controllers) for LFO or ADSR modules. Filter cutoff responds late to keyboard tracking, causing blips on attacks. No LFO sync to MIDI clock. Multiple sequencer modules can't start together.

One of the great things about the softsynth revolution is that every developer gets to stamp their creation with their own personal vision of what a synthesizer can and should be. As you'll see when you read this review from the July 2001 *Keyboard*, Tassman 2.0 doesn't have the full range of tools that I like to see in a modular instrument — but it does have some cool things that I wasn't expecting.

According to the Applied Acoustic Systems website, Tassman 3.0 is under development. It includes a much-enhanced 16-step sequencer and an ADSR envelope whose segments can be modulated individually. Also, the Builder and Player are now integrated into a single program.

oftware-based synthesizers are popping up like mushrooms, but most of them follow the design of a traditional analog or sample playback synth pretty closely. So it's especially nice to see a softsynth that offers something different. Physical modeling algorithms have been around for a few years, but Tassman is the first program I know of that puts physical modeling — digital algorithms that duplicate the behavior of plucked and bowed strings, blown reeds, resonating tubes, and so on — in a design-it-yourself modular synth environment.

Overview. Like most softsynths, Tassman runs native on the computer's CPU, so you'll need a fast machine if you want a decent amount of polyphony and if you want to run it concurrently with audio tracks in a sequencer. It will run as a stand-alone application, as a VST plug-in under Cubase (a Logic-compatible version, which I used without any problems, should be out by the time you read this),

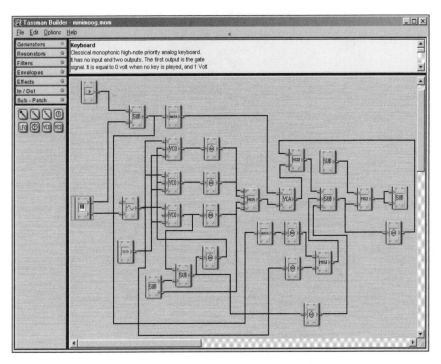

Figure 6-8.
To follow your dream of what a synthesizer ought to look and sound like, start by booting Tassman Builder. You can select the modules you need from the palettes at left, and connect them with graphic "patch cords" using the mouse. Pop-up tooltip labels appear over the modules' inputs and outputs when you position the mouse over them, which makes it easier to tell what you're patching to what. A brief explanation of the currently selected module, outlined in red, appears in the upper window area. By right-clicking on a module, you can open up a dialog box and edit its fixed parameters.

or as a DXi plug-in under Cakewalk Sonar. While DirectX is supported for audio I/O, the free-standing version is not yet ASIO-compatible. We're told ASIO support is in development.

If you're thinking ASIO compatibility is necessary for decent timing latency, think again. Using an 800MHz PC, I was able to get respectable performance out of a SoundBlaster Live card with Creative's latest DirectX driver and a Midiman 4x4 USB MIDI interface. "Respectable," in this context, means that I could feel the delay between key-down and the start of the note, but it was short — at a guess, in the 30–50ms range. (And part of that is due to the USB MIDI input. Applied Acoustics tells us they typically get 5ms latency on a 500MHz PIII.) [*Editor's note: This aside gives Applied Acoustic Systems the benefit of the doubt. Using a Midiman 2x2 USB interface on my home computer, I've never experienced any perceptible delay.*] Even if your computer/driver combination isn't this fast, you should still be able to get excellent timing — on playback, that is — by running Tassman as a plug-in in your sequencer.

Tassman consists of two separate applications — Tassman Builder (see the screenshot above) and Tassman Player (page 225). In Builder, you choose modules and connect them with graphic patch cords using the mouse. Each module has a few editable parameters as well, which are accessed from pop-up dialog boxes in the Builder.

Once you have a layout that you feel will be musically useful, you launch Player. Here, the modules appear in a rack panel arrangement. The patch cords are not vis-

Tassman at a Glance

System requirements	233MHz Pentium, 32MB RAM, Win95/98/2000/ME, DirectX sound-card, CD-ROM drive
Plug-in formats supported	VST, DXi
Synthesis types	analog modeling, physical modeling
Sample rate and bit depth	16-bit, 44.1kHz
Polyphony	system-dependent
Analog-type modules	VCO, FM osc, LFO, ADSR, filters (resonant lowpass, bandpass, highpass, comb), VCA
Physical modeling modules	mallet, noise mallet, plectrum; tube, flute, tonewheel organ, electric pickup; bowed and unbowed metal beam, marimba, membrane, plate, string
Effects	reverb, delay, flanger, phaser, chorus, stereo panner
Other modules	sample record and playback, 16-step sequencer, mixer, sub-patch I/O, inverter, attenuator, VU meter, etc.
Arpeggiator	none
Synchronization	none
Internal performance resampling	yes
Copy protection	challenge-response
Downloadable demo	yes

ible, however. To see how the modules interact with one another, you'll find it helpful to give them names.

The Player lets you choose the MIDI input(s) of your choice from a list of the MIDI devices installed in your computer. Curiously, you choose the MIDI channel in the Builder before launching the Player. The advantage of this is that each knob in each module can receive on a different channel if desired. Or you could set up a complex patch that would respond to both sides of a split keyboard at the same time. While knobs can be assigned to MIDI controllers, they don't accept input from velocity or note number — and they don't transmit MIDI. These are very significant limitations.

Installation. Tassman uses a challenge/response copy protection system. Once I had installed the software, I was able to go to Applied Acoustic Systems' website, enter the challenge, and get the response immediately from the Web page: I didn't even need to wait for an email to arrive.

I had problems on two different PCs getting Tassman to run reliably. On the first computer, a 600MHz Hewlett-Packard with a Creamware Pulsar II audio interface, Tassman exhibited major timing instabilities, stuck notes, and distorted sound quality. According to Applied Acoustics, the most likely culprit is the fact that the HP is set up as a dual boot machine with both Win98 and WinNT. They report that other users have had no problems running Tassman with Pulsar II.

On the machine I've been using at home, a 400MHz Dell with an Aardvark Direct Pro 24/96 interface, Tassman consistently crashed the machine, requiring a cold boot, when I tried to set it up for more than three-note polyphony. This problem was solved by installing the latest DirectX driver from Aardvark, but I still heard some timing instability when I played Tassman from Emagic Logic using Hubi's Loopback Device. (Using the plug-in version of Tassman eliminates the need for Hubi's.)

In order to evaluate the software properly, I asked Applied Acoustics to supply a computer on which their software was freshly installed and working properly. When this machine arrived, I was delighted to be able to make some actual music with Tassman. It ran without a hitch both stand-alone and as a plug-in under Logic, Cubase, and Sonar, all of which were installed by Applied Acoustics before the computer was shipped.

Sounds. The factory patches and programs supplied with Tassman are a mixed bag. On the good side, the analog filter resonance is fat to the point of being squawky. The fingerpicked electric bass is very solid and satisfying. The "ensemble2" patch does warm analog-style pads very satisfactorily. The Minimoog clone, while not entirely realistic, is a good source for synth basses and leads. Even better, to my ears, is the fat-sounding "tassman_se" patch. Some of the physical modeling modules can be pushed into doing far-out things.

The plucked and mallet percussion sounds are certainly usable. The vibes patch is perhaps a little tinkly at the high end, but it has a lovely metal bar resonance in the lower range. I especially liked the conga drum — again, it may not be utterly realistic, but with slightly different overtones from key to key, it sure doesn't sound sampled. When [*Keyboard* associate editor] Ken Hughes heard the Tassman attempt at a Rhodes patch, he said, "Hey, that's a pretty good Wurlitzer." The Hammond is closer to the real thing: It certainly isn't going to fool a Hammond snob, but I'd use it in a backing track.

The flute is clearly based on a physical model, not sampling, and has a nice breathy quality — but the factory patch can't track the keyboard without overblowing and producing odd pitches, so it's not very usable.

Physical Modeling. Physical modeling is a type of digital synthesis in which a computer algorithm "models," in one way or another, the actual behavior of an acoustic (or analog electronic) object. With well-written algorithms, it's a powerful technique — but physical modeling algorithms are not always easy for the user to control so as to get the desired sounds. Some parameter input values can "break" a physical model, causing either no sound at all or sounds that you wouldn't want to hear.

Tassman provides a number of physical modeling modules. The three main generators are a mallet, a "noise mallet," and a plectrum. There's also a tonewheel model.

The list of resonators includes bowed and unbowed metal beam, marimba, membrane, plate, and string, as well as tube, flute, and organ models. An electric guitar pickup model is tucked away in the effects palette.

In a typical physical modeling patch, a generator will be followed by one or more resonators, though it's just as easy to use a resonator in an analog-type patch. I set up a basic plucked-string patch using a plectrum generator, a string resonator, and a pickup. After a bit of tweaking I had a reasonable-sounding plucked-string synth up and running. I also tried running a couple of VCOs through string, plate, and tube resonators in parallel, which gave me a variety of timbres similar to fixed comb filtering, but with some unusual colors — rather as if I were using a steel drum for a speaker cone.

The string model includes an inharmonicity parameter, which added to the richness of my string sound. This parameter has no realtime input, unfortunately. I found it difficult to control my string synth with velocity in a smooth manner: Getting three or four distinct timbres at different velocity levels was easy, but getting smooth transitions as I played harder or softer was not.

The tonewheel oscillator has a couple of excellent features. You can use as many or as few tonewheels as you need, conserving your CPU cycles if appropriate. Each "wheel" has a bunch of radio buttons on its panel, allowing it to be set to any of the standard drawbar settings. There's also a four-position switch for key click, and another four-position switch labeled "flute reed" for adding a couple of overtones. In the factory Hammond patch the percussion is provided by a mallet model, and the low and high Leslie rotors by separate flanger modules.

In my experiments, the bowed resonators seemed to be among Tassman's more potent resources. The bowed membrane gave me some unearthly and hair-raising tones. The bowed models require no input from a generator: Any high-level signal will excite them. An ADSR set to a medium-slow attack and high sustain is ideal. These modules have several front-panel knobs, several more editable non-realtime parameters, and an internal noise source for roughing up the tone.

The tube resonator has only one front-panel knob, which controls decay time. In the Builder, you can edit both the length and diameter of the tube, and doing so will change its resonant properties. The fact that you can't get at these parameters while listening to the tone is a bit frustrating. The "tube 4" module combines four of these tube models in a single module. I was able to get some nice resonances out of the tube 4, but again, I was frustrated by only having one knob to play with.

Analog Modules. Tassman has the basic modules needed for analog-type synthesis, including a VCO with sawtooth, pulse, sine, and noise waveforms, an LFO, an ADSR envelope generator, and several different filters. Setting up a multi-oscillator, multi-filter patch with LFO crossfading and similar effects is pretty darn easy. Even so, the design of the modules falls way short in some areas. If your main inter-

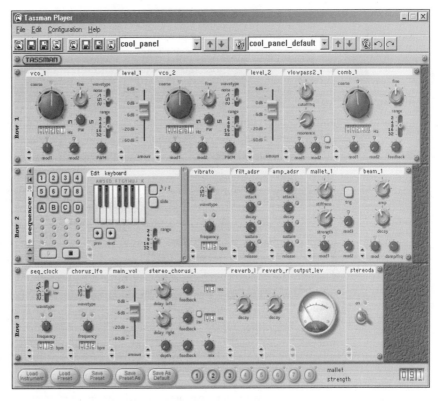

Figure 6-9.
Not hardware, but close: The Tassman Player software gives the modules an industrial-strength brushed-aluminum look. Data values for a few knobs are shown as "odometer dials" within the module, but with most knobs you read the current value by clicking on the knob and then looking at the readout in the lower right corner. The Player window can't be resized or scrolled: It shows three of the eight possible rows of modules at any given time. You select the rows you want to look at with the row of eight buttons along the bottom.

est is the outer reaches of modular analog modeling synthesis, I'd recommend Reaktor rather than Tassman.

Neither the ADSR nor the LFO in Tassman has any patchable modulation inputs. You can control envelope attack, for example, from an external MIDI controller message by assigning MIDI to the panel knob, but you can't control attack from key velocity or key position, which is a pretty fundamental aspect of sound design. Nor can you modulate one LFO's rate from another LFO.

A conventional ADSR is Tassman's only envelope. Attack rates below 40 (in a possible range from 0 to 127) are so fast as to be virtually instantaneous. When I tried modulating VCO pitch with an ADSR that was set to a fairly slow decay and zero sustain, I heard an audible pitch "bump" at the end of the decay portion: The decay ramp doesn't level out smoothly into the sustain segment.

The LFO can't be synced to MIDI clock. A "clock LFO" module is available, but this provides a clock output signal for the sequencer module. It has no MIDI clock input. The LFO's rate readout is nominally in bpm, but the utility of this feature is undercut by the lack of a fine-tune knob. You can set the LFO to 117 bpm, for instance, or to 124, but not to any values between 117 and 124.

The resonant lowpass filter exhibits an unfortunate fault: The cutoff frequency is not updated until after the note starts. Let's say you've set up a patch so that filter cutoff tracks the keyboard (a very typical sort of patch). Because the cutoff doesn't respond instantly to the new note's pitch, some of the notes will have clicks or thumps at the beginning.

The highpass filter module has no resonance and no control inputs except the cutoff knob on the panel. There's no oscillator sync. The oscillator will do pulse width modulation, however, via a patchable input.

The modulation input on the lowpass filter is not fast enough to allow you to modulate the cutoff frequency with an audio rate oscillator (again, this would be a fairly typical analog patch). Setting up this type of patch sweeps the filter cutoff only at an LFO rate.

Most of the modulation inputs are unidirectional, though one of the filters' two inputs has an invert button, allowing you to flip the polarity of the modulation. If you need to invert the input to an oscillator (to create a downward pitch enve- lope, for instance), you can insert an inverter module in the signal path. If you want to be able to program an upward-going pitch envelope in some patches and a downward one in others, a more complex patch has to be created, using a mixer, an inverter, and a couple of switches or sliders — a fairly cumbersome procedure to put together something that many modular synthesizers provide right out of the box.

A better option, I found, was to create my own sub-patch with a useful set of signal routings. It only took me a couple of minutes to put together a dual-oscillator sub-patch with bidirectional modulation amounts via two sliders. Now I can use it in any patch. An added bonus with the sub-patch approach to voice design is that Player's panel allows you to open and close sub-patches, vastly increasing the available window space.

Setting up a standard MIDI sustain pedal in a Tassman patch turned out to be an undocumented procedure. I couldn't figure out how to do it using the existing modules. Turns out there's a factory sub-patch that contains the needed circuit design. All it took was a quick phone call to the manufacturer, and my pedal was hooked up and working.

Digital Audio. Tassman has an audio recorder module, with which you can easily capture its output to disk. There's also an audio playback module, which allows you to run existing audio, such as a sampled loop, through Tassman's filters while gating it from the keyboard using a VCA module. By using a playback module in place of an oscillator, you can create patches with sampled attack transients. Multisample layouts are not possible, however, as Tassman includes no facilities for cross-switching from key position or velocity.

The playback module has to be regarded as a work in progress — it has a patchable input for retriggering playback, but no input to stop playback. You can stop playback from a panel button or a MIDI controller message, but not by lifting your finger from the keyboard.

Sequencer Module. After years of being thought old-fashioned, step sequencers have once more become *de rigueur* in modular synthesis, and a rudimentary 16-step model is included in Tassman. Individual steps can be rests or notes, and each step can be given a glide output. The glide button both lengthens the gate for the step and provides a separate trigger signal that can be sent to a portamento module on its way to the oscillator — not entirely a simple or intuitive patch setup, but workable.

Applied Acoustics tells us the sequencer module is slated for an overhaul. That's good to hear. Other than allowing you to save and load banks of preset patterns (32 patterns per bank), the sequencer is distinctly short on features. There's no MIDI clock sync. Swing/shuffle rhythms? Forget it. Inputting notes is done with the mouse using a little onscreen keyboard — don't look for MIDI step input.

The sequencer module has only one row for pitch output, rather than two rows for pitch and velocity. I tried to remedy this by hooking up two sequencers and using the pitch output of the second one to modulate filter cutoff, rather the way velocity might be used. I was unable to get the patch to work reliably: The filter and envelopes responded in a laggardly manner to my kludged-together "velocity" data.

I found a bug that prevented me from starting and stopping the sequencers in tandem using a MIDI sustain pedal as a start/stop trigger. Applied Acoustics confirmed the bug, and gave me a workaround: If there's a keyboard module in the patch, the sequencer will receive the MIDI start/stop command.

Effects. What would a synthesizer be without built-in effects? Tassman provides reverb, delay, flanging, phasing, chorus, and stereo panning. The available parameters are minimal and not easy to program, and frankly the effects don't sound all that rich. For many Tassman users, the effects won't be an issue: If the synth is instantiated as a plug-in, you can easily use the high-quality effects plug-ins of your choice.

Tassman's reverb has only a single front-panel control — a decay knob. At minimum decay the output appears to be effectively dry. If you need a separate wet/dry control, though, you can easily patch it together. In the Builder, you can enter values for six more reverb parameters, which are described as the lengths and diameters of three tubes. At normal decay times, the factory settings produce a distinctly metallic, sproingy sound. The module sounded better when producing short reverbs in some of the supplied sound programs.

With a sustained FM sound I got decent swirling out of the chorus. It has a wet/dry knob, delay time and feedback controls, and a modulation input that can be patched to an LFO.

In Use. To take Tassman out for a spin, I recorded a song in Logic, using Tassman for the plucked bass and Minimoog lead tracks, and a Korg Karma for drums and chord comps. By the time I added a little compression to the bass and a delay to the lead, Tassman sounded very good in the context of the song. Using two (monophonic) Tassman instances with two tracks of stereo audio didn't pose any problems for the 800MHz machine.

The only call I had to make to Applied Acoustics came when I saved my song, exited Logic, and then booted it again. The two Tassman instances appeared in the song with a default sound rather than the sounds I had been using. The procedure for insuring that your chosen programs will be saved with the song file was not explained in the documentation I received, but it does work. Applied Acoustics tells me the information will be on their website by the time you read this.

Conclusions. When I looked at Tassman 1.0 a few months ago, I felt it wasn't quite ready for prime time, so we put the Keyboard Report on the back burner. But when 2.0 shipped, this review became a higher priority.

As a plug-in synth that can add a few lead or bass lines to a song, Tassman performs well. Its best modules are in the physical modeling area: They can produce some evocative, detailed sounds, and there's nothing else on the market quite like them. If you're looking to go beyond the "normal" synthesizer sound palette, Tassman is certainly worth a look.

In other respects, though, I'm still not convinced this synth is ready for prime time. The factory sounds are not consistently inspiring, important modules like envelope generators and LFOs are missing the functionality I'd hope to see in a modular synth, and the user interface needs streamlining. On top of which, the program didn't run reliably on two of the three computers I tried it on, for reasons that were difficult to diagnose.

The good news is that Tassman is available as a downloadable demo. If you're interested in physical modeling synthesis, the program definitely has enough features to make it worth tying up your modem for an hour or so. And while it may not meet the needs of professionals until it's given an overhaul, it has some real educational value for those who are new to the software synthesis game. —*JA (July '01)*

Software Technology VAZ Modular
MODULAR SYNTH WITH POP-UP MENUS FOR PATCHING

stand-alone (Win)
$329 box, $279 download

Pros: Multiple driver options. Low latency with suitable soundcards. Accepts DirectX and VST plug-ins. Can load microtuning files. Compact code. Wealth of useful modules, including fairly esoteric ones. Easy to use. Flexible matrix modulation patching scheme. "Learn" mode for controller assignment to parameters. Internal mixer with multiple insert points (and dual aux buses) for plug-ins. Multitimbral operation. Includes arpeggiator and three pattern-based sequencers.
Cons: Stair-stepping noticeable when some parameters are adjusted during playback. Parameters expressed in arbitrary numbers rather than familiar units. No resource

consumption meter. Help file vague on applications. No processing for individual samples within a multisample.

I'm delighted to have Craig Anderton as one of the contributors to this book. Craig has been writing for music magazines for as long as I have (well, almost . . .), and his knowledge of technology is at least as broad-based as mine. This guy even knows how to wield a soldering iron; I don't.

I have something of a reputation as a dour, hard-to-please product reviewer, but Craig's outlook is a bit sunnier. I suspect if I had been writing the review of VAZ Modular 2.1 for *Keyboard*'s July 2000 issue, I would have gone into more detail on some of the features. Those "control voltage" processors, for instance. But maybe not. While I shouldn't admit this in a book full of product reviews, it can be darn hard to tell from reading a review where the rubber hits the road (or misses it) in a complex product. At least, that's my observation from reading other people's reviews. Somebody else will have to tell me how my reviews look from the outside.

In the two years since this review was written, VAZ Modular has not advanced past version 2.1 — but according to Software Technology, version 2.5 will be out by the time you read this. It will allow the program to be run as a VST or DXi plug-in, and will incorporate what they describe as numerous "minor improvements." You'll have to consult their website for details. It appears that during the intervening period, Software Technology has been con-

Figure 6-10.
A truly weird VAZ Modular patch. The modules with red title bars create a control signal for the Wavetable 2 oscillator: a ring mod processes a sine and triangle LFO, and a flanger processes the ring-modulated control signal. The modules with blue title bars produce a sample-and-hold control. The vowel filter receives modulation from both groups. Meanwhile, there's reverb, delay, a meter that shows how the flanger output fluctuates, and an oscilloscope that shows the stereo output signal.

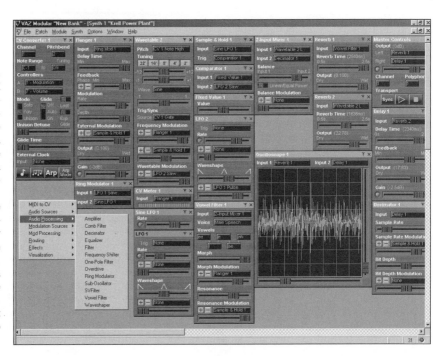

centrating on other products, such as their VAZ 2010 (not reviewed in this book, unfortunately). VAZ 2010 is a three-oscillator modeled analog synth that can run stand-alone or as a plug-in.

I've lusted after a full-blown modular. My lust was eventually sated by a combination of PAIA and do-it-yourself modules, but that solution never really had the cachet of Bob Moog's costly, complex, and seductive monster.

Now the same digital technology that fueled the decline of the analog modular synth has allowed it to flourish again in software form. The VAZ Modular synthesizer is one of the more recent entries. It's not too low-level, making it easy to use right out of the box (or after downloading the last byte), yet it offers serious capabilities and excellent sound quality. Plus, it's just plain fun to use. I must confess that writing this review was a model of inefficiency, because I just had to check out all the modules. I kept coming up with bunches of cool sounds that didn't provide a whole lot of incentive to go back to the word processor.

VAZ isn't just a synthesizer. It also makes a great processor for digital audio files. Between the conventional audio effects, the control signal processors, the option to load third-party plug-ins, and ability to capture a sound to disk, you can warp existing samples beyond recognition. Loopmeisters will no doubt burn many hours as they transform existing loops.

Installation. VAZ Mod is a compact (2.3MB) program; you can download a demo that saves but doesn't load patches, times out after 30 minutes, and can be used only 16 times. Still, that should be enough to let you know whether VAZ is your cup of tea. You can then purchase it online by getting a password to unlock the full feature

VAZ Modular at a Glance

System requirements	Pentium 200 (Pentium II or faster recommended); ASIO, MME, or DirectSound-compatible soundcard; Windows 95/98/NT
Plug-in formats supported	DirectX, VST
Synthesis types	modeled analog, sample playback, granular
Sample rate/bit depth	variable 16- to 64-bit internal, 16-bit output; 11.025, 22.05, 32, 44.1, or 48kHz (up to 96kHz with ASIO)
Compatible sample formats	16-bit mono or stereo WAV
Internal performance resampling	yes
Polyphony	variable (depends on CPU speed, patch complexity, latency setting)
Sequencers	3 multi-row 16-step sequencers
Arpeggiator	up, down, up/down, random note order, 1–4 octave range
Copy protection	password
Downloadable demo	yes

set. A boxed version is also available, but as there's no paper manual anyway, going the Internet route saves about $40.

Installation of the fully functional version is painless — double-click on the .exe file, enter the password, and go. After which, it's a good idea to open the help file for the "getting started" section and tutorials.

Your first step is to set preferences: Choose the MME, DirectX, or ASIO driver for your audio hardware, then set the sample rate (11/22/32/44/48). There's a slider for setting the size of the audio output buffer; this setting in turn determines the latency (the lag between when you play a MIDI note and when you hear it). The help file recommends starting off with the worst-case settings, just so you can make sure everything is working. Don't be discouraged if the latency is horrible, as you'll probably be able to trim it way down. Although most people will want to play VAZ with a MIDI keyboard, there's also a virtual keyboard mode that allows you to use your computer's QWERTY keyboard to check out sounds.

Surprisingly, my best-case latency wasn't bad — 17ms with Frontier Design's Dakota card in ASIO mode. This is not as good as what you'll get with a hardware synth being driven by MIDI, but it's certainly good enough for realtime playing. This figure held up fine to about eight voices on my 450MHz overclocked Celeron A (equivalent to a PII) when I played a patch of average complexity (three oscillators, two envelopes, a filter, etc.). Twelve voices started to break up, producing gargling and spitting noises. Even with MME (which the manual warns as being more latency-prone, aside from a few boards such as Gina), I found the latency acceptable. Again with the Dakota board, minimum latency was around 20ms with fairly involved patches and two or three voices. Setting the buffer to give around 37ms of delay was pretty fail-safe, even with 16 voices.

Note, however, that not only your CPU, but your soundcard and drivers, have a huge effect on both available polyphony and latency. The unfortunate aspect of all this is that you set the buffer size (latency) in the Preferences box, and the setting doesn't change when you load a new patch. You may be able to get latency down below 20ms with a monophonic bass patch, but need to reset it manually to as high as 300ms each time you load a complex patch with which you need to play eight voices. It would be helpful if the latency setting were stored with the patch.

Of course, latency is mostly an issue with realtime playing. If you're doing sound design, you can bypass the latency problem altogether by using the program's "capture" mode to save a sound as a WAV file.

The help file is reasonably good; its weakest point is superficial descriptions of some of the more unusual modules — examples of applications would have been useful here, although there are 65 factory patches you can analyze to learn more about how to use the various modules. The two tutorials are helpful, but a program this deep would be well served by more extensive applications info for those unfamiliar with modular synthesis.

Although Software Technology offers tech support, I never needed it. Everything went as expected.

Architecture. There are three main windows: the modular synth construction window (**Figure 6-10**, page 229), mixer, and sequencer (**Figure 6-11**, page 234).

VAZ can do multitimbral operation. You can create multiple synths, assign each to one of the usual 16 MIDI channels, then route the outs to the mixer. Synth patches can be saved individually (and I do mean individually — you can't save, for example, a set with a bunch of patches based on the same layout of modules). A particular combination of synths, mixer settings, and sequencers becomes a bank.

The mixer has several points of entry for plug-ins: two aux busses, master effects slots, and individual channel inserts. VAZ's emphasis on integrating signal processing into the synthesis process carries through the entire program: You can insert an effect anywhere in the signal path of a synth voice.

Patching. When you call up a new patch, you're presented with a Master Control window that has stereo outs, sequencer master transport controls, an output level slider, and MIDI channel/polyphony selection. Individual synths can have up to 16 voices, but as mentioned, various factors influence how many voices you can actually obtain.

You add modules by right-clicking in the work area to see a pop-up menu of available options. Select a module and place it as desired. You can add or delete modules at any time, and change module values as needed. However, there's no way to copy the parameter settings being used by a module if you want to "clone" one. Most of them are simple, though, making it easy to copy the settings by making a visual comparison of the sliders.

VAZ retains analog synth nomenclature — it considers MIDI signals as something to be converted into "control voltages," and requires that you route "gates" and "triggers" to modules. Of course, a software synth isn't control-voltage-based, which may confuse those who have never worked with a real modular synth. For synth veterans, though, VAZ works just as you'd expect it to. In addition, it adopts the MIDI lexicon where appropriate, such as when dealing with controller data.

Your first module will probably be the CV converter, as it allows you to bring data from a MIDI keyboard or sequencer into VAZ. This module is very much like the "global" page on a typical keyboard synth — set the MIDI channel, mode (unison with optional detune/mono/poly), pitchbend interval, note range, glide (with glide time slider), external clock enable/disable, and two MIDI controllers that will be available for use by other modules. Once that's set, it's sound construction time.

Patching is via a matrix modulation-type protocol. Each module input (signal or modulation) has a pop-up menu that selects the signal source. As you add new modules, the menu automatically adds more choices. Although you don't see the signal flow as easily as if you were using patch cords, the menu approach reduces screen clutter, because there are no "patch cords" getting in the way. Tracing signal flow can be time-consuming with complex patches. (Here's a tip: Tracing the flow backwards from the final output is much easier.) Conversely, setting up patches is very fast if you have a pretty good idea of what you want beforehand.

It's entirely possible to go nuts and create a huge sound with lots of modules (255 max). As another anti-clutter measure, each module has a "windowshade" button that folds the module into its title bar. With a complex sound, it's easier to "uncollapse" a module each time you want to work with it, and then fold it away afterward. There's also a degree of color-coding, as you can choose one of six colors for the title bar.

Although you can use a hardware slider box to control the individual mixer channel levels, there's an even hipper variation on this concept: Any onscreen slider or switch can be MIDI-controlled. Just right-click on the parameter to put it into "learn" mode, diddle your controller of choice, and next thing you know, the "learn" alert box disappears and your controller now varies the parameter. There are two limitations to this process: You can't gang multiple parameters to the same controller, and VAZ recognizes only controllers as parameter inputs (not pitchbend or aftertouch, for example, although you can use these as standard modulation sources). Still, controllers are so easy to set up, I found myself doing some realtime tweaking of crucial parameters for just about every patch.

Signal Sources. Although the oscillators are fine, the ability to use samples as oscillators means more flexibility. VAZ doesn't disappoint, offering three different ways to load samples. The sample modules default to a sine wave oscillator with no samples loaded, which also makes up for the lack of a sine wave option with the standard oscillators.

I particularly like the Wavetable source, as it lets you load samples into defined key ranges, and can loop or play one-shot files (stereo or mono). Even better, you can vary the loop position within the file, which changes the spectrum in a manner conceptually similar to hard sync (and yes, the oscillators offer hard sync). However, if you want separate processing for each sample in the multisample keymap, you'll need to access them as individual samples rather than using the multisample module. The simpler, mono sample module works fine for this type of application; it's especially good for creating drum kits.

Many of the modules are overachievers. When you see something like "Filter," you might think it's not too special — until you open it up. There are eight response types, including two different sets of two-pole lowpass, bandpass, and highpass filters (each set handles resonance differently, with one group fixed and one variable), and a standard two-pole or four-pole lowpass filter. There are several other filter modules as well.

All this wouldn't mean much if the filters didn't sound good, but they have a rich, clean sound. Although not quite as "dark" as real analog filters, they're not as brittle as some digital implementations.

The rich selection of control voltage generators and processors is also wonderful, especially for creating long, evolving sounds. Outputs can feed back to inputs,

Figure 6-11.
VAZ Modular's step sequencer. Control A controls filter cutoff elsewhere in the synth, while Control B affects the gate time.

and you can apply audio processes to control signals (as is done in **Figure 6-10**). Go ahead and flange an LFO — it's an interesting effect. Conversely, control processors work with audio. For example, although there's no phase inverter, the control inverter works well with audio, as long as there aren't too many high-frequency harmonics (spiky sounds tend to bleed through).

Presets. For the modularly challenged, the 65 factory presets are really quite excellent. Most of the list leans toward classic lead, bass, and pad sounds, with a few arpeggiated and effect patches thrown in. I suspect that if a non-programmable VAZ with a few hundred presets as good as the ones here existed, it would sell.

The presets are indeed analog-sounding, although to me, the exciting part of VAZ is that you can go where synthesists have not gone before. Okay, so it makes a killer TB-303 sound. So does ReBirth. Get creative and use the existing patches as guides, not ends unto themselves.

Sequencing. Three 16-step sequencer options are included, and each synth can use any of these. Because multiple sequencers can start and stop at the same time, they're even usable in multitimbral, bank-oriented contexts.

The main CV/Gate Sequencer is an analog-style sequencer with one row of sliders to set notes and two more rows to generate controller info (for example, send one to control filter resonance, the other to affect gate time). Other controls are typical of the genre — rests, slides, accents, 16 individual patterns you can link into songs, forward/backward cycling, and the like. The Control Sequencer is similar, but has four control outputs. This is optimized for sequencing controllers rather than notes. The Trigger Sequencer resembles that of a Roland TR-808 drum machine, and is optimized for creating drum machine patterns. As VAZ Modular creates fine analog drum sounds, this is a logical and useful addition.

The sequence control sliders' "gang" feature is particularly well implemented. Suppose Control A sets filter cutoff, and you want to slowly increase the overall cutoff frequency in real time. You hit the Gang switch, grab a slider, and they all follow along. If you grab the lowest-value slider, then move it all the way up, all sliders will now hit max. Now suppose you want to bring the cutoff back down for a more muted effect. The sequencer remembers the original slider positions, and as you bring the slider down, they all fall back into the same proportional levels they had originally — brilliant.

As to the arpeggiator, it's fairly basic: up, down, up/down, and two random options, over a range of 1–4 octaves.

Incidentally, driving VAZ from a sequencer within the same computer requires patching the MIDI out physically back to the MIDI in, or using an internal software MIDI loopback utility. The help file includes info on how to use and install Hubi's Loopback Device, which is available for free on the Software Technology website. [*Editor's note: Since version 2.5 can operate as a plug-in, this workaround is no longer needed.*]

Conclusions. If you love unusual sounds and enjoy an anything-goes experimental workspace, you owe it to yourself to discover modular synthesis. Want to use noise as a modulation source for a chorus? Go for it. Does it fluctuate too rapidly? Add a lag processor. Gee, let's throw a delay line in there . . . or how about using strange control signals with the granular synthesis module? Audio and control signals are interchangeable in VAZ, so you can even ring-modulate control sources if you're so inclined. The possibilities are deep.

My complaints are minor. VAZ seems to have an engineer's sense of graphic design — functional and clean, but lacking inspired visuals. Also, while it does make some nice analog-sounding noises, nothing that has stair-stepping artifacts will ever feel like a "pure" analog synth to me. I'd love to see interpolation added in a future version to smooth out the stepping a bit on parameters like filter frequency.

So what does VAZ sound like? Frankly, like just about anything you want. It certainly has an analog vibe, although effects such as reverb are more "digital." And of course, modules like the decimator (which alters sample rate and bit depth) impart sounds that could exist only in digital. So basically, you have the coolness of an analog synth with the depth of control associated with digital. There's a comparison on the Software Technology website of patches from real analog synths compared to versions programmed on VAZ, and believe me, you'll have a hard time detecting any difference at all.

One thing's for sure: This program is not coming off my hard drive, period. It's fun, but in a challenging way that exercises my brain rather than dulling it. With VAZ

Modular, you can get everything from the same old boring analog patches that everyone else has to sounds that I guarantee no living being has ever heard before.

Finally, I have that monster analog synth I always wanted — except it has way more modules than I could afford in a hardware synth, doesn't drift out of tune, will never have its patch cords or jacks break, speaks MIDI, includes a decent mixer and set of step sequencers, and costs less than 2% of what a basic Moog Series III would have cost. VAZ is not the only software modular synth in town, but if you find a more usable and cost-effective one, I'd sure like to know about it. —*Craig Anderton (July '00)*

Percussion Modules

7

Given the importance of rhythm in pop music, maybe it's surprising that there aren't *more* softsynths dedicated to producing percussion tracks. Blame it on the ubiquity of sampled loops: Programming your own beats takes a little more time than importing loops (and requires a modicum of musical creativity, to say nothing of production chops).

Most general-purpose synths have a few presets with which you can churn out the inevitable throbbing kick drums and electonic hi-hat "tssss" noises, and the virtual rack systems in Chapter 4 have dedicated drum modules. But the programs in this chapter are all percussion, all the time.

Broadly speaking, there are two ways to generate drum and percussion sounds: by playing back samples, or by synthesizing the tones on the fly. Two of the instruments reviewed in this chapter use sample playback, and one is a pure synthesizer.

In the pre-MIDI days of the late '70s and early '80s, you could buy hardware drum machines that used either method. Roland produced a number of beatboxes that used analog synthesis. At the time, rock musicians dismissed these devices as sounding hopelessly cheesy — but in the late '80s and early '90s, long after they had gone out of production, they suddenly became a hot ticket in the underground techno music scene. Today, a hardware Roland beatbox, if you can find one in good condition, will command a high price. Fortunately, software replicas are available.

The first drum machines that were taken seriously by pro musicians used samples of real drums. The first models introduced by Roger Linn, the LM-1 and LinnDrum, were expensive and much sought after. They included eight or nine short samples in all — kick drum, snare, a couple of tom-toms, open and closed hi-hat, and a few other items. At the time, their 8-bit samples were state-of-the-art. What these drum machines and the Roland boxes had in common was a *step sequencer,* with which you could program your own beats. After recording a few patterns (of one or two bars each), you'd switch to song mode and string the patterns together end to end to produce the drum track for an entire song.

With the exception of ReBirth and the drum modules in virtual rack systems, software drum synths generally eschew the step sequencer, because modern software sequencers offer so many tools with which to accomplish the same thing. This is kind of a shame: It seems to me a new generation of interactive step sequencers might offer musicians some interesting tools. At present, the only way to create something of this sort is with a program like Cycling '74 Max (see Chapter 6).

If you're not a drummer, you may be entirely unaware of the kinds of expressive variations in sound a trap kit — or for that matter a hand percussion instrument — is capable of. But when you listen to a sample playback drum module whack the same snare drum sample over and over and over and over, your eyes will start to glaze over. For some pop arrangers, of course, that's exactly the intended effect. But even if you're working in a rigidly repetitive style, you'll probably find that introducing subtle variations into the beat will make your music breathe and come alive.

Sample-based drum modules allow you to do this with a technique called *velocity cross-switching.* This technique was discussed in the "Multisampling" section of Chapter 5. To create a setup that allows for velocity cross-switching, the sound developer records a snare drum being played at three, eight, or even 20 different loudness levels. The recordings have to be carefully matched: The microphone position has to be consistent, and the drummer needs to hit the drum in precisely the same spot.

The various samples are then assigned to a single MIDI note, drum pad, or equivalent. Depending on the MIDI velocity of the note you play, the drum module will choose a different sample. In order for this technique to work well, at least two things need to happen: The drum module needs to provide a decent number of velocity zones (Native Instruments Battery lets you program up to 127 velocity zones, Steinberg LM4 Mark II up to 20), and the sound library provided with the drum module has to have a selection of well-matched samples for each drum that does velocity cross-switching.

Another important technique for drummers is working the pedal of the hi-hat while playing it with the stick. A hi-hat consists of two cymbals on a stand with their concave sides facing one another. When the pedal is down, the hi-hat is said to be *closed,* because the edges of the two cymbals are pressed against one another. Hitting a closed hi-hat with the stick produces a short, chopped-off sound. When the pedal is up, the hi-hat is open, allowing both the upper and lower cymbals to ring freely.

A standard technique is to hit the open hi-hat with the stick and then close the hi-hat with the pedal, producing the *sshhhh-tchk!* sound beloved of funk drummers. This is generally done in a rhythmic way, with an eighth-note or sixteenth-note of open hi-hat followed by the pedal-closing sound on the next beat. This raises a tiny problem for a sample-based drum module: The sound developer doesn't know the tempo of the tune you'll be recording, so it's not possible to specify ahead of time how long the hi-hat needs to stay open or, in consequence, how long the open hi-hat sample needs to be.

The solution, which has been used since the earliest days of drum machines and is still found in today's drum module software, is to assign the open and closed hi-hat sounds to a single electronic *voice channel*. A voice channel can only make one sound at a time, so whenever you trigger the closed hi-hat sound, it will chop off the open hi-hat sound. Some percussion-oriented products let you set up a number of these "hi-hat groups," each group being independent of the others. You'll be able to assign any sounds you want to them, not just hi-hats — which might or might not be useful, depending on the musical effect you're after.

All three of the reviews in this chapter were penned by frequent *Keyboard* contributor Francis Preve. As a professional dance remix producer, Francis knows his beats. Not included in this chapter because I couldn't round up decent reviews in time to meet the deadline:

■ Propellerhead ReBirth RB-338 was one of the earliest realtime softsynths, and a runaway success. It modeled three classic hardware beatboxes by Roland — the TR-808 and TR-909 drum machines, and the TB-303 monophonic bass synth. The downloadable demo (also available on the CD-ROM that comes with this book) runs for only 15 minutes, just long enough to give you a taste.

■ LinPlug Element P is a VST plug-in, and does synthesis rather than sample playback. Parameters can be automated, and Element P is eight-part multitimbral. There's a downloadable demo, and the cost is only $39.

■ The FXpansion DR-008 is a powerful percussion-oriented sample playback module that supports up to 96 sounds at once. According to the FXpansion website, it can import drum kits in both LM4 and Battery format, will run as a VST or DXi plug-in in Windows, and has eight hi-hat groups and up to eight stereo outputs. Parameters are automatable. Both velocity cross-switching and velocity crossfading are supported. Cost is $149, and the downloadable demo expires after four hours.

■ Muon Software's SR202 is a Mac/Windows VST plug-in. It makes noises via sample playback, and it has lowpass and highpass filters. Oh, and you can't buy it: It's a freebie made available exclusively to readers of England's *Computer Music* magazine (www.computermusic.co.uk). Muon's product line is not well represented in this book, sad to say. They make several affordable plug-in synths, such as the Electron, Atom Pro, and Tau Pro.

Waldorf Attack
MODELED ANALOG DRUM MODULE

Figure 7-1.
Attack's beauty is matched by its powerful synthesis engine. Each drum patch is accessed by clicking on a key on the stylized vertical keyboard at left. The graphic keyboard and horizontal pitch wheel at the bottom respond to the mouse. The Edit button at the top left corner pulls down a menu of cut/copy/paste/compare functions, while the Preset button accesses a list of templates based on classic beatboxes.

VST (Mac, Win)
$149

Pros: Very flexible modeled analog synth architecture. Functions as both drum synth and multitimbral polysynth. Dual syncable delays. Tempo-synced filter LFO. Three assignable hi-hat cutoff channels. Continuously variable decay/release curve.
Cons: Bizarre multitimbral implementation. Two-pole filtering only. No hard sync or glide. Limited pitch LFO functionality.

As revealed in this August 2001 review, Attack is mainly, though not exclusively, a modeled analog drum module. It's the only one of the three programs that I've used myself, so I can confirm that Francis's observations are on the money. For synthetic-sounding percussion tracks, Attack is surprisingly versatile.

Now that Steinberg's VST Instrument spec has become a *de facto* industry standard, the gold rush is on to see who can make the coolest new tools. Some software slavishly follows the hardware paradigm, but software manufacturers are quickly finding ways to create instruments that simply could not exist as hardware (or would be prohibitively expensive).

Waldorf's new Attack plug-in is a terrific example. Ostensibly, Attack is targeted at musicians who are looking to create future-retro drum sounds for modern dance tracks. But there's more to it than that. The synth architecture is so well rounded and flexible that Waldorf wisely decided to make it playable polyphonically as a melody/chord instrument. When you look at the two sides together, Attack is a remarkably powerful plug-in that breaks the mold of what a plug-in instrument should be.

Installation. Installing Attack is a no-brainer — a few clicks and the installer does the rest. The copy protection consists of CD-ROM authorization once during the install process, so it takes a few minutes longer to complete. But once it's done, you're set. No random "insert CD now" challenges or dongles, thank goodness. [*Editor's note: A few programs insist on seeing their original installation CD from time to time.*]

Attack comes with a printed multilingual manual that covers the essentials — and then some — in clean, concise fashion. But Attack is so well laid out that I only had to crack the manual once or twice. There's also an array of tutorials, explaining in some depth how various vintage beatbox sounds, such as 808 claps and Simmons drums, were created.

Factory Kits. Attack's factory kits really show off the horsepower lurking under its hood. Some of the sound effects are incredibly intricate, with a hard-edged sheen that cuts through a mix. While many of the patches have a "hey, look at what I can do" feel — which isn't necessarily conducive to sitting well in a mix — a few kits are knockouts, and totally usable right out of the gate.

The [Roland] CR-78 kit is a dead ringer for the original, all the way down to the insectile tambourine and hi-hats. The Latin kit offers a neat spin on thwacky synth congas along with a sweet triangle emulation. The New Style kit is a punchy, hard trance kit that virtually screams Timo Maas, while the Straight Attack kit blends nicely without being generic in any way. There are also a few really wild kits — notably Electro FX2 and 3 — that should work well for tracks in need of creative analog spice. That said, I could live without the Arcade Fever kit, which seems pretty kitschy and throwaway compared to the others.

The TR-808 and -909 kits are accounted for in a big way. Waldorf obviously knows their market, because both of these classic beatboxes — along with the Simmons SDS-5 — are included in the factory initialization templates. Via a pulldown menu, you can access these kits as starting points for your own creations. This feature is a great way to jump-start the sound design process.

Interacting. Attack's stylized user interface is immediately understandable. Along the left side is a list of the sounds in a kit, laid out as a vertical two-octave keyboard. The main body of the interface consists of a panel of knobs, buttons, and two graphically editable envelopes. Click on one of the keys in the keyboard list and the knobs and switches immediately jump to the values associated with that sound. The array of cut, copy, paste, and compare functions is equally welcome. If only the multitimbral key layouts in other synths were this easy to manage!

Attack at a Glance

System requirements	Mac: 604e/250MHz (G3 or better recommended), 64MB RAM, Mac OS 8.0 or higher; PC: Pentium 266MHz (Pentium II/400MHz or better recommended), 64MB RAM, Win95/98/ME/2000; VST-compatible host application
Synthesis type	modeled analog (plus hi-hat and crash cymbal sample playback)
Oscillators	2: triangle, sine, square, sawtooth, sample-and-hold, noise, closed hi-hat, open hi-hat, crash
Oscillator sync	none
Waveform modulation	ring mod, FM
Filter	2-pole resonant low/high/band/notch with overdrive, semi-parametric EQ, shelving EQ
Envelopes	2: ADR/ASR with variable response curve
LFOs	2: triangle wave and sample-and-hold for filter, sawtooth for amplitude
Syncable functions	filter LFO, delay times
Polyphony	64 voices (processor-dependent)
Multitimbral features	13-way multitimbral: 24 sounds per kit, 12 pitched sounds playable via MIDI
# of factory kits	29 (16 loaded into RAM at once)
MIDI control	all parameters addressable via MIDI controllers or sys-ex automation
# of audio outputs	8 (2 stereo, 4 mono)
Built-in effects	2 modulated delays
Copy protection	CD-ROM verification
Downloadable demo	no

The first octave of sounds in a kit is fixed-pitch. That is, the sounds can be triggered by MIDI note-ons, but can't be used for melodies or chords. The second octave contains sounds that can be played melodically and polyphonically in the upper octaves. These patches can be anything: basses, leads, effects, even pads.

The way Waldorf handles MIDI input is quirky. I had to grab the manual after a few minutes of head-scratching. Here's the skinny: The first two octaves of the standard five-octave keyboard let you play the entire drum kit, while the octaves above are assigned to one of 12 patches drawn from the second octave of drums. The assignment depends on which channel Attack is receiving on. For example, if you want to play a riff using a conga (or synth patch) assigned to D2, you'll need to transmit on channel 3. To access the patch on E2, switch to channel 5. Controller reception is arranged in a similarly oblique fashion on channels 13–16. In light of the excellent design elsewhere in this plug-in, this approach seems needlessly convoluted.

Voicing. The Attack voice architecture is pretty standard stuff. Two oscillators feed a mixer that includes ring modulation. The mixer is followed by a multimode filter/EQ section that feeds the amplifier and two discrete delay effects with modulation. Nothing really new here, but every section includes a few niceties (as well as a few omissions) that set it apart from the crowd.

Each oscillator features nine waveforms: sine, triangle, sawtooth, square, sample-and-hold, noise, closed hi-hat, open hi-hat, and crash cymbal. The standard analog waves have a slightly meaty quality to them, with a bit of lower-mid oomph and softened — but not dull — highs. I compared the waveforms to those in the Steinberg Model-E and PPG plug-ins and found Attack to be a tad more aggressive than either.

The noise waveform is accurate, too, with the pitch knob continuously shifting the color from pink (emphasized lows) to blue (emphasized highs). The sample-and-hold waveform will do vintage arcade game explosions.

The inclusion of cymbal samples is a mixed blessing. Hi-hats and other cymbals are tricky to synthesize well, so having these waves available speeds up kit construction. All three samples are suitably generic, so there's ample frequency content to shape with the filters and other processing tools. There's no ride cymbal, though, which is a drag. What really bugged me is that these options show that Attack's synth engine is capable of using sampled waves. So why didn't they include additional drums or, better yet, the ability to import your own percussion samples? File this one under "tease."

Both oscillators' pitches can be modulated by either of the envelopes or velocity. Oscillator 1 also includes FM input from oscillator 2, which adds a ton of flexibility for coming up with metallic and otherwise grungy textures. FM amount can be modulated by the envelopes as well. Since this is a drum synth, there's no pitch LFO to be found anywhere. This isn't a big deal, because tuning oscillator 2 to a low frequency and using it for FM gives you much the same effect, though you can't use this approach with dual-oscillator tones. This pseudo-LFO can't be synced to tempo, either.

Also missing are hard sync and glide functions. I can understand the absence of glide on a drum synth, since pitch envelopes will serve a similar purpose in a pinch. But I definitely miss having hard sync.

The mixer section includes controls for adjusting the volume of each oscillator and applying envelope and/or velocity modulation to the amplitude of the second oscillator. Other parameters include ring modulation and a unique new tool called crack modulation. (There's a really bad joke in here somewhere, but I ain't touching it.)

Crack modulation is Attack's secret sauce for emulating handclaps. In essence, it's a sawtooth LFO that modulates the mix output. A timed gate controls the duration of this modulation, after which the sound returns to its un-cracked state. Attack's crack modulator provides control over the speed of the LFO (which can extend into the audio range) as well as the duration of the gate. This is one of those nifty synthesis tools that is highly specialized, but so unusual that it's great for "how'd they do that" textures.

Filtering is another area where Attack really shines. Lowpass, highpass, bandpass, and band reject modes — all with self-oscillating resonance — are represented. Either envelope can modulate cutoff frequency, and the filter section also includes its own tempo-based LFO for synchronized filter sweeps. The LFO sweep is limited to triangle wave modulation, but there's a sample-and-hold mode that randomly changes cutoff with each trigger. Nice touch. Additionally, all patches in the second octave have cutoff frequency hardwired to the mod wheel. Since I routinely set up synth patches in this manner, I was delighted by this setup.

On the downside, all filter modes are strictly two-pole (12dB per octave). If you're looking for the beefier sound of a four-pole lowpass filter, this will be an issue. Overdrive can be added, if you're after those classic distorted kick drums or crunchy leads. The distortion algorithm adds considerable volume to the overall signal, which can be problematic if you're not careful.

Attack's envelopes are, again, oriented toward percussion work: They're neither ADSR nor multi-stage rate/level affairs. What you get are controls for attack, decay, curve, and release. The curve parameter is exceptionally useful, as it's continuously variable between exponential, linear, and inverse exponential. If you've ever tried to program a percussive synth patch using sluggish envelopes, you'll immediately fall in love with this feature. Exponential decay curves can be incredibly punchy and snappy. At first I was annoyed by the apparent absence of a sustain parameter. How on earth was I supposed to create pads? Fortunately, these ADR envelopes become ASR (attack-sustain-release) when decay is set to maximum and release is set to anything other than zero.

The amplifier section allows adjustments over volume, pan, effects send, velocity (negative and positive), and output routing. There are two stereo and four mono outputs, which is more than enough for all but the most elaborate mixes. Additionally, this is where the three XOR (hi-hat cutoff) groups are selected.

In addition to these synthesis tools, Waldorf has included two tempo-syncable, LFO-modulated delays. These are useful for everything from rhythmic echoes to flanging and chorusing to more exotic effects like pitch/time swept delays. The delays are hardwired to ouputs 1–2 and 3–4, respectively.

In Use. With all this synthesis horsepower at my disposal, I was itching to see how Attack would perform. I decided to base my experiments on Attack's prefab 909 kit template and create a trance beat using the standard sounds.

I began with the kick drum, modifying the tuning and adjusting the envelope to give it more boom. I opted to replace the hi-hats with a hard metallic texture. I ditched the existing open hi-hat and replaced it with an FM-based patch with a touch of ring mod, followed by a resonant highpass filter and a bit of distortion. When I was satisfied with the sound, I copied it to the closed hat key and fiddled with the envelope's decay and curve controls to get more clickiness.

I love the 909 snare for rolls, so I kept it basically the same, adding a bit more pitched tone and tweaking the envelope to give it some snap.

After some listening, I decided that the claps on two and four were sounding a little too vanilla for the track. I eliminated most of the crack processing, retuned the pitch of the FM carrier oscillator, added very resonant filtering, adjusted the envelopes, and ended up with a poppy little noise burst.

At this point, the rim shot was getting lost in the hats. What to do? Mutate the heck out of it! I went wild with FM, threw in some ring mod, and gave it a hyper-resonant zap via the filter envelope. Then, using the onboard effects, I mixed in a bit of synchronized delay to make the part bounce around the stereo field.

How did Attack fare overall? Brilliantly. Retro '80s drum and synth sounds almost fall out of this app with minimal effort. Hard, modern electronica textures lurk just beneath the surface. Tweaking and assigning the patches was a nearly painless process. Attack will definitely find a home on several new tracks I'm working on — what more could a person want?

Conclusions. It's a drum module! It's a synth! It's a drum module! Hey, wait. Waldorf's Attack is both a killer source of modeled analog drum tones and a flexible polyphonic synth. Sporting a diverse collection of features wrapped in a sexy and generally intuitive interface, Attack is useful for everything from classic drum machine emulations and boomy basses to crunchy leads and smooth pads. Not being able to import samples is a bummer, but there's still a lot of power here. Attack is a Swiss army knife you'll definitely want to check out if you're looking to add beefy analog textures to your virtual instrument collection. —*Francis Preve (Aug. '01)*

Native Instruments Battery
SAMPLE PLAYBACK DRUM MODULE

stand-alone, VST, DXi, DirectConnect, MAS (Mac, Win)
$199

Pros: Intuitive user interface with drag-and-drop addition of samples. Comes with a great selection of high-quality kits. Compatible with a wide range of sample and sequencer formats. Up to 128 velocity-switched (or crossfaded) samples per keymap. Can be used stand-alone or as a plug-in.
Cons: No filters or LFOs. Some kits require up to 86MB RAM.

Battery goes the opposite direction from Attack: Here, sample playback is the noisemaking method. Most sample-playback synths, it has to be said, include some form of filters. If you're new to the world of synthesizers, you might not appreciate what a serious weakness the absence of filtering is: It would dissuade me from using either Battery or LM4 Mark II (see below) for any but the most basic percussion chores. But in this review, from the September 2001 *Keyboard*, Francis Preve found some features to be enthusiastic about.

A footnote: I went to the Native Instruments website to find out if filters have been added to the latest version. Apparently not — filtering is not mentioned in the discussion of Battery's features. The site does say this, however: "Each instrument offers a complete set of sound parameters. . . ." I hate to rake Native Instruments over the coals, because I love their software, but this is a prime example of why you should never trust a manufacturer's claims about their own products. To any knowledgeable outside observer, "a complete set of sound parameters" would absolutely include filters.

The software synthesizer market is definitely heating up. Nearly every form of synthesis imaginable has been digitized and made available as a plug-in. From mind-blowingly accurate emulations of classic synths like the PPG, Prophet-5, and Minimoog to ultra-flexible modular synths that stretch the limits of sound design, the virtualization of musical instruments is in full swing.

One of the fastest-growing categories of synth plug-in is the drum module. Steinberg started the ball rolling with their retro '80s-style LM4 (see page 251), which was followed by FXpansion's DR-002/DR-005/DR-008 products. Then came Nexoft's Loopazoid, Steinberg's LM9, and most recently Waldorf's Attack (see page 240). Each of these plug-ins approaches percussion synthesis from a different perspective. Some are straightforward sample-playback plugs, others are full-featured analog-modeled synths, and still others blend sampling with synth functionality.

Designed by Nexoft for Native Instruments, and based in large part on Loopazoid, Battery arrives on the scene with an unusual and flexible approach to

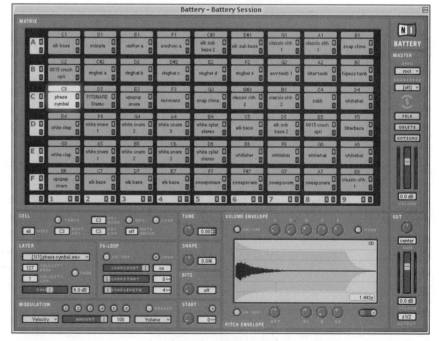

Figure 7-2.
Battery's user interface provides instant access to nearly every parameter. Each cell or row in the 6 x 9 matrix can be soloed or muted during performance. Layering, sample-editing, and processing tools are located at the bottom of the window.

sample playback and processing. When it first showed up, I brushed it aside as another me-too sample-based drum machine. Its user interface belied the power that lurked underneath. Only after several weeks of on-and-off fiddling with its extensive collection of high-quality drum kits did I begin to appreciate the effort and insight that went into creating this virtual instrument.

Battery is a quirky blend of innovation and unusual shortcomings. Still, its ability to import and process samples and soundsets from a wide variety of sources makes it worth a close look.

Compatibility. Battery is compatible with a wide range of virtual instrument formats, including Steinberg's VST 2.0, MOTU's MAS (Digital Performer), Digidesign's DirectConnect, and Microsoft's new DXi instrument spec. Battery can also function as a stand-alone instrument, which is very handy if you simply want to create a bunch of new patches or kits without opening your sequencing environment. All software manufacturers should provide this level of flexibility for their plug-in instruments.

Installation. Battery comes on two CDs. One contains the software, the other a collection of 31 kits totaling over 580MB of sample data. Installing the application is a no-brainer. Pop the CD in, enter your serial number, and you're set; no timeout challenge re-authorizations either. The installer provides options for nearly every sequencer and places directories and plug-ins in the appropriate locations.

Adding kits from the soundware CD is just a matter of dragging the desired kits to any hard drive location on your system. Since some of the kits are huge (several are over 80MB), some users will want to keep the kits on a separate drive, so this is a thoughtful approach.

The multilingual printed manual is pretty good overall, but not nearly as comprehensive as it could have been. Some aspects of Battery prompted moments of head-scratching, but I was able to track down the necessary info in the manual. There's a handy tips and tricks section at the end of the manual that covers techniques ranging from adjusting sampled loops to getting punchy drum mixes.

Included Kits. Battery's soundware CD features a huge selection of top-notch drum kits, as well as a variety of synth effect sounds. These sound sets cover virtually every musical genre and then some — one of the most comprehensive and flexible collections of drum kits I've heard in years. In fact, some users may never need to purchase third-party soundware for Battery. The kits are well recorded, and there are several samples that had me thinking, "Wow! How'd they do that?"

There's at least one kit for nearly every form of dance music, past and present. I noticed a strong European influence in quite a few of the patches. Industrial and hard electro sounds are well represented by the Destinct, Alkaloid, and Alais kits, which feature distorted, in-your-face percussion elements that could rock a Munich dance hall or a steel mill with equal aplomb. The French kit includes an array of fizzy synth splats of the Mirwais/Daft Punk variety, and is perfectly suited to flavor-of-the-nanosecond progressive house tracks.

If you're looking for more traditional dance music kits, Battery's got these covered too. The Dance 2 kit is perfect for Chicago house and trance grooves without resorting to me-too TR-808/909 patches. Sure, they've included the venerable 909 snare and hats, but these are paired with a super-thwocky kick drum and an array of useful percussion. Drum 'n' bass, trip-hop, and big beat are also represented with outstanding authenticity, and wedding bands will go wild for the '80s electro kit, as it includes classic new romantic sounds from the Roland CR-78 and Simmons SDS-5.

Battery also has acoustic kits galore, some with sample data for velocity-switched patches covering as many as ten discrete samples on some drums. The rock and "'60s Garrage" (that's how they spelled it) kits are terrific examples of this attention to detail. Other standout kits that could easily fool discerning listeners if played correctly include '70s reggae and the gorgeously ambient basic kit.

But wait, there's more! Native Instruments has also thrown in a few electronic kits that defy easy categorization and are genuinely inspirational to use. The aptly named Reaktor kit features bizarre, but eminently usable, sounds generated by NI's modular software behemoth. The Earth kit straddles the line between ambient sci-fi soundtrack and mutated ethnic percussion and would work great for both film production and electronica.

Other kits include a jazz setup and dirty vinyl emulations. The obvious genre omissions are country, Latin, and orchestral percussion, which was disappointing in light of the rest of the collection's usefulness. Producers looking for a wide range of classic acoustic sounds may be a tad disappointed, but remixers will be in heaven.

Importing. Battery can import a wide range of sample and instrument formats, including AIFF, WAV, Akai S1000 sampler instruments, Steinberg's LM4 and LM9 kits, and Creative's SoundFont format.

AIFF and WAV format samples are a breeze to drag and drop into an existing kit, and my collection of LM4 kits loaded without a hitch. LM4 users who crave a more robust sound design environment will be delighted with the ability to tweak their kits. If you currently use Cubase 5 and want more juice out of the included LM9 kits, bring them into Battery and adjust away.

Akai S1000 CD-ROMs (but not floppy disks, due to format issues) can also be imported. Their zone, volume, layer, tuning, and envelope properties remain intact.

Just to see how far I could push the format conversion algorithms, I found a bunch of freeware SoundFont 2 patches through SynthZone (www.synthzone.com/soundfont.htm) and tested them. Despite Battery's divergent architecture, most sounds survived the translation relatively unscathed. Keymaps and relative volumes were maintained, and the envelopes were closely approximated.

Battery at a Glance

System requirements	Mac: 300MHz (450MHz G3 or better recommended), 64MB RAM, Mac OS 8.0 or higher; PC: Pentium or K6 300MHz (Pentium III or Athlon, 500MHz or better recommended), 64MB RAM, Win95/98/ME/2000
Synthesis type	sample playback
Included DSP	bit reduction, waveshaping, looping, random modulation generators
Envelopes	2 AD with breakpoint for pitch, AHDSR for amplitude
Polyphony	up to 128 voices (processor-dependent)
Multitimbral features	16-way multitimbral
Sounds per drum kit	54 keymaps per kit, each with up to 128 velocity-switched (or crossfaded) layers
MIDI control	all parameters addressable via MIDI controllers, key position, velocity, aftertouch
# of audio outputs	8 stereo or 16 mono (configurable)
Compatible file formats	AIFF, WAV, Akai S1000/3000, Reaktor sample map, SoundFont 2, LM4/LM9, Loopazoid
Plug-in compatibility	VST 2.0, DirectConnect, MAS, DXi
Audio driver compatibility	ASIO 2.0, MME, DirectSound, SoundManager
Copy protection	CD-ROM verification on install
Downloadable demo	yes

User Interface. Battery's UI is organized as an array of 54 cells (six rows, nine columns). At first glance, it seems each cell is assigned to a single key and sample. In fact, each cell represents a keymap that can span multiple keys and overlap with other keymaps (more on this below). While this may initially seem counter-intuitive to users looking to create keyboard-oriented patches, it's no more difficult than wrestling with a hardware sampler's LCD screen.

Individual cells can be either soloed or muted while your sequencer plays the pattern, as can each of the six rows of cells in its entirety. While I rarely used the row mute/solo feature, for some types of workflow it could be quite handy. Cells can be highlighted in rows or columns to allow quick editing of groups.

At the bottom of the Battery window are the processing and modulation assignment tools. To the right of the window are the master volume, panning, and output assignment controls, as well as saving, loading, and preferences menus. Generally, I was quite happy with this interface, as nearly every parameter was exposed, sparing me the hassle of having to hunt through menus and additional windows searching for a given tool.

Voice Architecture. Each Battery cell can access up to 128 samples via velocity switching or crossfading. The contents of a cell can span multiple keys, and the pitch tracking can be switched on or off. Adding a sample is accomplished by simply dragging an AIFF or WAV file onto the desired cell.

The cells feature individual signal paths, which affect all velocity layers equally. While it would have been nice to have separate paths for each layer, you can work around this by manually assigning your layers to different cells and adjusting the velocity parameters accordingly.

Battery's array of processing tools veers away from traditional synthesis functions, instead focusing on modifiers that its designers deemed most important for creating cool drum kits.

Samples can be tuned via one of three methods: semitone, percentage, or note value. When using loops, the latter allows Battery to match the tempo of your sequencer to specific note durations (including triplets), provided your samples are edited to the exact length of one or more beats. This function worked fairly well, and I was able to quickly set up one-bar loops with a minimum of fuss. That said, the semitone and percentage tuning modes were a bit too coarse for my taste, despite the fact that higher resolutions are apparently available in the note duration mode. In certain situations, this posed some difficulty when I attempted to tune pitched content to a given track. [*Editor's note: According to Native Instruments, the pitch can be edited in finer increments by holding the shift key, and precise data values can be entered by typing. It's possible that Francis was aware of this when he wrote the review and was dissatisfied with the best possible resolution of the parameter. Or possibly not. It would be difficult, at this point in time, to resolve such a picky question.*]

Sample start, loop start, loop length, and number of loop iterations are all individually adjustable, with the zoomable wave display showing each parameter's position with solid accuracy. A snap to zero-crossing function is handily included as well.

A sample's dynamics can be modified via Battery's waveshaping function, which operates much like an expander (negative values) or a compressor (positive values). The manual states that this tool works on the individual bits of a sample rather than on the overall sound. But to my ears the effect was nearly identical, allowing the creation of really punchy drum sounds with minimal effort. Good stuff.

Also included is a bit-reduction parameter, which allows continuously variable control over the resolution of a sample. Integer values add some retro dirt to the signal, while fractional amounts deliver a grungy, digital distortion effect that I found super-useful for creating industrial effects.

Pitch and amplitude envelopes are also available. The pitch envelope is a basic two-stage AD envelope with an adjustable breakpoint for the two segments. Envelope polarity can be positive or negative.

The amplitude envelope is of the attack-hold-decay-sustain-release variety. The addition of a hold segment is a nice touch, as it can add punchiness to samples when used in conjunction with a quick decay. A mode switch shuts off the sustain and release segments, resulting in an AHD envelope for strictly percussive effects.

Realtime performance modulation abounds. Pretty much everything under Battery's hood can be modified via velocity, key position, or MIDI continuous controller data. This is great stuff for adding realistic articulation to percussion performances, such as controlling a drum's decay with the mod wheel or adding more pitch envelope when a key is struck harder. The realtime modulation of loop parameters is quite clean, exhibiting no crackling artifacts or glitching, even at extreme settings. Some unusual effects can be achieved using the random modulation sources. Modulation destinations include volume, pan, all envelope parameters, pitch, waveshaping, bit reduction, start point, and the various looping functions.

What's missing? Filters and LFOs. While Battery's sound shaping tools are certainly capable of twisting and warping sounds in interesting and unusual ways, the software is definitely optimized for drum processing, not full-featured instrument sampling. Granted, there are quite a few freeware and commercial filtering plug-ins out there, so it's possible to further transform your percussion parts within your sequencer's mixing environment. Still, it would have been nice to see these features incorporated within Battery itself. Even a nonresonant lowpass filter for removing some of the highs (preferably with velocity control) would have made a big difference.

In Use. Over the past month or so, I've found myself relying on Battery quite often for my drum and percussion tracks. Previously, I'd used LM4 and ReBirth for the majority of my drum parts, but since Battery can easily import LM4 kits — and allows for much more advanced editing of individual drums — the LM4 is collecting virtual dust in my VST Instruments directory. Battery's flexibility and comprehensive library of kits is growing on me quickly. I just wish it had a more powerful synthesis engine.

Conclusions. As a sampled drum instrument, Battery is a solid performer. Creating kits from scratch is an intuitive and painless process. Migrating from Akai samplers or other percussion plugs is surprisingly easy. The included kits cover almost every form of dance music currently in vogue, and then some. Battery is quite useful when it comes to melodic playback of pitched samples and drum loops, but due to its lack of filters and LFOs it's not really a replacement for a full-featured sampler, virtual or otherwise.

Some users are bound to be put off by the absence of these synthesis tools, but there are workarounds as long as you have a decent collection of effects plug-ins. If you're in the market for a drum sampler to add to your collection of virtual instruments, you'll get a charge out of Battery. —*Francis Preve (Sept. '01)*

Steinberg LM4 Mark II
SOFTWARE UPDATE OF A CLASSIC
HARDWARE DRUM MACHINE

VST (Mac, Win)
$149

Pros: Intuitive user interface. Adjustable envelope curves. Wide variety of kits. Drag-and-drop velocity switch editing.
Cons: No filters. No envelope velocity response. Processing and envelopes are global for each pad.

Steinberg's LM4 is modeled, visually at least, on Roger Linn's LM-1 and LinnDrum. Modeling the limitations of the original, however, such as 8-bit sound, non-replaceable samples, and only two dynamic levels for each drum, would have been pointless. As revealed in this June 2002 review, the LM4 Mark II comes with a healthy supply of meticulously recorded drumkits. It resembles its inspirations, however, in the fact that it doesn't have any filters.

Francis Preve alludes below to the fact that the LM4 Mark II records controller moves into its host sequencer as MIDI system-exclusive data rather than as MIDI continuous controller data. This is an important distinction. All of the sequencers I'm aware of allow controller data to be edited in some simple graphic fashion, usually using a mouse-based pencil tool. To animate the sound of the instrument, you can draw a controller curve by hand, or you can record it while listening to the music by moving the mouse on the knob or slider you want to control, and then edit the curve afterward if necessary. It's not usually possible to edit sys-ex data after the fact in this way: If you don't get the knob or slider move recorded correctly the first time, you have to erase it and try again — a slow and awkward process, especially since the mouse is not an ideal performance interface for musical gestures.

Why do some manufacturers prefer to use sys-ex rather than controller data? One reason is because controller data is limited to a resolution of 128 possible values. If a parameter can be set to 200 or 300 different values, sys-ex offers a way to control it precisely. Sometimes the limitations of MIDI force developers to make hard choices . . . or do they? MIDI allows controller data to be handled with 14-bit precision (that's 16,384 possible data values). I guess I'm mystified about why Steinberg chose to use sys-ex. Doubtless they had some reason they felt was compelling. When you get this deep into critiquing software features and implementations, clearcut distinctions disappear in a fog of personal taste and programmers' mumbo-jumbo. Let's be grateful that you can automate LM4's controls, and leave it at that.

Has it really been three years since the introduction of the ubiquitous VST Instruments plug-in format? [*Editor's note: This review was written in early 2002.*] Back in 1999, Steinberg announced the VSTi format, then promptly released the first plug-in drum machine: LM4.

For its time, LM4 was revolutionary. Users could import WAV, SDII, and AIFF format samples — at up to 24-bit resolution — and then sequence the sounds via an old-school LinnDrum-inspired pad interface. [*Editor's note: The pads transmit*

Figure 7-3.
The LM4 Mark II's performance buttons (the two rows along the bottom) mimic the appearance of the plastic buttons in the original Linn drum machines. Velocity, tuning, and pan can be adjusted per pad using the sliders at upper left. ADSR envelope segments can have independent linear or logarithmic curves. Using the Zoom button (top center), the envelope can be zoomed for minute adjustments. Samples can be reversed using another button, and the Bitcrusher can mangle the sample resolution, creating noise or retro-beatbox sounds. Each of the ten groups (assigned just below the Bitcrusher) can have its own polyphony setting. Each pad can use up to 20 velocity-switched layers, which are assigned in the column along the right side.

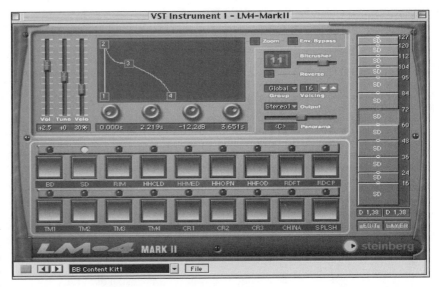

MIDI notes to the host sequencer for recording. LM4 doesn't have its own step sequencer.] Individual samples could be tuned, panned, and sent to specific mixer channels within any VST 2.0–compatible sequencer.

At the time, this was truly revolutionary: It enabled producers to dispense with the vagaries of collecting drum machines, instead keeping their favorite drum samples neatly organized on their hard drive. What's more, Steinberg threw in a massive collection of wonderfully sampled kits that covered a wide range of styles.

But LM4 was not without quirks or — more accurately — issues. Rolling your own kits was not for the faint of heart. Users could either learn Steinberg's scripting language and write code that told LM4 how to assign the various samples, or they could use Wizoo's handy, but limited, freeware kit creation tool. In 1999 this was a bottleneck. By 2001, as more comprehensive drum samplers arrived on the scene, it had become downright unacceptable.

Having used LM4 for some time, I was eager to see how LM4 Mark II addressed these shortcomings. I'd since switched to Native Intruments Battery (see page 245), Muon SR202, and Propellerhead Reason (see page 99) for my drum programming (while keeping the samples in LM4's tastier kits handy for importing into other programs), but the idea of a next-generation implementation of LM4 was tantalizing, as I'm not nuts about Battery's method of assigning multiple samples to various velocities, and SR202 is hardly robust in the stability department.

Getting Started. As with most Steinberg plug-ins, installation was a breeze. No dongles or challenge/response authorizations, not even a serial number. Just pop the CD in, wait for the installer to verify the entire CD (which can take from three to eight minutes, depending on your drive speed), and you're ready to start making beats. This is by far my preferred method. There's nothing more irritating than sitting in a

LM4 Mark II at a Glance

System requirements	VST host application, 64MB free RAM; Mac: 300MHz G3 or better, MacOS 8.0 or better; PC: 300MHz Pentium or K6-2 or better, Windows 98/ME/2000
Synthesis type	sample playback
Included effects	bit reduction
Envelopes	1 ADSR with continuously variable linear/logarithmic curves
Polyphony	up to 64 voices (CPU-dependent)
Sounds per drum kit	18 keymaps per kit, each with up to 20 velocity-switched layers per pad
MIDI control	tune, volume, pan, envelopes, and Bitcrusher automatable via sys-ex
# of audio outputs	3 stereo and 6 mono
Plug-in compatibility	VST 2.0
Copy protection	CD-ROM verification on install
Downloadable demo	no

coffeehouse, grooving to a new track on your laptop, when suddenly you're prompted to cough up your original install disk. Big thumbs-up to Steinberg on this point.

Kits can be placed on any local hard drive, making life much easier for those of us with multiple drives. If LM4 Mark II encounters difficulty locating needed samples, it can search any drive or folder for the necessary kit components.

The multilingual printed documentation is brief but thorough. Every parameter is covered in fair detail, and there are a few handy kit construction and manipulation tips at the end of the manual. Even without the documentation, I had little trouble sussing LM4mkII's features: The user interface is blissfully straightforward.

Included Kits. All 20 of the original LM4 kits from Steinberg and Wizoo are still here. While many of these kits have a distinctly retro flavor, the Electro 1 and 2 kits are well suited for trance and progressive house, and the Heavy and Power kits added some spice to a big beat track I was working on when I first installed LM4. Good stuff. The ten 24-bit kits from Wizoo sound awesome. The Acid Jazz and Hip-Hop kits are standouts, but their beauty comes at a price. They consume a whopping 375MB of disk space and take a fair amount of time to load. However, in these times of 20GB hard drives, this may seem trivial to some.

Upping the ante, LM4 Mark II also includes a stellar set of more contemporary kits, running the gamut from tight acoustic sessions to gargantuan big-beat bombast, as well as a few "kits" devoted to piano, guitar, and vinyl hits. For an extra $50, you can get the LM4 Mark II XXL ($199 retail), which comes with 2GB of samples rather than the standard version's 1GB. (All of the kits discussed below are in the standard version.)

Many users will no doubt find the new kits eminently useful for everything from jazz to seriously authentic rock, as quite a few include compression and other processing, making it a simple task to audition the kits while a sequence plays and choose the patch that best suits your song, without taking the time to add insert effects.

The Gator and Headbangers sets are perfectly suited for hard rock or nu metal, while the Loop kit has a '70s rock feel, complete with a ringing ultra-tight snare. The Reso, Small Ambience, and Compressor kits have a natural, slightly vanilla sound that works well for classic studio drum sounds, while the Big Arena kit is swimming in hall reverb, which can quickly be transformed to a choppy gated reverb via the Mark II's envelopes.

Other standouts include the Mod kit, which bathes acoustic drums in a flanger/phaser hybrid that sounds a lot like Waves' Enigma plug-in, with wonderfully resonant and synthy results. I also really got into the Metallic Grunge kit, which combines the best of industrial and EBM processing with a crunchy, pitched room reverb.

Also included are several brilliant velocity-switched kits from Bit Beats. Some drums are over ten samples deep! These studio kits are capable of incredible subtlety. Played idiomatically, they can quite accurately recreate the sound of a live drummer. The trick is in understanding how a real drummer plays and not adding tom fills and cymbal crashes while the hi-hats and snares continue playing.

Thankfully, many of these kits adhere to the General MIDI drumkit layout where possible, making it a fairly simple task to transfer existing sequences and grooves to the mkII. This kind of foresight is a nice touch. Other manufacturers might want to take note.

Rolling Your Own. The LM4 Mark II kit editor is a joy to work with. As in most other modern drum machine plugs, samples can be assigned by simply dragging them onto the desired pad. Volume and tuning can be adjusted from the main panel, but output routing and pan have moved to the edit page. Since the edit page is a single mouse-click away, this isn't a big deal.

The edit page is where the real sound design happens. Pads can be organized into up to ten color-coded groups, and each group can have its own polyphony settings. Setting a group to one-voice polyphony allows for realistic hi-hat and triangle cutoffs as well as cymbal chokes, but I also found it useful for restraining sets of toms with long decays.

A four-stage ADSR envelope can be directly edited by clicking/dragging with the mouse, as well as by dialing in values with the associated knobs. What's more, you can adjust the linear or logarithmic behavior of each envelope segment individually by dragging the curve in the desired direction. This is a wonderful touch, as it allows you to create super-spiky attack transients and pseudo-compression effects. On the downside, there's no way to control envelope rates from velocity.

Other tools include the requisite sample-reverse switch and a variable Bitcrusher that lowers the resolution of the selected sample. While the Bitcrusher is useful for recreating vintage drum samples, I wish Steinberg had also included a sample-rate division effect like the one found in Cubase 5.1, as this would have helped nail that E-mu SP1200 sound. [*Editor's note: The sound of the out-of-production E-mu SP1200 drum machine is prized in hip-hop circles. One reason for its distinctive tone is that its sample playback engine operated at a somewhat lower rate than today's 44.1kHz standard.*]

Surprisingly, LM4 Mark II eschews filtering of any sort. This is a total drag, as resonant filters and drum samples go together like milk and cookies. Sure, you can always add filtering in the mixer, but a little-known fact is that insert effects in Cubase VST are not delay-compensated for VST instruments (this compensation works on audio tracks only). So adding filters via the Cubase mixer is a risky proposition for drums, unless you render the instrument as an audio track first. Otherwise, your sample-accurate 157 bpm 32nd-note fill may end up a little late. Applying processing like reverb or delay via the aux sends doesn't introduce any timing problems.

Each drum pad can access up to 20 velocity-switched samples, which is more than enough for even the most detailed kits. New sample layers are added by dragging the samples into the layer area, then dragging their upper and lower limits. Layers can also be reordered by option/alt-clicking and dragging to the desired position. All layers inherit the envelope and other processing parameters for the pad.

Nearly all of these parameters (except for layering options) can be controlled in the sequencer via sys-ex commands. While this isn't as sexy — or as easy to edit — as Battery's ability to assign MIDI controllers to multiple parameters simultaneously, it still allows for pitch-swept snare fills (a favorite of mine) and dynamic adjustment of kick and hi-hat decays. I'm happy to see this included, as it's very handy.

In Use. I was working on an original track when LM4 Mark II arrived, and I needed a breakbeat-style loop for a section toward the end of the track. All too often, drum machines can sound a bit stiff for this type of part.

After auditioning various kits, I narrowed my choices down to three. Each kit gave the breakdown a distinctly different feel, while sounding surprisingly authentic with only minimal editing and processing. The original LM4 kits seemed a trifle flat for my track. The vinyl kit had a distinctly street appeal that I liked, but it wasn't a good fit for the pattern. I ended up using the Mini kit, applying a few minor tweaks to get it to sit correctly in the track.

I have to say that I missed being able to filter several of the drums, notably the snare and hi-hat parts, so I rendered them as audio tracks and processed the results with NorthPole (a freeware VST filter). It took a bit longer, but I got the effect I was after.

Conclusions. LM4 Mark II is a big step forward from its predecessor. By including variable curve envelopes, a wide array of kits that cover most styles, extensive grouping and layering options, and a super-intuitive interface, Steinberg is showing that they're listening to their users. While Native Instruments Battery is more powerful in some ways, LM4 is easier to use for most common drum tasks — and cheaper too. The absence of filters is a missed opportunity to leapfrog the competition, and may be a deal-breaker for some, but all of the essentials are in place. If you're shopping for a virtual drum module that's a breeze to program, or for a collection of eminently usable kits for importing into an LM4-compatible sampler, this instrument is definitely worth checking out. —*Francis Preve (June '02)*

Synthesizer Concepts

8

If you're new to the world of synthesizers and wanting to learn how to create your own personal sounds using those bewildering banks of knobs and sliders, I can tell you two things:

First, the best way to learn is by doing. Reading a bunch of abstract concepts, even in a well-written book like this one, is just going to make your eyes cross and give you a throbbing headache. Fortunately, with some very capable software instruments available on the CD-ROM that comes with the book, there's no excuse (assuming you have a computer and some sort of audio output device at your disposal) for not rolling up your sleeves and digging in.

Second, if you don't have a grasp of the technological underpinnings of synthesis, trying to learn by doing is just going to make your eyes cross and give you a throbbing headache. In the real world, synthesizers have a bewildering variety of features. The only way to understand what's going on in a synthesizer is to study the theory.

Confused? Good. You're ready to start learning. What I'm driving at, of course, is that you need to do both at once. Study the concepts, and find an instrument or two on which you can try them out. Try things out in an orderly, methodical way, listen to the sound, and then go crazy and try a few experiments that aren't in the manual.

In just one chapter at the end of an already thick book, I can't possibly explain every detail of how synthesizers operate. That would require a whole book in itself. What's worse, the owner's manual of the synth you're using may not explain the concepts fully — or even accurately. Some owner's manuals are very good indeed. (The award for Best Manual goes to Cycling '74 for their Max/MSP documentation, which includes dozens of tutorials and an online help system in which functioning Max objects have been embedded.) Others seem to have been slapped together as an afterthought, and then translated into English by someone who wasn't being paid well enough to do a thorough job.

Many real-world instruments will provide advanced variations on the basic concepts discussed here, or whole new wrinkles I haven't even touched on because they won't be invented until next week. But once you have a conceptual framework — once you understand signal flow, modulation, filtering, envelopes, and so on — none of the esoteric features a manufacturer can shoehorn into a synthesizer is likely to throw you for long. So let's get started.

The big picture

To qualify as a synthesizer, a software (or hardware) device needs three things: It needs one or more *audio signal sources,* one or more *audio signal modifiers,* and one or more *control signal sources.* Often, these are represented on the panel of the synth as separate sections called *modules.* When the synth is making a sound, a signal of some sort is generated by an audio signal source. The signal then passes through the audio signal modifier(s) on its way to the output. While this is happening, at least one con-

THE FREQUENCY SPECTRUM

The fluctuations in air pressure that we call sound waves (discussed in Chapter 1) can be fast, slow, or somewhere in between. We can measure the speed of periodic (repeating) fluctuations. The utterly useless but ubiquitous term Hertz (abbreviated "Hz") is used to refer to frequency measurements. Hertz is synonymous with "cycles per second" – 1Hz means "one cycle per second," 1,000Hz means "1,000 cycles per second," and so on, a "cycle" being one complete repetition of a repeating event.

Fast frequencies are usually referred to as "high," and slow frequencies are "low."

Rather than use long strings of numerals to refer to high frequencies, we can make our lives easier by referring to the numbers in kiloHertz, abbreviated kHz, megaHertz (MHz), or even gigaHertz (GHz) units. The prefix "kilo" means "thousand," "mega" means "million," and "giga" means "billion." (That's American billion – "thousand million" to you Brits.) So a sound with a fundamental frequency of 2,300Hz would more likely be referred to as being at 2.3kHz.

Frequencies below 20Hz are so low that human ears can't hear them. You can feel them in your gut if they're loud enough. Frequencies above 20kHz are so high that, again, human ears can't hear them. Thus the range of human hearing is conventionally referred to as 20Hz-20kHz. In reality, though, older people often lose the ability to hear frequencies above 10kHz.

trol signal source of some sort sends a control signal to one or both of the other modules, altering their behavior in some way.

That's pretty abstract. **Figure 8-1** makes it only slightly more concrete. To understand this diagram, which shows the simplest possible synthesizer, you need to know a couple of things:

First, in a conventional synthesizer block diagram, audio signals flow from left to right. They emerge from the right side of a module and enter the left side of another module. (Modules are represented as boxes. I'll bet you figured that one out by yourself.) The panel of an actual synthesizer may not be arranged in this manner, however. We're in concept territory here.

Second, control signals flow *upward*. They emerge from the top of a control signal source, and flow into the bottom of some other module.

In the diagram you'll see one of each type of module, and an absolutely minimal set of signal routings. An audio signal (a sound, in other words) emerges from

Figure 8-1.

The simplest and most abstract possible synthesizer. The audio signal flows from left to right across the top row. Control signals flow upward from the control signal source. They enter the control inputs of the other modules and influence their behavior in some way. At this level of abstraction, we don't even know whether there will be a control signal routing from the control source to the audio source. In a real-world instrument, however, there would be several such routings — and several control sources as well.

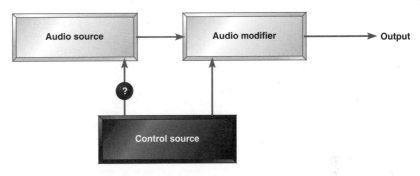

the audio source and enters the audio modifier. A modified version of the sound then emerges from the audio modifier and is sent to the output so we can listen to it. The control source is sending a signal to the audio modifier, causing the modifier to change its activity in some way. (At this level of abstraction, we don't even know what it's doing.) The control source may or may not be sending another signal to the audio source — that's why there's a question mark in that signal path. An extremely simple audio source might not even have any control inputs.

The diagram will make more sense when we give the modules concrete names and behaviors.

Audio signal sources are of two types. Either the synth generates an audio signal internally, or it receives an audio signal from the outside world. (In the latter case, technically the synth is operating as an *effects processor,* but let's ignore that distinction.) A module that generates an audio signal internally, within the synth, is called an *oscillator.* We'll have more to say below about oscillators.

Audio signal modifiers are of many types, but amplifiers, filters, and effects are the most common. An amplifier makes a signal louder or softer. A filter is a *frequency-dependent amplifier* — that is, it changes the loudness of different frequencies passing through it in different ways. For instance, it might boost the bass (the low frequencies) while attenuating (that's a fancy word for "reducing") the treble (the high frequencies). Effects do all sorts of things — in fact, this is a grab-bag category that covers just about everything that doesn't belong in any other category. We'll have more to say below about filters and effects.

Like audio signals, control signals can be generated within the synthesizer, or can arrive from the outside world. The most common internal sources of control signals are *envelope generators* and *LFOs* (low-frequency oscillators). And you guessed it, we'll have more to say below about both of these. External control signals usually arrive in the form of MIDI data.

In **Figure 8-2**, I've replaced the abstractions in Figure 1 with actual modules. The oscillator is making a tone. Because it has no control inputs, it's just making the same tone endlessly. The tone is passing through an amplifier, which has the power to make it louder or softer. The LFO is outputting a slow repeating signal that changes over

Figure 8-2.

Here, the abstractions of Figure 8-1 have been replaced by actual synthesizer modules. The oscillator is creating a tone, which is passing through the amplifier. The LFO (low-frequency oscillator) generates a square wave, which alternately sets the amplifier output to a high level and a low one (probably zero). This chops the oscillator's continuous tone up into separate notes.

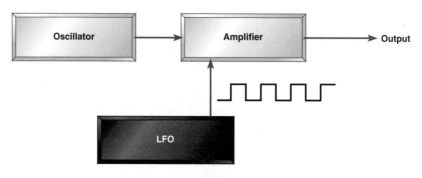

the course of time — perhaps a square wave that goes from a low value to a high value and back again once every second. The shape of the square wave is shown, purely for visual clarity, next to the signal routing along which it's traveling. When the square wave is in the high portion of its repeating cycle, the output of the amplifier is at a high level, so that we can hear it. When the square wave is in the low portion of its cycle, the output of the amplifier is at a low level, probably at zero. The result of the square wave modulation, then, is that we hear the tone of the oscillator starting and stopping. The tone has been chopped up into separate notes.

Please don't try to use this synthesizer as the basis for a pitch to a venture capitalist to fund your music software company. It couldn't possibly be any more primitive. A real synth will typically have anywhere from one to four oscillators, from two to seven or eight modifiers, and from three to a dozen control sources. The modules can be connected to one another in a bewildering variety of ways. The more modules of all types it has, and (crucially) the more control inputs each module has, the more sonic variety the synth will be capable of. In the next few sections, we'll look more closely at the possibilities.

Oscillators

The analog oscillators in first-generation synthesizers created very simple, repeating waveforms. Today we'd call them *single-cycle* waves; **Figure 8-3** should make it easy to see why. It was practical and economical to build analog electronic circuits that produced sine waves, sawtooth waves, triangle waves, and square waves, so analog synths produced their tones using combinations of those waves. As it happens, all four of those waves have interesting and useful harmonic spectra — a topic that

Figure 8-3.
The waveforms produced by early analog synthesizers were simple to generate electronically, but they had useful harmonic properties. The sine wave (a) has no overtones. Its sound is extremely muted and pure, making it suitable for reinforcing the fundamental pitch of a complex tone or adding a sub-octave. The triangle wave (b) is also muted, but has a few overtones. The sawtooth wave (c) has a bright, buzzy sound in which all of the harmonic overtones are present — the higher the overtone, the lower its amplitude. The square wave (d) contains only the odd-numbered harmonic overtones. In many synths, the width of the square wave can be varied, producing a narrow pulse wave (e). The pulse wave has only a few high harmonics, but they're loud enough to give the pulse wave a distinctive biting, reedy character.

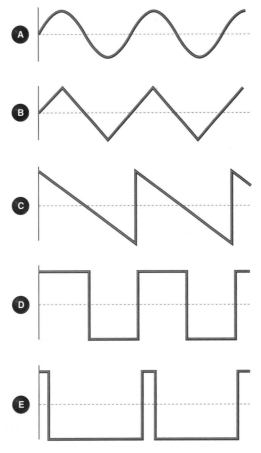

Figure 8-4.

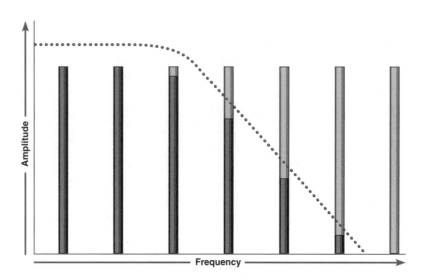

The frequency response of a lowpass filter. The overtones in the input signal are represented here as vertical bars. Low frequencies are to the left and higher frequencies to the right. The amplitude (loudness) of each overtone is shown by its height. The action of the lowpass filter in reducing the amplitude of the higher overtones is represented by the dotted line. The slope (angle) of the dotted line is referred to as the filter's rolloff slope. The portion of each overtone that succeeds in passing through the filter is shown as a solid black bar, and the portion that has been filtered out is shown in gray. In the case of a real input signal, the overtones in the input signal most likely wouldn't all be at the same amplitude. The steepness of the rolloff slope is described in deciBels (dB) per octave. A two-pole filter has a 12dB-per-octave slope, while a four-pole filter has a 24dB-per-octave slope.

would take pages to explain. Basically, "harmonic spectrum" is another way of saying "overtone series." All sounds except sine waves have one or more *overtones*. The quality of the sound, as we perceive it, has everything to do with which overtones are present in the sound, and how loud they are.

Around 1980 it became practical to build digital oscillators that could produce a much wider variety of waveforms. At first, these were still single-cycle waves: They generated a simple repeating pattern over and over. Their harmonic spectra were more interesting than the spectra of sawtooth and square waves, which is why they were useful.

Before long, digital sampling came into play. In sampling, an entire digital recording of an actual sound (a trumpet or piano note, for instance) could be played back by the oscillator. Today, sample playback oscillators are very widely used, and the character of the sound they produce depends entirely on what sample is currently playing.

An oscillator typically has several modulation inputs. A couple of them will be used to control the frequency (musical pitch) of the wave. At least one frequency modulation input is used to tell the oscillator what pitch to play: That's how you get the oscillator to play a recognizable melody. Another pitch control input is typically used to add *vibrato,* a repeating change in the pitch.

Most oscillators also have control inputs that can change the shape of the waveform. One of the earliest types of waveform modulation, found on many analog synths, was called *pulse width modulation.* In pulse width modulation, a square wave (also known as a pulse wave) would be controlled in such a way that it spent more of its time in the "high" part of its cycle, and less of its time in the "low" part. Again, explaining what this means in terms of timbre would take us rather far afield, but the concept is illustrated in Figure 8-3. If you're curious, track down a basic modeled analog softsynth with pulse width modulation (such as the freeware Soundforum synth on the CD-ROM that accompanies this book) and try it out for yourself. The point you need to understand is that waveform modulation is a way of adding *animation* to the otherwise deadly monotonous buzz of an oscillator.

A modern digital synth may offer quite a number of types of waveform modulation. In synths like Malström, which is part of Propellerhead Reason, the expressive possibilities of waveform modulation are taken to an extreme.

Another technique used in early analog synths to add more tone color resources to simple oscillators was oscillator sync. Again, oscillator sync — also called "hard sync" — is still found in some analog-type synths today. Don't confuse oscillator sync with MIDI clock sync. The latter has to do with the tempo of your song. In oscillator sync, the synced oscillator is locked to the pitch of another oscillator. You can still modulate the pitch of the synced oscillator, but when you do so, you don't hear a change in pitch — you hear a change in timbre (tone color).

Filters

The main purpose of a filter is to remove (*i.e.*, to filter out) some of the overtones from a sound. Synthesis that uses filters is sometimes called *subtractive synthesis* for that very reason. Filters are of various types: The name tells you what the filter does.

- A *lowpass* filter allows low frequencies to pass through, but blocks high frequencies.
- A *highpass* filter does just the opposite — it allows high frequencies to pass through, while blocking low frequencies.
- A *bandpass* filter allows frequencies within a specific frequency range (band) to pass, while filtering out both higher and lower frequencies.
- A *band-reject* filter (also known as a *notch* filter) does just the opposite — it filters out frequencies within a given range, but allows both the higher and lower frequencies outside the band to pass.

Most synthesizer filters are dynamic. That is, over the course of time (such as while you're playing a note) they can change the frequency range(s) they're filtering out and allowing to pass. This is why we use filters: They allow us to give the sound of the synth a dynamically changing shape. In order to see how a filter can be made to respond dynamically, we need to look at a couple of specific features.

Lowpass and highpass filters have a parameter (usually visible as a knob or slider) called *cutoff frequency*. The cutoff frequency is the frequency at which the filter starts to do its thing. If a lowpass filter has its cutoff set to 1,500Hz, for example, it will filter out the portion of the harmonic spectrum above 1,500Hz, while allowing any harmonics below 1,500Hz to pass. Conversely, when a highpass filter's cutoff is set to 1,500Hz, *only* the frequencies above 1,500Hz will be allowed to pass through the filter. (Please refer to the sidebars "The Frequency Spectrum," page 258, and "Overtones," page 268, if you're hazy on the concept of frequencies.)

The reality is a little more complex than what I've just described. It's not practical to build a filter that lets frequencies of 1,499Hz pass without any reduction in volume, while completely blocking frequencies of 1,501Hz. Actual filters operate in a more gradual, smooth (and more musically pleasing) manner. If the cutoff is set to 1,500Hz, frequencies around 1,500Hz will be reduced slightly, those at 2,000Hz will be reduced somewhat more, those at 2,500Hz will be reduced still more, and so on. This concept is illustrated in **Figure 8-4**.

The other vital parameter of lowpass and highpass filters is *resonance*. When we turn up the resonance, the filter doesn't simply cut off frequencies above (or below) its cutoff frequencies. While continuing to do this, it also amplifies a narrow band of frequencies that fall near the cutoff frequency. **Figure 8-5** illustrates this idea. As the resonance is turned up, the sound emerging from the filter will begin to take on a nasal or "peaky" character. If the resonance is turned up high enough, the filter will begin to squeal. If you're exploring a new synthesizer and aren't sure yet what its filters can do, it's generally a bad idea to edit filter resonance while wearing headphones. An unexpected resonant peak could even damage your hearing.

Filters can be used to color a synthesizer's tone statically, in a set-it-and-then-forget-it way. More often, you'll use the filter's modulation inputs to change the cutoff frequency — or, less often, the amount of resonance — during the course of each note. By modulating a resonant filter with an envelope generator, you can produce a classic "filter sweep" effect. Modulating a filter with an LFO produces a "wah-wah-wah" sound that can be used in a subtle way to add animation, or in a drastic way for a special effect.

Much more could be said about filters. We could talk about rolloff slope and keyboard tracking. We could define the word "formant," or discuss state-variable filters. We could discuss the merits of instruments in which you have two or more fil-

Figure 8-5.
When the resonance is turned up in a lowpass filter, a band of frequencies around the cutoff frequency is boosted: If the input signal has any overtones in this band, they'll get louder, resulting in a nasal or whistling sound. As the resonance is turned up, the peak gets higher.

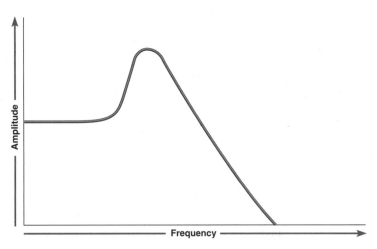

Figure 8-6.

The classic envelope generator, which has been around since the '60s, is called an ADSR, because it has controls for attack, decay, sustain, and release. Three of these are time controls, but the sustain parameter is a level control. When you play a key, the envelope rises from its initial level (zero) to its maximum level (an arbitrary value — use any number you like). The speed with which it rises is controlled by the attack time parameter, and we call this the attack stage of the envelope. The envelope then falls to the sustain level, which is some percentage of the maximum level (from 0 to 100%). The rate at which it falls is determined by the decay time parameter. When it reaches the sustain level, the envelope does nothing further — the envelope generator continues to output a static signal — until the key is released. When the key is released, the envelope falls from the sustain level back to zero, at a rate determined by the release time parameter.

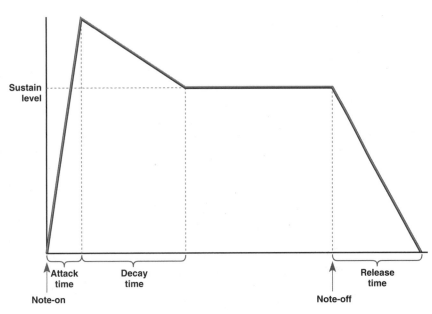

ters and can route signals through them in various ways. But since this chapter is no more than an overview, let's rush onward heedlessly.

Envelope generators

The most important modulation source in a synthesizer is the envelope generator. All synths have at least one, and many have three or four. The purpose of an envelope generator is to generate a control signal called an envelope. "Envelope" is simply a fancy term for "shape." Typically, the envelope generators (EGs) will generate a new envelope for each note you play, but your synth may have switches that will let the EGs do other things. You may be able to have a single envelope continue over the course of several notes, for instance, if the notes are played *legato* (so that they overlap).

It's important to understand that the envelope itself isn't a sound, and isn't the shape of anything in particular. It's a complete abstraction. Depending on the type of modulation routings your synth provides, an envelope can be used to modulate just about any aspect of the sound. An envelope typically starts at a level of zero at the beginning of the note, rises to a peak value, and then falls back toward zero. It may make some detours along the way, but that's the basic idea.

An envelope generator will give you a number of parameters with which to adjust the shape of its envelope. The classic envelope generator, which has been around for 40 years and is still found in many synths, is called an *ADSR,* because it has four parameters: *attack, decay, sustain,* and *release* (see **Figure 8-6**).

Many synths offer variations on the ADSR template. You may find a delay stage before the attack stage (DADSR), or a hold stage between the attack and decay (AHDSR). The sustain level may not in fact be level: Instead, you may be able to program the envelope so that it rises or falls during the "sustain" portion.

In the DX7 (which appeared in 1983), Yamaha introduced the concept of the *rate/level* envelope. In place of the four-parameter ADSR, the DX envelopes had eight parameters — four levels and four rates. The envelope would begin and end at level 0 (that's just the number of the level — the value of the parameter didn't have to be zero), rise or fall to level 1 at a speed determined by the rate 1 parameter, then go on to level 2 at a speed determined by the rate 2 parameter, and so on. You'll find rate/level envelopes, sometimes with far more than four rates and four levels, on some softsynths.

As a side note, there's no agreement among manufacturers on the subject of whether an EG's timelike parameters — attack, decay, and so on — are expressed as *times* or as *rates*. This is sort of an academic distinction, but not entirely: If an EG uses time parameters, large numbers (such as 99 or 127) will most likely produce long, slow envelope slopes. But if it uses rates, large numbers will most likely produce quick slopes.

Before we touch on some of the other features found in envelope generators, we need to say a bit about what you can do with an envelope. Going back to the block diagram in Figure 8-1, an EG is a modulation source. What can it modulate?

If we send the envelope to an amplifier, the envelope shape will control the loudness of the note — its amplitude envelope. This is pretty basic. A synth without some form of amplitude envelope either won't make any sound, or its sound will be going all the time and you'll never be able to shut it off.

Bear in mind, however, that the amplifier doesn't create a signal: It only controls the loudness of whatever signal it's receiving. If the oscillator happens to be playing back a sample of a percussive sound, such as a snare drum, the sound will stop when the oscillator gets to the end of the snare sample. At that point, it doesn't matter whether the amplitude envelope is still at its sustain level. The amplifier will be amplifying the signal it receives from the oscillator, all right — but the "signal" will be silence, so you won't hear anything.

By using an envelope to control filter cutoff frequency, we can shape the overtone content of the sound. Many types of acoustic sounds, especially struck and plucked sounds like piano and guitar, start with lots of overtones, but as the sound dies away the acoustic energy drains out of the upper overtones first. The sound not only gets quieter, it gets more muted as it decays toward silence. Simulating this effect with a filter is easy: Simply set the filter envelope to a very fast attack, zero sustain level, and a long decay. (You may have to fiddle with the filter's cutoff parameter as well.)

Envelopes can also be applied to oscillator pitch, oscillator waveshape, left/right panning, and so on. Consult your synth's manual for information on which parameters you can control with envelopes.

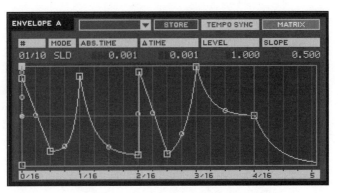

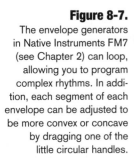

Figure 8-7.
The envelope generators in Native Instruments FM7 (see Chapter 2) can loop, allowing you to program complex rhythms. In addition, each segment of each envelope can be adjusted to be more convex or concave by dragging one of the little circular handles.

In some synths, you can control individual envelope parameters — attack, decay, and so on — from other modulation sources. A standard synth programming trick is to control envelope attack time from MIDI key velocity. When you do this, you can create a sound program that has a smooth, gentle attack at lower key velocities and becomes progressively harder and "snappier" as you play harder. Or you might like to modulate envelope decay from velocity, so that when you play lightly the notes will decay to silence more quickly, while harder notes will ring out and last longer. This mimics the response of acoustic instruments like guitar and piano.

It's a dirty little secret of synthesizer design that some manufacturers won't let you do both of the types of modulation I've just described at the same time. Instead of letting you modulate each envelope parameter individually, they may give you one modulation input that affects *all* of the EG's rate parameters. If velocity modulation speeds up the attack time, it may also speed up the decay and release times. There may be no way to have velocity speed up the attack while also slowing down the decay and/or release. This sucks, but apparently synth designers think musicians don't care.

In software-based instruments, we're starting to see more EGs with user-adjustable envelope slopes. In the graphic envelope edit window (see **Figure 8-7**), you may be able to drag a handle on each envelope segment up or down, giving you a concave, convex, or linear (flat) slope. The difference in sound will be subtle, but if you listen you'll be able to hear it.

Starting, I believe, with the Sequential Prophet-VS and its successor, the Korg Wavestation, we began to see a few instruments in which envelope generators could be looped. Rather than cycling through once to the sustain level and then "hanging" until you release the note, a looping envelope will cycle through two or more stages over and over. In effect, this type of EG becomes an LFO with a programmable waveshape. Which brings us, naturally, to the subject of LFOs.

LFOs

An LFO (low-frequency oscillator) is a modulation source that produces a regularly repeating signal (the oscillation). An LFO will probably offer you a choice of waveforms, including many of the same options found in analog-style oscillators — sine, triangle, square, sawtooth, and so on. LFOs are typically used to modulate oscillator pitch, filter cutoff frequency, loudness, panning, and other aspects of the sound.

LFO pitch modulation is known as vibrato — unless the LFO is producing a square wave, in which case you'll hear a trill. LFO modulation of filter cutoff produces a "wah-wah-wah" effect, as noted above in the section on filters. LFO modulation of loudness is called *tremolo*. LFO modulation of panning doesn't have a name; assuming you're listening to the sound in stereo, you'll hear it sweep back and forth from side to side.

The "low-frequency" part of the name means that an LFO's waveform repeats at a sub-audio rate — that is, at less than 20Hz. Vibrato, for instance, typically has a speed of between 4Hz and 6Hz. Some LFOs can be cranked up above 20Hz, however. When you do this, you won't hear the individual oscillations anymore: The modulation will turn into a buzzy change in tone color.

OVERTONES

A French mathematician named Jean-Baptiste Joseph Fourier (1768-1830) developed mathematical tools by means of which all sounds can be described as consisting of one or more sine waves. This technique is called Fourier analysis. The abbreviation FFT (Fast Fourier Transform) is used to describe a software process that analyzes the harmonic content of complex sounds.

Since a true sine wave is a mathematical abstraction that can be generated only by an electronic oscillator, all real-world acoustic sounds contain multiple sine waves at various frequencies and amplitudes (loudness levels). In fact, by describing the changing frequencies and amplitude levels of the sine waves, we can create a complete description of the sound quality that we actually perceive in a bird's chirp or a door slamming. The sine waves in a sound are often referred to as overtones, harmonics, or partials.

In most musical instrument tones, the overtones are distributed in a fairly simple mathematical way – as whole-number multiples of the frequency of the fundamental. For instance, if a cello is playing a note whose fundamental frequency is 100Hz, the tone will contain overtones at 200Hz, 300Hz, 400Hz, 500Hz, and so on. These overtones are called the natural harmonic series. They won't all be at the same loudness level, however, and their loudness levels will fluctuate during the course of a single note. The changes in the loudness of the overtones are what gives a sound its expressive character.

A synthesizer's sawtooth wave contains all of the harmonic overtones. A square wave contains only the odd-numbered overtones, however: If the fundamental is at 100Hz, the overtones will be at 300Hz, 500Hz, 700Hz, and so on. This is why the square wave sounds hollow, while the sawtooth wave sounds fat.

If the overtones don't fall in the natural harmonic series – for example, if a sound has a 100Hz fundamental and overtones at 257.3Hz, 309Hz, 546Hz, and so on – the sound is described as clangorous. This term is used because the overtones in a church bell don't follow the natural harmonic series.

LFOs often have other waveform selections. In the *sample-and-hold* effect (abbreviated S&H or S/H), the LFO steps through random values. Some LFOs will produce noise waves, which can be used to add a rough, dirty type of modulation.

Some LFOs have a delay parameter. With this, you can delay the onset of the LFO modulation until after the note starts. This is how many acoustic instrumentalists, such as violinists and trumpeters, play: A note is attacked with a clean, straight-ahead tone, and then vibrato is added to give an expressive shape to an otherwise static tone. Your LFO may also have a fade-in parameter, with which you can control how long the swell takes to move from zero to full depth.

These days, most LFOs can be synced to the tempo of a sequencer. This is useful if you're using an LFO to add long, slow filter sweeps and you want the sweeps to last for exactly two bars, but I'm inclined to feel that LFO sync is a bit overrated as a feature.

Many LFOs have modulation inputs, with which you can change the LFO's speed or depth while the note plays. Being able to modulate LFO speed is especially desirable, it seems to me. When playing solo lines, acoustic instrumentalists often give a shape not only to vibrato depth but to vibrato speed.

In a polyphonic synth (about 98% of the synths on the market are polyphonic), each voice will have its own complement of LFOs. Which raises an interesting question: What happens when you play two notes at once? If you've assigned a sine or triangle wave LFO to modulate pitch in order to generate vibrato, will the waveform of voice 1's LFO be moving upward while the waveform of voice 2's LFO is moving downward? If so, your two-note interval will get wider and narrower with each cycle of the LFOs. This may be perceived as an out-of-tune quality, which may not be what you want.

A well-designed synth will give you two choices: You can either allow the LFOs of the various voices to free-run (which will most likely result in the phenomenon described above), or you can sync them to one another, so that they'll all move up and down together. This switch is sometimes referred to as a choice between multi (or poly) and mono LFOs.

From time to time you'll find LFOs with other exotic features, such as the ability to retrigger the waveform starting at a certain spot in its cycle each time a new MIDI key is pressed. Have fun exploring them!

Modulation routings & external control

Now that you understand envelopes and LFOs, you're ready to start whipping your synth sounds around the room like a champ. Every synthesizer will give you some method with which to assign envelopes and LFOs so that they'll modulate various sound parameters. It may be useful to understand that there are two ways to do this. Some instruments provide *fixed* modulation routings, while others provide an open-ended *modulation matrix*. Many instruments give you some modulation routings of each type.

A fixed modulation routing pairs a source and a destination. For instance, you may see a section of the front panel labelled "filter EG." This means that the output of this envelope generator is permanently assigned to the filter's modulation input, and is used to modulate the filter cutoff frequency. (The term for this type of connection is "hard-wired," a holdover from the days of analog synthesis, when such a connection was indeed provided by a piece of wire.)

The advantage of a hard-wired connection is that it's easy. You never need to worry about it; it's just there, ready to use. The disadvantage is that it's not very flexible. What if you want to use that envelope generator for something else instead?

In a modulation matrix, you're given a list of modulation sources and another list of modulation destinations. It's up to you to choose the source-destination pairs (also called "routings") that you want in order to create a particular sound. In a synth with matrix modulation, you may not see an envelope generator called "filter EG." Instead, you may find EG1, EG2, and EG3 in the list, and you may be able to route any of them (or all of them) to the filter. The advantage of matrix modulation is that it's capable of more kinds of sounds. The disadvantage is that you have to do a little extra work to create a given type of sound.

Whether you're using fixed or matrix modulation, each modulation routing will typically have an *amount* control. This is essential: You may want only a little vibrato on some sounds, and a lot of vibrato on others. It's desirable as well — and this feature is not, I'm sorry to say, found on all synths — for the modulation amount controls to be *bidirectional*.

Why is having a bidirectional modulation amount control so useful? How can you have less than zero modulation, anyway? Well, if the modulation amount control is bidirectional — if it can be set, for instance, from –100% to +100% — a negative amount inverts the direction of the modulation. For instance, let's suppose you want to sweep the pitch of an oscillator with an envelope. If the amount of modulation is positive, the pitch will sweep upward. If the amount is negative, the pitch will sweep downward.

LFOs and envelope generators are not the only possible modulation sources. Another important source is incoming MIDI data. For instance, you may want to assign your keyboard's modulation wheel or lever (which will most likely be sending MIDI continuous controller 1 messages) to control filter cutoff. Once you've set up this routing, moving the mod wheel will open up the filter.

In some synthesizers, modulation from external MIDI sources doesn't sound very good because of a phenomenon called *zippering* or *stairstepping*. Standard MIDI controllers only have a 0–127 range. If you've programmed the mod wheel to make major changes in filter cutoff, each time the wheel jumps from one value to the next (say, from 16 to 17) the filter cutoff may jump audibly. Move the wheel rapidly and you'll hear a quick, gritty series of jumps, hence the term "zippering." A few synthesizers solve this problem by smoothing the modulation.

That is, they interpolate extra data values between the MIDI controller values. Controller smoothing is an advanced feature that I hope to see trickle down into less full-featured instruments.

As with LFOs and EGs, some synths provide hard-wired MIDI modulation routings, while others let you assign any type of MIDI data you like to control various parameters. For instance, you may be able to assign MIDI key number to envelope attack time, so that low notes will have slow attacks while high notes have quick attacks.

Let's dig a bit deeper: Modulation amount itself is a parameter that can in turn be modulated by a second modulation source. The best known example is using the mod wheel on your master keyboard to add vibrato. When the wheel is in the "down" position, you won't hear any vibrato, but as you push the wheel up, the MIDI data coming from the wheel is used to change the amount of LFO modulation being applied to the oscillators. In a synth with truly flexible modulation features, you'll be able to apply this concept in just about any way you can imagine.

A few synths (the Kurzweil K2000/2500 series on the hardware side, and Fruityloops on the software side) allow you to process your controller signals in complex ways using mathematical formulas. Here's a simple example: You might be able to have a given controller routing ignore the mod wheel until it outputs a value of at least 64, and respond to mod wheel messages between 64 and 127. Not a useful concept, considered in isolation — but if the mod wheel is being used to control three or four different types of sonic changes at once, you may want different changes to start at different points in the wheel's travel.

Effects

The purpose of effects processors is to enhance the signals being routed through them in some way. There are numerous types of effects, some generic and nearly universal, others quite specialized and rare. Generally speaking, any audio signal, be it a synthesizer sound or a recording of some other sound source, can be processed by an effect.

Some softsynths have built-in effects. This offers several advantages. First, the settings of the effect parameters can be stored as part of a given synthesizer preset: Each preset can have its own customized effects settings, which will add a lot to its essential character. Second, the softsynth may allow effects parameters to be modulated by control signals coming from elsewhere in the synth. You may be able to control the depth of the chorus effect from an envelope generator, for instance. Third, if the softsynth is being used in stand-alone mode rather than as a plug-in, there may be no convenient way to use plug-in effects with it.

The other way to apply effects to the sound of a softsynth is, as I just implied, by using plug-ins. If the synth is operating as a plug-in within a host application such as a sequencer, you'll be able to instantiate effects plug-ins in order to process

WHAT'S A VOLTAGE?

The first commercially available synthesizers, back in the 1960s, used analog control signals called voltages. In some synths, the control voltages were routed internally, and all the musician had to do was move knobs, sliders, and switches on the front panel to change the voltages. In other instruments, voltages were routed from one module to another (for example, from an LFO to an oscillator) using patch cords.

The synths discussed in this book are all digital, which means they don't use control voltages. Even so, the term "voltage" occasionally creeps into owners' manuals, because it's a convenient way to talk about control signals. You'll even see digital synths from time to time with modules called VCAs. That's an acronym for "voltage-controlled amplifier." In an analog synth, a VCA is used to shape the amplitude (loudness) of a signal passing through it. The control voltage sent to the VCA tells it how much to amplify.

the output of the synth. The advantage of this approach is that you can use high-quality effects plug-ins from other manufacturers. You're not limited to the effects provided in the softsynth itself.

A third possibility is using the softsynth itself as an effect plug-in. If the softsynth provides one or more audio inputs, you'll be able to route other audio tracks (vocals or drums, for instance) through its filter and built-in effects. This type of setup can provide some powerful resources for shaping a mix, but the details are beyond the scope of this book.

When using effects, it's important to understand the signal routing, as the routing can have a major impact on how the effect sounds. When instantiating an effect in your sequencer's mixer, for example, you'll probably be able to choose whether to use it as an *insert effect* or as an *auxiliary send effect*. Some effects, such as EQ and distortion, should usually be set up as inserts, because you want the entire sound of the mixer channel to be processed. Other effects, such as reverb, are sometimes better assigned to aux buses, because this allows several mixer channels to use the same effect.

When two effects are set up in a series routing, it can make a huge difference which effect goes first and which goes second. Feel free to experiment with this on your own.

Broadly speaking, we can divide effects into four types: time-based effects, frequency-based effects, amplitude-based effects, and distortion. Explaining all the parameters you may find on various types of effects would add many pages to this book. The list below explains what effects do in only the most basic way.

One parameter needs to be mentioned, however: Almost all effects offer a *wet/dry mix* control. The "dry" signal is the uneffected signal arriving at the input of the effect, and the "wet" signal is the output of the effect process itself, *without* any dry signal. If you like, you can think of the wet/dry parameter as controlling the amount of the effect. If this parameter is set to 100% dry, the effect won't do anything, no matter how you set its other controls. With some effects, such as chorus, the sound will actually be more "effected" if the wet/dry mix is set to 50% rather than to 100% wet.

■ *Delay.* The simplest time-based effect is delay (also called a delay line). A delay effect produces one or more separate, discrete echoes of the input signal. The delay time can often be set to a rhythmically meaningful value, and separate delay outputs, called "taps," can be panned to different positions in the stereo field. A delay is a great way to add rhythmic animation to a simple part.

■ *Chorus and flange.* In chorusing, one or more copies of the input signal are delayed only slightly (a few milliseconds), and the amount of delay is constantly modulated by an LFO. Chorusing adds a rich swirling quality to the sound. Flanging is produced by a similar mechanism, but the delay time is usually shorter. A flanger makes a "whooshing" sound that rises and falls.

■ *Phaser.* Though technically not a time-based effect, phasing sounds similar to flanging. In its customary usage, a phaser affects mainly the higher frequencies and makes a metallic whooshing sound.

■ *Reverb.* Reverb (reverberation) simulates the mass of overlapping echoes heard when a sound is played in a real room. Typical controls include decay time (how long it takes the reverberant sound to die away) and early reflections (discrete echoes that are blended in with the wash of reverberant sound). Reverb is one of the most important effects for giving an electronic mix a sense of being "real." Purists will doubtless argue with this usage of the term "real," but we all know what I'm talking about. Reverb can also be used in creative ways that don't sound real at all.

■ *Equalization (EQ).* An equalizer boosts or cuts certain frequencies in a signal, without affecting it in any other way. A typical software equalizer offers from three to five separate frequency "bands," each with its own parameters. For each band you'll be able to set the center frequency of the band, the bandwidth, and the amount of boost or cut. EQ is the kind of effect that your listeners will seldom even notice, but giving each track the right EQ can have a huge impact on the quality of a mix.

■ *Pitch-shifting.* A pitch-shifter can move the pitch of a signal up or down. More often used on vocals than on synth sounds, pitch-shifters can correct out-of-tune notes so subtly no one but the producer knows for sure. They can also be used to give a vocal a robotic, "computerized" quality.

■ *Distortion.* Adding some amount of controlled distortion to a signal can make it sound more aggressive, or give it added presence and "authenticity" (for instance, by making a guitar track that were recorded by plugging the guitar directly into the mixing console sound as if it were recorded using a real amp and speaker cabinets). Adding distortion to a softsynth can give the tone more "crunch" and "bite," which will help it sound less sterile.

■ *Compression/limiting.* The purpose of compression and limiting (closely related processes that are often found in a single effect unit) is to make the music sound louder without actually being louder. The effect processor performs this trick by taming (compressing or limiting) the loudest peaks in the sound while ignoring lower-level portions of the sound. Once the loudest peaks have been squashed, the whole signal can be boosted. At this point, the loudest peaks will be at the same level they were before, but everything else will have been brought forward in the mix. Compression is sometimes applied to an entire mix rather than to individual tracks or instruments.

■ *Ring modulation.* In some synths, ring modulation is considered an effect; in others, it's part of the oscillator setup. A ring modulator requires two inputs, and the output includes all of the sums and differences of the two input frequencies. Ring-modulated sounds tend to have a bell-like quality.

Figure 8-8.

In FM synthesis, modu-
lating a sine wave (left) with
another sine wave creates a
more complex waveform
(middle). As the amplitude
of the modulating wave is
increased, more peaks and
valleys are added to the
wave (right). We perceive
this as an increase in brightness (high frequencies).

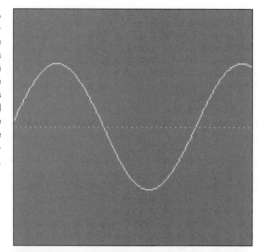

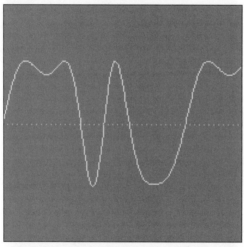

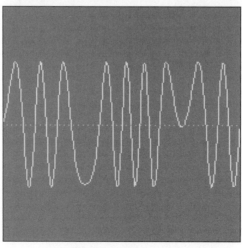

■ *Vocoding.* A vocoder is a popular effect for making synth sounds, wind, and other source material "speak" recognizable words. It needs two input signals: a speech signal (which contains the words) and a carrier signal (the signal on which the words will be imprinted). Some synths have built-in vocoders.

FM synthesis

Since the very beginnings of digital synthesis, way back in the 1950s, software engineers have been trying to devise ways to make more vibrant, expressive sounds. A breakthrough came in the 1970s, when Dr. John Chowning, working at Stanford University, published a paper describing the technique of frequency modulation (FM) synthesis. Chowning's patented FM algorithms were used in the hugely popular Yamaha DX7. In the software realm, FM is used not only in Native Instruments FM7 (see page 55), which is closely patterned after the DX7, but in many analog-style instruments, where it supplements other types of tone generation.

Basic FM requires two oscillators, which are called the *carrier* and the *modulator*. The tone we can hear comes from the carrier, but the tone color of the carrier's waveform is decisively influenced by the modulator.

Technically, using an LFO to add vibrato to an oscillator's tone is a form of frequency modulation. The frequency (pitch) of the oscillator is being modulated — that is, it's rising and falling — under the influence of the LFO. In FM synthesis, the same type of modulation is used, but the modulator is not a low-frequency oscillator. Instead, its frequency is in the audio range. As a result, the modulation isn't perceived as changing the pitch of the carrier oscillator. It's perceived as changing the timbre. **Figure 8-8** will give you an idea of what happens to a sine wave when it's frequency-modulated.

By putting the output amplitude of the modulator under the control of an envelope generator, we can shape the timbre of the carrier during the course of the note. In effect, the modulator's amplitude envelope functions more or less the way a filter envelope functions in an analog-style instrument: As the envelope signal gets higher, more overtones are added to the carrier, because the modulator is getting louder, thus adding more modulation. As the envelope falls, the modulator is tamed, so the tone of the carrier becomes more muted.

There's much, much more to FM synthesis than this simple description would indicate. An FM synth often includes four or even six oscillator/envelope pairs, which can be combined in various ways — for example, two modulators both feeding into one carrier. The relative tuning of the carrier/modulator pairs also has an enormous impact on the tone of the carrier.

FM synthesis is capable of producing fairly realistic emulations of some types of instrument sounds, especially tuned percussion like vibraphone, xylophone, marimba, and electric piano. It's less successful with complex sounds like string orchestra and acoustic piano.

Granular synthesis

Granular synthesis is frankly an experimental technique. It's well suited to producing hazy clouds of sound, but it wouldn't be my first choice for a sound that needs pinpoint clarity, such as a melodic synthesizer patch. It's sometimes used for time-stretching and pitch-shifting complex sampled sounds, such as drum loops, but in my experience the results tend not to be very convincing. Your mileage may vary.

In granular synthesis, a source waveform (usually a sample) is chopped up into a large number of tiny "grains." A new sound is synthesized by recombining these grains in various ways. You may be given control over the grain size, the tuning of individual grains, the amount of overlap, the order in which the grains will be played back, the density of the playback, the amount of randomness in any of the above, and so on. By modulating these parameters during the course of a single "note" (though the concept of what's a note can get pretty vague once a granular process gets under way), you can create effects like having a spoken voice emerge from a swirling cloud of seemingly random hash.

Physical modeling synthesis

Touted ten years ago as "the next big thing" in synthesis, physical modeling has proven unexpectedly resistant to mainstreaming. This may be because there are cheaper ways to get approximately the same musical results, because physical models are harder to control and use expressively than other kinds of synthesis, or because there's less need for synthesizers that simulate acoustic instruments than for synths that make bold new sounds.

In physical modeling, a software engineer develops a mathematical model that describes, in more or less detail, how an acoustic instrument produces its tone. A model of a trumpet, for instance, would probably include parameters for the lengths of tubing, the actions of the valves, the buzzing of the player's lips in the mouthpiece, the amount of wind being propelled through the tube by lung pressure, and so on. The physical model produces a tone by a series of calculations that includes these elements as factors, and the tone can be varied by changing the parameters. For instance, once the model has been developed, it might be fairly simple to program a trumpet with a tube that's only three inches long and a mouthpiece that's a foot in diameter, being played by a player whose lungs have the capacity of a NASA wind tunnel.

As you might imagine from this example, some of the inputs you might give to a physical model will "break" the model, producing either no sound at all or a sound you won't want to listen to. When well programmed, though, a physical model can do realistic effects that can't be achieved by any other type of synthesis. With a physical model, you can make a trumpet or flute sound "overblow" in a realistic and convincing way. Seer Systems Reality (found on the CD-ROM) includes physical modeling, along with other synthesis techniques.

I've also seen the term "physical modeling" used optimistically to describe less complex electronic processes, such as mixing in a sample of an acoustic piano's harp resonance when the player steps on a MIDI sustain pedal. Marketing departments are always looking for an edge.

Related to physical modeling and additive synthesis (see below) is a new technique that might be termed spectral modeling. As seen in Steinberg Plex, which was released too late to be reviewed in this book, spectral modeling resynthesizes sounds using models (analyses) of the harmonic spectra and envelopes of existing sounds. Plex includes about 90 analysis files, and allows you to recombine the upper harmonics, lower harmonics, and harmonic evolution (filtering) of different sounds. In my initial, all too brief experiments, it appears Plex is best at rich, swirling sounds, many of them quite breathy. There's no module for analysis of user-supplied sounds, but if you think about it, there are 90 to the 3rd power possible combinations just with the factory palette, so it's not likely you'll exhaust the possibilities anytime soon. It's too early to say whether Plex represents a real breakthrough or is simply an odd offshoot, but if you're on the lookout for fresh sonic resources it's certainly worth giving a listen to. Plex, by the way, is the first Windows softsynth I've seen that has bailed on Windows 98 compatibility. Guess it's time for me to migrate my creative work over to Windows XP.

Additive synthesis

While not used in many software synthesizers (or in many hardware instruments, for that matter), additive synthesis is worth at least a quick look. As mentioned in the "Overtones" sidebar on page 268, it's possible to describe any sound as a collection of sine waves, each having a different pitch and amplitude (which may change during the course of the sound). That being the case, shouldn't we be able to synthesize any sound at all with nothing but a big bank of sine wave oscillators and envelope generators?

Technically, yes. There are two difficulties with this approach, though. First, some sounds will require a pretty hefty bank of oscillators, as well as envelope generators with lots of segments. ADSRs just aren't going to cut the mustard. Second, once you've set up your oscillators and envelope generators, you're going to have to program them. Creating interesting sounds with additive synthesis turns out to be prohibitively complex and time-consuming. Techniques like FM will give you musically interesting results with far less work, and they also put less strain on the CPU.

In a more strategically limited and less cumbersome implementation, though, additive synthesis techniques can be quite useful. For instance, you might use two oscillators and a filter to produce the body of a tone, and another oscillator or two, routed through a separate filter and amplifier, to produce only some very quick attack transients at the start of each note. This hybrid approach, in which several complex signals are layered in a single note using both additive and subtractive synthesis, is a great way to produce expressive sounds.

Polyphony & multitimbrality

Before we leave the wonderful world of synthesizer features, we need to touch on one other aspect of instrument design that can easily trip up the unwary.

First of all, most synths are *polyphonic.* That means they can play more than one note at the same time. In the case of a hardware synth, the total polyphony (also called the voice count) will be fixed. In a computer-based synth, on the other hand, it's likely to be dependent on the speed of the computer's CPU and the number of other tasks the computer is being asked to perform at the same time. If you ask a softsynth to play too many notes at once, the sound will start to break up, or possibly shut down entirely.

In the most basic configuration, all of the notes played by a polyphonic synth will sound the same — more or less. A lot depends, it's true, on the nature of the sound program you've chosen. If you're using a sample playback synth, and if it's set up with a separate drum sound mapped to each MIDI key, then the notes won't sound anything like one another. What matters in this case is that all of the notes are being triggered by messages on the same MIDI channel, and that all of the drum samples are ultimately assigned to one sound program.

When the synth is operating in *multitimbral mode,* things get more complex. You may be able to select four, eight, or 16 separate sound programs and assign each program to its own MIDI channel. The total polyphony of the synth hasn't increased — that is, it can still only play the same total number of notes at once that it could play before. But now those notes can be divided up amongst various MIDI channels, and can use various different sound programs.

With a multitimbral synth, you can build up an entire musical composition, including melody, chords, bass, drums, and what-have-you, using only a single instrument. This is an effective way to work, especially if your budget is limited, but I've found that every synthesizer has, to some extent, its own sonic character, which it stamps on every sound it makes. Assigning tracks to several different synths can make your music sound just slightly bigger and more interesting, even if the tracks themselves are the same as before.

The virtual rack systems in Chapter 4 take the concept of multitimbrality a big step further. The individual synths in a program like Propellerhead Reason are not multitimbral, but you can instantiate as many copies of a given synth as you like (or as many as your CPU and RAM will support), and assign each to its own MIDI channel. You can even have several different synths operating on different MIDI channels, all within Reason.

Final thoughts

In this chapter we've covered only the rock-bottom basics of electronic sound synthesis, omitting many details. Such details often spell the difference between a riveting sound and a flaccid, wimpy one. Likewise, this book as a whole doesn't cover all of the software synthesizers that are available today (at the end of 2002), much less the instruments that will be introduced next month or next year. Once you start getting into synthesizers — especially the software kind — you'll realize there's no end to the possibilities.

The biggest challenge, it seems to me, is not making awesome music with software. The biggest challenge is finding a way to get your music heard by the public. This is not easy at all. Most of the talented musicians I know have day jobs. Some of them operate small independent record labels out of well-equipped garage studios, but even with a low overhead and years of back catalog to sell, most of them are not making a living with their music. The radio waves, meanwhile, are dominated by ultra-conservative corporate interests. The music that gets heard is high-quality, but it's also safe and predictable, because playing music by independent musicians might mean a loss in profits for the radio station. (In this context, "safe" can include gangsta rap that advocates violence. Advocating violence is a form of titillation, and titillation produces profit.)

The Internet may appear to offer an alternate avenue through which you can reach listeners with your music. But the same avenue is open to about 10,000 other musicians, all of whom are equipped with the same advanced music gear. Rising above the noise floor and getting noticed is difficult.

I don't expect to see this situation change any time soon. As much as I hate to end this book on a downer, I wouldn't want anyone to be dazzled into thinking that software synthesizers (or anything else) can provide a shortcut to fame and fortune. I once asked Wendy Carlos how music software has changed the creative process, and she was adamant that it hasn't. "Creating good music," she said, "is just as hard as it ever was." The process of creation is internal. It's mental and emotional (spiritual if you prefer), and has little or nothing to do with the tools that happen to be available. If you want to have a little fun, go for it! But if you hope to achieve anything significant as a musician, dedication and years of hard work will be required.

If anything, today's music tools give us too many options. It's easy to get paralyzed. You can waste hours trying to find exactly the right settings for a compressor or EQ, or simply devote weeks and months (as I have, I'm sorry to say) to exploring cool new synthesizers rather than to composing music. There's something to be said for choosing a platform for music creation — be it a virtual rack system like Reason, Storm, or Fruityloops, a multitrack sequencer with a stack of plug-ins, or a string quartet and a pile of score paper — and sticking with it for an extended period, without allowing distractions to creep in.

My wish for you is that, having experimented a bit with some of the software resources described in this book, you'll choose a working environment that seems congenial, spend a few years honing your skills at composition and arranging, and then find an outlet through which you can share your music with the world. Even if you never get rich or famous as a musician, I think you'll find that your life has been enhanced in ways that you never dreamed.

CD-ROM Contents

All files are demos unless otherwise noted. The limitations of the demo format vary from product to product: Some include an audible beep in the output, some won't save files, some quit after 20 minutes, some include only a few of the instrument files provided with the full version, and so on. The method by which a fully functioning copy can be purchased also varies, so you'll need to consult the manufacturer's website for details.

Our apologies to the other manufacturers who graciously offered to provide demos for the CD-ROM, especially Cakewalk and Steinberg. We packed as much stuff in there as we could, but some very cool programs had to be omitted.

Ableton
Live! 1.5.2 for Macintosh (OS9, OSX) and Windows (stand-alone).

Antares
Kantos 1.0 for Macintosh (RTAS, MAS, and VST plug-ins), plus three mp3 music demos.

Arturia
Storm 2.0 for Macintosh and Windows (stand-alone, plug-in, ReWire), plus two mp3 music demos.

BitHeadz
Unity Session 3.0.4 for Macintosh (OS 9, OS X; stand-alone, MAS, VST, RTAS, DirectConnect, ReWire).

IK Multimedia
SampleTank Free (Windows) is a fully functioning sample playback instrument, but it will load only content provided by IK Multimedia. (The CD-ROM contains 79MB of playable instruments.)

LinPlug
FreeAlpha (Mac, Windows) and RM F (Windows) are fully functioning synths. Also on the CD-ROM are demos for CronoX (Windows), daOrgan (Mac, Windows), Delta III (Mac, Windows), Element P (Mac, Windows), and RM 2 and RM III (Windows).

Native Instruments
The Soundforum synth (Mac, Windows) is fully functioning freeware. Demos for Absynth, B4, Battery, Dynamo, FM7, Pro-52, Reaktor, Spektral Delay, and Traktor (Mac, Windows); Kontakt and Kontakt Demo Instruments (Windows only); and Battery Studio Collection (Mac only). Music demos also included.

Propellerhead
Reason 2.0 (Mac OS 9 and OS X, Windows). ReBirth 2.0.1 (Mac, Windows).*

Seer Systems
Reality and SurReal (Windows).

Software Technology
VAZ 2010 and VAZ Modular 2.1 (Windows).

VirSyn
Tera (Mac, Windows).

Resources & Contacts

Now that I've got you all fired up, you're probably wanting to know, *Where can I find out more, Jim? Where can I buy all this cool stuff?* Not that I want to sound like a salesman — I really don't care whether you buy anything or not. Even if you're just vaguely curious, though, the various manufacturers' websites would be a great place to start. The URLs in the list below are current as of October 2002.

Ableton, www.ableton.com; U.S. dist. by Midiman, www.midiman.com

Antares, www.antarestech.com

Applied Acoustic Systems, www.applied-acoustics.com

BitHeadz, www.bitheadz.com

Cycling '74, www.cycling74.com

Digidesign, www.digidesign.com

Edirol, www.edirol.com

Emagic, www.emagic.de

FXpansion, www.fxpansion.com

GMedia, www.gmediamusic.com

IK Multimedia, www.ikmultimedia.com

LinPlug, www.linplug.com

Muon Software, www.muon-software.com

Native Instruments, www.nativeinstruments.de

Propellerhead Software, www.propellerheads.se

Seer Systems, www.seersystems.com

Software Technology, www.software-technology.com

Steinberg, www.steinberg.net

Tascam, www.nemesysmusic.com (for GigaStudio)

VirSyn, www.virsyn.com

Waldorf, www.steinberg.net (software with the Waldorf name is currently available exclusively through Steinberg; Waldorf's own site, www.waldorf-gmbh.de, provides information on their hardware instruments)

GET THE LATEST NEWS AND UPDATES ON
SOFTWARE SYNTHESIZERS
To join the email list for news related to this book,
including updates, changes, and new editions, send
a blank email to: softsynth@news.backbeatbooks.com

Index

Serious Keyboards.

Keyboard has all the information you need to be a serious music maker.

Years of editorial "hands-on" experience • Everything you need to know about the latest synths, samplers, music software, digital recording, players and remixers • Instructional columns, lessons, tips and techniques • Hands-on tests and extensive product information to help you find the gear you need • If you want to get serious about keyboards and electronic music production, check us out at your nearby newsstand or visit www.keyboardonline.com.

WHEN IT COMES TO MUSIC, WE WROTE THE BOOK.

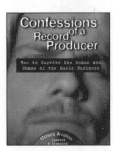